Deciding What's News

Deciding What's News

A Study of *CBS Evening News,* *NBC Nightly News,* *Newsweek,* and *Time*

Herbert J. Gans

Vintage Books
A Division of Random House
New York

Vintage Books Edition, April 1980
Copyright © 1979 by Herbert J. Gans
All rights reserved under International and Pan-American
Copyright Conventions. Published in the United States by
Random House, Inc., New York, and simultaneously in
Canada by Random House of Canada Limited, Toronto.
Originally published by Pantheon Books, a division of
Random House, Inc., New York, in April 1979.

Library of Congress Cataloging in Publication Data
Gans, Herbert J.
Deciding what's news.
Bibliography: p.
1. Journalism—United States. I. Title.
[PN4867.G3 1980]   070.4'3'0973   79-22849
ISBN 0-394-74354-7

Manufactured in the United States of America

FOR DAVID AND LOUISE

Contents

List of Tables

Preface

Walter Cronkite has, for several years, been one of the most trusted men in America; and he, as well as some other national journalists, have become celebrities. But the fact remains that they, and the 99 percent of journalists who are not celebrities, are the prime regular suppliers of information about America for most Americans.

That fact is the subject of this book. Part 1 describes how America is reported in the popular national news media; Part 2 indicates why it is so reported; and Part 3 proposes some other ways of reporting it.

The idea for this study dates back to the early 1960s, when the Cold War was at its height and the Cuban missile crisis brought the end of the world in sight. At that time, I thought about studying how the news media covered these events, how the news affected the audience, and how that audience, in turn, affected the decisions that were being made in Washington. However, by the time I was ready to begin work on the study in 1964, I realized that I could not, by myself, deal with all these questions. Also, the international situation had improved, the Vietnam escalation not yet having begun in earnest, and I had become more interested in what was going on inside America. Accordingly, I sought to study what this society tells itself about itself through the news and why, and I decided to focus on domestic news reported by the national news media.

What news media are truly national can itself be debated, since none reaches the majority of Americans. I wanted, however, to study those which sought to reach a nationwide audience—a large, general group rather than a small, specialized one. (This ruled out such quasi-national newspapers as *The New York Times* and *Washington Post,* as well as *The Wall Street Journal,* and the weekly or monthly journals of opinion, such as *The Nation* and *National Review.*)

My criteria were best met by the three network evening news programs and the three major weekly newsmagazines (ABC, CBS, and NBC; *Newsweek, Time,* and *U. S. News and World Report*). Detailed audience data can be found in Chapter 7; but according to W. R. Simmons & Associates Research, the average adult audience for the trio of network evening news programs (counting only weekday programs) was, day in and day out, almost 33.5 million people in 1977.

According to Simmons, the combined readership for the three news-magazines came to 47.3 million adults per week that year. Even so, the total number of viewers and readers is more modest than the 103.5 million adults Simmons reports as having looked at a daily newspaper in 1977. However, the daily papers are a mixture of national and local news, while the television newscasts and the newsweeklies reach the people who presumably want purely national (and international) news. But of course, some people keep up with all three types of news media, as well as local television and radio news.

Ultimately, I chose to study only two news programs and news-magazines, mostly for lack of time: the *CBS Evening News* and the *NBC Nightly News,* leaving out ABC because, when I began my work, it had a much smaller audience and staff; likewise, *Newsweek* and *Time,* excluding *U. S. News and World Report* because it served a smaller and more specialized readership. Methodological details can be found in the introductions to the three parts of the book, but most of my work, as reported in Part 2, was devoted to studying the journalists in these four news organizations to discover how they selected the news and what they left out; how they reported the stories they selected; why they chose as they did; and what kinds of people they were.

Having done several community studies using fieldwork or partici-pant-observation methods, I used basically the same approach to study four "journalistic communities" in their New York studios and offices. I observed how the journalists worked, talked with them about their story decisions, sat in on editorial meetings, and joined informal discussions in and out of the office.

I visited each of the four news organizations for several months between 1965 and 1969; but after shelving two drafts of the book in the early 1970s, I thought my data were too old. Consequently, I spent another month at NBC, *Newsweek,* and *Time* in 1975, and inter-viewed at CBS. As it turned out, the world had changed between my two fieldwork periods, but the way journalists work had not; the book, therefore, is based on both sets of fieldwork data and some last-minute interviews to update them, conducted in June 1978.

Nevertheless, the book is not really about the four news organiza-tions but about national news, journalism, and journalists in general. Marshall McLuhan notwithstanding, I soon learned that despite the differences between the electronic and print news media, the similari-ties were more decisive. Television favors news that produces dra-matic, action-packed film, but the newsmagazines emphasize stories that lend themselves to dramatic narrative, interspersed with vivid quotes and illustrated with action-packed still pictures. Moreover, both types of news are selected and produced by journalists who, for a variety of reasons, look at America in much the same way.

To be sure, having been impressed by the similarities between television and the newsweeklies, I underplayed the differences, although such differences, as well as specifics about each news organization and its people, are reported when they are crucial to how news is selected. Even so, I write part of the time about a generalized construct (or what sociologists call an ideal-type): the national journalists (and the national news organization). And I am more concerned with their differences in responsibility and power—whether they are executives, editors, or reporters, for example—than whether their final product is on film, tape, or paper. (Incidentally, I use the term "journalist" because "newsmen and women" is too unwieldy, and I do not like the sound of "newspeople," "newspersons," or "newsworkers." "Newsmakers" is more mellifluous, but journalists already use this word to describe the people about whom they report. I also dislike the term "news media" but have not found a suitable substitute.)

While individual magazines and networks are named, individuals are not, except when they have expressed their thoughts publicly, in print or on the air. I told the people I studied I would not use names; and besides, anonymity is an old fieldwork tradition. Sociologists are more concerned with the roles people perform and the positions they occupy in an organization than with individual personalities. Obviously, journalists are, in the end, individuals, but news organizations are also sufficiently bureaucratized that very different personalities will act much the same way in the same position. Some of the people I studied will nevertheless recognize themselves and their colleagues, although sometimes I have altered identifying data—but not quotes—in order to preserve their anonymity.

I came to the study without much knowledge of how journalists work. Like many of the people I studied, I had discovered journalism in high school and planned to become a journalist, but that was in 1945, and subsequently, I discovered sociology in college. I also approached the study without prior explicit values, and when I started my work, I thought I would need to deal only with the value problems that had come up in earlier community studies. I quickly learned otherwise, however, for I began my study during the emergence of the pervasive critique of the professions, the social sciences, and of America generally, in the mid-1960s. I became aware of how my own values affected my analyses, and a little of the resulting self-examination is in the book.

Another value problem followed from the realization, soon after my fieldwork began, that in some ways, sociology and journalism are similar. They both report on American society through the use of empirical methods, despite their very different aims, deadlines, and audiences. Among other things, they face similar dilemmas in dealing with values, for both aim to be objective, even if neither can finally operate without values or escape value implications, however much the actual empirical work is value-free or, as journalists put it, detached. Also, being similar, sociology and journalism are, to some extent, in competition, so that not much love is lost between them. Journalists make their opinions clear in the snide asides which they add to their occasional stories about sociology; sociologists regularly measure journalism against their own discipline and find it wanting. I faced the same temptation, and I doubt that I have overcome it entirely; but I have tried to deal with it, at times by comparing how the two disciplines work and how they confront similar difficulties.

This book, then, is one sociologist's attempt to understand journalists. Coming from the community-study tradition, I have tried to report what I found relevant in the communities I observed, but I have concentrated, in Part 2, on the informal rules that guide news judgment. In fact, one of the journalists put it nicely when he said I was writing down the unwritten rules of journalism. But rules contain values, and the book is also about the values and the ideology of a profession which deems itself objective and nonideological. And because I also traced the commercial, political, and other forces that produce the rules and values, the book examines the sources, audiences, and powerholders that impinge on journalists from outside their news organizations. A general argument about the role of journalists and the news in America runs through the book and is summarized in Chapter 9.

Having finished my work, I now think the book is also a study of a national profession; and what I have to say—for example, about how professional standards incorporate efficiency criteria and the realities of power—may provide clues to how other national professions function. Journalists are, among other things, producers of symbolic consumer goods; and what I learned about how they serve their audience without paying much attention to it may be relevant for understanding other commercial producers of consumer goods.

Last but not least, the book is a visitor's report about the innards of one part of the Establishment and about individuals who are often thought to be glamorous and powerful. I found, however, that the national journalists are hard-working, often harried people with little time for, and even less patience with, glamor; they are dedicated professionals ever conscious of their responsibilities to journalism and their audience. They have more power than the rest of us, but mainly because they express, and often subscribe to, the economic, political, and social ideas and values which are dominant in America. Indeed, as I was writing about the journalists, I felt that my book was as much about the dominant culture in America, and about its economic and political underpinnings, as about them.

Like all participant-observers, I wrote the book partly for the people I studied, telling them what I learned to reciprocate for their allowing me to observe them and talk with them at length. While I was observing, a few said that they could not make sense out of the enterprise in which they are engaged and wished I would do it for them; I hope that I have done so. The book is also for the general reader and for my fellow sociologists; but in the last analysis, I wrote it for myself, trying to understand the news we all watch and read.

Acknowledgments

My first thanks must go to the people I studied; without them and their help, this book could not have been written. I am equally grateful to Stimson Bullitt, who as head of the Bullitt Foundation of Seattle, provided the funds with which I began this study. That was long ago, at a time when the news had not yet become a subject of study; nevertheless, he gave me a grant almost by return mail.

The study was later supported by grants from the Ford Foundation and the National Endowment of the Humanities, and I finished the last draft while I was a Guggenheim Fellow. My findings do not, of course, necessarily represent the views of the agencies which funded me. Other forms of support, and pleasant working conditions, were provided by the three research centers where I worked on this study: the Center for Urban Education, the MIT-Harvard Joint Center for Urban Studies, and, above all, the Center for Policy Research. I am especially grateful to it and its director, Amitai Etzioni. I am also indebted to James Crispino, Nigel Fisher, and long ago, Charles Gillett, who helped in various ways as my research assistants.

Invaluable editorial help came from my wife, Louise; my editor, André Schiffrin; and my copyeditor, Donna Bass. They helped me tighten my argument, clarify my ideas, and improve my writing style. Audrey McGhie and Evelyn Ledyard typed and retyped the manuscript with their usual patience and efficiency. My son David helped with the search for a title; his father is responsible for the faults of the book.

HJG
June 1978

Part 1
The News

Introduction

Part 1, "The News," describes the picture of America as nation and society that appears in the national news media I have studied. Before reporting how I developed that picture, some basic information about the television evening news programs and newsweeklies may be relevant, at least for readers of this book who do not keep up with either.

The half-hour news programs, which actually contain 22½–23 minutes of news, combine filmed (now often taped) stories with what television journalists call tell stories; these are presented by one or two anchorpersons, with still pictures, maps, and graphs in the background. Each program is divided into four or five sections, interrupted by commercials. Typically, it consists of five or six filmed stories, each running 1 to 2 minutes, of "hard" news, about that day's events; and one or two "features," of somewhat longer duration, that do not carry an implicit "dateline." Tell stories, which take up about 6 minutes of each program, run from 15–30 seconds; introduce and end a film story, updating it with yet more recent information; and provide a "headline service," summarizing foreign or domestic stories that do not lend themselves to filming or are not deemed sufficiently important.

The news program is structured like a newspaper. The day's most important story is the lead, and the first two sections are generally devoted to the other important hard news of the day. Most of these stories are domestic news, usually about political or economic happenings, much of it originating in Washington. Features, which take up the remaining sections, are more often on topics of social importance or interest, such as health; and television journalists like to end the program with an amusing human-interest anecdote, of the "man bites dog" genre. When events that journalists deem to be world-shaking take place, however, the normal daily format may be set aside, with 8 to 10 minutes or more given to one story.

By and large, the three newscasts report virtually the same stories, but because they compete with each other, there are also some differences; and there may be additional ones by the time this book is published. Until Eric Severaid retired in 1977, *CBS News* ran his commentaries on the news three times a week; and it still runs, from time to time, a segment, anchored by Charles Kuralt, called "On the Road," with human-interest stories, particularly from rural America. *NBC News* introduced a nightly "Segment 3" earlier in 1977; it is sometimes devoted to investigative reporting, exposing what I shall later call moral disorder, but often it is a somewhat longer treatment of a currently topical phenomenon or controversy. About the same time, *ABC News* began to feature interviews with leading public officials, domestic and foreign, and it has also de-emphasized the anchorpersons, giving more play to its major reporters.

The newsmagazines run to about fifty pages of news columns a week. As I noted in the Preface, they combine dramatic narrative with dramatic still pictures, the latter taking up at least a third of the total news page (or "newshole"), and sometimes there are several pages of pictures. The magazines classify the news into regularly appearing and titled sections. The "front of the book" includes national and international news sections and a business section. The "back-of-the-book" sections are more numerous; as a result, many appear only once or twice a month and usually include only two or three stories. These sections report on a number of institutions-*cum*-professions, such as the law, religion, education, the press, medicine, science, and sports; but they also carry reviews of the latest books, films, and art exhibitions. From the point of view of the editors, the most important section is the weekly cover story, which is announced, with an illustration, on the magazine's cover; it may deal with an event in the headlines, a current political controversy, or a longer treatment of one or another back-of-the-book topic. The cover story can appear anywhere in the magazine, but the front and back sections are usually divided by a gossip section, which *Time* calls People and *Newsweek,* Newsmakers; it reports the latest doings of photogenic celebrities. Finally, there are brief feature sections, one of which reports the deaths of well-known people, and at least a couple of pages of letters.

My study, being primarily about domestic news, concentrates on the national news sections, called Nation at *Time* and National Affairs at *Newsweek.* These usually contain a half-dozen stories of varying length, some with "sidebars" reporting related information on major stories. Most are on hard-news topics, but there is always room for one or more "light" human-interest features. Since the magazines come out after all the headlines are known, they review the major events of the week, summarizing and integrating the daily newspaper and television reports into a single whole, and speculating, when possible, about the future. They also add details that their daily peers may have ignored or failed to notice, notably biographical details about people who make headlines, and data or speculation about their motives, when these are available. Unlike television, which eschews opinions, the newsmagazines sometimes conclude their stories with evaluations, although during the 1960s, first *Newsweek* and later *Time* gave up hard-and-fast judgments; now many stories end with what some writers call on-the-one-hand, on-the-other-hand conclusions. Additional opinions enter in through "Time-style" writing, the clever, often ironic style invented by Henry R. Luce, Briton Hadden, and the Ivy League English majors they first hired to write *Time*.

Like the networks, the two magazines report roughly the same stories. *Newsweek* publishes several regular columnists, as well as an invited guest columnist, every week; *Time* runs a weekly essay, usually written in-house. The magazines compete with each other largely through their cover choices, but during the last couple of years, competition has extended to running excerpts from controversial or attention-getting books prior to publication. These changes may constitute the beginning of a trend away from the traditional concept of the newsweekly as a magazine "of record" for the major news of the week.

The Content Analysis

The two chapters which follow report on a content analysis of what is in the news, indicating what news journalists have selected over time, not how they have selected it. The analysis proceeds on the assumption that the news contains a picture of the nation and society, but journalists are not paid to present such a picture. Their task is to create "stories" about what they have observed or whom they have interviewed. Nevertheless, the outcome of their work can be viewed, over time, as a picture of America.

This implies a further assumption: that a content analyst can observe recurring patterns in the news and can find a structure in its content. That structure is not solely a figment of the analyst's work, for journalists, being unable to report everything that happened in America, must select some actors and activities from the many millions they could choose. The result is a recurring pattern of news about a fairly small number of actors and activities.

Still, this pattern is also partly a function of my method, for my content analysis looked at the news with very general categories, deliberately constructed to abstract specific stories from their immediate contexts. For example, all protests and demonstrations were placed in one category, even if they had different targets and participants. (This method also calls attention to the similarities between electronic and print media, which I mentioned in the Preface.)

Needless to say, the picture of nation and society that emerges from the next two chapters is by no means the only one that could be sketched. News, like other kinds of symbolic fare, consists of innumerable bits of explicit and implicit content, and no single content analysis can grasp them all. Also, my analysis follows from the concepts and categories with which I looked at the news, and concepts contain values or have value implications. Because I also looked at what is left out of the news, the findings may at times strike journalists as a critique of their work, but my intent was analytic, not critical. (My critique of the news will appear in Chapter 10.)

Although I glimpse a picture of nation and society in the news, I do not assume that the audience sees the same picture. I am not even sure whether it sees any picture. This is especially true for the large number of viewers and readers who pay only irregular attention to the news. Audiences never look at the news as regularly or as closely as researchers; and insofar as reading or viewing the news is also a form of content analysis, audience members bring their own concepts and categories to bear and may draw a variety of conclusions from the news.

The methodology of my content analysis is in large part qualitative, resulting in a set of hypotheses based on over ten years of watching television news and reading the newsmagazines. Here and there, my observations are supplemented by some quantitative data, drawn from a six-month sample of stories appearing in alternate months during 1967, 1971, and 1975. (For some stories, I also included data from 1969.) I chose these years partly to avoid presidential election years, in which the campaigns drive much other news out of the news media. I also limited myself to domestic activities and actors. I should also note that the quantitative analysis omitted both the Vietnam War and domestic news directly connected with it because I wanted to focus on recurring patterns within America itself; the analysis thus ignores the fact that overseas wars are a recurring phenomenon with many domestic consequences. Some of these consequences did become part of my analysis; although I left out news about policy conflicts on the Vietnam War, I included news about policy conflicts that indirectly stemmed from the war, such as federal domestic expenditures. (How the omission of war and war-related news affects the findings will be indicated in several places.)

The quantitative content analysis is simple; in most instances, I analyzed stories only in relation to one or two categories. The unit of analysis, for both news media, was the individual story, and I classified stories by which actor and activity dominated each. (When two or more actors and activities were dominant, I split the story over the relevant categories by the amount of time or space given to each.) The data on television news came from *CBS News,* and I chose that network because in 1967 it was the only one to have complete scripts available. The choice of newsmagazines was made by flipping a coin, and the coin picked *Newsweek.* Had I chosen another network or magazine, however, the data would have come out virtually the same. Incidentally, analyzing the television scripts was so time-consuming that I could do it only for one year. (Nor did I attempt to analyze videotapes, but I had seen virtually all of the programs in my sample when they were first shown.) In fact, I found that for the general categories with which I am concerned, even analyses by minutes or, in the case of the magazines, by columns were unnecessary; percentages based on the number of stories were almost entirely the same. Because I had planned to compare the electronic and print media, the 1967 television programs and magazine issues were chosen to cover exactly the same time periods. To make the results more comparable, I limited the television analysis to domestic news, and the *Newsweek* analysis to stories in its National Affairs section and cover stories related to it. The 1971 and 1975 magazine samples covered the same months as the 1967 sample.

I should add that the content analyses to follow are at best suggestive; they only begin to hint at how the news portrays America. Obviously, much more needs to be done. I wish that literary analysts, particularly, would apply their insights and methods to news stories that reach tens of millions of people, and devote less effort to the works of "serious" minor writers of the past.

1

Nation and Society in the News

During the late 1960s and early 1970s, the news was dominated by the war in Vietnam; by the ghetto disturbances and their consequences for race relations; inflation and unemployment; and by such always prominent topics as presidential elections and crime. In order to understand the picture of nation and society that appears in the news, I chose not to focus on the specific topics that became newsworthy; instead, I began by looking at the people, or actors, who populate the news, and the activities that become newsworthy.[1]

Actors in the News

Journalists often say that the news ought to be about individuals rather than groups or social processes; and by and large, they achieve their aim. Most news is about individuals, although they may be in conflict with groups or impersonal forces such as "inflation" and "communism."

National news is, by definition, about the nation, and so the most frequent actors in the news are inevitably individuals who play a role in national activities. Which national actors are reported however, is, not inevitable. They could be well-known people, whom I call Knowns; or they could be Unknowns, ordinary people prototypical of the groups or aggregates that make up the nation. The Knowns, furthermore, could be political, economic, social, or cultural figures; they could also be holders of official positions or powers behind thrones who play no official roles.

Knowns in the News

As I have categorized them, Knowns are a combination of people. Some are assumed by journalists to be familiar names among the audience; others have appeared frequently in the news and are therefore well known to the journalists. Some are not necessarily known by name but occupy well-known positions, like governor of a large state or mayor of a troubled city.

In American news, as in the news of all modern nations, the people who appear most frequently in the news are Knowns, and, for the most part, those in official positions. As Table 1 shows, during the time of my study, they took up between 70 and 85 percent of all domestic news, while Unknowns occupied about a fifth of the available time or space. The remainder was given over to animals, objects (such as boats or hurricanes), and abstractions (such as inflation).

TABLE 1: Types of People in the News

| | Percentages | | | |
| | Television Stories | Newsmagazine Columns | | |
	1967	1967	1971	1975
Knowns	71	76	72	85
Unknowns	21	18	23	10
Animals, objects, and abstractions	8	6	5	5
Total stories or columns	1290	645	753	795

Altogether, five types of Knowns dominate the domestic news, although as Table 2 (p. 10) indicates, the percentages vary with the years, as different Knowns become newsworthy.

1. *Incumbent presidents.* The single individual who appears in the news most often, year after year, is the president; and normally, he appears without fail in every issue of the newsmagazine and on virtually all television news programs. In 1975, he took up 23 percent of all magazine space about the well-known and almost 20 percent of all domestic news. Unlike other people who get into the news only when they are involved in unusual, innovative, or dramatic activities, he is the only individual whose routine activities are deemed newsworthy.

2. *Presidential candidates.* The presidency is so central to national news that every presidential hopeful—provided he is affiliated with one of the two major parties—enters the news when he begins to act

TABLE 2: Knowns in the News

| | Percentages | | |
| | Television Stories 1967 | Newsmagazine Columns | |
		1967	1971	1975
Incumbent presidents	11	12	20	23
Presidential candidates	4	17	12	7
Members, House and Senate	16	10	12	4
Other federal officials*	22	9	16	20
Kennedy family members	3	4	9	4
State and local officials	11	13	16	11
Alleged and actual violators of the laws and mores**	10	9	7	22
Astronauts	1	4	0	0
Professionals	9	11	5	3
Business and labor leaders	7	1	0	3
Civil rights leaders	4	7	2	0
Other Knowns	2	3	1	1
Total stories or columns	918	490	544	674

*Also includes members of the Supreme Court, vice-presidents, and past presidents and vice-presidents.

**Some were federal officials, but I coded them as law violators regardless of their official position.

like a candidate and stays there as long as he appears to have a chance at the nomination. During presidential election years, the candidates sometimes obtain more space and time than the incumbents; and in the magazines, far more than in television, news about hopeful candidates begins the year before the election.

3. *Leading federal officials.* Altogether, federal officials appear in the news more often than the president, but on a per capita basis, they of course obtain much less time or space. Even so, the total number of such officials is small; they include the leaders of the House and Senate, the heads of the major committees, and selected cabinet members.[2] Given the role wars and the Cold War play in domestic news, the secretary of state is in the news more than any other cabinet official, even before and after Henry Kissinger's incumbency; during the economic difficulties of the 1970s, the secretary of the treasury appeared frequently.

In recent years, leading members of the White House staff also surfaced in the news; but while they have played a central role in the federal government for a long time, it took the Watergate scandals to make them newsworthy. When the Supreme Court announces its decisions, it, too, breaks into the news, although normally only in brief stories. The Court is also one of the few major federal agencies to be treated as a group, and usually individual justices are in the news only when they are appointed to or retire from the bench. Other federal officials are almost always agency heads, who enter the news when they announce a new policy or come into conflict with the president.

Incidentally, ever since the presidency of John F. Kennedy, members of the Kennedy family have often appeared in the news. Many of the stories are aftermaths to the assassinations of John and Robert Kennedy; but when Robert Kennedy was alive and before he was a presidential candidate, he was in the news more frequently than any other senator of equal seniority.[3] Despite his occasional disappearance from the news in recent years, Edward Kennedy also remains unusually newsworthy, while Jacqueline Kennedy Onassis and the younger members of the family have been virtually the only celebrities to appear in television news and in the magazines' domestic news sections.

4. *State and local officials.* Most of the nonfederal officials in the news are governors and mayors, primarily from the larger states and cities, although they do not come into the news merely because of the offices they hold. In the late 1960s, they appeared in the news mainly because they were nominally in charge of dealing with the ghetto disturbances (which the news media called riots) and their consequences; in the 1970s, because they were responsible for dealing with urban fiscal problems and school bussing. A large number of black mayors have been in the news, however, inasmuch as the election of a black mayor, even in a small city, was (and still is) deemed national news.

5. *Alleged and actual violators of the laws and mores.* In this category, I have included well-known people who get in trouble with the law or become enmeshed in political scandal, as well as ordinary people such as Charles Manson and the presidential assassins, who become Knowns because they have murdered well-known people. Both news media follow trials and congressional investigations at length—for example, those of Adam Clayton Powell and Daniel Ellsberg in the 1960s, the Watergate defendants in the 1970s—and high state and local officials accused of corruption or malfeasance.

Ordinary people who violate the laws or mores also appear in the news, but most violators are Knowns. In 1967, 81 percent of television news and 61 percent of magazine coverage of violators was devoted to Knowns; in 1975, the figure for newsmagazines rose to 89 percent, as Watergate and other governmental scandals drove most unknown violators out of the domestic news arena.

Altogether, a very small number of Knowns, probably less than fifty and most of them high federal officials, are repeatedly in the news. Conversely, others who are often thought to play important roles in the nation do not enter the news very often. For example, the economically powerful, such as officers of large corporations and holders of great wealth, are filmed or written about rarely, and then usually for reasons having little to do with their economic power—primarily when they are involved in some conflict with the federal government or are having legal difficulties. The leaders of business organizations, such as the Chamber of Commerce, the National Association of Manufacturers, or the Committee for Economic Development, are not newsworthy at all. Labor leaders appear more often, but typically in the person of George Meany. Still, over time, James Hoffa probably received more attention than Meany, although not as a labor leader. He was first newsworthy as a defendant and prisoner, and then as a kidnap and murder victim. (Business and labor leaders, however, do appear in the business sections of the magazines but were not included in the analysis reported in Table 2.)

Other seemingly powerful or important individuals on the national scene who rarely appear in the news include generals and admirals, although they were covered during the Vietnam War, and political party leaders, who are briefly newsworthy during election years. Informal holders of political power, such as large campaign contributors and heads of significant local and state political machines, particularly rural ones, are generally ignored, especially between elections. Business lobbyists are accorded much the same treatment as campaign contributors, except when they become actual or accused violators of corruption laws and mores. So-called public-interest lobbyists appear somewhat more often, recently most notably in the person of Ralph Nader.

Political leaders not affiliated with the major parties usually come into the news when they become embroiled in political conflict or legal difficulties with the federal government. As Table 2 indicates, leaders of or speechmakers for civil-rights organizations were in the news during the 1960s but have almost entirely disappeared in the 1970s. The heads of minority parties and more informal political groups receive attention when they lead protest demonstrations or are associated with civil disturbances; those who do not are absent from the

news. The Socialist party became newsworthy over the past decade
only in connection with the death of Norman Thomas; the Socialist
Workers party only when its infiltration by the FBI became known.
Nazi parties and the Ku Klux Klan make the news; conservative and
ultra-conservative groups which eschew what journalists call trouble
do not.

The heads of national voluntary associations, secular and sacred,
receive attention when they act or comment on important or controversial federal issues, such as abortion, and in the last ten years, when
they were involved in issues of sexual or racial equality. The League
of Women Voters was in the news when it permitted men to become
members, and then again when it sponsored the 1976 presidential
debates. Religious bodies are generally covered (other than in the
magazines' Religion sections) when they admit or fail to admit women
to their priesthoods.

Unknowns in the News

Ordinary people, including low-level public officials like policemen
or rank-and-file federal "bureaucrats," obtain about a fifth of the
available time or space, and most of that is devoted to five types of
Unknowns:

TABLE 3: Unknowns in the News

| | | Percentages | |
| | Television Stories | Newsmagazine | Columns |
	1967	1967	1971	1975
Protesters, "rioters," strikers	42	43	40	32
Victims	33	20	25	21
Alleged and actual violators of the laws and mores	8	23	14	17
Voters, survey respondents, and other aggregates	3	2	11	14
Participants in unusual activities	7	12	6	7
Other	7	0	4	9
Total stories or columns	266	118	171	80

1. *Protesters, "rioters," and strikers.* Unknowns appear in the news
most often when they act in opposition, especially against government

policies. In 1967 and 1971, this category constituted 40 percent of all ordinary people in the news, and the proportion would have been higher had I included anti-war demonstrators. In 1967, the newsworthy were largely black participants in the ghetto disturbances; that year, blacks took up 58 percent of all magazine columns devoted to Unknowns, as compared to 12 percent of all columns about Knowns. Television gave them relatively less time: 22 percent of all minutes about Unknowns and 11 percent of all minutes about Knowns. Almost half of the television stories in this category were about strikers, whom the magazines cover in their business sections. By the 1970s, the ghetto disturbances had virtually ended, but protesters remained in the news, principally whites protesting school or residential integration.

2. *Victims.* The next most newsworthy Unknowns are victims of natural or social disorders, most often of crime, and on television, of tornadoes, floods, fires, plane accidents, and other natural or technological disasters. In 1967, however, the victims were primarily people who were killed or injured, or who lost property during the ghetto disturbances; in the years since, they have increasingly been victims of unemployment, particularly people who held steady blue-collar or white-collar jobs in better times. Both news media pay regular attention to victims of bureaucracy, people who suffer from red tape and other bureaucratic phenomena, which are usually depicted as irrational. In the late 1960s, when the permanently poor were newsworthy, stories about them often dealt with their victimization by government agencies or by "the welfare mess," but only rarely with their exploitation by or uselessness to the economy.

3. *Alleged and actual violators of the laws and mores.* Although Unknowns who get in trouble with the law wind up in the news about as often as the Knowns, they are accused or convicted of very different crimes; most of them are kidnappers, mass murderers, or murderers who kill individual victims in unusually grisly ways. Since their victims are also Unknowns—or else they themselves would quickly become Knowns—their actions are usually reported more often than their court trials. Knowns, on the other hand, are more often in the news while standing trial. Ordinary people who carry out nonviolent crimes or violate the mores rarely appear in national news.

4. *Participants in unusual activities.* Unknowns also make the news if they engage in new or bizarre fads, participate in exotic cults or clubs, or develop unusual hobbies. When Unknowns depart from expected roles—for example, old people acting like youngsters or children displaying adult skills—they become eligible for man-bites-

dog stories. Charles Kuralt's *CBS News* feature "On the Road" is normally devoted to such Unknowns, particularly older people.

5. *Voters, survey respondents, and other aggregates.* Unlike the previous four types of Unknowns, who are almost always named individuals, Unknowns also get into the news as aggregates, and then often as statistical ones. The most frequent are voters and poll respondents, the latter appearing with increasing frequency as the news media report poll data on topics other than national elections. Since the onset of the country's economic problems, the unemployed have appeared regularly in unemployment statistics, as have consumers in stories chronicling rising prices. Nonstatistical aggregates, such as nonprotesting parents and children in school-bussing stories, are also in the news from time to time.

The Unknowns who appear in the news are, by most criteria, an unrepresentative lot; and most ordinary people never come into the news, except as statistics. How ordinary people work, what they do outside working hours, in their families, churches, clubs, and other organizations, and how they relate to government and public agencies hardly ever make the news.

The point is obvious, for it is built into the definition of news. Perhaps the place of ordinary people in the news is most dramatically illustrated by the day in 1974 when Congress approved a change in the pension law that affected millions of workers, and all news media, daily and weekly, gave far more space or time, as well as headlines, to the appointment of Nelson Rockefeller to the second-highest office in the land.[4]

Activities in the News

A related way of looking at the news is in terms of the activities reported most often. By "activities," I mean a variety of behavior patterns ranging from political disagreements to deaths; moreover, I deal with the activities themselves, even though in many cases the stories featured a reporter or an interviewee discussing the event.

This analysis, like the one of actors, excluded domestic activities connected with the Vietnam War, whether by public officials or protesters; however, I did carry out a separate tally of the ratio of such news to other domestic news. The National Affairs section of *Newsweek* devoted 19 percent of the section columns during the sample months of 1967 to war-related domestic activities; in 1971, the proportion dropped to 16 percent; and in 1975, to 5 percent, all of these stories reporting the final "winding down" of the war. An analysis of one month of *CBS News* programs in 1967 showed that 26 percent of domestic tell stories and 35 percent of filmed stories were related to the Vietnam War. (For both news media, my tally excluded stories about the battles and other details of the war itself.)

Table 4 indicates the major nonwar domestic activities that appeared in the news, without distinguishing whether they involved Knowns or Unknowns. Of these, eight are most frequent or important.

1. *Government conflicts and disagreements.* Year in and year out, about 15 percent of the domestic news is given over to disagreements and conflicts within and between parts of government and the public officials who personify them. Because the news pays so much attention to the president, much of this type of news reports his disagreements

TABLE 4: Activities in the News

	Television Stories 1967*	Percentages Newsmagazine Columns		
		1967	1971	1975
Government conflicts and disagreements	17	16	17	13
Government decisions, proposals, and ceremonies	12	10	13	13
Government personnel changes, including campaigning	6	22	26	22
Protests, violent and nonviolent	10	13	13	3
Crimes, scandals, and investigations	28	18	17	34
Disasters, actual and averted	14	5	1	1
Innovation and tradition	8	2	4	0
Rites of passage—births, weddings, and deaths	4	5	4	0
Biographies (only in newsmagazines)	0	6	1	9
Unusual activities	2	2	4	2
Other	0	1	0	3
Total stories or columns	392	645	753	795

*This analysis was limited to two sample months of television news.

and conflicts with Congress. The specific topics of conflict vary over time, but since the start of the 1970s, they have primarily been focused on economic policies.

2. *Government decisions, proposals, and ceremonies.* A somewhat smaller proportion of stories deals with less conflict-laden government activities, reporting government decisions—which are, of course, often the resolution of conflicts—and proposals. Most of these are announcements, by the president or other executive-branch officials, of new government policies, although some may later appear as conflict news. Congressional approval of new legislation and Supreme Court decisions also fall into this category. Some journalists call these input stories, as compared to output stories, which report the actual implementation of the proposals and legislation, and appear in the news much more rarely.

3. *Government personnel changes.* In the newsmagazines, the most numerically frequent government news story concerns personnel change, although most of these stories are about the campaign activities of presidential hopefuls, which, as I indicated earlier, television news does not stress in pre-election years. In addition, this category includes the appointments, resignations, and dismissals of high public officials, mostly cabinet secretaries and federal agency heads, and occasionally high state and local officials.

4. *Protests, violent and nonviolent.* In 1967 and 1971, around 10 percent of the activities in the domestic news dealt with demonstrations and disturbances, most often related to racial issues; the proportion would have been higher had I included anti-war protest. If protest is defined as citizen-government conflict, and is combined with intragovernment conflict, political conflict becomes the single most frequent activity in the news. The numbers would have been even higher had war-related conflict been included.

5. *Crimes, scandals, and investigations.* Almost a fifth of the domestic activities in the news is about crimes, scandals, and their investigations, although in 1975, this activity was, thanks to the Watergate and CIA scandals, the most newsworthy. Until then, the typical story concerned the financial misbehavior of government officials, and the investigations and trials connected with them.

6. *Disasters, actual and averted.* Television news gives a good deal of attention to small and large disasters, and to human efforts to avert, control, and explain them. Long-lasting natural catastrophes, or disasters with a heavy toll of lives, are also reported in the newsmagazines, but disasters that claim only a few victims, unless these are Knowns, are usually not reported.

7. *Innovation and tradition.* A regularly appearing, though not very frequent, set of activities has to do with social, cultural, or technological innovation on the one hand, and the decline and disappearance of traditional social practices and technological objects on the other hand. These activities could also be described as "first and last" news, for innovation is often reported as a first; for example, the first woman to be allowed entry into a previously all-male occupation or the debut of some new technological device. Nelson Rockefeller's appointment to the vice-presidency was so newsworthy because he was the first vice-president in American history to have been appointed to the office by a president who was himself appointed to the office.

A related "first" activity, not listed in Table 4, is the record-setting activity, when widely used statistical indicators reach a new high or low. Thus, new highs in unemployment or inflation rates are given special prominence in the news, as were record-setting body counts during the Vietnam War. Concurrently, the news pays regular, if not frequent, attention to the disappearance of traditions, as when old-fashioned army uniforms or prison behavior regulations are abolished, or when a famous ocean liner or train makes its final trip.

8. *National ceremonies:* Even though it does not appear in Table 4, one of the most important activities reported in the news is the national ceremony. The principal ceremony is the national presidential election, which is seen as an indicator of the effectiveness of American democracy. Other recent major ceremonies include the landing of the first astronauts on the moon and the Bicentennial celebrations. The news also features minor ceremonies, such as official visits from foreign heads of state.

Tragic events are treated as national ceremonies, notably the assassinations of John Kennedy and, to a lesser extent, those of Robert Kennedy and Martin Luther King. The mourning of John Kennedy was generally viewed by the news as a time of national cohesion and rededication, as were, in a somewhat similar vein, the 1967 ghetto disorders, once they were concluded; and the Watergate scandal, once Gerald Ford was inaugurated.

Ceremonies are activities which represent the nation or the idea of the nation; and their importance is signified by the fact that the news media frequently break out of routine formats to deal with them at greater length: in "specials" on television and in special sections in the magazines.

Nation and Society

Despite the explicit concern with people and their activities, the recurring subjects of the news are nation and society—their persistence, cohesion, and the conflicts and divisions threatening their cohesion. Strictly speaking, the news is principally about the nation, with what sociologists call society being reported in "soft" news, or features, both on television and in the magazines' back-of-the-book sections. The nation, in turn, is operationally defined as the federal government, and is often signified by the president and the presidency; but it also includes both nationwide and local institutions which are, in effect, "nationalized" by the news.

Thus, the nation is made up of such symbolic complexes as Government, Business and Labor, the Law, Religion, Science, Medicine, Education, the Arts—complexes that have also become sections in the newsmagazines. New complexes are added as new actors and activities come to the fore. The civil-rights marches and the ghetto disturbances were generalized and symbolized into black-white relations—what *Time* later called the Races—while women's liberation led to news about the Sexes. The Cities and the Urban Crisis were other symbolic complexes produced in the sixties. Hippies, the anti-war protesters, the increasing use of marijuana, and changing sexual practices among the young in general added a complex on Youth, while campus protests nationalized the University. The stagflation of the early 1970s brought the Economy into prominence; and in recent years, changes in the traditional nuclear family have raised that institution to complex status.

Many other such complexes exist, some of long standing. Often the subject of magazine cover stories and television documentaries, they also serve as leads to more routine news stories, with actors, activities, or statistics becoming newsworthy by virtue of their shedding some light on the condition of one or another complex. Although Watergate led to considerable copy about its consequences for the most significant such complex, the Presidency, all but the most routine activities of the president may be treated in that way. Since 1975, stories about child abuse and wife beating have appeared in the news, not because they are new or even rapidly increasing phenomena, but because they relate to concerns about the maintenance of the Family. Similarly, a wide variety of once unrelated stories are now connected to a symbolic complex called the Environment.

Conversely, some institutions which are viewed as symbolic or real complexes by others do not enter into the news; thus, there are no stories or magazine sections about what sociologists call the Social Structure (although, to be truthful, sociologists are not agreed on what it is or how it is defined); nor about more easily grasped complexes such as the Class Hierarchy or the Power Structure. Also, while corporate mergers are often newsworthy, there is little news about corporations per se, with the notable exception of multinationals; consequently, a decade's content analysis of the news would not easily show the extent to which the economy is dominated by oligopolies.

The Nation as a Unit

Because the symbolic complexes are components of the nation and reflect on the nation as a unit, threats to them become newsworthy. Furthermore, the stories I earlier called national ceremonials, as well as major wars, scandals, and disasters, focus attention directly on the nation as a unit, since specific stories often judge individual happenings in terms of their consequences for the country as a whole. Foreign news involving American foreign policy readily invites a view of the nation as a unit vis-à-vis other units as well, and some domestic news takes a similar perspective.

Typically, such stories conceive of the nation in anthropomorphic terms; and when the news is tragic or traumatic, it becomes the nation-*cum*-individual whose character and moral strength are tested. After the assassination of John Kennedy, the nation was viewed as being "in mourning"; after Watergate, it was seen as "cynical"; and one magazine described the *Mayaguez* incident as "a daring show of nerve and steel by a nation whose will, after Vietnam, had come under question around the globe." The positing of a national will that needs to be exerted is, to be sure, a conventional rhetorical concept not distinctive to journalists, for politicians often apply it as a solution to conflicts and crises. But then, many of the concepts that appear in the news are not journalistic monopolies.

Ceremonial events, on the other hand, are indicators that the nation remains a unit. The coverage of the July 4, 1976, Bicentennial ceremonies moved the normally objective anchorpersons to express their feelings of pride in the nation on the air, while the otherwise anonymous editors of the two newsmagazines contributed signed articles along the same line. *Newsweek* had established a special Bicentennial section during 1975 and 1976, which frequently dwelt on the commercial and political exploitation of the anniversary; but in its special issue for July 4, 1976, its editor introduced "a group portrait of our people, unadorned by rhetoric or ideology,"[5] which the chief writer of the issue described as "a kind of American chorus, diverse in origin and station, and yet strikingly one at heart."[6] Noting that the "common wisdom of the day pictures Americans as a people sunk in malaise," the magazine argued that "they see themselves, still . . . as a nation born perfect and aspiring to progress," and concluded that "we are . . . a nation haunted by a dream of excellence. We have not yet despaired of making the dream come true."[7] Likewise, the managing editor of *Time* published a two-page essay entitled "Loving America," which dealt at length with the conflicts in "the American self-image" but concluded that "we must deeply believe, and we must prove, that after 200 years the American promise is still only a beginning."[8]

Other journalists also saw America as a cohesive chorus that day. As far as I can determine, none of the major national news media noticed a lack of enthusiasm for or consensus about the Bicentennial on or after July 4, 1976. *The New York Times* carried a story headlined "Few Blacks Inspired by Bicentennial" four days later but placed it on page 62, amidst the shipping and weather news of the day.

On ceremonial occasions, the nation is not only a unit but a Platonic one, defined by the American "spirit," as *Time*'s editor put it, and aspiring to hallowed ideals, as the quotes from both magazines suggest. Of course, Bicentennial stories could not help but be focused on the extent to which America had lived up to the ideals of the Founding Fathers; but even at other times, the ideals that appear in the news are traditional ones, and the stories assess contemporary reality in relation to them.[9] I noted earlier that elections are seen as proving the effectiveness of the democratic forms created by the Constitution. This practice extends beyond ideals, however, for in the news, contemporary events are often compared to traditional practices, in the process hiding the evolution of new solutions. The resignation of Richard Nixon was interpreted as a sign of the continued viability of the presidency rather than, like Lyndon Johnson's decision not to seek a second term, as a new method of forcing an unpopular president to leave office. During the period of campus unrest, interpretative stories were more apt to worry whether the elite universities could continue to train the nation's leaders than to notice that the unrest had resulted in some students taking on national leadership roles.

Divisions in Nation and Society

Because the news is dominated by stories about conflict, and because of its concern with unity and consensus, or the lack thereof, the overall picture is of a conflicted nation and society. Instead of focusing on the more obvious and topical divisions in the news—for example, the conflict between the White House and the Congress, or during the war, between the hawks and doves—I took a more demographic approach. Thus, my content analysis sought to see what divisions in the population appeared in the news; I did so also to shed more light on an earlier topic: what types of people, particularly among the Unknowns, are likely to be newsworthy. Although many divisions could be so studied, I deal here only with those of race, class, sex, age, and ideology.

Race

Over the last ten years, perhaps the primary societal division in the news has been racial, although this was largely a consequence of the ghetto disorders of the late 1960s. In the sample six months of 1967, 1969, and 1971, *Newsweek* carried 180 articles in which blacks were centrally featured. Of these, 22 percent (taking up 30 percent of all columns about blacks) were directly concerned with racial disturbances, particularly in the urban ghettos of the larger cities but also on college campuses and in prisons. Although by 1975 the racial division had not ended, the amount of news devoted to it had decreased considerably; during the sample six months of that year, the magazine published seven articles which centered on blacks and two others in which blacks were targets of white protests, mostly in urban school-integration disputes.

The news coverage of the uprisings has been well studied, notably by the Kerner Commission; and although I will discuss it briefly in Chapter 2, here my analysis will focus largely on racial news unrelated to the disturbances. Television stories in 1967 often dealt with the legal and political difficulties of Congressman Adam Clayton Powell and heavyweight boxing champion Muhammed Ali, but of 288 *Newsweek* columns devoted to racial stories (other than disturbances) during 1967, 1969, and 1971, 30 percent centered on governmental and private integration efforts. Integration has been newsworthy ever since the 1954 Supreme Court decision on school integration; and about half of the integration stories in my three-year sample focused on schools. Many of the integration stories involved whites, just as many of the special reports following the ghetto disturbances were concerned with what whites should be doing for blacks. Consequently, in 38 percent of the stories in my magazine sample, the major actor was white.

Still, the racial news in my sample hardly ignored black activities and actors. Fourteen percent of the columns reported the electoral activities of black politicians; another 8 percent, black organizational activities. Many of these stories were about the Black Panthers, however, and were often critical in tone. Conversely, 11 percent of the columns reported activities to advance black capitalism, culture, and identity, while only 4 percent dealt with social and other pathologies among blacks.[10] By 1975, however, news about black business and cultural activities had been integrated into the relevant back-of-the-book sections; as a result, most of that year's racial news stories were about black criminals, rioters, gangs, and disaster victims.

Generally speaking, then, the national news features middle- and upper-middle-class blacks who have overcome racial, economic, and especially political obstacles, with less affluent blacks more often newsworthy as protesters, criminals, and victims. Blacks already integrated into national institutions and those who make no attempt to enter them tend to be left out of the national news, as are poor blacks simply because they are poor. While the news about the ghetto disturbances and their aftermath included economic explanations of these phenomena, between 1969 and 1971 *Newsweek* carried only one brief story about black poverty that was not tied to the disturbances. Racial news featuring whites reflects a similar dichotomy, with public officials and upper-middle-class citizens who seek to advance racial integration and less affluent whites who demonstrate against it being deemed most newsworthy.

Class

The news pays attention to racial differences, but it does not often deal with income differences among people, or even with people as earners of income. Brief stories about the American distribution of income crop up from time to time when a high public official or other well-known person brings it up; and since the 1970s, stories about unemployment and inflation generally report how these affect various income groups. Still, income appears most frequently in the news in connection with the publication of polls, which now regularly use income as one demographic category.

Class, class groupings, and class differences are, however, rarely reported. Foreign news is different; for example, the political news from Chile prior to the military coup d'état in 1973 regularly described demonstrations by and conflicts among upper-class, middle-class, and working-class groups, although more attention was given to upper-class and middle-class protest against the Allende government than to working-class support for it. Other foreign events are sometimes couched in similar class terms, but these terms are not applied to domestic events, except when a particularly far-fetched Marxist analysis of American society in a Soviet or Chinese publication is quoted to show how incorrect it is.

Still, over the last ten years, the notion of class has begun to creep into the news, although less in economic and political stories than in features on lifestyles and fashions, so that it is used principally as a cultural concept. Perhaps the prime exception is the term "Middle American," coined by columnist Joseph Kraft to refer to what most sociologists would call the working and lower-middle classes. The term originally appeared as a synonym for the Silent Majority, Richard Nixon's label for his intended new conservative constituency. It gained further currency in stories about the white urban backlash against the ghetto uprisings and the War on Poverty. As a result, it became a quasi-political term to describe white ethnics who opposed racial-integration policies.

Insofar as the news contains a conception of the stratification system, it recognizes four strata: the poor (now sometimes called the underclass), the lower middle-class, the middle class, and the rich. "Lower middle-class" is the journalistic equivalent for what sociologists generally call the working class; "middle class" usually refers to the affluent professionals and managers sociologists call upper middle-class. I do not mean here to suggest that sociological terms are necessarily better or more accurate but that the class system in the news leaves out the sociologists' lower middle-class: the skilled and semi-skilled white-collar workers who are, next to blue-collar workers, the largest class in America, however they are labeled. In eschewing the term "working class," the news also brings blue-collar workers into the middle class; and by designating upper middle-class people as middle class, it makes them appear to be more numerous than they actually are.

Journalists shun the term "working class" because for them it has Marxist connotations, but even non-Marxist notions of class conflict are outside the journalistic repertoire of concepts. Strikes are, of course, reported as conflicts between labor and management; but they, as well as disputes between cities and suburbs, or growing and declining regions, are seen as incidents soon to be resolved rather than as permanent conflicts of interest. Moreover, the news is not often couched in terms of economic or other kinds of interests to begin with. To be sure, lobbyists are identified with the clients they represent, and elected politicians become newsworthy when they are shown to have close ties to individual firms or entire industries; but politicians who represent unorganized or less visible economic interests are rarely so identified. Neither are ordinary people viewed as having class interests. When the so-called ethnic revival was in the news, the extent to which ethnic organizations were making economic demands rather than—or as well as—ethnic ones was not emphasized. When ethnic homeowners fought to keep black tenants out of their neighborhoods, the racial conflict made the news, but the endemic homeowner-tenant struggle did not. Nor did anyone notice that Middle American ethnics had economic interests different from those of affluent members of the same ethnic group.

Regardless of how class is conceptualized, the news media do, of course, cover the various income groups and classes in America, and they do so differentially. Most news is about affluent people, almost by definition, since the main actors in the news are public officials, whose incomes are in the top 1 to 5 percent of the income distribution. To be sure, they are not reported as people with high incomes but as people in public roles—except when newly appointed cabinet secretaries must divest themselves of their stocks or put their outside income into blind trusts. However, when the salaries of senators and representatives were raised in 1977, only a few columnists commented on the fact that their salaries were already considerably above the national median. In fact, public officials are distinguished by their geographical, racial, ethnic, and religious background far more often than by their economic background. Their social-class background tends to be even less newsworthy, except perhaps when an elected or appointed official comes from an "old family" (a synonym for the sociologists' upper class) or from a very poor one.

Conversely, other people of unusually high income or prestige appear only when they clash with the government—say, in their role as corporate officers—or when they are found to have violated the laws and mores. Sometimes their May-December marriages or their consumption practices are made into humorous but scornful light stories. When a New York restaurant opened some years ago with a *prix fixe* dinner of $100, its opening was reported with the thinly veiled value judgment that no one should spend that much for a restaurant meal

—or be affluent enough to do so. A 1977 television feature on a new Chicago magazine, with a readership whose median income was over $80,000, treated the publication and its readers as objects of hilarity, and the anchorman introducing it smiled after the feature ended, even though his income made him more than eligible to become a subscriber.

The poor appear in the news less often than the upper class, for while many of the people who are participants in or victims of crime are poor, their income is rarely relevant to the story. The incomes of rich criminals may appear in the news; those of the poor do not. Stories about the poor or about poverty are also rare; in 1967, less than 1 percent of the television news, and from 1967 to 1971 a similar percent of the newsmagazine columns, were devoted to stories centering on the poor or poverty, and most of these were about the federal War on Poverty or anti-hunger policies. Subsequently, the poor have dropped out of the news, except as law violators. When President Jimmy Carter held a news conference on August 6, 1977, to announce his proposals for welfare reform, none of the sixteen questions asked by reporters touched on what the program would do for the poor, although one reporter wanted to know whether it would help keep families together; however, half of the questions concerned the cost of the program, the elimination of fraud, and relief for local and state taxpayers.

Ordinary working-class people once got into the news only as strikers and victims of occupationally connected accidents, e.g., mine disasters, construction accidents, or deaths in the line of duty on the part of policemen and firemen. The ethnic revival, the attempts of Governor George Wallace and former Vice-president Spiro Agnew to speak for Middle America, the violence at the 1968 Chicago Democratic Convention, and the demonstration of the "hard hats" on Wall Street that same year combined to bring working-class people into the news, though mainly as often violent opponents of anti-war demonstrators. But by the mid-1970s, working-class people—and ethnics—had virtually disappeared from the news.

Television and the newsmagazines diverge, however, in their treatment of the middle-class population, for the individuals who appear in the newsmagazines are more often of the upper middle-class, while those on television are frequently of the lower middle-class. For one thing, the magazine's back-of-the-book sections deal primarily with the professions; in fact, many of the section titles are named for the more prestigious ones. The magazines report regularly on medicine but not very often on dentistry; and while breakthroughs in the sciences are covered, those in plumbing or auto repair are not. Members of high-status professions, such as lawyers and doctors, are newsworthy, whereas members of less prestigious professions, such as accountants and nurses, are rarely mentioned. The arts reviewed in the so-called critical sections are those appealing to well-educated audiences; however, the popular television programs most people watch and the novels that become big bestsellers either are not reviewed or are panned.

The magazines tend, actually, to universalize upper-middle-class practices as if they were shared by all Americans. A significant example took place in the early years of the Vietnam War, when anti-war protest was limited almost entirely to students on elite campuses but was, by implication, projected to the entire college population. More often, the universalization is limited, however, to the back-of-the-book news about social problems and new fads or fashions. For example, a cover story on child rearing was devoted to that minority of American families with two breadwinners in which both spouses are sufficiently well educated and affluent to be embarked on careers; but that same year, a front-of-the-book cover on the unemployed dealt with poor and working-class people, and made only passing reference to joblessness in the upper middle-class.

The upper-middle-class monopoly on new fads and lifestyles was nicely illustrated by a 1976 *Newsweek* column about California, written by Mary Kellogg, a reporter who had just returned to New York after a 2½ year "tour of duty" in the San Francisco bureau. The article was critical, as is most writing about California life, and the author drew her observations from "former IBM executives . . . now happily making candles, . . . former college professors who till the soil in wine country, . . . advertising executives who . . . drive cabs, [and] former rat-race proponents who have left to paint driftwood."[11] Cultural innovations by less prestigious people are not in the news very often, however.

Television news, lacking a back-of-the-book section, does not often have as much room for features, but its equivalent stories normally focus on lower-middle-class people. Many features are actually devoted to matters of health; and while the main actors are apt to be professionals, the patients are hardly limited to the upper middle-class. Stories of fads run to things like skateboarding, hang-gliding, and surfing. As in the newsmagazines, these are the fads of an innovating minority, but not of the upper middle-class.

Perhaps the class differences between the two media are best shown by their coverage of school news. In 1967, when education was often newsworthy, 60 percent of the television news stories on education were about public schools, as compared to 23 percent in the magazines; 37 percent of television news dealt with colleges, as compared to 63 percent of the magazine stories. (The analysis excluded news about school desegregation and anti-war protest.) Television's college stories were almost equally divided between public and private schools, with the news about the latter being drawn mostly from Catholic colleges; the newsmagazine reported nearly twice as often on private schools, particularly those in the Ivy League.

Sex

If the primary national division featured in the news of the 1960s was between the races, that of the 1970s has been between the sexes. Although most of the people who appear in the news continue to be men, the news—in both media—has regularly reported on women's liberation and the feminist movement, as well as on male-female relations and other related problems. A large proportion of the stories has dealt with the successful entry of women into previously all-male occupations and institutions; also, the election of a woman politician or the appointment of a female public official is given the same attention as the elevation of a member of a racial minority. In fact, women have become the latest newsworthy minority; and like other minorities, they have come into the news because of their distinguishing minority characteristic.

There are other parallels in the news coverage of the two minorities. As in the case of the races, coverage of the women's movement began with demonstrations, then moved on to organizational activities and the successful entries of leading individuals into important national positions. As a result of the emphasis on politics and professions, the activities of the organized women's movement and the forward march of professional women have shown up in the news more often than either the feminist activities of unorganized women or the concerns of working-class feminists. As in the case of the civil-rights movement, coverage of the women's movement has also emphasized the differences and the conflicts between the militants and the moderates. Feminist critics have pointed out that little change has taken place in the newsworthiness of pinup girls or in the way prostitution is reported, but the depiction of poor black criminals has also remained the same.

Age

Since most news is about politics, in which age divisions are not normally of great significance, the news takes little notice of age groups. With most public officials middle-aged or older, and with most ordinary people involved in crime or protest either adolescent or young adult, the majority of news stories are about these age groups. Personnel replacement stories sometimes note when younger leaders replace older ones, especially in the Congress; and television news, which appeals to a predominantly older audience, runs comparatively more features about older people than do the newsmagazines, which write more frequently about the young, notably of college-student age.

Both news media cluster college students in "generations" of varying lengths. After World War II, they were defined as returning war veterans, eager to learn; during the 1950s, they were a silent or apathetic generation; and in the 1960s, they began as a set of idealists responding to John Kennedy's appeal to get the nation "moving again," and ended as rebels and protesters. When the 1970s began, students were once again seen as pranksters, even if they streaked rather than swallowed goldfish; but this image quickly gave way to a generation of "silent," hard workers, competing feverishly for good grades and for jobs in a shrinking labor market. Generations, then, are not people of similar age but symbolic complexes that typify a period of years and are formed in reaction to major events of that period, such as World War II or the Eisenhower-Joseph McCarthy era. Student behavior, like that of other ordinary people, is thought to be shaped by headline-making events and by national leaders.

Young people, especially affluent ones, are also depicted as violators of adult traditions and adult restraints.[12] During the sample months of 1967, for example, young people, other than those protesting segregation or the war, appeared in *Newsweek* as hippies, pot smokers, student mystics, and lemming-like participants in the annual, sometimes riotous spring vacation trip to southern beaches, which television also reported. Poorer youngsters appeared principally as gang members or individual delinquents.

Ideological Divisions

In the news, ideology is defined as a deliberately thought-out, consistent, integrated, and inflexible set of explicit political values, which is a determinant of political decisions. As a result, ideology is deemed significant mainly in Communist nations and among parties and adherents of the Left and the Right, both overseas and here. Given that definition, most American political groups are thought not to be ideological; and the news does not accept the possibility that sets of less deliberate or integrated political values are also ideologies. Although the news distinguishes between conservative, liberal, and moderate politicians and party wings, these are perceived as shades of opinion; and being flexible, they are not ideologies.

Nevertheless, the news also applies the conventional European ideological spectrum; and even though it is slightly Americanized, it often fits poorly. During Jimmy Carter's first year in office, for example, attempts to categorize him as a liberal or conservative had to be revised frequently; in earlier years, there were problems categorizing working-class organizations which were liberal on economic issues but conservative on "social" issues.

The spectrum used in the news spans seven ideological positions. On the Far Left are the "radicals," democratic socialists and revolutionaries who advocate public ownership of major resources and industries. Then come "left-leaning" liberals, also called ultraliberals, who make up the "McGovern wing" of the Democratic party; they are thought to favor an egalitarian welfare state that stops short of public ownership. "Liberals," who favor the New Deal or its latter-day version, are, by and large, northern Democrats, but this category is very broad, encompassing as well such politicians as Governor Edmund G. (Jerry) Brown, Jr., of California and Governor Hugh Carey of New York, who favor cutbacks in welfare expenditures (and who might more properly be called right-liberals).

"Moderates" are people in the center who take a pragmatic rather than an ideological position and engineer the compromises between liberals and conservatives. "Conservatives," typically Republican, are defenders of private enterprise who are willing to accept some government intervention in the economy but favor subsidies to business as a means of achieving welfare goals. "Ultraconservatives," on the other hand, are adherents of the free market in America, with government intervention limited to foreign policy. On the Far Right are the "right-wing extremists," a term usually reserved for American Nazi parties and the Ku Klux Klan.

Positions on the spectrum are not always described in neutral terms, however. All the major news media approve the moderate core, which includes liberals, moderates, and conservatives; adherents to other positions are treated less favorably, but generally, those on the Right are labeled more politely than those on the Left. Ultraliberals may be called left-wingers, but ultraconservatives are rarely described as right-wingers, and never as reactionaries. Radicals, being "extremists," are labeled as if they were nearly equivalent to Nazis. In addition, the news media do not distinguish between democratic and revolutionary socialists; nor, among the latter, between those who preach revolution and those who actually practice or condone violence. The ultraconservative label also fails to distinguish between those who favor government aid to private enterprise and the libertarians, who advocate a completely free market as well as a turning over of many public services to private industry. But ultraconservatives are set apart from Far Right groups which condone or practice violence. Groups which support violence are always considered extremists, but those which condone violence on the part of government agencies are not.

The World: Domestic Themes in Foreign News

Although this book is concerned with news about America as nation and society, a brief review of major themes in foreign news is relevant for two reasons. First, in some respects, foreign news deals with the same kinds of people and activities as domestic news, but since it does so in fewer and shorter stories, it also brings the priorities in domestic news into sharper focus. Second, foreign news is generally treated with less detachment, and explicit value judgments that would not be considered justifiable in domestic news appear in stories about the rest of the world, particularly from Communist countries. Thus, foreign news makes overt some of the values in the news that will be considered in the next chapter.

Most news in America, as elsewhere, is domestic; in 1967, 14 percent of all television news in my sample was foreign, as compared to 28 percent of all front-of-the-book magazine news.[13] Moreover, like domestic news, foreign news is concerned largely with the nation. Three types of countries dominate foreign news: America's closest or most powerful political allies, especially in Europe; the Communist countries and their major allies; the rest of the world, which is reported only sporadically. Over the years of my study, most foreign news has been about England, France, West Germany, Italy, Japan, Israel, Egypt, the Soviet Union, and mainland China, although not always in that order. Other countries typically make the news only when they are the site of unusually dramatic happenings, such as wars, coups d'état, or major disasters. Calvin Coolidge's observation, made in 1926, that "readers of our newspapers might have imagined revolutions and volcanic disturbances were the chief product of Latin America," remains true fifty years later and applies as much to television and the newsmagazines as to the daily press.[14] Whether countries appear in the news frequently or not, most foreign news stories fall into seven categories.

1. *American activities in a foreign country.* Probably the most time or space is given to what Americans do to, for, and in other countries, notably when American presidents and secretaries of state visit, and when American diplomats participate in carrying out American foreign policy. In addition, the news covers the activities of federal and corporate officials involved in foreign trade, and sometimes those of well-known American entertainers, as well as tourists who get into trouble overseas. Stories in this category are, in fact, often treated as domestic news. For example, in 1967, 75 percent of the newsmagazine stories from Vietnam were about Americans fighting or working there; by 1971, the proportion had risen to 88 percent. But then all news media paid only passing attention to the South or North Vietnamese, and considered Vietnam a domestic story.

2. *Foreign activities that affect Americans and American policy.* Foreign countries also become newsworthy when their activities affect Americans or American interests—for example, if individual Americans are imprisoned or killed, and if American firms are harmed. When a country's foreign policy comes into conflict with American foreign policy, political or economic, or when individual politicians who are known to be particularly anti-American come to power, even small countries may appear in the foreign news.

When newsworthy American happenings surface elsewhere, they often become foreign news. In 1973 and 1974, European inflation was important foreign news because of America's own inflation; in 1975, rising unemployment became news because it mirrored events here. A significant proportion of such stories are likely to come from countries in which American firms are active and from those visited by large numbers of American tourists. (Indeed, these countries provide an additional category of foreign news: tourist stories. The newsmagazines, more than television, not only deal with travel experiences and problems of American tourists, but also keep track of the fate of landmarks, such as the razing of London's Covent Garden and Paris' Les Halles, and the deterioration of Venice.)

Foreign events are also of interest when they represent convergences with American phenomena. England is newsworthy simply because it is thought to converge culturally with the United States; but when other countries adopt American election strategies, incorporate American words into their language, or establish American-type goods and stores, the event is likely to be reported.

By the same token, foreign crime usually becomes newsworthy only if it copies American crime or violates American mores. When European juvenile delinquents use American methods, they may break into the news; so may foreign crimes which accord with American expectations, such as Sicilian family vendettas and Mafia murders. The biggest foreign crime-story in recent years, however, was the report of grafttaking by European and Asian political leaders, but the news dealt largely with payments made to them by American companies. Yet, when political leaders take money from other foreigners, it is not often newsworthy.

3. *Communist-bloc country activities.* Although a considerable amount of foreign news is devoted to keeping up with Soviet Russia, mainland China, and their allies and satellites, the stories deal primarily with two general topics: (1) activities perceived to involve their relationship to the United States; and (2) internal problems or difficulties that reduce their military, economic, or political power vis-à-vis the United States. In fact, almost everything that happens in the Communist bloc is thought to affect Americans or American policy, which helps explain why so much of the foreign news comes from countries within that bloc.

Even in America, the government's failures are more newsworthy than its successes or its routine activities. On the other hand, news from Russia and China is concerned almost entirely with those governments' problems and failures; if successes are reported, these are apt to be labeled suspected propaganda. Political unrest in the Communist countries is news, whereas similar kinds of unrest in other countries is not. In 1967, the revival of the Cultural Revolution in China was covered in so much detail that it was the major foreign-news story of the year.

Although change in top leadership is a major staple of foreign news in all countries (see below), when such changes take place in Communist countries, they are interpreted either in terms of what they might mean for future relations with the United States or as power struggles indicating internal political weakness. The possibility that personnel turnover and succession struggles may reflect domestic policy disputes or prosaic factional politics is rarely considered.

When personnel changes in non-Communist countries involve

Communists, or "leftists," they become as newsworthy as if they were taking place inside the Communist bloc. Consequently, foreign elections in which Communists participate are, as a rule, more newsworthy than others. Ever since the mid-1970s, the major political news from Italy and France has been the possibility—or more correctly, the danger—of a Communist victory. Even British politics, which is usually reported in more detail than that of other foreign countries because England is regarded as an ally and cultural kin, is certain to get into the news when Communists or the left wing of the Labor party wins a political victory.

The official decline in the Cold War brought about a considerable change in the news from Communist countries, especially mainland China, which, for a time after President Nixon's visit, was depicted in a much more favorable light. Although reporters allowed to travel through the country continued to note the monotonous, shabby, and "gray" ambience, which they attributed to egalitarian policies and the regimentation they observed in China's institutions, typically the schools, they also reported the economic and social benefits which the revolution had provided for ordinary Chinese people. They celebrated the enthusiasm and public-spiritedness of the Chinese citizens they observed, particularly their willingness to work hard and to make personal sacrifices in the public interest. In fact, at the time, some commentators noted that these were virtues which had once existed in America, were now lost, and should be revived. After the Chinese welcome to American visitors lost its novelty, however, the news about China again began to emphasize the problems and shortcomings of the country's government.

The reportage from Soviet Russia was much less affected by the official American shift from Cold War to détente; even when Washington and Moscow were proclaiming their friendship for each other, the news continued to report in great detail Soviet violations of civil liberties, the ill-treatment of Jews and intellectuals, and the protest activities of dissidents. Since these phenomena are interpreted as signs of government weakness or immorality, the victims of Russian totalitarianism are treated as heroes or martyrs; and unlike American dissidents, Soviet dissidents are always reported favorably. However, once dissidents come to America, they are viewed from a domestic perspective. When Alexsandr Solzhenitsyn was expelled from the Soviet Union, he was first lionized by the American news media for his courageous exposure of Soviet brutality, but only until American journalists discovered that he did not believe in freedom of the press and was far from enthusiastic about American democracy.

4. *Elections and other peaceful changes in government personnel.* This category of foreign news, like the others to follow, deals with news not of direct relevance to Americans and American policy. Like domestic news, foreign news keeps up with government personnel change, but it is limited to the elections or appointments of de facto heads of state, except in allied countries. Ceremonial presidents in countries governed by prime ministers are rarely deemed newsworthy.

Conversely, foreign news has a sentimental attachment to European royalty, particularly those who serve as figureheads in otherwise democratic countries. The news about European royalty is dominated by two themes. On the one hand, it focuses on pomp and ceremonies, with the marriages and anniversaries of British royalty being given considerable television time and pictorial layouts in the newsmagazines. English monarchs and their ceremonies are viewed both as providing cohesion to a nation in economic and political difficulties, and as symbolizing the nation as a unit for American audiences. News about Scandinavian monarchs, on the other hand, concentrates on their populist impulses and actions, and their respect for democracy. However, when monarchs, ex-monarchs, or any of their relatives perform no useful royal functions and also practice conspicuous consumption, they fall subject to the scorn the news often displays toward the idle rich. While the news media have treated Queen Elizabeth of England deferentially, they have often looked askance at her sister, Princess Margaret.

Non-European royalty receives less respect, and African dictators who appoint themselves kings or emperors are reported as comic figures. Dictators of royal lineage, however, are reported sympathetically, the best example being Haile Selassie, who did not lose the heroic image he received during the Italian invasion of Ethiopia in 1936 until after his deposition, when his autocratic regime was acknowledged *ex post facto.* Similarly, for many years, stories about the Shah of Iran dealt only with his dedication to modernization policies, and news about his brutal treatment of political opponents and intellectuals was still sparse. Because the news has a short memory, the facts that he is a second-generation king and that his father was a dictator who crowned himself are not deemed relevant.

5. *Political conflict and protest.* While foreign news displays the same interest in political conflict as domestic news, foreign conflicts must be more dramatic and usually more violent than their domestic equivalents in order to break into the news. By and large, peaceful demonstrations are rarely covered, unless they are anti-American.

Wars, civil wars, coups d'état, and revolutions are reported from countries large and small; smaller countries, especially in Latin America or Africa, generally break into the news only under such conditions. However, continuous coverage of these events is reserved for conflicts involving American or Communist allies, such as the Mideast wars, and more recently the wars in Angola and the Congo; and to a lesser extent, for conflicts producing racial violence between whites and blacks, as in Rhodesia and South Africa.

Left-wing coups d'état and revolutions often receive more attention than their right-wing equivalents, even when Russia or China is not involved, unless there is widespread killing of civilians or torture of political prisoners. The Cuban revolution was a major foreign story even before the United States and Russia nearly went to war; since then, Chile has probably received more time and space than any other Latin American country because of the rise and fall of the Allende government and the brutalities of its successor.

6. *Disasters.* Foreign disasters must also be more serious than equivalent American ones. An American airplane crash that claims the lives of five or more persons is apt to be reported on television; but a foreign plane crash must involve a much larger loss of life, unless Americans or heads of state are among the victims. Generally speaking, the farther from America the country is geographically, politically, culturally, or racially, the larger the number of victims necessary for the story to receive attention.[15]

The same yardstick applies to other disasters. Floods, earthquakes, and famines which may kill tens or hundreds of thousands of people in Africa and Asia are reported, but normally only once or twice. Tribal or religious wars which lead to the deaths of huge numbers of people also receive less emphasis than the loss of life involved, unless they have political significance for America or unless Americans become seriously involved in helping the victims. The massacres in Biafra became newsworthy for this reason, but also because the Ibo were sometimes described as being culturally similar to Americans. Equivalent massacres in India, Pakistan, Indonesia, East Timor, and other far-off countries were not reported in the same detail. Genocidal wars and nationwide famines may receive little attention in the news because they are unknown in America; the same is true of problems and policies which are foreign to the American experience, such as feudal land-ownership practices and land-reform measures.

7. *The excesses of dictatorship.* The only foreign-news category which lacks a parallel in domestic news consists of stories about

foreign dictators; but these stories concern themselves mainly with the violation of American political values by dictators, and thus illustrate once more the extent to which American ideas and values dominate the reporting of foreign news.

Foreign news is fascinated with dictatorship, and the stories are openly critical of undemocratic practices. Dictators are viewed as having total power; they do not need to worry about compromises or other political processes connected with democracy. Communist dictators engineer cults of personality or resort to terror; non-Communist dictators also maintain their power by bribing financial elites. Although the relationship between national poverty and dictatorship is sometimes noticed, dictatorship is generally perceived to exist because dictators amass personal or military power.

All other things being equal, foreign news gives the most critical attention to dictators who are unusually brutal and openly antagonistic to democracy. During the last several years, Uganda's Idi Amin, currently the prototypical dictator, has been newsworthy on both counts, while some years earlier, former Vice-president Nguyen Cao Ky virtually monopolized the news about South Vietnam, particularly on television, by his readiness to make scornful statements about democracy. Dictators who are not known to be brutal are treated more sympathetically or are not in the news at all, notably Portugal's Salazar and Spain's Franco in the past, Paraguay's Stroessner today, and for a long time, Philippine President Marcos. Conservative dictators who are not brutal are apt to be treated more kindly than socialist ones, either because they are American allies or because they maintain public order; however, in recent years, critical comments have been made about the economic policies of right-wing Latin American dictators, such as Nicaragua's Somoza. Black critics of the news have noted that nonwhite dictators are often reported more negatively than whites and are accused of tribal allegiances that make them appear primitive.

In essence, then, foreign news deals either with stories thought relevant to Americans or American interests; with the same themes and topics as domestic news; or when the topics are distinctive, with interpretations that apply American values. Because American news media devote less air time or print space to foreign news than to domestic news, they often limit themselves only to the most dramatic overseas events. In addition, they tend to follow American foreign policy, even if not slavishly, but they hew closer to the State Department line on foreign news than to the White

House line on domestic news. Foreign news adheres less strictly to objectivity than domestic news; but as the next chapter will show, the values it applies are not very different from those that appear, less explicitly, in domestic news. As in most other countries, American foreign news is ultimately only a variation on domestic themes.

2

Values in the News

Journalism is, like sociology, an empirical discipline. As a result, the news consists not only of the findings of empirical inquiry but also of the concepts and methods which go into that inquiry, the assumptions that underlie concepts and methods, and a further set of assumptions which could be tested empirically if journalists had the time. These assumptions being mainly about the nature of external reality, I call them reality judgments. Chapter 1 can therefore be read, in part, as an analysis of some of the reality judgments in the news.

Like other empirical disciplines, the news does not limit itself to reality judgments; it also contains values, or preference statements. This in turn makes it possible to suggest that there is, underlying the news, a picture of nation and society as it ought to be. The values in the news are not necessarily those of the journalists, nor are they always distinctive to the news. As I shall suggest in Part 2, many are shared by or originate with the sources from whom the journalists obtain information and other sectors of America.

The Analysis of Values

Journalists try hard to be objective, but neither they nor anyone else can in the end proceed without values. Furthermore, reality judgments are never altogether divorced from values. The judgment that the president and leading public officials represent the nation, for example, carries with it an acceptance of, if not a preference for, this state of affairs; otherwise, stories which investigate whether the president does, in fact, represent the nation would be more numerous.

The values in the news are rarely explicit and must be found between the lines—in what actors and activities are reported or ignored, and in how they are described. If a news story deals with activities which are generally considered undesirable and whose descriptions contain negative connotations, then the story implicitly expresses a value about what is desirable. In the process, the news also assumes a consensus about values that may not exist, for it reminds the audience of values that are being violated and assumes that the audience shares these values. When a story reports that a politician has been charged with corruption, it suggests, *sotto voce,* that corruption is bad and that politicians should be honest. Much news is about the violation of values; crime and disasters are not reported because these phenomena are desirable, which is why journalists and audiences alike speak of bad news.

Nevertheless, because journalists do not, in most instances, deliberately insert values into the news, these values must be inferred. Since inference cannot take place without an inferrer, however, and different people come to the news with different preconceptions, they may infer many different values from what they see or read.[1] Also, the analyst's own values make him or her more sensitive to some values in the news than to others; as a result, content analysis is often a comparison of the analyst's values with those that "exist" in the content.

Furthermore, even if the values *in* the news could be inferred unambiguously—that is, if all inferrers agreed about them—there are also values that stem *from* the news. There is a difference between the values in the news and the value implications of the news; but while the former may ultimately originate with the journalists, the latter do not. Journalists are sensitive to the difference between the news and its implications, but critics and content analysts are not always equally so, and the values they may see in the news and among journalists are actually implications. Ephron analyzed the network television news about the 1972 presidential election in terms of whether stories would help or hurt the candidates. She studied the implications of the content rather than the content, however, and concluded, on the basis of her own values, that the networks were engaged in a vendetta against Richard Nixon.[2] Other conservative critics have attacked the news media for their coverage of the ghetto disturbances and the anti-war demonstrations, maintaining that these stories, by publicizing dissent, had negative implications for the status quo. Critics on the left do likewise, for they perceive stories that fail to report the faults of capitalism or that ignore the activities of radical activists as holding back drastic change. Although the dividing line between values and value implications is not always easy to maintain, my analysis will eschew the latter as much as possible.

Even so, identifying values in the news is a virtually impossible task because there are so many of them; indeed, every story expresses several values. Consequently, I shall employ a narrow definition of values, examining only preference statements about nation and society, and major national or societal issues. I also distinguish between two types of values, which I call topical and enduring, and I will analyze only the latter. Topical values are the opinions expressed about specific actors or activities of the moment, be they a presidential appointee or a new anti-inflation policy. These manifest themselves in the explicit opinions of newsmagazine stories and television commentary, as well as in the implicit judgments that enter into all stories. Enduring values, on the other hand, are values which can be found in many different types of news stories over a long period of time; often, they affect what events become news, for some are part and parcel of the definition of news. Enduring values are not timeless, and they may change somewhat over the years; moreover, they also help to shape opinions, and many times, opinions are only specifications of enduring values.

The list that follows is limited to the enduring values I have found in the news over the last two decades, although all are probably of far more venerable vintage; obviously, it includes those which this inferrer, bringing his own values to the task, has found most visible and important. The list does not claim to be complete; and since I undertook no quantitative analyses, it does not suggest which values appear most frequently.

The methods by which I identified the values were impressionistic; the values really emerged from continual scrutiny of the news over a long time. Some became apparent from the analysis of Chapter 1; others came from the ways actors and activities are described, the tones in which stories are written, told, or filmed, and the connotations that accrue to commonly used nouns and adjectives, especially if neutral terms are available but not used. When years ago the news reported that Stokely Carmichael had "turned up" somewhere, while the president had, on the same day, "arrived" somewhere else; or when another story pointed out that a city was "plagued by labor problems," the appropriate values were not difficult to discern, if only because neutral terms were available but were not used. However, sometimes neutral terms are simply not available. The news could have called the young men who refused to serve in the Vietnam War draft evaders, dodgers, or resisters, but it rarely used the last term. Of course, individual words only provide clues to values, not conclusions about them; also, newsmagazines are more easily analyzed by this method because they eschew neutral terms for stylistic reasons, although all of the above examples are from television.[3]

Enduring Values in the News

The enduring values I want to discuss can be grouped into eight clusters: ethnocentrism, altruistic democracy, responsible capitalism, small-town pastoralism, individualism, moderatism, social order, and national leadership. These last two are more striking than the rest and will therefore be described in greater detail. There are many others, of course, which I shall leave out either for reasons of space or because they are taken for granted, even though they are values. Among these, for example, are the desirability of economic prosperity; the undesirability of war *sui generis* (which does not always extend to specific wars); the virtues of family, love, and friendship; and the ugliness of hate and prejudice.[4] The news often supports the kinds of values sometimes unfairly belittled as "motherhood values."

Ethnocentrism

Like the news of other countries, American news values its own nation above all, even though it sometimes disparages blatant patriotism. This ethnocentrism comes through most explicitly in foreign news, which judges other countries by the extent to which they live up to or imitate American practices and values, but it also underlies domestic news. Obviously, the news contains many stories that are critical of domestic conditions, but these conditions are almost always treated as deviant cases, with the implication that American ideals, at least, remain viable. The Watergate scandals were usually ascribed to a small group of power-hungry politicians, and beyond that, to the "Imperial Presidency"—but with the afterthought, particularly following Richard Nixon's resignation, that nothing was fundamentally wrong with American democracy even if reforms were needed.

The clearest expression of ethnocentrism, in all countries, appears in war news. While reporting the Vietnam War, the news media described the North Vietnamese and the National Liberation Front as "the enemy," as if they were the enemy of the news media.[5] Similarly, weekly casualty stories reported the number of Americans killed, wounded, or missing, and the number of South Vietnamese killed; but the casualties on the other side were impersonally described as "the Communist death toll" or the "body count."

Again, as in war reporting everywhere, the committing of atrocities, in this case by Americans, did not get into the news very often, and then only toward the end of the war. Seymour Hersh, the reporter credited with exposing the Mylai massacre, had considerable difficulty selling the story until the evidence was incontrovertible.[6] The end of the war in Vietnam was typically headlined as "the Fall of South Vietnam," with scarcely a recognition that by other values, it could also be considered a liberation, or in neutral terminology, a change in governments.

Altruistic Democracy

While foreign news suggests quite explicitly that democracy is superior to dictatorship, and the more so if it follows American forms, domestic news is more specific, indicating how American democracy should perform by its frequent attention to deviations from an unstated ideal, evident in stories about corruption, conflict, protest, and bureaucratic malfunctioning. That ideal may be labeled altruistic democracy because, above all, the news implies that politics should follow a course based on the public interest and public service.

The news tends to treat politics per se as a contest, identifying winners and losers more than heroes and villains. Although the news has little patience for losers, it insists that both winners and losers should be scrupulously honest, efficient, and dedicated to acting in the public interest. Financial corruption is always news, as is nepotism, patronage appointments, logrolling, and "deals" in general. Decisions based, or thought to be based, on either self-interest or partisan concerns thus continue to be news whenever they occur, even though they long ago ceased to be novel events.

Politicians, politics, and democracy are also expected to be meritocratic; the regular activities of political machines are regularly exposed, and "machine" itself is a pejorative term. Although the news therefore regards civil-service officials more highly than "political appointees," the former are held to a very high standard of efficiency and performance; as a result, any deviant bureaucratic behavior becomes newsworthy. "Waste" is always an evil, whatever the amount; the mass of paperwork entailed by bureaucracy is a frequent story, and the additional paperwork generated by attempts to reduce the amount of paperwork is a humorous item that has appeared in the news with regularity over the years. Officials, whether elected or appointed, are also expected to be spartan in their tastes; consequently, in 1977, Secretary of H. E. W. Joseph Califano got into the news when he hired a chef for his official dining room. The story lasted longer than a concurrent report that he had hired a combination bodyguard-office manager, at almost four times the cook's salary.

The same high standards apply to citizens, however. Citizens should participate; and "grassroots activity" is one of the most complimentary terms in the vocabulary of the news, particularly when it takes place to foil politicians or bureaucrats, or to eliminate the need for government action. Ideally, citizens should help themselves without having to resort to government aid, and occasionally stories of such an occurrence suggest a revival of a past and now extinct tradition. As a result, the news seems to imply that the democratic ideal against which it measures reality is that of the rural town meeting—or rather, of a romanticized version of it. Citizen participation should also be as unselfish as that of politicians. Organized lobbying and the formation of pressure groups in behalf of citizens' self-interest is still reported in suspect tones, though not as suspect as when corporate lobbyists are covered.

The support for altruism correlates with an emphasis on what one might call the official norms of the American polity, which are derived largely from the Constitution. Consequently, the news endorses, or sets up as a standard, the formal norms of democracy and the formal structures of democratic institutions as established by the Founding Fathers. Concurrently, it treats as suspect the informal norms and structures that have developed in the polity to allocate power and resources; in effect, the news defends democratic theory against an almost inevitably inferior democratic practice.

In the process, the news keeps track of the violations of official norms, but it does so selectively. Over the years, the news has been perhaps most concerned with freedom of the press and related civil liberties; even recurring local violations, by school boards which censor library shelves, have often become national news. Violations of the civil liberties of radicals, of due process, habeas corpus, and other constitutional protections, particularly for criminals, are less newsworthy.

Another official norm to which the news pays frequent attention is racial integration. Because citizens are expected to live up to these norms altruistically and because the norms are viewed as expressions of the public interest, the violations of the legal and political rights of blacks in the South were news even before supporters of the civil-rights movement began to demonstrate. While attention has now shifted largely to the North, the election of any black official continues to be news, since it is treated as an affirmation and realization of the official norm.

Activists who strive for the realization of democratic norms are often described in the news as extremists or militants, but the activists supporting racial integration were never so labeled, much to the dismay of southern television stations affiliated with the networks. Conversely, black-power activists were newsworthy in part because they rejected integration; they were almost uniformly labeled militants, with equally activist supporters of integration described as moderates.

Actually, the news tends to treat all formal governmental goal statements, and even campaign promises, as official values, and reports when these are violated. In particular, politicians who run campaigns emphasizing their honesty are closely watched, and the deviations from their own stated ideals by Eugene McCarthy, George McGovern, and Jimmy Carter consequently became headline news.

While—and perhaps because—the news consistently reports political and legal failures to achieve altruistic and official democracy, it concerns itself much less with the economic barriers that obstruct the realization of the ideal. Of course, the news is aware of candidates who are millionaires or who obtain substantial amounts of corporate or union campaign money, but it is less conscious of the relationship between poverty and powerlessness, or even of the difficulty that Americans of median income have in obtaining political access. That economic power affects the achievement of the democratic ideal continues to be viewed more as a southern populist campaign theme—as it was again during the 1976 election campaign of Jimmy Carter—than as a fact of life, for in the altruistic and official democracy valued by the news, economics are, and should be, kept separate from politics.

The relative inattention to economic obstacles to democracy stems from the assumption that the polity and the economy are separate and independent of each other. Under ideal conditions, one is not supposed to affect or interfere with the other, although typically, government intervention in the economy is more newsworthy and serious than private industry's intervention in government. Accordingly, the news rarely notes the extent of public subsidy of private industry, and it continues to describe firms and institutions which are completely or partly subsidized by government funds as private—for example, Lockheed, many charitable organizations, and most privately run universities.

Responsible Capitalism

The underlying posture of the news toward the economy resembles that taken toward the polity: an optimistic faith that in the good society, businessmen and women will compete with each other in order to create increased prosperity for all, but that they will refrain from unreasonable profits and gross exploitation of workers or customers. Bigness is no more a virtue in business or union organization than in government, so that the small and family-owned firm is still sometimes presented as the ideal. While monopoly is clearly evil, there is little explicit or implicit criticism of the oligopolistic nature of much of today's economy. Unions and consumer organizations are accepted as countervailing pressures on business (although the former much less so than the latter), and strikes are frequently judged negatively, especially if they inconvenience "the public," contribute to inflation, or involve violence.

Economic growth is always a positive phenomenon, unless it brings about inflation or environmental pollution, leads to the destruction of a historic landmark, or puts craftsmen or craftswomen out of work. In the past, when anchormen gave the stock market report, even the most detached ones looked cheerful when the market had had a good day, assuming this to be of universal benefit to the nation and the economy.

Like politicians, business officials are expected to be honest and efficient; but while corruption and bureaucratic misbehavior are as undesirable in business as in government, they are nevertheless tolerated to a somewhat greater extent in the former. For example, the January 2, 1978, issue of *Time* included a three-page critique of government bureaucracy, entitled "Rage Over Rising Regulation: To Autocratic Bureaucrats, Nothing Succeeds Like Excess"; but a business-section story reporting that General Motors had sent refunds to the purchasers of Oldsmobiles equipped with Chevrolet engines was only one column long and was headed "End of the Great Engine Flap." Actually, the news often fails to notice that corporations and other large private agencies are also bureaucracies given to red tape.

Time tends to be somewhat more tolerant of private enterprise and more critical of government activities than is *Newsweek;* then, too, business sections in both magazines are still dedicated to the celebration of entrepreneurs and innovators, as well as corporate executives who show themselves to be able managers. Although this endorsement is less enthusiastic than it was in the 1950s and 1960s, innovation and risk taking are seen as more desirable in business than in public agencies. Consequently, governmental demonstration projects must succeed the first time around, while the failure of business experiments is treated with greater tolerance, even if the public pays the bill in both instances.

Domestic news has by now acknowledged the necessity for the welfare state; even in the good society, the market cannot do everything. The term "welfare state" itself is reserved largely for foreign countries, however, and attitudes toward it are more clearly evident in foreign than in domestic stories. These tend to dwell more on its problems and failures than on its successes, most recently in England and Sweden, where the welfare state is particularly seen as a threat, from high tax rates and public control over investment, to the ability of the economy to provide sufficient incentives for economic growth. In America, the welfare state is expected to aid people who cannot participate in the market or who are hard-pressed by inflation; that government can provide useful services, or that it can sometimes do so more effectively than private enterprise, is not often acknowledged.

It is now accepted that the government must help the poor, but only the deserving poor, for "welfare cheaters" are a continuing menace and are more newsworthy than people, other than the very rich, who cheat on their taxes. Public welfare agencies are kept under closer scrutiny than others, so that although the news reported on the "welfare mess" in the 1960s, it did not describe equivalent situations in other government agencies in the same way. There was, for example, no "defense mess," and what is "waste" in H. E. W. programs is "cost overruns" in Pentagon programs.

American news is, of course, consistently critical of Communist and democratic-socialist economies.[7] In fact, foreign news is more worried about the political and cultural shortcomings of socialism or communism. To be sure, both are suspect because public ownership and other socialist programs will do away with private property and impair productivity and growth; but descriptions of existing income distributions, in America and elsewhere, now regularly imply that economic inequality is undesirable, even if income redistribution is not the right solution. Still, the primary dangers of socialism are cultural homogeneity, the erosion of political liberties, and the burgeoning of bureaucracy.

Although domestic politicians who criticize governmental welfare measures as socialistic or communistic no longer get the attention they once did, domestic news also remains critical of American socialism.

More correctly, the news ignores it, for socialist critiques of the American economy, as well as the activities of America's socialist parties and informal groups, are not newsworthy. The socialist factions in the protest movements of the 1960s, and in the feminist and other movements of the 1970s, have also been ignored. At the same time, however, libertarian groups, which advocate a return to complete market competition, get equally little play in the news.

Small-town Pastoralism

The rural and anti-industrial values which Thomas Jefferson is usually thought to have invented can also be found in the news, which favors small towns (agricultural or market) over other types of settlements. At one time, this preference was complemented by a celebration of the large city and of the vitality of its business and entertainment districts; but the end of this period can be dated almost exactly by *Life*'s special issue on the cities, which appeared in December 1965.

Although the belief that cities should be fun places and that large, central business-district renewal projects should "revitalize" them still continues to be held, for the last ten years cities have been in the news almost entirely as problematic, with the major emphasis on racial conflict, crime, and fiscal insolvency. Suburbs are not often newsworthy, despite the fact that a near majority of Americans now live in them, and they, too, have generally received a bad press. During the 1950s and 1960s, suburbs were viewed as breeding grounds of homogeneity, boredom, adultery, and other evils; since then, they have come into the news because they are suffering increasingly from "urban" problems, particularly crime, or because they keep out racial minorities and stand in the way of racial integration.

During the 1960s, new towns (like Columbia, Maryland) were welcomed precisely because they were expected to overcome the faults of both city and suburb, restoring the more intimate social relationships and sense of community ascribed to small towns; but that hope was lost when they also encountered fiscal problems and manifested racial conflict and other "urban" ills as well. As a result, the small town continues to reign supreme, not only in Kuralt's "On the Road" but also in television and magazine stories about "the good life" in America. Stories about city neighborhoods judge them by their ability to retain the cohesiveness, friendliness, and slow pace ascribed to small towns, and during the period of journalistic interest in ethnicity, to the ethnic enclaves of the past.

Needless to say, the pastoral values underlying the news are romantic; they visualize rural and market towns as they were imagined to have existed in the past. Today's small towns are reported nostalgically; and their deaths, or their being swallowed up by the expanding suburbs, is a frequent and sentimental story. During the 1960s, the youthful exodus into the hinterlands of Vermont and California was first welcomed as a small-town revival. In recent years, the growth of small towns, especially in the South, has also been reported as a revival; but generally, economic growth is viewed as a danger to "community," even if it is valued in the abstract.

Small-town pastoralism is, at the same time, a specification of two more general values: the desirability both of nature and of smallness per se. The news dealt with the conflict between the preservation of nature and the activities of developers long before the environment and ecology became political issues; and more often than not, the news took at least an implicit stand against the developers. The post-war developers of suburbia were seen as despoiling the land in their rapacious search for profits; that they were concurrently providing houses for people was rarely noted. The arrival of the energy crisis and the decline of economic growth have forced the news into an agonizing choice, however, between its defense of nature and the need for more jobs or fuel.[8]

The virtue of smallness comes through most clearly in stories that deal with the faults of bigness, for in the news, Big Government, Big Labor, and Big Business rarely have virtues. Bigness is feared, among other things, as impersonal and inhuman. In the news as well as in architecture, the ideal social organization should reflect a "human scale." The fear of bigness also reflects a fear of control, of privacy and individual freedom being ground under by organizations too large to notice, much less to value, the individual. As such, bigness is a major threat to individualism, an enduring value in the news, to be discussed below. Consequently, the news often contains stories about new technology that endangers the individual—notably the computer, which is viewed anthropomorphically, either as a robot that will deprive human beings of control over their own lives or as a machine endowed with human failings, which is therefore less of a threat. In any case, there is always room for a gleeful story about computers that break down. The news has, however, always paid attention to the dangers of new technology: when television sets were first mass-produced, they were viewed as dehumanizing because they robbed people of the art of conversation; related fears were expressed at the time of the institution of digit-dialing in telephones.

Conversely, the news celebrates old technology and mourns its passing, partly because it is tied to an era when life was thought to have been simpler, partly because it is viewed as being under more individual control. Sentimental features about the closing of a business based on craftsmanship and about the razing of architectural land-marks, including the industrial mills that were once hated symbols of an exploitative industrialism, are commonplace. Even more attention is paid to the berthing of an ocean liner or the elimination of an old railroad train. The Cunard flagship is in the news about as often as the Queen of England; and the captain of an ocean liner is a far more admired figure than the pilot of a jumbo jet, even if both now use radar to steer their vehicles, and the vehicles themselves are both owned by large corporations.

Small-town pastoralism and old technology may in the end be surrogates for a more general value: an underlying respect for tradition of any kind, save perhaps discrimination against racial, sexual, and other minorities. Tradition is valued because it is known, predictable, and therefore orderly, and order is a major enduring news value. Novel phenomena are, despite their being the basic raw material of news, potential threats to order. Thus, California, which is, from the Eastern perspective of the news, still a new land, is viewed as the fountainhead of bizarre new ideas.[9]

Individualism

It is no accident that many of the characters in Kuralt's pastoral features are "rugged individualists," for one of the most important enduring news values is the preservation of the freedom of the individual against the encroachments of nation and society. The good society of the news is populated by individuals who participate in it, but on their own terms, acting in the public interest, but as they define it.

The ideal individual struggles successfully against adversity and overcomes more powerful forces. The news looks for people who act heroically during disasters, and it pays attention to people who conquer nature without hurting it: explorers, mountain climbers, astronauts, and scientists. "Self-made" men and women remain attractive, as do people who overcome poverty or bureaucracy. Still, the most pervasive way in which the news pays homage to the individual is by its focus on people rather than on groups.

Conversely, the news also continually deals with forces that may rob people of their initiative as individuals. The fear of new technology is, on one level, a fear of its ability to emasculate the individual; computers and data banks invade the privacy that enables people to act as individuals. Communism and socialism are viewed similarly, and capitalism is valued less for itself than for the freedom it offers to at least some individuals. During the 1950s, the suburbs were thought to induce conformity, which would stifle individuality; in recent years, various youth cultures and community developments in the Sunbelt have been criticized in the same fashion. In writing her farewell to California, Kellogg prefers "New York's chaos to ennui," and worries that the easy life of the West would result in "letting the spark die."[10] Her spark is the struggle not only against conformity but against laziness. Individualism is also a source of economic, social, and cultural productivity. The news values hard and task-oriented work, and is upset about the decline of the "work ethic."

Individualism is, in addition, a means of achieving cultural variety, and variety is in turn another weapon against the dangers both of bigness and conformity. The small town is a last hiding place of the stubborn eccentric, and ethnic enclaves consist of people who try to stave off complete Americanization. The news is fearful of mass society, although it neither uses that term nor worries that the masses will overwhelm high culture.

Moderatism

The idealization of the individual could result in praise for the rebel and the deviant, but this possibility is neutralized by an enduring value that discourages excess or extremism. Individualism which violates the law, the dominant mores, and enduring values is suspect; equally important, what is valued in individuals is discouraged in groups. Thus, groups which exhibit what is seen as extreme behavior are criticized in the news through pejorative adjectives or a satirical tone; in many spheres of human activity, polar opposites are questioned and moderate solutions are upheld.

For example, the news treats atheists as extremists and uses the same approach, if more gingerly, with religious fanatics. People who consume conspicuously are criticized, but so are people such as hippies, who turn their backs entirely on consumer goods. The news is scornful both of the overly academic scholar and the over-simplifying popularizer: it is kind neither to highbrows nor to lowbrows, to users of jargon or users of slang. College students who play when they should study receive disapproval, but so do "grinds." Lack of moderation is wrong, whether it involves excess or abstention.

The same value applies to politics. Political ideologists are suspect, but so are completely unprincipled politicians. The totally self-seeking are thought to be consumed by excessive ambition, but the complete do-gooders are not to be believed. Political candidates who talk only about issues may be described as dull; those who avoid issues entirely evoke doubts about their fitness for office. Poor speakers are thought to be unelectable, while demagogues are taken to be dangerous. Those who regularly follow party lines are viewed as hacks, and those who never do are called mavericks or loners—although these terms are pejorative only for the politically unsuccessful; the effective loner becomes a hero.

The political values in the news will be discussed at the end of this chapter, but they are dominated by the same principle; in fact, insofar as the news has an ideology of its own, it is moderate. Since the ideology in the news is implicit, however, and not a deliberate or integrated doctrine, the political values may even be derivative, reflecting a belief in the virtue of moderation that extends across all human activities.

Social Order and National Leadership

If one looks at the actors and activities which have dominated the news over the years, it is possible to divide much of what appears on television and in the magazines, particularly as hard news, into two types of stories. One type can be called disorder news, which reports threats to various kinds of order, as well as measures taken to restore order.[11] The second type deals with the routine activities of leading public officials: the day-to-day decisions, policy proposals, and recurring political arguments, as well as the periodic selection of new officials, both through election and appointment. These story types in turn suggest two additional values: the desirability of social order (but as will be seen, of a certain type) and the need for national leadership in maintaining that order.

Disorder and Order

Disorder stories fall into four major categories: natural, technological, social, and moral. Natural disorder news deals with natural disasters, such as floods and earthquakes, as well as industrial accidents which can be ascribed to natural forces, such as many but not all plane crashes or mine cave-ins. Technological disorder concerns accidents which cannot be ascribed to nature. Social disorder news deals with activities which disturb the public peace and may involve violence or the threat of violence against life or physical property; it also includes the deterioration of valued institutions, such as the nuclear two-parent family. Moral disorder news reports transgressions of laws and mores which do not necessarily endanger the social order.

These categories are not used by journalists, nor are they hard and fast. A major fire may first be reported as a natural or technological disaster, but if there is evidence of human failure or arson, it soon becomes a moral disorder story. Similarly, once social disorder ends, the news looks for the responsible parties and identifies agents of moral disorder. Conversely, when high officials are guilty of moral disorder, the news may raise the possibility of resulting social disorder. If people lose faith in their leaders, there is fear that the social fabric may unravel.

Social Disorder News

American news media have always emphasized stories of social disorder, both at home and abroad.[12] Foreign news is, as I suggested in Chapter 1, limited to violent political disorder, but domestic news also keeps track of nonviolent and nonpolitical demonstrations. (Conflict among public officials is reported so matter-of-factly that it is a routine activity story rather than disorder news; the conflict is expected; and because it involves officials rather than ordinary people, it is not treated as a threat to the public peace.)

During the 1960s, domestic social disorder news was dominated by the ghetto disturbances and by anti-war marches, demonstrations, and "trashings." Marches and demonstrations are, from one point of view, protest activities, but the news almost always treated them as potential or actual dangers to the social order. In the beginning, the television cameras focused mainly on bearded and other unusual-looking participants who were, in those days, assumed to threaten the social order by their very appearance. Later, when demonstrations became a conventional strategy, they became particularly newsworthy when reporters noticed trouble.

At first, "trouble" was defined as stone throwing and other physical or verbal violence against the police, or fights between demonstrators and hecklers, often from the American Nazi party. Marches, especially those involving large numbers, were deemed potential threats to the social order because so many people were involved; consequently, trouble was almost inevitable, and if it did not take place, that fact was also newsworthy. "Violence," as well as trouble, was perceived as action against constituted legal authority; and until the 1968 Chicago Democratic Convention, police violence against the demonstrators was viewed as action taken to restore order and was rarely called violence. What the demonstrators described as police brutality was at best shown in passing on television, while day-to-day police brutality in the ghettos was not normally news, perhaps because it was routine.

The turning point in the treatment of anti-war demonstrators came in Chicago when the behavior of the police was reported almost universally as a "police riot." Still, earlier events, and news about them, contributed to the change, for after the ghetto disturbances, police brutality against its residents began to be newsworthy. More important, perhaps, earlier in 1968, most national news media had been persuaded by the Tet offensive that the Vietnam War could or should not be continued. From then on, the news started to see the demonstrators more as protesters, and to pay closer attention to the middle-class, middle-aged, and conventionally dressed young marchers. Eventually, some demonstrations even began to be seen as responses to the moral disorder on the part of the president and his hawkish policy makers.

Disorder news could, of course, be analyzed as valuing disorder, and some critics of the news media have charged that overly liberal journalists have done so to justify the need for political change. Actually, however, domestic disorder stories are, except in unusual circumstances, as much concerned with the restoration of order by public officials as with the occurrence of disorder. For example, the Kerner Commission study of the network television coverage of the 1967 uprisings showed that only about 3 percent of the sequences were devoted to what it called riot actions, 2 percent more to injuries and deaths, and at least 34 percent to what I call order restoration.[13] Although the emphasis on order restoration could be explained by the inability of television to gain immediate camera access to the disorder, the newsmagazines were not hampered by such considerations. Even so, Newsweek's ghetto-disturbance stories, in my 1967 sample, devoted four times as much text to police and army attempts to restore order as to descriptions of the disturbances.

After the disturbances had ended, the concern with order restoration continued, for television documentaries and special sections of the newsmagazines suggested, without condoning participants in the disturbances, that racial segregation and, to a lesser extent, economic inequality, had helped to bring them about, the implication being that government and economic reforms were necessary to prevent their recurrence. On both practical and moral grounds, the news argued for a more altruistic democracy and a more responsible capitalism. By the start of the 1970s, however, the fear of ghetto disorders had disappeared, and so had the pleas for reform, although they returned briefly after the looting that accompanied the 1977 power failure in New York City. This time, the looters were criticized more harshly than in the 1960s because they had taken advantage of the city's disability, were thought to be employed, and were taking luxury goods rather than necessities. Even so, *Time* called once more for reform, in a cover story entitled "The Underclass," although the magazine treated that class more as a racial group than as an economic one.[14]

Another illustration of the value placed on order restoration can be found in the news about events that do not, on the surface, deal with disorder. A television report covering a demonstration outside the White House moments after Richard Nixon made his resignation speech emphasized that the demonstration was quiet and that there were no signs of incipient panic or violence. Likewise, in the hours after John Kennedy's assassination, network anchorpersons and reporters frequently pointed out that the country was not panicking. Later, I learned that they were, in fact, worried about possible panics and immediately looked for stories which would indicate that none were taking place. They also sought to allay panic by reporting that the transition of Lyndon Johnson to the presidency was taking place quickly and in an orderly fashion.[15] For the same reason, the anchorpersons also took pains to dispel a rumor that the Russians were about to take advantage of the president's death to launch a war.[16]

I do not mean to suggest, however, that the fears of a Russian move originated with the journalists; in describing Richard Nixon's inability to govern during his last days in the White House, Woodward and Bernstein suggest that then Secretary of State Henry Kissinger was considering "the possibility that some foreign power would do something foolish."[17] Still, the fears expressed in the news underline the generic concern with order and suggest the extent to which order is thought to depend upon the president, which reflects, among other things, the value placed on his leadership.

Moral Disorder News

The moral disorder story is a hallowed tradition in modern American journalism, prototypically taking the form of exposés based on investigative reporting. Such exposés reveal instances of legal or moral transgression, particularly by public officials and other prestigious individuals who, by reason or virtue of their power and prestige, are not expected to misbehave.

The prime exposé of the 1970s was Watergate. Although defenders of the Nixon Administration have accused the news media of exaggerating the transgressions involved in the events and of blowing up the story in order to drive a president disliked by many journalists out of office, the story was a prototypical exposé, which would have been dealt with in much the same manner had the scandals been committed by a more popular president. Later investigations of CIA and FBI scandals, which implicated Presidents Kennedy and Johnson, were carried out just as energetically. Some observers have also suggested that the news exaggerated Nixon's transgressions by combining individual and often unrelated activities into a single scandal; but exposés are, by their nature, structured to point the finger at a morally disorderly leader, and sometimes, investigative reporting efforts do not see the light of day until a villain is found. Traditionally, exposés have concentrated on politicians or other public officials resorting to nepotism, unethical campaign practices, bribery, and taking money out of the public till, although sometimes, exposés are more institutional, dealing with the failure of public agencies to serve their constituents or clients, or more frequently, with wasting the taxpayers' money.

Nevertheless, the vast majority of moral disorder stories do not involve investigative reporting; often they deal with routine phenomena, such as violent or nonviolent crime or political acts, which are treated as violations of altruistic democracy. Such common practices as logrolling, deals, patronage appointments, or the failure of election candidates to abide by campaign promises are reported in such a way as to indicate that these practices are immoral.

In most moral disorder stories, the values being violated are never made explicit, and that they are being violated is not discussed. Still, the participants in a moral disorder story know they are being identified as transgressors and react accordingly. After an election in New Jersey, supporters of the losing candidate, who was then on trial for bribery and had been accused of conducting a racist campaign, smashed television cameras and attacked reporters. The values in the news, against corruption and for racial integration, had led to campaign stories which the candidate and his supporters felt were responsible for his defeat.

News stories which are announced, or in Erving Goffman's terminology, "framed," as exposés make the search for moral disorder explicit, forcing those identified as transgressors into the difficult position of defending their practices, while at the same time reaffirming the moral values on which the exposé is based. Few people can do so without being defensive, particularly on television documentaries, which are television's primary genre for exposés. Among recent examples are "Migrant," in which fruit-company executives had to react against the documented exploitation of migrant workers; and "The Selling of the Pentagon," in which Defense Department officials had to respond to what the documentary makers considered deviant public-relations practices. If the transgressors refuse to be interviewed, their refusal is also reported and becomes a virtual admission of guilt.

In such instances, the news media become guardians of a moral order; as a result, reporters are generally viewed as representatives of that order, even if they are not looking for moral disorder news. Consequently, when they, and especially television camera crews, arrive on a scene, people begin to perform not only physically for the camera but also morally, denying or eliminating behavior that could be judged as moral disorder. Beatings or tortures of prisoners did not take place in South Vietnam or the American South when cameras were present. Public and private agencies spruce up their physical environment when reporters are expected, just as the Chinese authorities temporarily "opened" their society when American television crews arrived to film life in China during and after President Nixon's visit. Berelson's classic study of the 1945 New York City newspaper strike showed that when the newspapers were not publishing, politicians sometimes ignored the honesty values which are defended in and guarded by the news media.[18]

The Nature of Order in the News

The frequent appearance of disorder stories suggests that order is an important value in the news, but order is a meaningless term unless one specifies what order and whose order is being valued. For one thing, there are different types of order; a society can have violence in the streets and a stable family life at home, or public peace and a high rate of family instability. Also, what order is will be judged differently by different people. To the affluent, the slums will appear orderly as long as there are no disturbances and crime does not spill over into wealthy districts; but for slum dwellers, order cannot exist until exploitation, as well as crime, is eliminated. For the parent generation, adolescent order exists when adolescents abide by parental rules; for the young people, order is also freedom of interference from adults.

What Order in the News?

The conception of order in the news varies with each type of disorder. In news about natural disasters, order is defined as the preservation of life and property; despite the concern for nature, flood stories do not often worry about how the flood may harm the river. Among technological disasters, plane crashes are usually more newsworthy than the winter breakdowns of tenement furnaces, even if they result in the same number of deaths. Yet, here as elsewhere, disorder news is affected by whose order is being upset.

Social disorder is generally defined as disorder in the public areas of the society. A protest march in which three people die would be headline national news, whereas a family murder that claimed three victims would be a local story. Disorders in affluent areas or elite institutions are more likely to be reported than their occurrence elsewhere. In the 1960s, the looting of a handful of stores on New York's Fifth Avenue received as much attention as a much larger looting spree taking place in a ghetto area that same day. Peaceful demonstrations on college campuses, especially elite ones, are usually more newsworthy than those in factories or prisons. But the major public area is the seat of government; thus, a trouble-free demonstration in front of a city hall or a police station is news, whereas that in front of a store is not.

Still, the most important criterion of worthiness is the target of the demonstration. Ultimately, social disorder is equated with political disorder; similarly, social order is viewed as the absence of violent or potentially violent threats to the authority of public officials, particularly the president. The anti-war demonstrations of the past decade were covered as disorder stories because they were aimed at presidents, and campus protests against government war policies were more often reported than protests against college-administration policies. Likewise, the 1978 coal strike did not become a magazine cover story until it involved the president. Just as low-level public officials and corporate leaders get into the news only when they quarrel with the president, the activities of ordinary people must also touch the Oval Office before they are newsworthy.

Even so, the conception of political order in the news transcends public officials and even the president. Now and then, such officials are themselves treated by the news as potential threats to order, either because they resort to "demagoguery," which may stir up the passions of their followers—as in the case of Governors George Wallace and Lester Maddox—or because they act in ways that may encourage ordinary people to question the legitimacy of authority, and subsequently to ignore the rules which underlie the political order. In the waning days of the Nixon Administration, the news frequently expressed concern about the possibility and consequences of widespread cynicism toward and lack of trust for the presidency (rather than toward the incumbent president); and when Richard Nixon was reported to have underpaid his taxes, there were stories which speculated whether ordinary taxpayers would follow his example.

Beneath the concern for political order lies another, perhaps even deeper concern for social cohesion, which reflects fears that not only the official rules of the political order but also the informal rules of the social order are in danger of being disobeyed. This is apparent in the nonpolitical stories that either become or do not become news. Hippies and college dropouts of the 1960s were newsworthy in part because they rejected the so-called Protestant work ethic; even now, drug use by the young, and its consequences, is in the news more than alcohol use because it signifies a rejection of traditional methods of seeking oblivion or mind expansion. Indeed, the news evaluates the young almost entirely in terms of what adult rules they are in the process of rejecting, be they of dress, decorum, or sexual behavior. Rising divorce rates, falling rates of marriage and fertility, and increasing cohabitation without benefit of clergy, all of which suggest a rejection of the conventional rules of family life, are therefore more frequently in the news than family conflict (other than wife beating and child abuse). Whatever its effect on family life, conflict is not viewed as indicative of the decline of the family. The romanticization of the past as an era in which formal and informal rules *were* obeyed betrays the same fear of contemporary disintegration, and the frequent celebration of past ways in the news may reflect an implicit ideal for the future. As Eric Severaid put it during the live television coverage of the marriage of Princess Anne of England: "A people needs the past to hold them together."

Moral disorder stories are, in the end, cued to much the same concern for social cohesion, particularly those stories which report violations of the mores rather than the laws. Such stories are based on the premise that the activities of public officials, public agencies, and corporations should derive from the same moral and ethical values that are supposed to apply to personal, familial, and friendship relations. Even if every political reporter knows that politicians cannot operate with the same ideal of honesty as friends, the failure of politicians to do so continues to be news. In fact, insofar as the news conceives of nation and society anthropomorphically, as having a will and as being held together by moral fibers, the social order persists because it is based on moral values, and the violation of these values is thus an invitation to political and social disintegration. In the last analysis, the values underlying social and moral disorder news are the same, although the two types of news differ in subject and object: social disorder news monitors the respect of citizens for authority, while moral disorder stories evaluate whether authority figures respect the rules of the citizenry.

Whose Order in the News?

National news is ostensibly about and for the entire nation; therefore its values pertain to national order. Since one person's or group's order may be another's disorder, however, and since the news does not, as I suggested in Chapter 1, report equally about all parts of nation or society, it cannot possibly value everyone's order. Thus, it is relevant to ask whose order is being valued.

Much of the answer has already been suggested. Most of the routine —and thus, by presumption, orderly—activities which appear in the news are carried on by elected and appointed public officials, whereas social and moral disorder news involves, by and large, ordinary people, many of them poor, black, and/or young. Moral disorder stories, however, also identify public officials who have violated the laws or the enduring values. In other words, the news supports those public officials who abide by the enduring values against misbehaving peers and deviant ordinary people.

In addition, the news upholds the legitimacy of holders of formal authority as long as they abide by the relevant enduring values, both in public and private realms. It also pays respect to the more prestigious professions, although its members must not only abide by the enduring values but must also carry out innovative activities. The news reports more about progress in physics than in plumbing, but it pays no more attention to the routine activities of physicists than of plumbers.

In social and economic class terms, then, the news especially values the order of the upper-class and upper-middle-class sectors of society, though it may make fun of some of their very rich members. Although it does not often concern itself with either the social order or the values of the middle and working classes and the poor, it supports the classes when they respect the enduring values; but it can be critical of their popular culture, and among whites, their prejudice toward blacks. The defense of the upper middle-class is stronger in the newsmagazines than on television, but it is common to both.[19]

The news also tends to value the social order of the middle-aged and old against the young. Most public officials, business leaders, and professionals do not act in newsworthy ways until they are in their fifties and sixties, so that the news cannot help but be dominated by this age group; even so, it is rarely reported that old leaders sometimes become senile in office. Similarly, the young are inevitably in the news because criminals or protesters are almost always youthful; even so, juvenile delinquency against adults is commonplace news, whereas adult delinquency against juveniles—other than child abuse—is much less so.

Furthermore, the news reflects a white male social order, although it sides with blacks and women who try to enter it and succeed. Nevertheless, its conception of both racial integration and sexual equality is basically assimilatory; the news prefers women and blacks who move into the existing social order to separatists who want to alter it.

With some oversimplification, it would be fair to say that the news supports the social order of public, business and professional, upper-middle-class, middle-aged, and white male sectors of society. Because the news emphasizes people over groups, it pays less attention to the institutionalized social order, except as reflected in its leaders; but obviously, the news is also generally supportive of governments and their agencies, private enterprise, the prestigious professions, and a variety of other national institutions, including the quality universities. But here, too, always with a proviso: obedience to the relevant enduring values. Equally obvious, however, is the fact that institutional obedience is monitored differentially, and the news is therefore much harsher on government than on the remaining sectors.

In short, when all other things are equal, the news pays most attention to and upholds the actions of elite individuals and elite institutions. It would be incorrect to say that the news is about elites per se or a single elite; rather, the news deals mostly with those who hold the power within various national or societal strata; with the most powerful officials in the most powerful agencies; with the coalition of upper-class and upper-middle-class people which dominates the socioeconomic hierarchy; and with the late-middle-aged cohort that has the most power among age groups.

Nevertheless, the news is not subservient to powerful individuals or groups, for it measures their behavior against a set of values that is assumed to transcend them. Moral disorder stories can bid the elites to relinquish, or at least hide, their moral deficiencies. To be sure, the values invoked in moral disorder stories are themselves often set by and shared by these elites. The president's policies are not often viewed from the perspectives of, or judged by, the values of low-income and moderate-income citizens; corporate officials are even less rarely judged by the values of employees or customers; or university presidents, by the values of students or campus janitors. Instead, the values in the news derive largely from reformers and reform movements, which, as I shall argue in Chapter 6, are themselves elites. Still, the news is not simply a compliant supporter of elites or the Establishment or the ruling class; rather, it views nation and society through its own set of values and with its own conception of the good social order.

Leadership

If the news values moral and social order, it also suggests how to maintain them, primarily through the availability of morally and otherwise competent leadership. As I noted in Chapter 1, the news focuses on leaders; and with some exceptions, public agencies and private organizations are represented by their leaders. In the past, magazine cover stories often reported national topics or issues in relation to an individual who played an instrumental or symbolic leadership role in them. When necessary, the news even helps to create leaders; in the 1960s, radical and black organizations functioning on the basis of participatory democracy sometimes complained that journalists would pick out one spokesperson on whom they would lavish most of their attention, thereby making a leader out of him or her.[20]

Although several practical considerations, to be discussed in Part 2, encourage the news media to emphasize leaders, the news is also based on a theory of society that would argue, were it made explicit, that the social process, above all others, is shaped by leaders: by people who, either because of their political or managerial skills, or personal attributes which inspire others, move into positions of authority and make things happen. A lengthy 1974 *Time* cover story that surveyed existing definitions of leadership concluded that most "emphasize honesty, candor, and vision, combined with sheer physical stamina and courage"; to which the magazine added that "courage without brains was [not] sufficient."[21] A leader must also be strong and able to control subordinates; their moral failings and inefficiencies are a sign of weak leadership.

Unlike sociology, which sees leadership as a role found in most groups and assumes that someone will inevitably take it, the news focuses instead on the personal qualities and psychological traits of the person taking it. Also, while sociology suggests that group members, in other than totalitarian situations, use formal and/or informal mechanisms for choosing leaders, thereafter influencing their actions, the news tends to treat group members as followers.[22] Moreover, sociology proposes that institutions require and therefore generate leadership; the news, however, sees institutions as "blocks" to it.[23] Whether sociologists or journalists are more correct is not at issue here, for both may be observing different aspects of the same phenomenon. Still, the news divides nation and society into leaders and followers, with the former not only initiating but also being given credit for the activities of the latter. Washington stories routinely tell of the statements or actions of official leaders, while equally routinely ignoring the fact that these are often the work of subordinates. In fact, although the news objectively reports the orders that leaders give, it looks askance at the government bureaucrats who carry them out.

The foremost leader in America is the president, who is viewed as the ultimate protector of order. He is the final backstop for domestic tranquility and the principal guardian of national security, his absence from the White House due to resignation or death evoking, as I indicated earlier, fears of an enemy attack or possible panic by a now leaderless populace. Through his own behavior and the concern he shows for the behavior of others, the president also becomes the nation's moral leader. He sets an example that might be followed by others: should he permit or condone corruption among his associates or appointees, he is suspected of moral disorder. Finally, he is the person who states and represents the national values and he is the agent of the national will.

The news describes the president as the person who actually performs, or who is expected to perform, these functions. Stories which indicate that decisions are actually being made by others, sometimes even without the president's knowledge, are written to suggest that such delegation of power is a departure from the norm and a potential cause for alarm. When a president takes a vacation, the news questions his control over the government during his absence; a presidential illness is always a major story; and his death is the biggest story of all.

Leadership in the News: A Case Study

The news reports not only on incumbent leaders but also on the recruitment of new ones. This emphasis is nicely illustrated by the aforementioned 1974 *Time* cover story, most of which was devoted to a carefully researched project to identify two hundred of the country's "rising leaders"—people under 46 years of age on the day the magazine appeared on the newsstands—in order to assess the future leadership of the nation. *Time*'s effort serves as a useful case study, for it not only offers insight into the magazine's conception of leadership but also suggests where the future leaders are now working, from where they originated, and where they were educated. As such, the story further elucidates the social order within which they are expected to operate later. Of course, the list represented the judgment of a small group of editors of one magazine, but I am convinced that most other national news media embarking on the same project would have come up with virtually the same people.

The story was not conceived to express *Time*'s preferences; the editors pointed out that it was neither "an endorsement . . . nor *Time*'s version of the 'Top 200 Americans.' "[24] Even so, some values went into the effort. For one thing, the candidates had to meet the qualities which the magazine associated with leadership (honesty, candor, vision, physical stamina, courage, and brains). During my fieldwork at *Time,* I learned that in winnowing the list of nominees, the editors eliminated some because their recent activities suggested a loss of dedication, "the spark that makes leaders," as one editor put it. Others were dropped because of alleged or actual scandals in their pasts.[25] Although a morally questionable history has not always prevented individuals from rising to leadership, *Time* assumed that in the future it would—or should—do so.

Still, the most significant selection criterion was institutional rather than personal, for the list was limited to people "whose touchstone was civic or social impact . . . politicians, government officials, as well as businessmen, educators, lawyers, scientists and journalists."[26] Although the purpose of this criterion was to exclude artists, "because they are basically soloists," it also restricted the list to a selected number of occupations, thus implying, at least, the value that leadership inheres in them.

As Table 5 indicates, most of the nominees came from the occupations quoted above; all who were not public officials were from upper-class or upper-middle-class professions or organizations. The leaders of the public-interest lobbies, for example, were Ralph Nader and the heads of NOW, ACLU, Common Cause, Consumers Union, and the Hastings Institute. Only one labor leader appeared on the list; and if teachers, beauticians, librarians, or veterans organizations had young leaders, they were not included.

The future leaders were already located at primarily national or "nationalized" institutions. Of the twenty-eight university officials and professors on the list, fifteen came from Harvard or other Ivy League schools. While only half of the public officials were in the federal government, most state and local officials were governors and mayors from the largest cities and states. Politically, the list was divided fairly evenly between liberals and conservatives, Republicans and Democrats. Several ultraconservatives, mainly politicians and

TABLE 5: Occupational Distribution of *Time*'s List of 200 Future Leaders

Occupations		Percentages
Public officials		49.0
Elected politicians	37.0	
Appointed officials	8.5	
Former politicians or officials	2.5	
Politically connected lawyers	1.0	
Professionals		24.5
University presidents and provosts	7.5	
Professors	6.5	
Journalists and editors	5.5	
Other professionals*	5.0	
Heads of businesses		17.5
Publishers and TV executives	5.0	
Other businessmen and women	12.5	
Public-interest lobbyists		4.0
Racial and ethnic leaders		3.0
Others		2.0
Total		100.0

*Five were ministers, two each were architects and athletes, and one was a doctor.

journalists, were included, but there were no socialists or representatives of the revolutionary Left.[27]

Despite an energetic search for black and female leaders, 91 percent of the nominees were white and male.[28] Not all the short biographies appended to each name provided details on the socioeconomic aspects of family background, but the majority for whom such data were available came from affluent homes. Ten percent were the children of very rich or very famous fathers, mostly the former. Conversely, only five of the two hundred had working-class fathers. Undoubtedly, some came from poor homes, notably among the nineteen blacks on the list.

Whatever their origins, most of the leaders were educated at prestigious schools. Of the 168 schools mentioned by the nominees, 42 percent were Ivy League schools—with Harvard far ahead of the rest—and 21 percent were other prestigious private colleges and universities, such as Northwestern or Stanford.[29]

Finally, the tendency of the news to focus on middle-aged people was reflected not only by the decision to set the age limit at 45 but by the concentration of people in their forties. Fifty-two percent of the leaders were in their forties, 46 percent were in their thirties, and 2 percent were in their twenties.

Taken as a whole, then, *Time*'s article illustrates not only the concern in the news with leadership but also the extent to which even nominally young leaders represent the public and professional occupations, the white male middle-age group, and the upper and upper-middle strata in society. And if the social order with which the news is concerned at all resembles the institutions which the two hundred leaders then represented, *Time*'s compilation reveals the extent to which that order consists of public agencies, national corporations, the prestigious professions, and the "quality" universities.

Leadership News and the Journalistic Process

I should like to note once more that the analysis of the *Time* leadership project—like the analysis in Chapters 1 and 2—is not meant to be either an analysis of the values of the journalists themselves or an exposé of their biases. Indeed, to anticipate some of the findings in Part 2, *Time*'s list of leaders was mainly a product of the sources and audiences with whom national journalists deal, and of the corporate environment in which they work.

The project was formulated after one of the regular, if infrequent, conferences of *Time* editors with professors at Harvard University.

During the conference, several professors expressed some concern about the next generation of leaders, a theme which had long been of interest to the editor-in-chief of Time, Inc. (the corporate executive, himself a journalist, who provides editorial supervision for all Time, Inc. magazines). However, the idea for the project came from *Time*'s managing editor; and after the conference, he and his colleagues decided to look into the supply of young leaders. The pool of names from which the two hundred were chosen was supplied by *Time* reporters, but the pool was a direct product of the people they consulted. As *Time* noted: "To create our portfolio, *Time* correspondents last April began gathering recommendations from university presidents and professors, Congressmen, church figures, industrialists."[30] These sources nominated individuals whom they knew or had heard of; they could not have been expected to know leaders from other than their own sectors of society.

Time's reporters chose the recommenders primarily on the basis of precedent; they consulted the people with whom they routinely keep in touch and who are regular and frequent sources for domestic magazine news—which also explains why the final list of leaders closely resembles the Knowns who appear in the magazine on a recurring basis. The editors, whose task it is to hold the attention and allegiance of a diverse, nationwide set of readers, strove for some degree of geographical and political balance; in addition, they sought to maximize the number of women and blacks, partly, but not only, to forestall criticism of sexism and racism. They also tried to maximize the number of business leaders, some corporate executives having evidently expressed concern about the small number of businesspeople on an early list.[31]

In short, the final list was not constructed to express the values that appear in the news, or even to express the editors' own values.[32] Rather, it emerged from a number of other, practical considerations, above all, the reliance on regular sources for recommendations. This is not to say the editors lacked values or excluded them; they themselves defined leadership, and they had reporters gather information on the honesty and dedication of nominees. I spoke at length with only one member of the small team of editors who made the final choices, and, with one exception, he was not aware of the extent to which the list expressed the values I have inferred. Feeling justly proud of the immense amount of work that went into the project, he regretted only the absence of labor leaders from the final list, an unintentional absence which no one noticed until later. I asked him why the list had not included leaders of the Left, but this appears to have been intentional. While he indicated that one bureau had "goofed" in failing to nominate a person who should have been on the list, that person was a recently elected liberal senator.

News Values and Ideology

If the news includes values, it also contains ideology. That ideology, however, is an aggregate of only partially thought-out values which is neither entirely consistent nor well integrated; and since it changes somewhat over time, it is also flexible on some issues. I shall call this aggregate of values and the reality judgments associated with it paraideology, partly to distinguish it from the deliberate, integrated, and more doctrinaire set of values usually defined as ideology, but it is ideology nevertheless. It also bears some resemblance to what Thomas Kuhn has called the dominant paradigm in the sciences, and what Alvin Gouldner has described as domain assumptions in sociology.

The paraideology can itself be placed on the conventional spectrum, but not easily, partly because, as I show in Chapter 6, the journalists are neither much interested in ideology nor aware that they, too, promulgate ideology. As a result, individual stories and journalists can span various parts of the spectrum, although their values rarely coincide with those on the Far Right or the Far Left. Even the news media as a whole, and the news, analyzed over time, are not easily classified, for the paraideology reflected in the enduring values moves within the boundaries of conservative and liberal positions.

In its advocacy of altruistic and official democracy, the news defends a mixture of liberal and conservative values, but its conception of responsible capitalism comes closest to what I described as the right-leaning liberalism of Governors Brown and Carey. On the other hand, in its respect for tradition and its nostalgia for pastoralism and rugged individualism, the news is unabashedly conservative, as it is also both in its defense of the social order and its faith in leadership. If the news has to be pigeonholed ideologically, it is right-liberal or left-conservative.

The News as Reformist

In reality, the news is not so much conservative or liberal as it is reformist; indeed, the enduring values are very much like the values of the Progressive movement of the early twentieth century. The resemblance is often uncanny, as in the common advocacy of honest, meritocratic, and anti-bureaucratic government, and in the shared antipathy to political machines and demagogues, particularly of populist bent. Altruistic democracy is, in other words, close to the Progressive ideal of government. The notion of responsible capitalism is also to be found in Progressivism, as is the dislike of bigness, the preference for craftsmanship over technology, the defense of nature, and the celebration of anti-urban pastoral society. Journalistic paraideology and Progressivism are further akin in their mutual support of individualism, their uneasiness about collective solutions, other than at the grassroots level, and their opposition to socialism. Moreover, the preservation of an upper-class and upper-middle-class social order, like the need for morally and otherwise competent national leadership, has its equivalents in Progressive thought.

The Progressive movement is long dead, but many of its basic values and its reformist impulses have persisted. Why the news is reformist and Progressive I will discuss in Chapter 6, but its being so helps explain why the news is not easily fitted into the conventional ideological spectrum. Of course, Progressive thought can be placed on that spectrum, although historians have not yet agreed whether the movement was liberal, conservative, or both. In any case, the news may be marching to a somewhat different drummer; and when journalists are unwilling to describe themselves as liberal or conservative, and prefer to see themselves as independents, they may be sensing, if not with complete awareness, that they are, as a profession, Progressive reformers.

= Part 2 =
The Journalists

Introduction

Despite my occasional tendency to anthropomorphize the news in the first two chapters, it is put together by journalists. The next seven chapters have two aims: to analyze how journalists work and to explain the findings of Part 1. My emphasis is on story selection, but I also cast a tangential glance at story production, for how journalists choose the news cannot be fully understood without considering how they report and write, or film, their stories. I omit, however, any discussion of dissemination, the technology-laden methods by which television scripts and films get on the air and magazines are printed; or of the business and advertising organizations which collect the funds, except when the people and processes involved are relevant to story selection and production.

My interest in story selection is, in turn, centered on the unwritten rules journalists apply, which I shall call considerations. However, the research would be dangerously narrow were it to look only at the journalistic rules. Consequently, I also report on the roles that information sources, audiences, and people who exert pressure to censor the news play in the total process, as well as on commercial and other considerations which stem from the fact that journalists work in news organizations for news firms. Since I am, furthermore, interested in why journalists use the considerations they do, economic, political, cultural, and other forces and agents outside the news firm are also drawn into the analysis.

In the Preface I indicated that I collected most of my data by participant-observation, but I did not participate in the work itself. For the most part, I observed what people were doing and then talked with them afterwards about the hows and whys. In addition, I asked questions about their past work, and historical and contemporary questions about their colleagues, bosses, and news organizations. I was also a participant in the many informal discussions, in and out of the office, that were always taking place. I talked with news executives; people in circulation, advertising, and research departments; with network documentary makers and foreign correspondents who came to New York; and with many journalists who had worked or were then working in other news media, local and national. In between, I kept up with the steadily growing popular, professional, and scholarly literature about the news.

I devoted most of my time to the people responsible for story selection, but I also spent time with those who actually produce the stories, occasionally went out with New York and Washington reporters, and spent a week at a network Washington bureau. Still, I learned more about what bureau reporters call New York than about the bureaus.

I said earlier that my fieldwork took place in two separate periods, but I should report the exact times of my visits, for while basic story-selection processes alter little over the years, the contexts in which they take place inevitably undergo change. The historical moments at which I did my fieldwork may therefore affect my findings.

I began my fieldwork at NBC and observed there from October 1965 to April 1966; I went to CBS on Thanksgiving Day 1966 and remained until the end of May 1967. At that time, both programs were riding high in all respects, including the ratings; as a result, they were virtually autonomous, with minimal supervision from news executives (the presidents and vice-presidents of the news division) or corporate officers.

My fieldwork at the networks was intermittent, as I was actually in each studio only about thirty days. Other work kept me busy at the time; but once I had learned the basic processes, which did not take long, I returned periodically to see how the journalists handled different types of stories. Sometimes, I came for several days at a time, however. Conversely, at the newsmagazines, my fieldwork was continuous, for in order to understand the evolution of a week's issue, one must be there virtually every day. In addition, the newsmagazine staff is several times the size of the television news program staff; thus, I had to study many more people. Most of my magazine fieldwork took place in the domestic-news sections, but I also observed and talked with journalists in the other sections, especially when they were dealing with news of domestic political and social significance—for example, in education. On the days when the magazine went to press, I walked back and forth among the journalists' offices and cubicles in order to keep up with what was going on in different sections.

I came to Newsweek in May 1968 and left at the end of August, just before the editors were leaving to attend the 1968 Chicago Democratic Convention; however, I did talk with them about it afterwards. Newsweek was then known as "the hot" magazine on Madison Avenue, approaching Time in advertising and prestige. I came to Time on April 1, 1969, and left in mid-July that same year. Henry Luce had retired as the editor-in-chief of Time, Inc. a couple of years earlier, and Hedley Donovan, his successor, had appointed a new managing editor in 1968. As a result, most of the practices and policies of the Lucean era had already been abolished. Even before I arrived, the explicit editorializing in behalf of the Republican party, the Vietnam War, and Generalissimo Chiang Kai-shek had ended, and the magazine no longer ran uncomplimentary pictures or stories about Luce's political enemies. In fact, the changeover was so complete that the new managing editor devoted most of his attention to making the magazine more competitive with *Newsweek.*

I kept in touch with one or two people at each organization in the years that followed and returned for a second period of fieldwork in mid-1975. I spent May 1975 at *Time,* June at *Newsweek,* and July at NBC. I had planned to observe at CBS in August, but its executives, feeling that they had been recently "burned" by journalist visitors, limited me to conducting interviews. Although I did talk with the executive producer and his assistants, interviewing people is never as productive as watching what they do. Inasmuch as a number of books about CBS News have recently appeared, I have drawn on them instead.

My approach to participant-observation among journalists differed little from that which I had used in my earlier books, the *Urban Villagers* and the *Levittowners.* Observing journalists is not very different from observing other people; the main thing I had to learn, other than the journalists' technical jargon, was to stay out of people's way when the selection and production processes became hectic. Also, when I studied communities, I could not always tell everyone why I was there, especially people I met at large meetings; in the newsrooms, however, I told everyone that I was a sociologist who had come to study them. Being there regularly, I had the freedom to observe everything and to talk to everyone. I was excluded from meetings in which an editor or producer dressed down a subordinate, and from some with executives; but in both instances, I had no trouble in finding out afterwards what had taken place.

I also observed myself or, rather, the role I played as an observer as best I could in order to understand how my presence affected the people I studied and what I learned. No doubt I had some effect, for they were pleased by the attention I paid them and their work, which may help explain why they allowed me to observe in the first place. The journalists I studied are responsible for much of the country's national news, but except for anchorpersons, they are still virtually anonymous and invisible. Although they work hard and take pride in their work, only their peers, families, and friends know what they do. I know they were pleased, for they told me so when I kept the same long hours as they did and showed up on weekends and holidays.

Incidentally, I had no difficulty getting permission to observe. I had met some of the television journalists while working as an interviewer in a study of the network coverage of John Kennedy's assassination, and in one case, I was introduced by a friend from college days. Elsewhere, I knocked on the door, but I chose my doors, getting permission from an editor or producer, and asking him to clear it with relevant executives. I had learned in earlier fieldwork that executives, who must safeguard the image of their companies, might more readily say no than yes when asked directly.

I also pleased the people I studied by being a new face. Time and other pressures keep the journalists in New York chained to their desks and isolated from outside contact. As a regular visitor, I sometimes became a sounding board for those who had gripes or who were thinking through ideas; one or two laughingly called me their analyst. At the start, I was occasionally an audience, a visiting academic for whom people performed, especially when explaining their decisions; but this ended once I became a fixture. Once or twice, people described me as their conscience, which made me nervous because it implied that I was forcing them to stick with rules they might otherwise have violated. But because I kept a low profile, neither being judgmental about their work nor expressing personal opinions that would give them any indication of how to perform in my presence, I doubt that my presence altered story choices. Besides, the journalists had so much to do and so little time that they could not do much performing in the first place.

Of course, I knew the people I studied only in their work roles; I did not study what they did or thought about at home, although I went for lunch, dinner, or drinks with them whenever there was a chance. I had a closer rapport with some than with others, but that always happens in fieldwork. While some people were close-mouthed, I could always find co-workers who would provide the needed information.

I also thought about how my own values affected the fieldwork. My goal, to understand story selection and production, was not, I think, influenced by conscious values; and I had no a priori hypotheses I wanted to test, so that I could not be blinded to data that would conflict with them. Since most of my political values and opinions are, roughly speaking, left-liberal, I did not share the right-liberal or left-conservative paraideology of the news, or of most journalists, and frequently I disagreed with their opinions. I had, however, previously studied people with whom I disagreed politically, and I had long ago learned to keep my mouth shut. When I was asked my opinion, I tried to avoid a direct answer but without alienating people with whom I was speaking; instead, I explained that fieldworkers must remain detached—and this the journalists understood because they, too, seek to remain detached.

I was privately unhappy when people did not see what I felt were obvious ideological implications that could be drawn from the news, or when they left out stories that they thought dull but I found sociologically fascinating. But I quickly learned that I was far more aware of ideological implications than they and that they were not working for an audience of sociologists. In the end, I think the fact that some of my values differed from those of the people I studied was helpful, for it made their values—and mine—more visible to me. The hardest task in fieldwork is to study people who are politically or culturally akin to the fieldworker and who take the same things for granted.

3

The Organization of Story Selection

In reporting the news about a nation of over 200 million potential actors in news stories, journalists could, in theory, choose from billions of potential activities. In fact, however, they can learn about only a tiny fraction of actors and activities; and having limited air time and magazine space, they must select an even tinier fraction. More important, they cannot decide anew every day or week how to select the fraction that will appear on the news; instead, they must routinize their task in order to make it manageable.[1]

Theories of Story Selection

Many theories have been put forth about how the selection of stories is routinized. One type of theory is journalist-centered: it argues that the news is shaped by the professional news judgment of journalists. Messrs. Nixon and Agnew applied a variant of this theory when they attacked the news media for choosing the news on the basis of deliberate ideological bias. Many politicians hold a somewhat similar view. Judging the news by its implications for their political careers, they blame journalistic bias when the news hurts them.

A second type of theory, favored by social-science studies, locates the routinization in the news organization and shows how story selection is influenced by organizational requirements. Some organizational theories focus on the news firm and emphasize commercial imperatives; others are more concerned with the news organizations themselves and look at how their structures and division of labor affect story selection.[2] The theories also vary by the degree of influence organizational requirements have on story selection. Some reify the organization at the expense of events, as if story selection were not affected by them; others forget that journalists, being professionals, also shape the organization and the news.[3]

A third approach is event-centered: the so-called mirror theory, which used to be popular among journalists, proposes that events determine story selection, with journalists simply holding a mirror to them and reflecting their image to the audience. Mirror theory began to weaken in the 1960s, as media critics pointed out what journalists did to and with events in transforming them into news, and called attention to events that failed to become news.

A final set of theories explains story selection with forces outside the news organization. Technological determinists, such as Marshall McLuhan, argue that the message is determined by the technology of the medium. Economic determinists view the national economy as molding story selection; and some Marxists treat journalists as the public-relations agents of monopoly capitalism. Similarly, ideological determinists believe that journalists align the news to the political ideology of those holding power in the country. Cultural theorists extend this, seeing journalists as selecting stories which accord with the values of the national culture. A related approach centers on the audience, as expressed in the notion that "we get the news we deserve." Another type of externally centered theory suggests that the news is shaped, above all, by the sources on which journalists rely; or, as Molotch and Lester argue, by those groups in society powerful enough both to create what they call "public events" and to gain access to journalists.[4]

These capsule descriptions of alternative explanations of story selection all contain some degree of truth. Journalists do apply news judgment, both as members of a profession and as individuals, but they are by no means totally free agents, and in any case, they rarely make selection decisions on overtly ideological grounds; rather, they work within organizations which provide them with only a limited amount of leeway in selection decisions, which is further reduced by their allegiance to professionally shared values.

Journalists do not hold up mirrors to events; nonetheless, mirror theory remains useful, for it reminds us that journalists do not make up the news but begin with what they deem an empirically graspable external reality. Phenomenologically inclined researchers have made a major contribution to understanding journalists and their work by showing that whatever the nature of external reality, human beings can perceive it only with their own concepts, and therefore always "construct" reality.[5] Even before phenomenological theories became popular, sociologists had shown that the events journalists ostensibly cover are themselves journalistic constructs that frame chronologically and otherwise related phenomena.[6]

While print and electronic news media rest on different technologies, every news medium uses its technology primarily to compete against other news media, and it does so selectively.[7] Television could limit itself to tell stories if it did not have to compete against the newspaper or the radio. Besides, the stories which different news media select are sufficiently similar to suggest that technology is not a determining factor. Economic determinists are closer to the truth; but even if the news is critical of socialism, journalists are not merely public-relations agents for capitalism. Insofar as they express the dominant political ideology, they often do so unconsciously. They work inside a national culture; but nations are aggregates of subcultures, and a relevant cultural approach would ask which subcultures are reported and ignored in the news. We do not get the news we deserve because we, the audience, are not directly involved in choosing it. Sources, however, are crucial.

My Own Approach

I view news as information which is transmitted from sources to audiences, with journalists—who are both employees of bureaucratic commercial organizations and members of a profession—summarizing, refining, and altering what becomes available to them from sources in order to make the information suitable for their audiences. Because news has consequences, however, journalists are susceptible to pressure from groups and individuals (including sources and audiences) with power to hurt them, their organizations, and their firms. By "sources," I mean the actors whom journalists observe or interview, including interviewees who appear on the air or who are quoted in magazine articles, and those who only supply background information or story suggestions. For my purpose, however, the most salient characteristic of sources is that they provide information as members or representatives of organized and unorganized interest groups, and yet larger sectors of nation and society.

Although the notion that journalists transmit information from sources to audiences suggests a linear process, in reality the process is circular, complicated further by a large number of feedback loops.

For example, sources cannot provide information until they make contact with a member of a news organization; and that organization will choose the sources it considers suitable for the audience, even as it is chosen by sources who want to transmit information to the audience. Sources are also an important part of the audience, particularly in Washington. The audience is, moreover, not only an information recipient but a source of income for the news firm; and insofar as its allegiance must be maintained, its viewing and reading behavior even affects, to some extent, the choice of sources by journalists. In effect, then, sources, journalists, and audiences coexist in a system, although it is closer to being a tug of war than a functionally interrelated organism.

Tugs of war, however, are resolved by power; and news is, among other things, "the exercise of power over the interpretation of reality."[8] Power is exercised by all participants in the transmittal of information; it is also in evidence inside the news organization, which is hierarchically organized.[9] Even readers and viewers have some power, expressed by protest against and refusal to accept what they read and see, which is why journalists often worry about their credibility.

Availability and Suitability

Since this book is based on a study of journalists and their organizations, I have chosen to cut into the circular process there. From this perspective, story selection is essentially composed of two processes: one determines the availability of news and relates journalists to sources; the other determines the suitability of news, which ties journalists to audiences. Sources and journalists, however, must have access to each other before information can become news; but that access is differentially distributed, depending in part on the social distance between sources and journalists, and even more so on their respective power. The economically and politically powerful can obtain easy access to, and are sought out by, journalists; those who lack power are harder to reach by journalists and are generally not sought out until their activities produce social or moral disorder news. In short, access reflects the social structure outside the newsroom; and because that structure is hierarchical, the extent to which information about various parts of America is available to journalists is hierarchically and differentially distributed. Even so, journalists almost always have more available information than they can use; consequently, they must also make suitability judgments, through which they winnow available information to select what they can cover with limited staffs and time, and what they can report in the equally limited amount of air time or magazine space.

The crucial word is "limited," because what distinguishes journalism from literary and social-science studies of America is the deadline, which is immutable in television and can be extended at the magazines only by high additional expenditures. Lack of time and staff also require the use of quickly and easily applied methods of empirical inquiry, and limited air time and magazine space restrict the number of findings that can be presented. This is one reason why news is basically descriptive; temporal and other resources that social scientists can devote to complex analyses and explanations are not often available.

On the Nature of Considerations

Availability and suitability judgments are guided by a large number of considerations, which I shall describe in the following chapters. I have classified them into seven sets: source, substantive, product, and value considerations; and commercial, audience, and political considerations. The classification scheme emerged from my fieldwork, but it is not rigid, for some considerations overlap and could be classified differently. The order in which I present them is deliberate, for I begin with the four sets that I saw journalists apply, and I end with the three sets that are, to some extent, imposed on them from beyond the newsroom. That these sets are reported in later chapters does not imply, however, that they are less important. In practice, all considerations are intertwined and interrelated, but books must impose linearity on reality. The labels for the considerations are mine, of course, for journalists do not deal in considerations; they make news judgments.

Story selection is a decision-making and choice-making process, but a hurried one. When Edward J. Epstein began his research at NBC News and asked the journalists how they made decisions, they would jokingly tell him that they were about to make one; at the same time, they were indicating that if they had to treat the hundreds of choices they must make every day as formal decisions, they would be unable to complete their work.[10] Instead, they act on the basis of quick, virtually intuitive judgments, which some ascribe to "feel."

As a result, the considerations must be quickly and easily applicable so that choices can be made without too much deliberation. Simple considerations also help journalists avoid excessive uncertainty about whether they have made proper choices.[11] Conversely, the considerations have to be flexible so that they can be adapted to the endless variety of available news; and they have to be relational and comparable, since the suitability of one story always depends on what others are available. In fact, there are considerations for adding stories or dropping them, which I call *inclusionary* and *exclusionary,* respectively. The considerations must also be easily rationalized so that if one story is replaced by another, an acceptable reason for doing so is always at hand. Last but hardly least, the considerations are designed for efficiency so as to guarantee the necessary supply of suitable news with the least amount of time, effort, and, if possible, expenditures which can wreak havoc with the budget.

The outcome is a large number of considerations, and every available story can be judged on the basis of several, some of them contradictory. To prevent chaos, the application of news judgment requires consensus among journalists, and perhaps even more so, a hierarchical organization in which those with more power can enforce their judgment as to what considerations are relevant for a given story.

I suppose the considerations could be called decision-making criteria, but that term is too formal. The same shortcoming applies to "policy guidelines" and "rules." "Conventions" is more informal, but the term connotes arbitrariness, whereas the unwritten rules of journalism are, as I will show, hardly arbitrary. "Norms" and "values" do not fit because they imply a measure of cultural or ideological fixity and sanctity, and besides I will later compare the role of values and other considerations. The term I have chosen is free of connotations. Considerations are not applied in a vacuum, however; thus, the analysis must begin with a look at the news organization, and from a number of angles.

The News Organization

Before the news organization comes the news firm. The organization that produces the *NBC Nightly News* is a small part of a large firm, NBC; likewise, *Time* is a news organization within Time, Inc.[12] The national news firms exist to make money, and the news organizations exist to produce a money-making product. But for reasons explained in Chapter 7, television and magazine journalists are not under constant pressure to increase firm income, partly because they do not know how, and partly because they have enough power in the firm to reject the supposedly sure-fire way of enlarging the audience: resorting to "sensationalism" and "yellow journalism." Only when the economic indicators fall drastically are journalists forced to alter story-selection practices, but none of the media I studied was in such dire circumstances at the time.

News organizations are, as I suggested earlier, bureaucracies staffed by professionals. (Incidentally, I consider national journalists to be professionals, even if they do not obtain all the perquisites and powers of the medical and legal professions.) Because they are bureaucracies, *Time* and *Newsweek* have often been criticized for practicing "group journalism," but all news organizations do so. More correctly, they practice seriatim journalism, as every story passes through several hands before it reaches the audience. For this reason, some journalists describe their organizations as assembly lines; as one executive producer put it: "The daily routine is like screwing nuts on a bolt." The analogy with the factory is not entirely accurate, for news is a more variegated product than an automobile; but like a car, the news program or magazine is assembled from many parts.

The hands through which stories pass in the various news media, the total number of nuts and bolts, and the assembly of parts are remarkably alike in all news organizations, but then they are all creating a roughly similar product under deadline conditions, and the workers are members of a single profession. News organizations differ most in the names they give to the same roles.

Formal Positions and Roles

The national news organizations all include the following roles, listed in order of decreasing rank and power: policy makers, top editors (or producers), section heads, reporters and writers (or film makers), and researchers. These are complemented by various supporting staffs, some of which play an indirect role in story selection.

Policy makers are divided into corporate and news executives, the latter almost always trained journalists who have moved up to "management." Corporate officers, personified in national journalism by William Paley and Henry Luce, can intervene in the news whenever they choose to, but as I will suggest below, they do so only rarely. Even the news executives, such as the president of the network news division or Time, Inc.'s editor-in-chief (who is, however, a corporate official, there being no news divisions at the magazines), while formally responsible for the product of their respective news organizations, participate only intermittently in determining the contents of the daily program or weekly issue.

Actual responsibility for the daily program or weekly magazine is lodged with the executive producer at the networks, the managing editor of *Time,* and the editor of *Newsweek*—and all generally have two or three assistants. At the magazines, the editor and his assistants are sometimes called the top editors, because they do the final, or "top," editing of all stories; consequently, I shall hereafter call them the top editors, and their equivalents at television the top producers, using the singular form of the title of top editor or producer when discussing the man in charge. (As of 1978, all the top positions were still held by males.) News organizations are not democratic; in fact, they are described as militaristic by some journalists, and the top editor or producer, and his assistants, have the power to decide what gets into print or on the air, at what length, and in what order, subject only to suggestions or vetoes from news and corporate management. At the networks, they must also share their power with anchorpersons, who can participate in story selection if and when they wish.

The section heads are called senior editors at the magazines and producers at the networks; they are responsible for selecting and readying stories in their own sections, with the advice, consent, and final review of their superiors. Television staffs are usually divided into only two sections—hard news and soft features—although there may be separate producers for hard foreign and domestic news. These producers also double as assistants to the executive producer in the story-selection process.

The magazines have about half a dozen section heads.[13] The front-of-the-book sections—national, international, and business—are each run by a senior editor; in the back of the book, a senior editor is usually responsible for three or four sections. The senior editor in charge of the national-news section has more power and prestige than the others and often eventually becomes a top editor. (Each senior editor, in turn, reports to one of the top editors, who divide the sections amongst themselves; but the top editor usually reviews the work of his assistants.)

The remaining journalists lack responsibility over story selection, although they suggest stories or propose dropping them if the required information is lacking. Their main role is story production, for they assemble the information that goes into a story, and write or film it. In television, story production is carried out by an associate producer, a reporter (who may double as associate producer) who writes and narrates the filmed story, and the cameraman and sound man, who make up the camera crew. ("Reporter" is both a role and a title, but reporters are eventually promoted to the position of correspondent.) The writing of tell stories is supervised by a news editor and carried out by writers.[14] Some anchorpersons write their own copy (David Brinkley); some write the leads and other major stories (John Chancellor). Walter Cronkite writes little copy but usually selects the tell stories and edits the writers' copy.

At the newsmagazines, story production is divided into two steps. Information is gathered by reporters and researchers (who supply background data from the morgue and library); this is then fed to writers (still called editors on *Newsweek*'s masthead), who actually write the story. They are complemented by the art staff, the photographers and researchers who take or find the pictures which illustrate newsmagazine stories; however, senior and top editors make the final picture choices.

Both in television and at the magazines, reporters are set apart organizationally from the rest of the editorial staff and are affiliated with a news service, having its own executive and bureau chiefs. The chief of the Washington bureau exerts some influence on story selection, since his bureau supplies the largest share of domestic news both for television and the magazines. At *Newsweek* he holds the rank of senior editor; and his story suggestions, transmitted by telephone, initiate the story-selection process at the start of the week.

The magazines' researchers play one further role; they "check" the "factual" accuracy of the writers' stories. Although the checkers are at the bottom of the editorial hierarchy (and therefore still mainly women), they have the formal right to override writers, and even editors, if they can supply sufficient convincing evidence of factual inaccuracy or lack of data to support an empirically based generalization—and if they can summon up the courage to contradict their superiors. Most actually do so because they can lose their jobs if ever-observant readers write in with too many factual errors. Checkers cannot, however, question writer assumptions or generalizations not involving researchable facts.[15] Reporters also participate in checking, for they review and must approve a writer's story, and they can question assumptions and generalizations. In television, news editors (and others) read the Associated Press and United Press International wires all day long, using them to check the reporters' films and texts for possible errors.

Although this account leaves out the nonjournalistic support, dissemination and business staffs without whom news could not come into being, two types of nonjournalists play a marginal role in story production and selection. Television film editors who cut, or help cut, film and tape shot by reporters may choose the scenes that are used, but they rarely determine or influence the main story themes. The magazine makeup staff helps top and senior editors to make up the pages, but the editors determine the order of the stories.

Functions in Story Selection and Production

As in any organization, formal positions never tell the whole story, and the news organization is no exception. It, too, can be divided into functional positions, which describe different roles in the process of story selection and production. The first step in that process is carried out by story suggesters, whose job it is to find or think up story ideas. Story suggestion is formally assigned to the reporters. They are required to keep up with what is going on in the beats they patrol or in the areas of the country assigned to their bureaus, and they are evaluated in part by their ability to suggest suitable stories. All other staff members, including top editors and producers, are also expected to come up with story ideas, and nonjournalists are encouraged to do so as well. At the magazines, the first meeting of the week of top and senior editors often begins with an informal review of their weekend activities and the topics discussed at dinner parties or public gatherings they attended, with the hope that it will produce story ideas.

The task of the story suggesters is facilitated by the wire services, which spin out stories twenty-four hours a day. These then become story suggestions for followup by magazine or television reporters. Equally important, story suggesters can rely on the continuing availability of "anticipated stories," identifiable events prescheduled by sources, such as news conferences, speeches, congressional hearings, and ceremonies. They are frequently called media events because some come into being principally to be covered by the news media.

Anticipated stories provide a predictable supply of potentially suitable news, with access and availability made certain in advance. This helps assuage the constant, if rarely justified, fears of the story selectors that there will not be enough news to fill the magazine or television program. Anticipated stories also enable news organizations to schedule the work of reporters and camera crews, spreading out their work so that it does not pile up to tax limited staff (or require the organizations to hire more people) and keeping them busy at all times.

Sources who want to get into the news and can afford to preschedule activities are aware of the journalists' dependence on anticipated stories and respond accordingly—for example, by providing advance information about the activities so that story selectors can try to assess whether they are likely to produce suitable news that is worth covering. Prescheduled events are also timed to conform to the work schedules of the news media, particularly television. Congressional hearings, for instance, are usually held in the mornings, when network camera crews are sure to be available; the most newsworthy witnesses always appear first, since camera crews often have other assignments and cannot remain for the entire hearing. During the 1960s, experienced organizers also scheduled demonstrations to fit the schedules of camera crews.

Not all anticipated stories are suitable, of course, but they are an important resource for all news media. Sigal found that of a sample of 3,000 stories which appeared in *The New York Times* and *Washington Post,* about two thirds were anticipated; but then most political happenings, even those which appear to be spontaneous, are planned with an eye toward getting them into the news.[16]

Once story suggesters have done their work, the story selectors make the final decision as to which of the suggested stories will be assigned to reporters and camera crews. Story selection is handled by the top producers at the networks, and by top editors and senior editors at the magazines, although usually with some consultation with reporters, writers, and others who have enough advance information about the potential story to decide whether it is actually available and feasible, that is, whether it can be reported and produced.

When story-selection decisions are complete and assignments to reporters, writers, and researchers have been made, one of the journalists, usually an associate producer or writer, becomes a story designer, drafting what are called queries at the magazines, which outline the major themes of the story and list the questions which reporters must ask. (However, often top editors and producers, as well as senior editors, make suggestions about story design at the time they select the story.) At this point, the story producers begin their work, but they and their stories remain under continuing review by story selectors. Stories may be "killed" or postponed because the needed information is not available in time, or because they require too much rewriting and editing, or, as often happens, because they turn out to be "stale" or no longer newsworthy. Concurrently, new stories are suggested continuously, and if time permits, they go through the same process.

Since both news media want to be as up-to-date as possible, that time is almost always found, and newer stories may "space out" older ones. Story selection is therefore an ongoing process, ending only when top editors and producers make the final choices and allow the disseminators to go to work.

Source and Audience-related Journalists

The way people function in the news organization can be looked at from another angle, for the organization is informally divided between journalists (notably reporters) who judge a story from the perspective of sources and those, such as top producers and editors, who look at it from the viewpoint of the audience. From that perspective, story selection begins with journalists who have varying relations to sources and ends with journalists who are charged with creating a news program or magazine for an audience. In reality, however, no one can ever afford to side entirely with either sources or the audience. For example, beat reporters (see Chapter 4) sometimes identify with the sources in their beats, thereby causing story selectors to discount or alter the reporters' suggestions; conversely, story selectors must pay some respect to sources, even if their main task is to supervise the summarizing and simplification of information to make it acceptable to the audience.

The tug of war between source and audience interests is played out mainly during story production. At the magazines, reporters gather information from sources and give it to writers, who adapt it for the audience. Even so, reporters must themselves begin to adapt. A young reporter once wrote what everyone agreed was a superb "file" on a new development in computer technology, but even though he had translated computer jargon into English, the writer could not understand the file. The reporter did not last long at the magazine. Reporters, in fact, are encouraged to write files as if they were writing the story in order to facilitate and speed up the work of the writers, and perhaps eventually to make writers superfluous. Nevertheless, even when files are story-like, a reporter may still be source-related; for example, when sources are medical researchers, a reporter may emphasize the advance in medical knowledge, whereas the editor may want to know how the research will benefit sick people.

The final shape of the story is often a compromise, but usually it is more audience-related, for top producers and editors have more power. It is no accident that audience-related journalists are at the top of the hierarchy. Nor is it difficult for them to be audience-related, for when they are not familiar with the detailed information provided by sources, and thus know little more about the story than the audience, they are in some ways like it. If they find the story interesting, they assume that the audience will respond in the same manner. At *Time,* sports cover stories are sometimes shown to editors totally uninterested in sports; if they are enthusiastic, the story is judged suitable.

Sellers, Buyers—and Highlighting

The people involved in story selection can be viewed as participants in a quasi-commercial transaction in which story suggesters are sellers, offering their ideas to story selectors acting as buyers. Story suggesters actually talk about "selling the story," and one executive producer of the 1960s used the old Hollywood expression "I'll buy that." The commercial terminology is not used because news is part of show business but because journalists operate within a supply-and-demand situation.

The news organization consists of people who are competing for a scarce resource: air time or magazine space; but the supply of story suggestions is always larger than the effective demand. Since story suggesters are judged in part by how many of their suggestions are chosen, they advertise their wares, trying their best to persuade selectors of the merit of their ideas. Specifically, they identify what they deem most salable—the most novel, dramatic, or unusual components of a story idea—in the hope of making a sale to a selector, who cannot buy everything that is being sold.

Like all other interactions and transactions within the news organization, selling is usually conducted in a casual manner. Although suggesters might like to resort to the hard sell, they do not yet know at this stage in the process what they can finally deliver in the way of a story; nor can they afford to oversell, for this casts doubt on their credibility. Consequently, they combine the most salient aspects of the advance information they have with what they know about the preferences of the buyers, short of falsely advertising their product. The seller's feeling about the story is also relevant, for story suggesters who are enthusiastic about their ideas are more likely to persuade the buyer, all other things being equal. Furthermore, buyers pay more attention if several suggesters independently sell the same story; and from time to time, reporters have gotten together and agreed to sell the same story for this reason.

Buyers are, of course, aware that they are being sold. Also, they prepare themselves for the transaction; before story selection begins, they will have read *The New York Times* and the *Washington Post,* and know, therefore, that their editors, who have already participated in a similar transaction, have bought or rejected the story idea.

Actually, the selling process begins long before story selection, with a source trying to sell a story idea to a reporter, who must then sell it to the bureau chief (in television), who, in turn, tries to sell it to a section head in New York. (At the magazines, reporters can sell directly, via memos, with copies being sent to senior editors, writers, and others.) Finally, section heads must sell to top producers and editors. In each stage of the process, the idea may be altered slightly, as different parts of the story are given more emphasis to make the whole more attractive to the later buyer.

I do not want to exaggerate the adversary nature of this transaction, for its participants have worked together for a long time and trust each other. Also, many stories virtually sell themselves, for buyers and sellers are, after all, fellow-journalists with a common conception of newsworthiness. In addition, some stories are installments of a "running story," such as a war, an election, a period of inflation, or bad weather. Others feature what might be called "running actors," like the president of the United States, who are almost always newsworthy. Not all installments of running stories wind up on the final story list, but they are, in a sense, pre-sold.

The selling-buying transaction involves not only story selection but the shaping of story content, for the sellers engage in highlighting: they select the highlights about an actor or activity, deleting the routine or expected, whatever is not sufficiently important, novel, dramatic, or distinctive to interest the buyer. But since an initially selected story is not guaranteed to appear on the final story list, highlighting is also an intrinsic part of story production.

The questions which go into the queries are drawn from the highlights that originally sold the story; thereafter, story producers, who are also competing with each other to get on the air or into the magazine, look first and foremost for highlights that will make their story survive to the final stage of story selection. For example, when television reporters cover speeches, they underline the most dramatic portions of the advance text and instruct the camera crews to shoot film only for them and for other portions of the speech which excite the speaker or the audience.

Over the span of the selection and production processes, highlighting proceeds in a spiraling manner, for by the time a suggested story is finished, only some of the initial highlights will remain. Television reporters in Vietnam primarily covered the war's highlights, such as battles and search-and-destroy missions; but when they or New York shaped the raw footage into a finished film, they chose only the most dramatic scenes to show on the air. Likewise, magazine writers select only some of the highlights from the reporters' files. News is thus often the highlights of highlights.

I fully appreciated highlighting after I accompanied a network reporter to a Washington press conference on hunger. The conference was attended by several major figures in the movement against hunger, some poor people who testified about the continued existence of hunger in their community, a congressman, and two senators, Jacob Javits and the late Robert Kennedy. Almost a dozen people made statements; but as soon as the conference was over, the reporter indicated he wanted to "do the piece with Bobby about twelve minutes in." In his sales pitch to the bureau producer, who would, in turn, have to sell the story to New York, he "offered" several other highlights, including arguments that had taken place at the press conference; and he proposed to interview two southern congressmen bitterly opposed to anti-hunger policies whose dramatic statements would enhance the story's salability. The producer bought only Kennedy's participation in the conference, as the reporter had expected from the start; later, he explained to me that since the press conference itself was not important and produced no previously unreported news about the anti-hunger movement, New York would consider the story only if it featured Kennedy, who was then always newsworthy. New York was sufficiently interested to "order up" a short film which not only highlighted the senator but limited itself to the most dramatic portions of his brief statement. Senator Kennedy's role in the actual press conference had been minor, but it became the centerpiece of the film. Nevertheless, at final story selection, it could not compete against the other films of the day and consequently was not shown.

Buying and selling lead journalists to construct a highlighted reality, which is, as in the case of Vietnam War news, an exaggerated summary of the observed events, at least by sociological standards of empirical inquiry. (To put it another way, whereas sociologists summarize from recurring patterns or random samples, journalists gravitate toward what sociologists term deviant cases.) At other times, as in the press conference, highlighting ignores the observed event entirely, with the journalist constructing a new story.

Selling, buying, and highlighting also help explain why the news is dominated by well-known public officials and stories of conflict and disorder. But the total explanation must include considerations to be described later, as well as the belief that the audience will pay attention to the news only if it is highlighted. Still, journalists are often not aware that they are highlighting or that external reality can be approached in other ways.

The Organizational Division of Labor and Power

I noted previously that organizational theories of story selection vary by how broadly they define the news organization. I shall use a narrow definition of the organization as a set of professionals, ignoring until later chapters how news organizations must deal with the commercial imperatives of their firms and therefore also with the political pressures that result. (I used the narrow definition because I was curious how organizational arrangements per se affected the news, and because journalists see commercial and political pressures as external to their organization; even so, I must occasionally mention some of these pressures here.[17]) When journalists make news judgments, they do not, of course, take the organization itself into account, but some of its requirements are, in effect, organizational considerations. Nonetheless, many organizational considerations come into being in response to the exigencies of story selection and production, and in the final analysis, the news determines the news organization more than the organization determines the news.

News organizations sometimes defy textbook generalizations about organizational practices, for while they are assembly lines and bureaucracies (complete with tables of organization, seniority, and other personnel rules and "channels"), they are staffed by professionals (many of whom are also union members). As professionals, they cannot be given direct orders but only "suggestions," to respect both their professional autonomy and their morale—and thus their productivity. And what they like least are suggestions that ask them to behave like bureaucrats.

Much of the discussion will be devoted to the magazine organizations, since they are much larger than their television equivalents. The evening news program is put together by less than twenty people in New York, while the magazine staff consists of about 130 journalists. Since television news is not as segmented by subject matter and lacks a back-of-the-book section, the organization also has fewer divisions. At the same time, television is dominated to a greater extent by the production process. Film or tape produced elsewhere can be edited in New York or over the phone, but it cannot usually be reshot. The daily deadline also limits the time for discussing changes, so that the television news organization is also a simpler and more flexible bureaucracy. (Ironically, the networks themselves are larger and more complex bureaucracies than those of the magazine news firms.) But in both electronic and print media, news organizations are hierarchical; consequently, the division of labor is also one of power, and my analysis begins with the people who have the most power.

Corporate and News Executives

Corporate and news executives "sit" outside the news organization, as I define it here. They also differ somewhat in terms of their responsibility and power, but they can be discussed jointly because, most of the time, their role in story selection and production is intermittent. As executives, they have virtually unlimited power and can suggest, select, and veto stories whenever they choose. But because they have other duties and because they are expected to abide by the corporate division of labor (and when they are nonjournalists, by the informal rules which give autonomy to journalists), they do not exercise their power on a day-to-day basis. Perhaps because they do not do so, the journalists pay close attention to their periodic suggestions, and at times, they overreact. When a new executive known as a "budget cutter" comes into office, top editors and producers may watch their budgets more carefully even without being asked to do so. As one editor put it: "It is not what [the executive] will do or will veto, but what we expect that he will do or veto; that's his influence."[18] But if expectations are not met, executives can obviously be more direct.

In practice, corporate and news executives play four roles. First, they exert power through budget and major personnel decisions. While they rarely make these decisions in order to alter story selection, some consequences for the news are inevitable. Lower budgets make it more difficult to cover the news; new top editors or producers appointed by the executive may come in with new ideas, especially if they have been brought in from the outside. This happens rarely, however, as almost all of the top producers and editors appointed in the last ten years have been promoted from within.

Second, corporate and news executives act to protect the commercial and political interests of the firm. Occasionally, they must settle disputes between competing news organizations in the firm; advise top editors or producers how to deal with—and sometimes kill—news that affects the firm's fortunes; or firmly suggest a story about changes in corporate management that the journalists, considering it a public-relations handout, would just as soon ignore. More often, executives defend journalists from commercial and political pressure (see Chapter 8).

Third, they make "policy." Although some organizations publish policy manuals, story selection and production are not governed by formal policies, as these would inhibit the journalists' flexibility and their ability to compete with rivals. Instead, executives make policy in response to specific events; in recent years, these have aimed to minimize the role (and visibility) of news organizations in social disorders. During the ghetto disturbances, executives set policies to ensure that the presence of the cameras did not encourage further disturbances or looting; more recently, they have issued rulings on the coverage of terrorists.

Most of the time, however, executives make policy by ruling on individual stories, but these rulings do not necessarily set a precedent. Top editors and producers consult with executives about "touchy" stories, which might generate audience or government protest; often they involve questions of "taste," as in the use of profanity, sacrilege, nudity, and the like (see Chapter 7).

At the magazines, executives are also consulted when the top editor wants to take a stand on a particularly visible issue. One top editor indicated in 1975: "If I suggested pulling troops out of South Korea, I'd have to check it out, or if I wanted to come out for price and wage control, but not about social policies such as crime." In the 1960s, however, he did not have to consult on economic policy stands, but then social policy stands, notably on race, required review. When top editors decide whether to endorse a presidential candidate, they discuss that decision, and the particular candidate, with superiors.

Fourth, news (but not corporate) executives supervise, meeting briefly with top producers daily, and with top editors weekly, in order to keep abreast of story selection. The meetings tend to be *pro forma,* but news executives also participate informally in story selection, sending in story ideas, suggesting preferences for leads or covers, and commenting critically on stories after they have appeared. How often they intervene is up to individual executives, although it happens more often when a new executive takes office, wanting to put his stamp on the organization, or when a new top producer or editor is appointed.

However, top producers and editors resent regular intervention, and news executives restrain themselves accordingly. In fact, although top producers and editors must obey their superiors, they tolerate intervention only because news executives themselves are trained journalists. Corporate executives, not being journalists, must therefore transmit their own suggestions through news executives, intervening directly only once in a long while. News executives also resent suggestions from their nonjournalistic superiors, and sometimes these are quietly ignored.[19]

Time's organization differs in some respects from that of other magazines. Since *Time* is conceived as speaking for Time, Inc., the corporate editor-in-chief and his assistants (all journalists) play a more regular supervisory role than corporate executives at *Newsweek*. The editor-in-chief receives all story lists and may review individual cover and lead stories that deal with subjects on which he wishes to speak for the corporation. Thus, he reversed the magazine's support of the Vietnam War in 1968; participated in writing *Time*'s 1973 editorial calling for the resignation of Richard Nixon; intervened in the 1974 leadership story described in Chapter 2 to make sure it included sufficient businessmen and women; and has edited a number of covers, including a 1975 cover on capitalism. From time to time, he or his assistants take over the top editorship when the regular incumbent is away on business or vacation.

The ultimate power of executives is perhaps best illustrated by the military or totalitarian labels with which journalists describe their superiors. At NBC, executives were generally referred to as "the brass"; at CBS, William Paley is known, according to David Halberstam, as "the Chairman, much as Mao Tse Tung . . . is known in China as the Chairman."[20] A top editor sometimes joked about his superiors as "the Soviet" or "the Politburo." A more measured description of the power of executives was provided by a top producer: "They can order me to do something on big or small issues, for after all this is a company and a business, but they rarely exert that influence. I am as autonomous as I could expect to be."

Top Editors and Producers

Magazine journalists sometimes liken their news organization to kingdoms or armies in which the top editor is the king or the general. In fact, a senior editor in charge of foreign news once explained that according to diplomatic protocol, the top editor is equivalent to a four-star general, outranked only by a news executive, who is a five-star general, the senior editor himself holding the rank of brigadier.

The power of top editors resides not only in their complete and final say over what appears in the magazine but also in their position as heads of bureaucracies. Communication with them must normally go through channels, although they are concurrently expected to maintain an "open-door policy." While some top editors do so with more enthusiasm than others, the mystique of the position is sufficient to intimidate journalists, especially those with little seniority, from ever approaching the open door. Consequently, top editors are sometimes viewed by their staffs as being "remote," the more so when they are shy.

The power of top editors (as well as of executives and senior editors) is furthered by the fact that they do not have to justify or explain their decisions or judgments. As a result, they can envelop themselves in a good deal of mystery, forcing underlings to guess what will please or displease them. The practice of not giving orders only enhances the mystery, as does the fact that promotions tend, as in every organization, to go to people who, among other things, please their superiors. News organizations, however, are pyramids, with only a limited number of top jobs. Writers who like to edit and want the higher income, status, and power that attend senior editorships know that they are competing for fewer than ten positions, while reporters compete for about twenty bureau chieftaincies. At the networks, the top jobs are also few in number.

Top-editor power is also furthered, if not deliberately, by the division of labor, which creates interest differences throughout the staff. Like all organizations with branches, news organizations experience endemic conflict of interest between New York and the bureaus, which often feel that their stories are not considered important enough in New York. Reporters want to see as much of their files in the writer's final story as possible, but writers must take into account the files of several reporters, as well as the demands of the format and the instructions of superiors. Writers compete with each other to get into the magazine, particularly the back of the book, whose sections must give up space to the front of the book virtually every week. Researchers with checking duties are beholden to their sources, thus opening up possible conflicts with writers, reporters, and editors.

Senior editors in many ways resemble foremen or forewomen; on the one hand, they must satisfy top editors, but on the other, they must defend the interests of their sections against story killings and cuts. Although they can argue with their superiors, they must ultimately accept their decisions. Their writers hold no power over them, but too much neglect of their interests will depress their morale, and senior editors do not allow top editors to forget this. Wise senior editors also place responsibility for decisions that hurt the section on the top editor, who then becomes the major target of resentment and hostility.

Last but hardly least, the power of top editors, and of superiors in general, is maintained by organization-wide pressures for conformity. Because news organizations are assembly lines on which people must work together to manufacture a product against a deadline, they almost always generate conformity. Few top editors are either sufficiently powerful or Machiavellian to manipulate the pressures for conformity, which actually originate in the production process; nevertheless, insofar as news judgment is filled with uncertainty, and top editors must, by virtue of their position, resolve uncertainty and decide which selection considerations have priority, they also set tones, and sometimes precedents, which then require conformity. Senior editors do much the same inside their sections.

Journalists do not seem to be aware of the conformity under which they labor. When things are going well at the end of the week, or at the end of the day at the networks, conformity actually takes the form of a cohesive and satisfying camaraderie, as colleagues work together to finish a product of which they are proud. Still, when a magazine goes to press, people who argue too fiercely about "edits," those who take too long to finish their writing assignments or are reluctant to help out with petty chores, are not popular with their colleagues and eventually find themselves isolated, transferred, or even jobless. News organizations generally hire people on a probationary basis, and newcomers who do not demonstrate the ability and willingness to cooperate rarely secure permanent jobs, whatever their journalistic skills. Prima donnas are universally scorned, and whenever journalists talk about now famous freelancers who had begun their careers at the magazine, they are apt to remember them as prima donnas who were uncooperative or whose work habits created difficulties during the rush to meet deadlines.

Conformity pressures required to get the work done expand into other areas as well, so that journalists who find fault with story choices early in the week, regularly avoid group lunches, and refuse to participate in the office banter are also looked at askance. Conformity further extends to values and ideology (see Chapter 6), and sometimes even to dress. During my fieldwork at one magazine, several of the men suddenly began to appear in shirts with epaulets, and the women went off to buy large glasses.

Top producers have the same kind of power as top editors, but because television staffs are smaller, they are more accessible and less mysterious. Much of the day, they may be working in the newsroom itself and are less approachable only when they retreat to their offices. However, they must share their power with anchorpersons; indeed, the latter are more than equals, for anchorpersons can recommend the firing of executive producers, but not vice versa.[21] Anchorpersons obtain power because most viewers hold them responsible for the content of the program, and because they attract a significant proportion of the viewers to the program in the first place. Some anchorpersons are too busy with other activities to participate regularly in story selection, but they can do so if and when they choose.[22] The ambiguous position of the anonymous top producer vis-à-vis the highly visible anchorperson was nicely put by one who told me: "It's still my show, but I let a star get his way unless it stinks up the show." Subsequently, however, his conflicts with a star resulted in his departure from the program.

Although the television organization is also divided into formal ranks, these are offset by the simpler division of labor. Like their peers at the magazines, reporters and bureau chiefs are not always happy with New York's decisions, but television writers play a very different role than writers at the magazines. They write tell stories for the anchorperson and thus are not working on their own stories or for themselves. Top producers have the same final voice in story selection as top editors, but some top producers make final story decisions with the entire staff present. Even so, rank and seniority determine actual participation much of the time, and the younger people are likely to defer to "the grownups," as one young associate producer at NBC called his seniors.

The organization's size and the daily deadline also require more group activity, and conformity pressures are, if anything, stronger than at the magazines. There is no time for argument, and there is no room for prima donnas. But in the hectic 60 to 90 minutes before air time (to be described further at the end of the chapter), the formal division of power and labor is virtually set aside, as are differences of age and rank. An associate producer may make last-minute story cuts when superiors are busy elsewhere, and the top producer may collate scripts if no one else is free to do so. Only anchorpersons occupy a privileged position. The "stars" are praised when they help out in a last-minute crisis and are criticized, out of earshot, if they come to the newsroom in late afternoon and suggest sudden changes in the story list.

Countervailing Powers of Underlings

Every journalist involved in story selection or production applies one overriding organizational consideration: pay close attention to the suggestions from superiors because they may be intended to set a precedent. But there is also a contradictory consideration: the suggestions from above can be questioned, within limits, for the power of top editors and producers is not absolute.

There are a number of ways in which this power is diluted. For one thing, neither a top editor nor a producer can do everything; consequently, he must delegate some story selection and editing decisions to assistants and section heads. During the 1960s, *Newsweek* became a "senior editor's magazine," enabling some senior editors to establish virtually autonomous "feudal baronies"; *Time,* on the other hand, followed the Luce tradition, with the managing editor delegating little and editing virtually every story. During the 1970s, however, a new editor at *Newsweek* recentralized the magazine, bringing in a new group of young assistants and senior editors loyal to him, while *Time*'s managing editor began to delegate some back-of-the-book story selection to an assistant.

The extent of delegation is partly a matter of organizational tradition and of top-editor personal style, but both are honored only as long as the magazine or program is doing well in its pursuit of the audience, and staff morale remains satisfactory. The changes at both magazines not only reflected the personal styles of the top editors but were also made to improve the quality of the magazines and to deal with morale problems.

Variations also exist at the networks, for at NBC the executive producer and the New York anchorman are in charge, while at CBS, the executive producer delegates much of the daily story selection to a senior producer. But at both print and electronic media, who makes the final story decisions has little impact on what decisions are actually reached, for all abide by the considerations that govern news judgment. That someone rules the roost makes a difference, but who rules it does not. Although top editors and producers can affect the value judgments in major stories and determine the fate of lesser stories, they do not determine what actors and activities routinely become newsworthy.

Individual Autonomy

Delegation of power also takes place because the news organization consists of professionals who insist on individual autonomy. Journalists claim freedom from interference not only by nonjournalists but also by superiors; they have the right to make their own news judgments, which is why they cannot be given orders. To be sure, individual autonomy is frequently illusory, especially in a group enterprise. Moreover, the suggestions of powerful superiors are, in fact, thinly veiled orders, requiring polite circumlocutions in which commands are phrased as requests. Still, a writer who had spent nearly twenty years at *Time* once said that "if people around here started giving orders, the whole system would collapse."

Reporters and writers play only a consulting role in story selection, but they have some autonomy in story production, the amount being a function of their seniority. Before writers begin to work on their stories, they discuss these with the senior editor. Senior editors generally decide how many words a story "deserves," although writers may later choose to exceed the prescribed length; and if the story is good enough, the writer's judgment is sustained. The tenor of the rest of the discussion depends both on the style of the senior editor and the status of the writer. A few senior editors virtually dictate the story to the writer, particularly if he or she is a novice; but one editor made himself unpopular by even dictating stories to senior writers. A few leave the story entirely up to the writer (other than the novice), and most offer suggestions about the organization of the story and a possible lead. "Star" writers are almost completely autonomous, however; they are treated as respectfully as bestselling or prestigious novelists, discussing the story with the senior editor only if they want guidance. Most of the time, senior writers are equally free, except when they are writing lead or cover stories; on the other hand, junior writers must earn individual autonomy by their performance.

Nonetheless, discussions with senior editors do not often concern story substance, for writers are entitled to select their own facts, draw their own conclusions, and come up with their own evaluations, although they may be edited later. When senior editors make substantive suggestions, writers can disagree, although senior writers are more likely to do so than juniors. In addition, the prevailing conformity discourages frequent disagreement. Even writers who have been at the magazine for several years must remember that "you can protest only so much; then you become a 'crank.' "

Wherever possible, differences of opinion about conclusions and evaluations are treated as differences of "fact" so as to uphold the autonomy of individual judgment. People argue for their ideas on the basis of available information; and more often than not, the final outcome is a compromise. The direction of the compromise is determined by the power and status of the participants, as well as by the intensity with which they defend their positions, the evidence they can bring to bear, and in the case of writers, by their writing skill as well. "You can get in what you want to say if you say it well," one writer suggested; and saying it well usually means a choice of words that can compromise or transcend disagreements and, in the process, save face for all concerned.

Even so, top editors have the last word, for if disagreements cannot be settled to their satisfaction, they can order rewrites or suggest, directly or indirectly, the point of view to be taken. Often, the suggestion is indirect; one writer, describing his top editor, pointed out: "He doesn't ask you to change your point of view; he just nibbles away at it by asking for a second version, or he will kill it and give it to someone else next week." Then, too, some top (and senior) editors are less diplomatic than others. Nevertheless, for writers and reporters, the prime fact of life about individual autonomy is its uncertainty. Superiors always have more individual autonomy than underlings, and the latter never know when their editors are likely to exercise their authority. "Anyone who believes writers have complete freedom," a senior writer pointed out, "also believes in the tooth fairy."

Writers, therefore, must combine their own judgment with what they think will please their editors; if they have no interest in a story or no firm point of view, they will write only to please them. Sometimes they will do so even when they have a point of view but do not want to work all night rewriting. Pleasing editors, however, is more difficult than might be imagined, because they do not always know enough about a story to develop their own judgments. An experienced *Time* writer once described the problem in an internal memorandum: "Every writer has a working knowledge of what his editor wants. Unless he's incorrigibly stubborn or independently wealthy, he tries to give it to him. But a senior editor doesn't always know what he wants. In the words of a senior editor . . . , 'I don't know what I don't want until I get the writer's story.' " Even when editors know what they want, however, they may not say so, partly to preserve the writer's autonomy, partly to see what the writer will add when they request a rewrite. At *Newsweek,* which gives bylines to all writers, those who feel that their stories have been edited too heavily can have their byline removed. Readers may not care or notice, but colleagues do, and a senior editor's byline is public notice of undue interference with a writer's autonomy.

Over the years, however, only a handful of senior-editor bylines have appeared in *Newsweek,* for most writer-editor disagreements are stylistic rather than substantive. Editors may suggest a different lead, ask the writer to place some information higher up in the story, or propose a reorganization to enhance the logical development of the narrative that would also shorten the story. Sometimes they will "soften" a harsh judgment or edit out a conclusion that could result in angry letters (see Chapters 6 and 8), but seldom do they suggest a different conclusion or evaluation. This is true even at *Time.* Although the magazine continues to follow the Luce policy of "speaking with a single voice," individual journalists can state their own judgments, which then become the corporate "voice." But on major issues of American policy, *Time*'s voice, like that of *Newsweek,* is determined by the top editor and, in some instances, his superiors.

At the networks, individual reporters have even greater autonomy because they film their stories far from New York, and films can rarely be redone. When the story is controversial, however, top producers work closely with reporters on their texts; and when time is short, producers are apt to make their suggestions more brusquely than editors. However, because television stories do not end with evaluations, the opportunity to exercise individual autonomy is more limited than at the magazines.

Power and Morale

The right of individual autonomy is, for top editors and producers, a major organizational consideration, although it plays a larger role in story production than story selection. Yet, an even more important consideration follows from the inherent contradiction between hierarchy and autonomy, which requires top editors and producers to uphold the morale of their staffs. This is particularly necessary at the magazines, for when morale is low, reporters and writers are less likely to exert the extra effort for informational and stylistic originality the magazines need in order to compete with each other.

Morale is largely shaped by a pleasant ambience (organizational mood) and good working conditions. Ambience, however, is often determined by factors over which top editors and producers have little control. For one thing, a news organization's mood suffers when it is doing poorly vis-à-vis its competitors. Also, the organization's ambience is created, to some extent, by that of its firm, and the mood is less pleasant in firms which pay respectful attention to bureaucratic rules. While I can only report personal impressions, CBS and Time, Inc. always struck me as more earnest and straight-laced places than NBC and *Newsweek*. Time, Inc. has long had a reputation for taking itself more seriously than other news media, while *Newsweek* seemed to operate in a more light-hearted fashion—or, as one editor suggested: "We use humor to lubricate the friction."

Still, each news organization also creates its own ambience, as do individual sections; thus, very earnest sections could be found at *Newsweek* and light-hearted ones at *Time*. Some top editors and producers, and section heads, maintain morale through charisma, others through the respect they command as journalists, and still others by the intentional or unintentional application of "human relations"; but many eschew any deliberate effort at leadership. Viewing themselves as journalists who have rejected bureaucracy, they prefer to forget that they have administrative duties and to use their private personalities in their public roles. Because of their power, their ways of handling social relationships strongly influence the morale of organizations or sections. The top producer's personality is particularly significant, given the small size of television organizations; however, the group mood is also affected by anchorpersons who behave too much like stars, and by excessive interference from executives.

Nevertheless, morale is primarily determined by the amount of control people have over their work and the ways in which superiors treat their work. Most journalists have a strong commitment to and identification with their product, but they easily become discouraged when their desire to perform well is restrained by what they consider unnecessary bureaucratic obstacles, the unwillingness of superiors to listen to them, and especially by undue interference with their autonomy. Magazine reporters are unhappy when too little of the information in their files winds up in the final story; writers complain when they are allowed too few words for complex stories or when their work is heavily edited, cut, or killed; their morale is lowered further when no explanation is given. Television reporters live more easily with cuts and kills, because air time is finite and all material is subject to these decisions.

Judging by the amount and frequency of griping I encountered during my fieldwork, writer morale is rarely high, but some organizational considerations exist to keep it from sinking to depression levels.

The magazines consist of so many sections that not all can appear each week, and many are "prekilled" at the start of story selection. Top editors, however, will not kill a section more than three or four times consecutively, and will assign at least one cover story to every section each year; these decisions are made principally to preserve morale. Editors and producers ensure that all bureaus, including those which rarely supply important news, see their efforts in print or on the air regularly. Features may therefore be assigned to a bureau that has not been on the story lists recently. In addition, stories of lesser importance are sometimes put on the story list on grounds of "diplomacy," to reward or please a colleague, or to make amends. If an enthusiastically proposed story idea is rejected or if a story is killed for lack of space, story selectors incur debts which they endeavor to repay whenever possible.

When morale is depressed by working conditions, and informal gripe sessions no longer suffice, journalists, at least at the magazines, may turn to organized protest. Magazine writers began to protest in 1968 at *Time*, and in 1969 at *Newsweek*; there, a group of young writers called themselves the April 26 Movement after the Castro revolution, although they had no intention of overthrowing the magazine. Many of the complaints at both magazines were similar; the writers wanted more time to think and a chance to write longer stories. They also wanted story selection to reflect more of their own interests and skills; instead of a "magazine of record," they wanted what *Newsweek*'s top editor later called "a weekly *Harper's* magazine." The *Time* writers also complained about heavy and unexplained editing by senior editors, the top editor's remoteness, as well as his practice of killing no back-of-the-book sections until all stories had been written, which meant that every week, many writers were working on stories that had no chance of ever being published.[23] In effect, the writers were demanding more individual autonomy and a reduction of the power of the top editor (as well as of senior editors), but they also asked that more writers be hired and that the magazines be enlarged.

The protests were presented in a friendly tone—"in a spirit of moving ahead together," as the *Newsweek* writers put it; nor were the top editors antagonistic, although both cautioned against the possibility of unduly rapid change. Reforms were made, although some only years later and in response to other pressures. *Time* soon transferred some overly autocratic senior editors; at both magazines, stories grew in length, and *Newsweek* eventually abolished the feudal baronies of the senior editors and gave bylines to all its writers. But top-editor power was not reduced, and costlier demands were not met; it took another protest by *Time* writers, in 1975, to institute prekilling of back-of-the-book sections before stories were written.[24]

Another wave of protest, in the early 1970s, came from researchers, who objected to the magazines' failure to allow them to become reporters, writers, or senior editors. Through organized protest—and at *Newsweek*, threatened lawsuits—the researchers won the right to train and compete for reporting and writing jobs. By the middle of the decade, a goodly number had moved into these positions, despite frequent hiring freezes, and each magazine had appointed at least one woman senior editor.[25] The women also complained about sexist terms and stereotypes in stories and the lack of news about women; as a result of constant reminders, these shortcomings have been slowly, if not entirely, overcome.

The ability of writers to protest and to win some of their demands reflected, in part, the expansion of journalistic job opportunities in the 1960s, the younger writers securing more power because the magazines were reluctant to lose them. Researchers are more easily replaced, however; it was no accident, therefore, that they had to resort to more energetic pressure.

During the 1970s, the labor market tightened up again, and the writers' bargaining position deteriorated. In 1976, Time, Inc. asked its unionized workers to accept some pay cuts and more corporate control over pay increases; the resulting strike was won by management.[26] Although not all journalists belonged to the union, the strike radicalized some, who now viewed themselves as "labor" vis-à-vis "management." Inside the news organization, however, the adversary relationship is hard to maintain. Top and senior editors are only nominally part of management and play no part in contract negotiations. Moreover, editors and their staffs must cooperate in order to get out the magazine.[27]

At the networks, organized protest has not developed so far, except among women, for all journalists are union members and can take their grievances to the union. With only three networks, moreover, the labor market for national television journalists is always tight. Jobs at local stations are often available, but few network journalists are ready to move "down" to the local level, with the exception of reporters who sometimes become highly paid anchorpersons at big-city local stations. Both internal and external pressures have resulted in the hiring of women reporters and producers. By 1978, women were also producing and anchoring the evening news but, except for Barbara Walters, mainly on weekend programs.[28] NBC journalists have struck twice in the last fifteen years, primarily because of money issues. They have long perceived themselves as labor, but like magazine journalists, they have little sympathy for other unions and have not developed pro-labor values as a result of their own protests and strikes.

Nonjournalistic Bureaucracy

News organizations are also subject to universal forms of bureaucratic practice which have no relation to journalism but do have some impact on story selection and production. For example, seniority principles are applied at both news media: senior writers and reporters are usually assigned the stories that are most likely to survive, while younger people are assigned those more likely to be spaced out. At the magazines, effective researchers may be rewarded by transfers to sections where they can occasionally work as reporters, one result being that the expertise they have developed in one section is lost to the magazine. The sectional division of labor and the overlapping mandates of some sections can encourage turf struggles, with senior editors selecting stories that enable them to enlarge their sections. Such struggles took place at *Newsweek* when it was a senior editor's magazine; but when power is centralized in the top editor, senior editors cannot easily compete with each other.

As in all organizations, some people are more ambitious and more competent, as well as more willing than their peers to please their superiors and to play organizational politics in order to rise quickly in the hierarchy. While promotions are regularized, in quasi-civil-service fashion, unusually rapid mobility takes place occasionally, especially when luck or skill enables a journalist to obtain a scoop or to be in the right place at the right time for a big story. During the 1960s, assignments to Vietnam sometimes enabled young reporters to make a name for themselves in a short time. Individuals may also be promoted over their seniors when a magazine or television program is in trouble.

Knowing and pleasing the right people, and coming from a prestigious background, do not hurt in the competition for promotions; still, because of widespread consensus about what constitutes journalistic merit, upward mobility unaccompanied by merit seems less frequent at news organizations. (Of course, as in all organizations, merit is defined and evaluated by superiors; but in a group enterprise, sharp disagreements about definitions and evaluations are unlikely to occur.) Upward mobility due to family background or success in organizational politicking is resented by others, but a rapid rise based on merit is not. Downward mobility is rare; instead, people are transferred to other parts of the news firm. There is also little "deadwood," for the intensity of the work pace forces the rapid extrusion of people who do not do their share of the work. It also exhausts people, so that by the time they reach their fifties, many find themselves jobs that are less demanding.

While news organizations are perhaps more meritocratic than others, they experience their share of factions, alliances, and power struggles. Gary Paul Gates's historical study of the internal dynamics of CBS News supplies many detailed case studies that attest to this fact; however, they also suggest that these struggles rarely concern issues of news judgment. Furthermore, in almost all instances, particularly at the executive level, such struggles are won by the individual or faction that wins rating successes: the most active political gamesmen will survive—even though their machinations are resented—as long as their decisions produce high ratings. Gates reports, for example, that two presidents of the news division were asked to resign—people are seldom fired—in the 1960s because they could not overcome the ratings dominance of NBC's *Huntley-Brinkley Report*. [29] Conversely, a news executive disliked by many of his colleagues and some corporate superiors for his internal political manipulations remained in his post until Sally Quinn, whom he had hired to co-anchor the morning news program, proved to be inadequate, her departure providing the justification for his. [30] Anchorpersons are rarely asked to leave, even when the ratings are low; like athletic teams, news organizations replace their coaches and managers in the hope that a change at the top will improve team performance. Less visible and prestigious reporters, however, may be forced out or demoted in the line of succession that forms behind incumbent anchorpersons, if they align themselves with a losing faction or anger their superiors.

Friendship cliques are to be found at news organizations, as are personality conflicts among people who must work together—although almost all conflicts, including those involving conflicts of interest, are ascribed to personality differences. Older hands, who arrived at the magazines when staffs were smaller, sometimes complain about overbureaucratization and the replacement of personal contact by memos; on the other hand, top editors and producers tend to make final decisions in small, ad hoc meetings, with the result that sometimes these decisions are not passed on to other people who need to be informed. Consequently, many journalists complain about communication difficulties and cannot understand why they, as professional communicators, should encounter such problems. They know they are working in bureaucracies, but being journalists, they also try not to remember it.

News Organizations as Assembly Lines

Ultimately, the divisions of power in news organizations are over-shadowed, and the divisions of labor determined, by the deadline. That deadline, furthermore, leads to story selection and production processes that become routinized and remain virtually unchanged over the years—which is one reason why journalists describe their organizations as assembly lines. The processes are almost the same at the two networks, and at the two magazines, for each organization independently develops a similar set of solutions to what is, after all, a common task.[31]

The daily television program is put together between 9 A.M. and 6:30 P. M.; and the magazines are assembled over a five-day period: Mondays to Fridays at *Time,* Tuesdays to Saturdays at *Newsweek.* But at both media, story selectors actually begin their work when they wake up, and start to read or watch the news; and at the magazines, some days can last fourteen to eighteen hours. Nor does the assembling process ever really stop, for someone is already planning tomorrow's program or next week's magazine as the current one is being finished.

The selection and production processes have been likened to a funnel, with many stories being placed on the assembly line at the start, of which only some remain at the end. But the funnel also resembles an accordion, for new stories can be added up to the last moment. The initial story lists are long because many suggested stories do not pan out. An anticipated story billed as an important speech by a newsworthy public official may turn out to be a virtual repetition of an earlier speech; a good story idea may have been based on erroneous advance information; sources may not make themselves available to reporters. Then, too, the list contains postponed stories, which were previously spaced out or which could not be completed because sources failed to supply the necessary information in time for the previous deadline. In addition, the list always includes some "timeless features," which are not "pegged" or connected to a specific event and can thus be run at any time; these are also called pegless wonders, or evergreens.

The list is purposely padded to include postponable items that can be scrapped to make room for "breaking" stories (news about unanticipated events), such as the death of a major public figure, a disaster, or the indictment of a leading politician. Breaking stories have first priority among story selectors; and at the magazines, they still sometimes "stop the presses."

Once all suggestions are in, they are winnowed to produce the first story list: by noon to 1 P. M. in television; before the end of Day 1 at the magazines. At the networks, the executive producer makes this list —a "lineup" or "rundown" (usually networks have different terms for the same operation)—in consultation with his assistants or the entire senior staff, depending on his personal style. At the magazines, senior editors make up lists for their sections and obtain a top editor's approval. These lists are still overly long, but by now story selectors have made priority decisions, knowing which stories they would prefer to use.

Top editors at the newsmagazines have a special winnowing problem not shared by top producers, for as I reported earlier, some back-of-the-book sections must be prekilled each week. The top editor makes this decision primarily on the basis of how important and interesting he finds the story lists that senior editors have submitted, and how often a section has appeared during the last month. (Reporters and writers of prekilled sections now have more time to prepare for next week and to come up with ideas that will entice the top editor.) One or two other sections, however, may "die" later in the week, even if their contents pass muster, because the front-of-the-book sections often require more space as new stories enter their lists.

Since 1977, newsmagazines have been able to use color photographs throughout the magazine; and "picture picking," previously done on Days 4 and 5, has been somewhat advanced. At the moment, the magazines can use only a dozen color pages per issue, and in "forms" or sets of four or eight pages; consequently, if color pictures are scheduled, say, for pages 13 and 14, they must also be used on pages 80 and 81. Since color pages go to press a day earlier than black-and-white pages, top and senior editors must keep in mind that sections using color pages have to be properly aligned. Although the advent of color photography has not altered the basic production process and has not significantly affected story selection (see Chapter 5), top editors are required to plan ahead more than in the past, and to coordinate and juggle pages in the final stages when story lists need to be updated. Eventually, however, color pages will go to press as late as others.

Choosing the Lead and Cover Stories

Top producers and editors must go through one additional sifting process: choosing a preliminary candidate for the lead for the evening program, and a cover subject for the magazine. Candidates for program leads are nominated early in the day, and a preliminary lead is chosen by the executive producer when he makes up the first story list. Choosing a magazine cover, however, is a more complicated process.

The cover story, deemed by the editors to be the most important story of the week, usually runs at least five or six pages. Both magazines hold weekly cover conferences, attended by the top and senior editors, in which a list of preliminary cover decisions is made for the next six to eight weeks. These meetings never produce final cover decisions, but they do offer an opportunity for "long-range planning," for senior editors to begin selling future cover story ideas to their colleagues and for the group to reject ideas that excite no one.

The choice of the current week's cover is made by the top editor, on Day 1, after quick, informal consultations with his assistants and some senior editors. More often than not, that decision remains preliminary, particularly if a back-of-the-book cover is chosen, for it may be eliminated by a breaking national or international story. Frequently, a final choice is not made until Day 4, when the cover itself (but not the story) must be sent to the printers.

Cover selection is a weighty decision because it represents the editor's judgment of what constitutes the most important story of the week, and he knows that many news media, people in Washington, and others are watching to see what he picks. Covers award power and prestige to the cover subject, at least momentarily; they also legitimate the chosen person or topic, and indicate to observers of the American scene what is currently important in the country. For the top editor, the cover also provides an opportunity for competition with the other newsweekly (see Chapter 5) and an instantaneous form of feedback from the readership (see Chapter 7).

The Final Stages of the Process

From about 10 A. M. to 3 P. M. at the networks, and from Day 2 to Day 4 at the magazines, New York waits for the reporters to produce their films and write their files, although many reporters have been at work on their stories long before then.

Television: The Last Three Hours

By 3:30 or so, the top producers know what stories have been filmed or are currently being shot; they have also been informed, by phone or telex, what the camera has captured and how long the film is estimated to run. Some films, features especially, are already completed. About 4 P. M., the executive producer prepares the first "published" story list, which is mimeographed and circulated around the network news division. He now decides on his lead, the film stories he plans to use, the order in which they are to run, and the amount of time to be devoted to tell stories. At CBS, the executive producer then divides the program into five segments with internal unity, separated from each other to create a "natural break" for commercials. At NBC, the 1977 format change into a four-segment program has simplified one of the producer's tasks, for "Segment 3" stories are often prescheduled for all or part of the week. Since these stories are long by television standards, however, he has fewer minutes at his disposal for the day's news than his peer at CBS; in that sense, his story-selection task has become more difficult. Both producers must also make certain that the films and tell stories they want to include add up to the 22 to 23 minutes available for news.

On most days, at both networks, the lineup is revised at least once or twice. It can be changed as late as 5:30, and new film and tell stories can even be inserted during the commercial breaks while the first segments of the program are already being broadcast.[32]

The final 90 minutes are devoted to translating the story list into a program. Then, film stories about the day's hard news are fed into the newsroom by closed-circuit television, and a top producer reviews each story with the reporter over the phone. In recent years, however, the networks have begun to shift from film to tape, which can be transmitted to New York more quickly and edited in-house. Still, the most important stories, from Washington, come in late so as to be as up-to-date as possible. In addition, a new breaking story may have to be fitted into the lineup or a scheduled story omitted because it is substantively or technically poor; equally often, a story is too long and it or others must be trimmed.

In any case, the final period is extremely harried, and everyone is tense, although no one shows it. Top and associate producers make or take one phone call after another, giving instructions to reporters, asking film or tape editors to cut fifteen seconds from a finished film, and worrying whether a foreign film transmitted over the satellite will look sharp enough when it appears on the air. Meanwhile, they discuss among themselves whether a last-minute story should be substituted for another and bark instructions to news editors and writers, for new tell stories may have to be written, and some will have to be dropped.

A minute or less before air time, the anchorperson or persons are made up, straighten their ties or dresses, collate their scripts, and focus on the teleprompters, from which they read most of the script. Calm and collected, they go "on the air," but the work pace in the newsroom remains feverish, as last-minute revisions are made and given to the anchorperson during commercial breaks.

The hectic pace ends at 7 P. M.. The executive producer and others may watch at least part of the competitors' programs; at that time, their and their rivals' mistakes and omissions are discussed. Since secretaries have left, writers and producers may be on the phone, answering calls from viewers, even getting involved in heated discussions over the inclusion or coverage of a specific story. By 7:30 P. M. everyone has left except the producer responsible for starting tomorrow's story list. But if an important story breaks, top producers may be on the phone during the night, making plans to cover it for the next evening's program.

Days 4 and 5 at the Magazines

At the magazines, the final stage is longer and less hectic, except for the top editors, who spend much of the final twenty-four hours reading and editing everything that their writers have produced. During Days 2 and 3, while reporters work on their files, writers and researchers keep busy with background reading for their assigned stories; senior editors continue to work on their story lists, for in the front of the book, these lists are revised and updated daily.

Every section works on a slightly different schedule; but in the domestic sections, some files have already come in by Day 3; and by noon of Day 4, reporters are expected to have sent in enough of their files so that writers can meet with the senior editor to discuss story content and length.

Now the doors of the writers' offices close, and they get to work. Although many have been writing for the magazine for years, few write easily. When a summer trainee wrote on her application that she enjoyed writing, the writers who saw it agreed that she was either stupid or lying. The difficult part is not writing but organizing, however: assembling the information from several files around a framework that flows logically, with the fewest number of words and without repetition or resort to unnecessary bridges that may add to story length or sound hackneyed.

Usually, the crucial files do not arrive until late on Day 4, and writers may be working until long after midnight. The finished story then goes to the senior editor and researcher, and is phoned or telexed to the reporters involved. Senior editors make some changes in almost all stories, if only, as writers argue, to show top editors that senior editors are earning their keep. Once approved by the senior editor, the story is reviewed by a top editor, who normally suggests only minor revisions, except for cover stories, which may be rewritten several times.

Meanwhile, once writers have judged whether they can meet the agreed-on story length, senior editors begin to think seriously about the section's final story list and their total page requirements. Should the number of pages assigned earlier in the week be insufficient, they can appeal to the top editor for more, and appeals from the front of the book are usually granted. This means cutting or killing more sections in the back of the book.

On Day 4, senior editors begin to plan their section makeup, deciding the order of their stories and determining, with top editors, which stories will be accompanied by color photographs. Their makeup plans remain preliminary, however, for the final decisions are made by top editors, and in the front-of-the-book sections, by the flow of events. In these sections, story lists are updated until the magazine goes to press, and even afterwards, should important stories break, although currently, the earlier closing of color pages restricts the updating to pages using black-and-white photographs. Since magazines appear on newsstands on Monday, and in the subscribers' mailboxes on Tuesday, the editors want to be as current as possible, if only to prevent being scooped by their rival.

Day 5 is sometimes described as cleanup day, when copy is "cleaned up" and final changes required by top editors, researchers, reporters —or by late events—are made. The office ambience becomes more informal, as does the mode of dress, but the cleanup can last late into the night. The cover-story writer may still be at work on the last draft, while other writers sit and wait as galley copy is "fitted" on "dummies," which may require them to add or cut some lines from their stories. During this period, senior editors take care of administrative chores and begin to think about next week's first story lists, for suggestions have already come in from many bureaus.

The two-day weekend break begins, late at night on Day 5 (Friday at *Time,* Saturday at *Newsweek*); the weekend skeleton crew, which includes a top editor, is responsible for last-minute corrections or additions. But if the story to be added is big enough, some people may be back in the office on Day 6; and as they go to work, they hope that their peers at the other magazine have stayed home, so that they can be the most up-to-date.

4

Sources
and Journalists

Journalists obtain the news from sources they observe or interview. A complete study of the news should therefore include an investigation of both the individuals who become sources and the 99 percent of the population that does not. Since sources represent organized and unorganized groups (if not always intentionally), the study would need to ask how and why they become sources, and how what they do and say as sources relate to the groups they represent. I have not carried out such a study, however; my observations are gleaned from what I learned about sources in studying journalists and from the sources I encountered during my fieldwork.

The relationship between sources and journalists resembles a dance, for sources seek access to journalists, and journalists seek access to sources. Although it takes two to tango, either sources or journalists can lead, but more often than not, sources do the leading. Staff and time being in short supply, journalists actively pursue only a small number of regular sources who have been available and suitable in the past, and are passive toward other possible news sources. In many cases, national news organizations depend on the wire services or other news media (local and national) to find them, after which they assign their own reporters to get another version of, or angle on, the story. In other instances, they wait for sources to make contact with a reporter, and to sell him or her a story idea. There are notable exceptions, of course, such as exposés, for which journalists will become exceedingly active in digging out sources; and the magazines compete in part by discovering new sources who can shed additional light on important stories of the week. But often, the national journalists follow the news.

This chapter deals with source availability—how sources and journalists obtain access to each other—and with source suitability—the considerations which determine the newsworthiness of available sources. Since journalists assume that they have a right of access to everyone, little needs to be said about the ways in which they gain it. Although I will report on some of the difficulties they encounter, my emphasis will be on how sources seek access to journalists.

Availability: Source-Journalist Relations

Journalists see people mainly as potential sources, but sources see themselves as people with a chance to provide information that promotes their interests, to publicize their ideas, or in some cases, just to get their names and faces into the news. In any event, sources can only make themselves available; it is the journalists who will decide if they are suitable. If so, the information offered is screened by the journalists' observations and interview questions. The source-journalist relationship is therefore a tug of war: while sources attempt to "manage" the news, putting the best light on themselves, journalists concurrently "manage" the sources in order to extract the information they want.

Looking at the tug of war from the perspective of sources suggests that their successful access to journalists is shaped by at least four interrelated factors: (1) incentives; (2) power; (3) the ability to supply suitable information; and (4) geographic and social proximity to the journalists. Of the four, the ability to provide suitable information is crucial, but the other three factors enhance that ability. In fact, Molotch and Lester have suggested that the news is determined largely by the power of sources to create suitable news.[1] Not all sources are as powerful as the ones they discuss; but in the end, power of one kind or another is highly instrumental, at least in the attempt to gain access.

Incentives: Eager, Agreeable, and Recalcitrant Sources

Since journalists must often let sources come to them, the news is weighted toward sources which are eager to provide information. Sources become eager either because they benefit from the widespread and legitimated publicity the news media supply or because they need the news media to carry out their duties.

Private firms can use advertising to obtain publicity, but even they prefer a news story about their activities, since it is more credible. Public agencies, voluntary and professional organizations, and most individuals either cannot afford or are not allowed to advertise; consequently, they depend on the news media for visibility. National politicians cannot long function without news publicity, while the power of federal agencies to command an increased share of the federal budget often depends on their ability to be in the news at the right time. The point is obvious: individuals and groups whose well-being is achieved and maintained by acting for or on behalf of constituencies must become eager sources in the hope of reaching their constituents as members of the audience. This helps explain why so much of the news centers on public and other agencies which serve constituencies.

Eager sources eventually become regular ones, appearing in the news over and over again. Most sources that appear intermittently are agreeable; they do not need the news to survive but enjoy the benefits, such as added prestige, that come from appearing in the national news media. Permanently recalcitrant sources are few, although many politicians and public officials who are normally eager sources will quickly become recalcitrant when the news hurts them or their cause. One permanently recalcitrant source is the organized or unorganized underworld; as a result, its leaders usually make the news only when they are murdered or imprisoned. Another group includes CIA and FBI officials responsible for "covert actions"; they were able to stay out of the news until congressional investigators and journalists armed with the Freedom of Information Act went to work.

Being a recalcitrant source is less a matter of incentive than of power to refuse access to reporters. Corporate officials and others who operate without public funds—and some who do—are often able to bar reporters, but public officials are legally required to be available for public inspection even if they try to circumvent the relevant laws. The privacy of private enterprise is less easily invaded, which is why the news contains fewer moral disorder stories about it than about the government. Still, even powerful recalcitrants, including private agencies, can bar journalists only at some risk, for nothing whets journalistic hunger for a good story as much as being denied access, which may result in the scheduling of an exposé.

The investigative reporting required for an exposé is expensive and not always productive, for reporters must usually be assigned to the story for weeks, if not months, thus making them unavailable for other stories; and sometimes, months of investigation may not produce a suitable story. As a result, most news media resort to investigative reporting only when they cannot obtain access any other way or, equally often, when they need a circulation or rating booster. However, some reporters who are refused access will work long overtime hours to pursue a recalcitrant source on their own.

The ability of recalcitrant sources to bar access is balanced by a countervailing process. Organizations often become recalcitrant because of internal controversy or turmoil, which may spawn sources inside the organization eager to leak information, anonymously, either to expose immoral behavior or to publicize their side of the controversy. During Watergate, the more the White House tried to prevent leaks, the more it increased the eagerness of other officials to supply news about people whom they wanted exposed and forced out of the government.

The Power of Sources

I noted earlier that while in theory sources can come from anywhere, in practice, their recruitment and their access to journalists reflect the hierarchies of nation and society. The president of the United States has instantaneous access to all news media whenever he wants it; the powerless must resort to civil disturbances to obtain it.[2]

Of course, powerful sources rarely use their power to bully their way into story lists; indeed, they use their power to create suitable news. Nor are story selectors easily bullied; they retain the right to choose suitable sources, and even the president is sometimes not deemed sufficiently newsworthy. Also, story selectors have little contact with sources, powerful or powerless; in fact, top editors and producers are quite isolated. Magazine editors do meet powerful sources at special briefings with the president or high federal officials, the luncheons and dinners they hold for presidential candidates or other notables visiting New York, and the parties they attend after working hours. These occasions do not, however, seem to provide the powerful with useful access, as editors attending these functions often complain that they are a waste of time. Television producers seldom have the time to attend such occasions and may never meet their most newsworthy sources; as one producer pointed out: "We work in hermetically sealed rooms." Anchorpersons are somewhat freer to get out of the newsroom, however. Whenever the evening news originates from Washington, the anchorperson has probably been invited to a White House dinner or a personal interview with a high official.

The hierarchical structure of the news organization has a similarly isolating effect, for contact with sources, powerful or not, is almost entirely left to reporters. To be sure, the president, or a corporation president, can get on the telephone and suggest a story directly to a top editor or producer; but for status reasons alone, powerful people generally call the corporate heads of the news firms. The executives, however, are restrained by the organizational division of labor, and they pass on the story suggestion in such a way as to enable story selectors to ignore it.

At the national level, power is generally exercised by refusing access and is the primary form of censorship. The White House, the Pentagon, the State Department, and a few other agencies can plead "national security"; although the plea has been abused by more than one government agency over the years, journalists still have to think twice before going ahead. During the Vietnam War, the military sometimes kept reporters away from battles which were going badly by withholding transportation to the war zone.[3]

The military, like other institutions Goffman has aptly called total, also has the power to discourage its members from talking to reporters. Through most of the war, reporters had difficulty interviewing enlisted men, who were generally less optimistic than officers about the progress of the war and the likelihood of eventual American victory. In 1967, only 13 percent of the quotes in Newsweek's war stories were from enlisted men. (Seventeen percent of the quoted sources were generals, 33 percent were other officers, 13 percent were noncommissioned officers, and 24 percent were civilian officials and "government spokesmen."[4])

Powerful civilians can achieve a similar effect by restraining underlings from providing information and by punishing miscreants. In 1969, a magazine reporter alerted his editors to the news that King Hussein of Jordan was receiving large amounts of money for personal use from various governments, but the reporter warned that under no circumstance could the story be published because the source would be "compromised." Not until 1977, when CIA files became available to American journalists, did the story become news. The more powerful a politician, the harder it is for a reporter to find someone who will talk; thus, one early indicator of Richard Nixon's declining power was the number of people ready and able to leak information. At the same time, reporters who come up with stories that are explicitly or implicitly critical of powerful sources must provide considerable evidence to substantiate their facts, for such stories will result in an angry call from the source, and executives cannot defend reporters whose evidence is not convincing.

Sources with less power can normally gain access only with an unusually dramatic story; on the other hand, as power decreases, so does the ability to bar access. Reporters can intrude on the privacy of ordinary individuals who have been struck by tragedy to ask them what they are feeling; they dislike the practice but continue doing so only for fear that their competitors will scoop them. Very poor people can stave off access, however, because reporters, like other nonpoor people, are reluctant to go into poor neighborhoods. The inability of white reporters to enter the ghetto slums during the disturbances of the 1960s thus created instantaneous jobs for black reporters.

Ability to Supply Suitable Information

Given the journalists' insatiable appetite for story ideas and stories, sources which are able to supply suitable news can overcome deficiencies of power. Even so, the ability to be newsworthy itself requires resources and skills, many of which go hand in hand with economic power, at least, and are possessed by only a few.

Perhaps the most able sources are organizations that carry out the equivalent of investigative reporting, offer the results of their work as "exclusives," and can afford to do so anonymously, foregoing the rewards of publicity. The FBI has often supplied detailed information about the misdeeds of American politicians whose political careers it wanted to end. In 1977, a story about the alleged appointment of a new head of the Mafia turned out later to have been leaked by the Drug Enforcement Administration. According to one reporter, the DEA supplied the story "because this is the hood they know a lot about, so when they bring him down, they can say: 'Oh wow! What a catch we got here. This is the boss of all bosses!' "[5] The news which these agencies supply always serves their organizational self-interest in one way or another; journalists may know this, but in return, they initially secure a monopoly on a sensational story and can thereby scoop their competitors.

A related practice, sometimes called news saturation, is the proliferation of so much information by the source that some of it cannot help but turn into news, concurrently placing less well organized sources with more accurate information at a disadvantage. The Washington and Saigon Pentagons were able to saturate the news media with inflated body counts and successes in winning the hearts and minds of the South Vietnamese population, whereas the anti-war movement lacked the resources to rebut more than a fraction of these reports, even when it had convincing evidence.

All organizations, including those with only minimal resources, can and do send "handouts" to the news media; but at the organizations I studied, these are seen only by secretaries, and often they go into the wastebasket unopened. Large corporations and government agencies send films and film clips, but the networks use them only when they cannot do their own filming. Stories about the air war in Vietnam were sometimes accompanied by Pentagon film because the reporters lacked their own planes and were unable to accompany pilots on bombing raids. Corporate film is generally unusable because it mentions or shows the company's product.

Still, affluent organizations have an advantage in the competition to gain access to journalists, for they can preschedule their activities so as to satisfy the news organizations' continued need for anticipated stories. A similar advantage accrues to organizations that can supply either newsworthy spokespersons or sources who are able to make themselves available to reporters at short notice, give them the time and information they need, and do so at no cost to the journalists.

News organizations are unique among commercial firms in that the raw material from which they produce the news is itself obtained without charge; except in the rare instances of "checkbook journalism," they do not pay their sources. Consequently, the news media are especially attractive to sources that need publicity but not money. Not paying sources for news thus produces an implicit class bias, although so would paying for the news. Journalists also object to helping publicity seekers, but if these persons can provide suitable stories, their motives are sometimes ignored. Public officials are not deemed to be publicity seekers unless they are unwise enough to supply information that only reflects glory on themselves. Because journalists do not pay sources, they often attract individuals and groups who are paid by someone else to be sources. Reporters try hard to avoid public-relations personnel, and instead gain access to agency heads and corporate executives, whose prime duty is also public relations.

Media Events

Sources also gain an advantage in the competition over access to journalists when they are sufficiently able and ingenious to create activities that exist solely, or mainly, to be covered by the news media —which are therefore called media events. However, not all media events are newsworthy; in addition, journalists object to being "used" by sources. If they suspect that an event is being staged for their benefit, they may refuse to cover it. In the 1960s, civil-rights and anti-war groups were sometimes accused of scheduling demonstrations solely for the television cameras. As a result, producers grew suspect of all but the largest demonstrations. Conversely, they were less reluctant to cover press conferences, hearings, or campaign stops and other media events created by official agencies. Not only are these agencies regular sources, but the events they create are frequently judged to be important news (see Chapter 5). In recent years, however, journalists have expressed their resentment over the proliferation of media events by turning the creation of a media event into a story. As party conventions and campaign whistle stops have been designed first and foremost for television, journalists report how and why they have been so designed. Voters are increasingly exposed to election stories that show how politicians use the news media to seek their votes.

Media events have also been criticized by nonjournalists. Boorstin has suggested that they, as well as many prescheduled activities that become anticipated stories, are "pseudo-events" and should not be treated as news.[6] Boorstin's critique expresses a meritorious bias for spontaneity. But a taboo on pseudo-events would limit journalists to covering breaking news, in which case none could ever fill their news-holes, and the news media would eventually disappear—as would many national organizations which stage media events to reach a geographically distant or scattered constituency.

Although media events *are* staged, the actual pseudo-event is the activity staged for the physically present audience, which serves only as a foil to reach the absentee audience. Presidential press conferences are not held for the attending journalists, nor are campaign whistle stops held for the people brought together by advance men and women. These are only occasions to enable politicians to communicate with the voters.

A general taboo on media events would also disadvantage sources that lack other means for supplying suitable news, such as groups with unpopular views and small constituencies which must organize protests staged for the television cameras, and powerless populations which can communicate their plight to the nation only by engaging in activities that become social disorder stories. Admittedly, journalists are put in a difficult position when terrorist groups or individuals commit crimes in order to attract attention to themselves or their demands from a large audience. Even so, a decision to ignore them is not only selective censorship but could lead to an escalation of terrorist acts, for the terrorists might then commit crimes of a magnitude which no journalist could afford to ignore.

In one sense, however, all activities that become news stories are media events; whether activities are spontaneous or staged is less important than whether or not they appear in the news. Of course, spontaneous events are not quite the same as staged ones; but the moment both types become news, they can affect the subsequent course of events.[7] In either case, the aim of journalists to avoid influencing the course of events is frustrated. While activities staged to reach a national audience should be identified in news stories as media events, the concern about such events seems to me to be misplaced. The more serious problem is that the ability of sources to gain access to journalists, either with staged or spontaneous events, is unequally distributed. (In Chapter 10, I shall argue that this ability should be equalized.)

A very different kind of media event occurs when journalists stage activities for their own benefit, either when they are short of news or are falling behind in the competition. Staging by journalists is strictly prohibited, and my impression is that it happens very rarely in the national news media. Reporters may occasionally resort to it when they think they cannot be detected; during the ghetto disturbances, they were accused of urging participants to throw stones for the benefits of the camera. Film editors usually can notice staging, and suspicious film is not used.[8] Hoaxes impair the journalists' credibility, and stagers are punished. (Restaging to improve the quality of a story is permissible, however, and will be discussed in Chapter 5.)

Geographic and Social Proximity

Sources may be eager, powerful, and ready to supply suitable information, but in order to gain access and overcome the isolation within which story selectors normally function, they must be geographically and socially close to the journalists. (Reporters must also be close to sources to which they want to gain access, but they are more mobile, at least physically, than sources.)

Geographical proximity is achieved, both for sources and journalists, by the establishment of bureaus. In his study of NBC News, Epstein showed that domestic news came mainly from or near the cities in which NBC had bureaus.[9] However, bureaus tend to be located where the most suitable news is likely to be gathered, and new bureaus are established when a critical mass of stories has appeared on story lists. In addition, the wire services have created a far-flung geographical network of "stringers," who fill many gaps left uncovered by bureaus. A mapping of all wire-service stringers would probably show that large areas of the country, especially rural sectors and low-income neighborhoods, remain uncovered.

Still, even geographical proximity cannot guarantee social proximity. Powerful or skilled sources know how to make contact with reporters; but many people—perhaps most—lack this knowledge. Few even know how to contact reporters affiliated with their local news media, and the reporters serving the national news media are socially and otherwise far more distant. In fact, many of the features about ordinary people that appear in the national news are brought to the attention of story suggesters by local Chambers of Commerce and similar organizations skilled in getting in touch with journalists.

Social proximity is, moreover, influenced by all the structural and demographic factors that shape other social relationships, thereby enabling people of similar backgrounds and interests to make contact, and obstructing those who differ. After all, journalists are also members of society. Upper-middle-class sources, for example, are not likely to have difficulty reaching reporters and may even have a mutual friend; people of lower social status often do not know how to deal with professionals, and fear rejection to begin with.

Class and other differences which restrain potential sources also create difficulties for reporters seeking access to sources. They find it easiest to make contact with sources similar to them in class position, as well as race, age, and other characteristics; they encounter the same communication problems, fears, and hostility as do other professionals when dealing with poor people. These barriers particularly intrude when a story requires contact with ordinary people. Reporters assigned to cover a new social problem or lifestyle often begin by calling up friends, asking them for the names of friends and acquaintances who can serve as sources. In the process, reporters inevitably select sources of roughly equivalent status, which helps explain, in part, why so many magazine feature stories are about the upper middle-class.

Upper-class people who are not eager to be sources have many means of preserving their invisibility, which frustrate both journalists and sociologists. Television news can call on anchorpersons whose celebrity status gives them instant entrée to famous, powerful, and prestigious people, whereas newsmagazines can normally rely on editors or writers from high-status backgrounds.

When the story calls for working-class or poor sources, reporters generally call up churches or branches of middle-class voluntary organizations located in poor neighborhoods, which then supply the people they know best, who are often the upwardly mobile joiners. A network reporter assigned to find people for a film on the unemployed had a more difficult time. She was reluctant to look for them on street corners or to knock on doors, and the local unemployment office would not supply names. After a week of failure, a colleague told her about a letter, written to the network by an unemployed viewer, which enabled her to contact a congressman mentioned in the letter, who in turn gave her the names she needed.

As a result, national journalists—but I suspect local ones as well— move within a relatively small and narrow aggregate of sources, which is dominated by the people they contact or who contact them regularly. When I began my fieldwork, I assumed that journalists, especially reporters, knew more about America than anyone else—or at least more than campus-bound sociologists—but this is not the case. Journalists obtain their information about America from their customary sources; from what they themselves read in the paper; and, because they have trouble crossing the social barriers that separate them from strangers, from what they learn from peers and personal contacts, notably relatives and friends.

Peer and Personal Sources

Peer sources are closest at hand, for story suggesters and selectors spend as much time as possible perusing other news media for their own use. Most often, they analyze an already published story for new "angles," different ways of conceptualizing or covering it; then they assign the idea to their own reporters as a new story.

Peer sources are useful in two other ways. First, the prior appearance of a story elsewhere means that a peer has already judged its availability and suitability, thus eliminating the need for an independent decision. *The New York Times* is a primary peer source inasmuch as the size and quality of its editorial and reporting staff are taken as guarantors of the best professional news judgment; but the *Washington Post, The Wall Street Journal,* and a few southern, midwestern, and western papers are also used for story ideas. Second, prior publication is taken to be a sign that the topic has audience appeal. This applies especially to "trend stories," which report the arrival of an up-and-coming politician, author, or entertainer; a new fad, lifestyle, or social problem.

Personal sources are primarily family members, other relatives, friends, neighbors, and people journalists meet at parties. If these people are talking excitedly about a new trend that has not yet been reported in the national media, a potential story is in the offing. Personal sources are useful in part because of their credibility, which accrues from their close association with the journalist. They are also considered representative of the audience; consequently, their excitement about a new trend leads story selectors to assume that the audience will be interested once the story appears.

Children and their friends are important personal sources, for they keep their journalist-parents in touch with what is going on in the nation's high schools and colleges; in addition, they are likely to be the "trend spotter's" first informants about a new teenage fad or popular entertainer. During the late 1960s, young people also pressured their parents into becoming more favorably inclined toward the anti-war protest, although most reluctant parents were converted by the police action at the 1968 Democratic Convention in Chicago. Some editors and producers were angered because the police beat up their reporters, but one senior editor adopted a more favorable view of the anti-war protesters because "those [beaten-up demonstrators] were our children."

Top and senior editors are expected to attend New York parties, where they can meet public officials, leaders of various professions, assorted celebrities, and, occasionally, intellectuals. One candidate for a top editorship was deemed ineligible by some of his colleagues because he refused to attend these functions. While journalists rarely come back with an immediately usable story idea, they nevertheless make contact with people who are often in the news, and they hear what newsworthy people are talking about. One magazine decided to run a cover on malpractice partly because an editor, who lived in a suburban community full of doctors, reported that it was a central topic of conversation at the parties he had attended.[10] Then, too, journalists have friendships that were made at college or at the start of their careers, and these individuals sometimes become exclusive sources. In 1975, *Newsweek* was able to run an exclusive cover story on the making of the film *Nashville* because its film critic was a friend of Robert Altman's; that same week, *Time* devoted its cover to the making of *Jaws,* its film critic being an old friend of Steven Spielberg's.

Journalists also treat themselves as sources. Although their long work hours do not leave them much time for other pursuits, what they experience at home and in their communities becomes grist for the story-selection mill. Journalists are not immune from familial problems; and while these are not often discussed at editorial meetings or in office conversations, their existence creates a ready interest in stories about the problems of two-career families, child-rearing difficulties, and adolescent "dropouts." The occasional but recurring interest of journalists in stories about "male menopause" may reflect the feelings of writers and reporters in their mid-forties who realize that they will never become editors or famous freelancers.

Logistics and Availability

I should note that the foregoing analysis has emphasized the social aspects of source availability, but in a production process dominated by deadlines, sources are sometimes unavailable for a variety of logistic reasons. People who want to be in the news or whom journalists want to reach may be out of town; camera crews may not be in the right place at the right time, often because there are too few of them, especially in Washington. Cameras can break down, and film is sometimes overexposed or underexposed; before foreign film was transmitted by satellite, Vietnam battle film occasionally could not be used because the couriers bringing it into the West Coast studios were caught in late-afternoon traffic jams in San Francisco or Los Angeles.

The networks suffer more from such problems than do magazines, but from time to time, all news media lose stories they want because the sources are unavailable. These difficulties loom large for journalists, but they are rarely publicized, for admitting to them reflects on the journalists' ability to get the news. However, they do dominate the post-mortem discussions that journalists hold when they are finished with their work and can see what their competitors have done; if problems continue, people are fired and production processes are reorganized.

Suitability: Source Considerations

The suitability of available sources is determined by the journalists, who make their judgments on the basis of a number of interrelated source considerations. The considerations are interrelated because they have one overriding aim: efficiency. Reporters who have only a short time to gather information must therefore attempt to obtain the most suitable news from the fewest number of sources as quickly and easily as possible, and with the least strain on the organization's budget.

Source considerations come into play at the start of story selection, when little is as yet known about the stories but the sources relevant to them may be familiar and can be evaluated. Even so, these considerations are always applied in conjunction with others, especially story suitability. Altogether, I identified six major source considerations at the news media I studied.

1. *Past suitability.* If sources have provided information leading to suitable stories in the past, they are apt to be chosen again, until they eventually become regular sources. However, regulars are liable to supply repetitious information over time; as a result, journalists become "bored" with some of them, dropping them from the news "because we've seen them too often lately." To be sure, story selectors cannot often be bored by the president of the United States, but they can be bored by sources representing single-purpose organizations, who must continually deal with the same issue. This helps explain why black militants and leaders of the poor during the 1960s were newsworthy for only a short time. Experts who dwell on the same theme continually suffer the same fate. In 1975, *Newsweek*'s top editors hung a map of a fictitious island in their editorial meeting room, to which they "banished" sources who, in their judgment, had appeared too often in their magazine. The normal term of banishment is one year.

2. *Productivity.* Sources are judged by their ability to supply a lot of information without undue expenditure of staff time and effort. Although reporters do not shrink from whatever legwork is necessary, they and their superiors must keep logistics in mind; as a result, they try to minimize the number of sources to be consulted. This partially accounts for the predominance of high public officials in the news: as spokespersons for their agencies, they can spare journalists time and effort by eliminating the need to interview other agency members. Productivity also explains the emphasis on government plans and new policies in the news; these can be obtained from the official announcing them, whereas stories about the implementation and effects of policies require interviews with many people. Of course, if the story calls for a large number of interviews, they will be done, in which case, reporters will seek out central clearing houses that can quickly supply names. In 1968, *Newsweek* planned an education cover that included, among other things, biographies of a number of college graduates. Bureau reporters who were assigned to locate possible candidates headed for the alumni offices of nearby colleges, which provided them with the names of their more successful alumni; this biased sample forced the senior editor to request a second round of interviews, to discover alumni who had not—or at least, not yet—achieved the American Dream.

3. *Reliability.* Story selectors want reliable sources whose information requires the least amount of checking. However, if a story or a

fact is controversial or not readily believed, reporters are then expected to gather proof from at least two separate and independent sources.

When reporters can explicitly attribute information to a source, they do not have to worry about reliability (and validity), the assumption being that once a story is "sourced," their responsibility is fulfilled, and audiences must decide whether the source is credible. A magazine writer once pointed out that "we don't deal in facts but in attributed opinions." Nevertheless, an unreliable source can damage journalistic credibility.

4. *Trustworthiness.* When reliability cannot be checked quickly enough, story selectors look for trustworthy sources: those who do not limit themselves to self-serving information, try to be accurate, and, above all, are honest. Reporters keep a continuing check on the honesty of sources, remember when they have been lied to, and inform story selectors accordingly while selling them story ideas.

Journalists harbor a pervasive distrust of their sources, since so many come to them with self-serving motives that they are not always inclined to be completely honest. Much of the cynicism attributed to journalists is actually their distrust of sources, and the greatest distrust is felt for politicians, who are deemed to be inherently "two-faced" and inconsistent.

Journalists often have difficulty in judging the trustworthiness of their sources. Those they talk with frequently can be evaluated over time, which is another reason why story selectors prefer regular sources. When they cannot get to know their sources and thereby get a "feel" for them, they rely on other indicators. Sources who cooperate with journalists and treat them cordially are apt to be trusted more than others; so are sources who take reporters into their confidence and explain why they must be inconsistent. Sources in positions of formal authority are considered more trustworthy than others; beyond that, journalists apply the same criteria professionally that they and others use in everyday life, placing greater trust in people who are similar to them. Accordingly, conservatives and liberals are trusted more than ultraconservatives and socialists, pragmatists more than ideologists; upper-middle-class people more than others. This is why socially proximate sources, such as peers and friends, are so frequently used.

5. *Authoritativeness.* All other things being equal, journalists prefer to resort to sources in official positions of authority and responsibility.[11] They are assumed to be more trustworthy if only because they cannot afford to lie openly; they are also more persuasive because their

facts and opinions are official. When stories become controversial, journalists can defend themselves before news executives by having relied on authoritative sources. Moreover, story suggesters can sell stories from these sources more easily than from others.

6. *Articulateness.* When sources are interviewees, they must be able to make their point as concisely, and preferably as dramatically, as possible. Television interviewers achieve conciseness to some extent by rehearsing; in fact, all interviewees, famous or otherwise, are normally "fed" questions off-camera until they have formulated a concise answer. Television reporters also look for interviewees who speak in the standard (national middle-class) English dialect that most of the audience is thought to understand most easily; unless absolutely necessary, they try to stay away from sources using lower-class dialects.

The newsmagazines also look for articulate sources, but conciseness and standard English can be achieved through editing. Editors are allowed to alter quotes accordingly, a practice one of them called "helping the quoted guy." Sources given to poor grammar or convoluted syntax are normally helped in this fashion; in 1968, a college president who was thought to have become incoherent as a result of student protest on his campus was edited to satisfy the expectation that college presidents are coherent.[12] Nevertheless, the magazines also prefer sources who speak standard English; an education editor pointed out that "the best schools give us the best interviews."

Beat Reporters and General Reporters

Source considerations are applied mainly in story selection, but sources also help shape the news during story production. I did not systematically study what sources do and say—or do not do and say—in front of reporters, but I was able to examine how reporters deal with sources.

Reporters are normally divided into two categories: beat reporters, who cover a specific and bounded turf; and general assignment reporters (here called general reporters), who cover everything else and therefore appear on many different turfs. Beat reporters and general reporters bring different levels of prior knowledge to bear on their contacts with sources and enter into different relationships with them, out of which come different kinds of information.

Most beat reporters are locational; they cover either a region or, in Washington, a federal agency. (The latter I shall hereafter call agency beat reporters.) Other beat reporters are substantive: they report on education, the law, science, or the economy.

A concurrent classification of reporters divides them into generalists and specialists; and while all general reporters are generalists, so are many beat reporters. The bureau staffers who collect the news from an entire region must keep up with so many different substantive topics that they remain generalists. Reporters with agency beats, such as White House correspondents, become specialists on White House politics but remain generalists about the specific issues with which the president deals from day to day. Substantive beat reporters are the only true specialists, but even they must range over wide territories. A science reporter who is a specialist in the natural sciences becomes a generalist when assigned to a story about the social sciences.

Only a few news media have set up substantive beats. Television is at one end of the spectrum; it has only a handful of substantive beats, in science, health, ecology, and the economy. The newsmagazines are at the other end of the spectrum, for the back-of-the-book sections are written by people who become specialists on most stories. Although they are not supposed to do their own reporting, they sometimes do so nevertheless, since the bureau reporters may not understand the experts who are the major sources for the back-of-the-book sections.[13]

While substantive beats have increased manifold in the last twenty years, all journalists are still expected to be generalists, able and willing to cover anything and everything at a moment's notice. (They are also expected to have one universal specialty: politics. This is one reason why domestic news pays less attention to issues than to the politics surrounding them.) General reporters may be assigned substantive beats without knowing anything about the subject and, consequently, do not become specialists until they have occupied the beat for some time. (Section writers at the newsmagazines sometimes go off to a relevant professional or graduate school for six months or a year to hasten the acquisition of specialist knowledge.) Nevertheless, specialists do not necessarily stay on a beat permanently; they may become bored with it, but more often, they give it up when it is no longer newsworthy. Education, for example, was a lively and prestigious beat during the period of campus growth and unrest, but during the 1970s, it has become a less desirable beat to cover.

Agency Beat Reporters[14]

Since the predominant amount of domestic news originates from Washington, the agency beat reporters who cover the White House,

Capitol Hill, and the federal agencies play a far more central role in national news than the reporters attached to other bureaus. Washington's agency beat reporters virtually live in and with their beat, and thus develop close relationships with their sources. They function much like participant-observers in sociology, and their sources become what sociologists call informants, keeping reporters up-to-date on what is happening inside the beat and supplying unofficial, "inside," and secret information to them. In addition, the beat reporter quickly picks up the gossip and rumors that are generated in every social setting.

Being on the inside enables beat reporters to gather information that lends itself to dramatic inside stories; but at the same time, they must concentrate on stories that please their sources, since angering them may endanger their closeness or rapport, thus ending the reporter's usefulness on the beat. As a result, beat reporters are drawn into a symbiotic relationship of mutual obligations with their sources, which both facilitates and complicates their work.

This symbiotic relationship develops in almost all beats, but it becomes particularly problematic for agency beat reporters whose stories have political implications. They can make news out of inside information that aids an agency in its competition with other agencies or helps it get its message into the White House, but they cannot so easily propose stories which can hurt the agency.

Consequently, beat reporters must often practice self-censorship, keeping their most sensational stories to themselves in order to protect their beat. Reporters have some leeway: if they cannot get newsworthy information, they cannot sell their stories, and thus their sources will not receive publicity. Sources must occasionally grin and bear it when reporters file displeasing news, especially if they need the reporters' good will—and the publicity. When all reporters on an agency beat have arrived at the same story, they can (and must) report it, for even if their sources are displeased, their displeasure is less serious than that of their editors or producers, who would not forgive them for failing to cover a story that everyone else has reported. Moreover, at the magazines, writers (who lack contact with or obligations to sources) can be more critical than beat reporters, and sometimes, beat reporters can feed them the necessary information without their sources holding them responsible. Television reporters cannot hide behind writers, however; and while they sometimes risk their rapport with sources for the sake of a scoop, the source may then put pressure on a news executive to restrain the reporter in the future (see Chapter 8). Indeed, presidents and other public officials have periodically tried to have uncooperative reporters removed from their beat, but they have rarely succeeded.

Nevertheless, sources have somewhat more power in the relationship than reporters, since they can punish reporters by withholding information, thereby putting them at a disadvantage with peers from competing news media. Consequently, beat reporters must frequently calculate the costs and benefits of displeasing their sources with a story, deciding whether to report it or to pass it up so as to maintain the relationship for another day, when a much bigger story may come their way that will justify the disruption of the rapport. Tom Wicker, in explaining the beat reporter's resultant emphasis on "official" information, has suggested that "the political reporter would not be allowed the kind of leeway that any critic of the arts is allowed."[15]

The need for beat reporters to censor themselves creates a vacuum in the news that is filled by such columnists as Jack Anderson and the late Drew Pearson. These journalists are free from any symbiotic relationship because they do not occupy beats; instead, they get their information from many sources, often on an unsolicited basis and as anonymous leaks. Although many of the journalists I studied disparaged people like Anderson as gossip-mongers, they fill an important role in national journalism, even if some of their revelations eventually turn out to be erroneous.[16]

Politicians, of course, are well aware of these symbiotic relationships and try hard to co-opt reporters for their own purposes, "wining and dining" them, giving them exclusive stories, or plying them with secret information they cannot publish. Experienced beat reporters seem to be able to escape co-optation, even while they enjoy being flattered with invitations and unpublishable secrets; and they learn to endure a politician's wrath when his or her flattery does not stave off a critical story.

In Washington, the greatest temptation is always offered by the president, for he can dispense exclusive interviews and invitations to private White House parties; moreover, even the most jaded White House reporter remains susceptible to the presidency's quasi-monarchical mystique. Some politicians use charm to attract reporters, just as they attract staffs and constituents; John Kennedy, for example, was able to form friendships with a number of journalists.[17] Surrendering to temptation may give reporters short-run advantages over their colleagues, but it is fatal in the long run, for once reporters have developed a reputation of having been co-opted, they lose the confidence of their peers and superiors, and eventually are transferred to another beat.

The White House beat is atypical, however; elsewhere, beat reporters are somewhat more likely to be co-opted. Some federal agencies demand agency loyalty from beat reporters; the Pentagon, for example, has long been known to withhold information from or to banish reporters who do not adhere to the Pentagon "line." In less visible or controversial agencies, co-optation proceeds almost unconsciously. Beat reporters become identified with the sources with whom they spend so much time, and they have little contact with an agency's adversaries. They may not personally share the political values and objectives of their sources, but they accept agency practices and let themselves be used to advance agency objectives, particularly when the result is a dramatic or exclusive story.

The reactions I have described are not unique to agency beat reporters, however, for bureau reporters covering a region begin to grow fond of it, and reporters who cover a war zone identify with the people to whom they are closest. An experienced war correspondent in Vietnam pointed out that despite his strong personal doubts about the Vietnam War, "you get caught up, you are involved with the people you are with—the GI's—not with the people being killed or the civilians, but the GI's and you can't help that."

Whether reporters are restrained by symbiotic relationships with sources or are co-opted or get "involved," their work may be affected in the same manner. A number of media observers have argued that the support of the national news media for the Vietnam War until the 1968 Tet offensive can be explained by the fact that as a result of symbiotic relationships or co-optation, senior Washington reporters communicated the government's information and line on the war to their superiors in New York.

While many Saigon reporters began to express their doubts that the war could be won long before the Tet offensive, their television reports and magazine files were given less weight in New York, partly because these reporters were younger and less experienced. Equally important, New York considered them too close to the war itself, too affected by the bloodshed they observed, and thus unable to obtain a sufficiently broad view of the overall war effort. In addition, the Saigon reporters were far away; and unlike their seniors in Washington, they could not make their case often enough and in sufficient detail with top producers and editors in New York. The Tet offensive had a traumatic impact on New York, and several national news media sent top people, including Walter Cronkite, to South Vietnam to assess the situation for themselves. Subsequently, virtually all of them began to question, in editorials or story conclusions, whether the war could be won. Some even suggested it should not be won, although none became so dovish as to agree with the anti-war protesters.[18]

A similar pattern developed at the time the civil-rights movement set up Resurrection City in Washington to dramatize the demands of the black poor. Reporters from the Washington bureaus, accustomed to the relatively tidy bureaucracies of their beats, were upset by the chaotic administration of Resurrection City, whereas Atlanta reporters on the scene were more tolerant, for having covered the civil-rights movement regularly, they were used to the chaos in which the movement, like all underfunded and understaffed groups, operated.

All bureaus see America from a somewhat different perspective, and New York always assumes that bureaus are too close to the trees to see the forest. New York is the final arbiter because it is "headquarters"; but some journalists argue that New York is the best arbiter because it is not a major source of national political news. As Harry Reasoner put it: "I think there is a kind of incestuous journalism in Washington. That's why I'm glad that . . . the network broadcasts come out of New York, which is a non-town. It's not anybody's hometown."[19]

New York recognizes the dangers of co-optation on some beats; as a result, war reporters, and White House and foreign correspondents are periodically rotated to other beats, as are reporters traveling with a presidential candidate, who are routinely switched to covering his opponent midway in the campaign. More often than not, reporters welcome the change in assignment, for many are generalists at heart and eventually become bored with contacting the same sources and doing what they perceive as the same story day after day.

Some reporters stay on the same Washington beat for many years, however; and because of their seniority and their ties to senior government officials, they become, and encourage their news organizations to become, a fourth branch of government.[20] Still, even beat reporters serving briefer terms are drawn into quasi-governmental roles, indirectly because their stories have implications for future agency decisions and directly because their sources may use them to fight their rivals or to launch policy trial balloons. Washington reporters also become representatives of the citizenry, for when the statements and actions of agency heads, particularly the president, are intended to affect public opinion, they are often designed most immediately to affect the reporters. The White House press corps is thus assumed to react for the country as a whole.

Substantive Beat Reporters

Substantive beat reporters—and at the magazines, section writers, who also occasionally function as reporters—are responsible for a very broad range of subject matter, since "specialties" such as science or education include many disciplines, agencies, and institutions, some local, some nationwide. Substantive beat reporters therefore cannot become participant-observers in one agency; instead, they must keep up with many more sources and on a less intense basis than agency beat reporters. They identify with their beats, but less so with individual sources. Nevertheless, they develop close relationships with a few regular sources, especially those knowledgeable about many subjects in the reporter's beat, which is, of course, why these sources are sometimes banished when they are interviewed or quoted too often.

Substantive beat reporters also develop symbiotic relationships with their most regular sources; but while they may gather "inside dope," it is normally of interest to so few people, among their superiors or the audience, that reporters gain little and lose much by disrupting their rapport with sources on whom they depend. Scandals in a public agency are always newsworthy, but those in a professional organization, an academic discipline, or a university are much harder to sell to story selectors, who must keep a lay audience in mind.

Substantive beat reporters are also co-opted but for a different objective. Insofar as they popularize technical knowledge and publicize experts, they become ambassadors to the lay world for the specialties they cover. When sources in these specialties value publicity, the journalists who cover them become more important than, say, Washington reporters, for there are relatively fewer journalists who report on religion or education to a large national audience than there are White House correspondents. Nonetheless, their ambassadorial power is always limited. While they are expected to report and write so as to maintain the attention and respect of experts, they are working primarily to inform a lay audience. Experts who would like to communicate their ideas and findings to the nation are often stopped short when reporters tell them that stories which may be highly newsworthy within the expert's circles cannot be sold to a producer or editor who must consider the lay audience. In recent years, many social-science disciplines have tried to bring their findings to the attention of that audience, only to discover that journalists are unable to help. Although both newsmagazines have established social-science beats (reported in *Time*'s Behavior and *Newsweek*'s Ideas sections), most of the stories originate from that nonacademic discipline called pop psychology. Economists have a somewhat easier time breaking into the national news media, but usually only those ready to be quoted on topics that interest consumers, victims of inflation, or investors.

General Reporters[21]

A sizable proportion of the news is actually suggested and produced by general reporters, and that proportion is dramatically increased by the many beat reporters who are themselves generalists about much that takes place in their beats.

General reporters differ from beat reporters in that they pursue their work without significant prior knowledge about their assignments. They neither know much about the sources from whom they obtain information nor spend much time with them. As a result, they do not become involved in symbiotic relationships and are thus free of the obligations to which beat reporters are subject. Like their eventual audience, general reporters are outsiders vis-à-vis most of the sources they contact, coming to them with the same kind of lay curiosity and knowledge. This affects what they observe, the questions they ask when they interview, and the stories they produce.

Except for the rare cases in which they have done prior legwork on stories they have suggested, general reporters come to their work *de novo*. They are briefed quickly by assignment editors, or at the magazines by the persons who have drafted the queries; but they themselves may be new to the story. In any case, general reporters almost never have time to read background materials; usually, they do not even have access to a morgue or library.

Some general reporting involves observation, but for the most part it requires interviewing sources. Unless general reporters have been instructed to interview specific people, they apply the source considerations. Not knowing the actors and activities they are to cover, they naturally head for authoritative sources, whose productivity and trustworthiness are assumed. These sources, who are often public officials, know that they are expected to give the reporter information without demanding time-consuming efforts at creating rapport; but in the process, they can also manage the reporter, who may lack the knowledge to ask searching questions.

When general reporters are observing, they add other reporters to the list of sources. Whenever I accompanied reporters on assignments requiring observation, they spent as much time as possible with peers. Competing reporters will not reveal information that promises to result in an exclusive or a distinctive angle, but they will exchange other observations, particularly on information about which they are uncertain. They swap impressions on the trustworthiness of sources and get together to try to make sense of ambiguous statements. At demonstrations they always compare crowd estimates, so that they can legitimate their own counts—or rather, guesses—by adjusting them to those of peers.

This practice, which is pejoratively called the herd instinct, or fraternization, is employed whenever uncertainty must be reduced, and by beat as well as by general reporters. Crouse has shown to what extent information and angles are swapped, compared, and agreed upon in the reporting of presidential campaigns.[22] Sometimes fraternization becomes a protective device for reporters who have unearthed a story that New York may not consider credible. When a number of Saigon reporters exposed the corruption of the Diem government in the early 1960s, I suspect that their stories would not have been believed if the men had been unable to exchange ideas. Given the strong denials from American officials in Saigon, their respective editors in New York must have been reassured that other reporters had reached the same conclusion.

When they are observing and interviewing at meetings, other public events, and demonstrations, general reporters also talk with people in charge and major speakers, but they rarely speak with ordinary people or even participants in a demonstration unless absolutely necessary. At anti-war demonstrations, television reporters sought out unusual participants, such as people carrying National Liberation Front flags, but they, and magazine photographers, normally stayed away from rank-and-file demonstrators. I once spent a day with a respected magazine reporter at a civil-rights march; although he was there to do a "mood piece," he never spoke with an ordinary marcher. The one time I did observe a reporter talking with everyone he could buttonhole was at a routine press conference held by a Democratic party leader; the reason he did so, he explained later, was that he was laying the groundwork for his forthcoming assignment as a beat reporter: coverage of the party in the upcoming presidential election.

The reluctance to make contact with other than official and familiar sources should not be surprising. Rushed reporters do not have time to develop rapport with unfamiliar sources and go through the routines by which strangers become informants. Even when rapport is quickly attainable, as it is for television reporters whose cameras offer the promise of getting on the air, unfamiliar sources may provide information that cannot be assessed, thereby creating uncertainty. Perhaps more important, unfamiliar sources may provide new or contradictory information that complicates the general reporter's ability to generalize and summarize. All journalists must resort to data limitation so as not to be flooded by more information than they can process quickly and fit into limited air time or print space. Producers encourage reporters not to shoot unnecessary footage for this reason, while editors ask reporters to keep their files short. But general reporters have a more urgent reason for practicing data limitation. Coming to their assignment with little advance knowledge, they have a slender repertoire of angles that can easily collapse under the weight of too much, or conflicting, information; moreover, they have little time to reflect on the information they have gathered before completing their story and going on to the next assignment.

The general reporters' lack of prior information also affects what they see when observing. For one thing, being new to the scene, they can be managed so that they observe only what sources want them to observe. Television reporters are most easily managed, since they are accompanied by highly visible camera crews. The occasional practice, by American troops, of cutting off the ears of dead North Vietnamese soldiers as souvenirs did not become news until very late in the war, partly because American soldiers did not do so when the cameras were around. But even print reporters are not likely to witness such scenes.

In addition, as transient and unprepared visitors, general reporters often observe only the dramatic incident, not the routine social process. To be sure, this is what they are assigned to look for in the first place; but even when their assignment is less specific, they are most sensitive to the unexpected deviations from what they know or consider to be an accepted value, or to behavior which is abnormal or unusually dramatic. In short, they see highlights.

In many ways, general reporters are like tourists, albeit in their own culture; they seek out what is memorable and perceive what clashes with the things they take for granted. Unlike sociologists, who can spend enough time in the field to distinguish recurring from idiosyncratic behavior, reporters can see only the latter. Sent to report on a political speech, they can observe the speaker becoming emotional, but they cannot recognize the hidden agendas in the speech or the phrases that have double meanings.

When they interview sources, general reporters work under similar conditions, with similar results. Assignment editors or queries arm them with a few questions, but many are made up on the spur of the moment. Some are standard questions, developed by the profession for specific types of sources; other questions derive from the reporters' own conventional wisdom and common sense. As a result, the questions often reflect their professional or personal values. When they interview experts, reporters draw on the lay knowledge they have of the interviewee's expertise; when they interview people whose values they do not share, their questions may be tinged with antagonism.

Because they deal with strangers, however, general reporters are freed from the restraints under which beat reporters operate; they do not have to worry about maintaining rapport with people they will never see again, and can more easily ask leading, loaded, or provocative questions. Sometimes, such questions merely demonstrate the lay knowledge of the general reporter, but often they are designed to draw out sources in order to obtain a dramatic television spot or magazine quote. A television reporter known for his bristling style explained: "You want to get questions that force the person you're interviewing to say something interesting; you have to do it to get him to expose himself, to get him angry so he'll say something interesting. We don't necessarily feel the way we sound." Beat reporters must remain more polite. White House correspondents, for example, need to maintain decorum, which puts them in a difficult bind. They cannot readily ask the president searching questions that will produce news, for these may anger him; and if the news conference is being televised, they themselves are likely to be accused of being disrespectful.[23]

The extent to which general reporters are free from restraints is illustrated by what happens when they come to a community to transform a local story into national news. National reporters are sent out mainly for social and moral disorder stories; but as strangers without prior knowledge, and lacking obligations to local sources, they are free to emphasize the highlights. Assigned to report the most dramatic incidents, they are often not around long enough to observe the less dramatic ones. More important, they can ignore local rules which obligate local reporters to minimize the disorder, either to prevent it from escalating or to preserve the positive image of the community.

The result almost always is a national story which, by local standards, is inaccurate and exaggerated. When the networks visited South Boston in 1975 to report on the interracial violence generated by school bussing, local reporters objected to the networks' failure to note the calm amidst the storm and to abide by local rules against escalating community conflict.[24] After Iowa school officials sought to bus Amish children from their own school to the public school, they complained that the networks showed only the children running away from the bus. According to a local journalist: "When our officials tried to enforce the school laws that the Amish were breaking, the national news media made it look like we were running a police state out here."[25]

The role that national reporters play is also demonstrated by their absence. In an exhaustive study of the newspaper coverage of the Santa Barbara oil spill of 1969, Molotch and Lester found that once the dramatic oil spill had been reduced to a prosaic but nonetheless permanent trickle, the out-of-state press withdrew its own reporters and stopped using the locally written reports. Instead, they returned to the sources they regularly consulted for stories on oil—the federal government and the national oil companies—and subsequently reported only their claims that the spill was no longer a problem.[26] As a result, local attempts to effect a permanent cleanup, as well as conservationist policies to prevent future spills, never received national publicity.

Although the national news media frequently come to highlight disorder, they may not always remain to see that in the long run order restoration can also be a return to the status quo. At the same time, they are often criticized for coming in the first place, for when disorder news publicizes the plight of the powerless, local power holders charge the national media with unwarranted meddling.

Finally, the general reporter's brief contact with unfamiliar sources helps explain the many inaccuracies—some major, most minor—that regularly creep into the news. Beat reporters also make mistakes, but general reporters have to work hard just to get names right, and they often lack time to be accurate about titles or biographical details. Not knowing their sources well enough to discount self-serving information, they may report an opinion or a hopeful guess—for example, the size of an organization's membership—as statistical fact. In this way, enterprising politicians sometimes get inflated estimates of their support into the news, thus making themselves seem more powerful than they actually are, while their opponents can only object to this misrepresentation. Occasionally, general reporters may cover only one side of a story without ever knowing that there are other sides. Consequently, controversies of great importance to a small number of people may be reported in the news from an unintentionally biased perspective; and unless letter writers provide corrective feedback, neither the reporters nor their superiors ever learn what they have done. And even when corrections are published, they rarely receive as much attention as the original inaccuracy.

Generalists and Specialists

Journalists commonly believe that America and other industrial societies are becoming ever more complex. Although this belief is hardly distinctive to journalists, journalism has been under pressure to make use of more specialists. Nevertheless, the news is still gathered mostly by generalists. One reason is economic, for general reporters earn less and are more productive. Beat reporters can rarely produce more than one story per television program or magazine issue, while general reporters can be asked, when necessary, to complete two or more assignments within the same time period.

Generalists also remain dominant because they are audience-related. Unlike specialists, they cannot become source-related, for their contacts with sources are far too fleeting. Also, insofar as their reporting relies on lay knowledge and preconceptions, they are likely to ask questions which at least some audience members may also have thought of asking. More important, the use of generalists ensures that the audience will not be given more information, especially technical information, than it is thought ready to pay attention to. According to one top producer: "If a reporter is too close to a subject, he is considered an expert. He does the audience no good, for he is too far away to communicate with it. . . . If the reporter moves into contact with the audience, however, he establishes some communication with it. Yet he is still closer to the news event than the audience. He is just lucky enough to be in a more informed position."[27]

Of course, even specialists must be able to communicate with their audience, and the specialists who write the magazine back-of-the-book sections are apprised by their senior editors when they become too "technical." Conversely, when important running stories dominate the story lists for a considerable time, they are usually assigned to generalists (both reporters and writers), who then become temporary specialists. Even so, they are eventually taken off the story, either because they become bored with it or because editors and producers want a "fresh approach" so as to retain audience interest in it.

The continued reliance on generalists is supported by the inclinations, and the audience-related tasks, of top producers and editors. Themselves generalists, they are never entirely comfortable with specialists. When an executive producer congratulated his economic reporter for a concise story on a complicated economic topic, he ended his praise by adding: "You scare me with your information; I think we'll put you on another beat." As a result, specialists always worry that they are becoming too technical for the audience or their superiors, and that they are being locked into a specialty that may lose its newsworthiness in the future. For status reasons alone, specialists cannot easily return to being general reporters; but at the same time, they are often not thought suitable for promotion to producer and editor positions, for these go to people who have remained generalists. At present, then, specialists lead an uneasy existence in a generalist profession.

Sources and the News

The means by which sources gain access to journalists, source considerations, and the relationships between reporters and their sources feed into each other to create a cumulative pattern by which journalists are repeatedly brought into contact with a limited number of the same types of sources. Eager and powerful sources which need to appear in the news first become suitable because they can always supply information, and then because they satisfy the source considerations for authoritativeness and productivity. The most regular sources develop an almost institutionalized relationship with the news organization, for beat reporters are assigned to them. The beat reporters become virtual allies of these sources, either because they develop symbiotic relationships or identify with them in a process that anthropologists call going native. General reporters usually go to the same kinds of sources and are managed by them as a result of their own transience and lack of knowledge.

There are exceptions, to be sure. When breaking stories develop, general reporters are freed to find the most relevant sources; and when powerless sources can supply dramatic news, the standard source considerations are temporarily set aside. Agency beat reporters can occasionally alienate their sources without suffering a permanent loss of rapport. Even so, on a day-to-day basis, they must side with their sources. The Watergate scandals were not uncovered by White House correspondents but by general reporters, who were then given the time and resources to develop the exposé. And when Watergate later became a beat, the reporters assigned to it did not gather their facts at the White House. During this period, White House correspondents could do little more than report the denials that came from the Oval Office whenever a new scandal was uncovered.

The cumulative pattern that determines availability and suitability makes the public official the most frequent and regular source. I did not count the number of times he or she appeared in television and magazine news; but Sigal analyzed the origin of 2,850 domestic and foreign stories that appeared in *The New York Times* and *Washington Post,* and found that public officials were the source of 78 percent of the stories.[28]

The reliance on public officials, and on other, equally authoritative and efficient sources, is almost sufficient by itself to explain why the news draws the portrait of nation and society I reported in Part 1. Sources alone do not determine the news, but they go a long way in focusing the journalists' attention on the social order described earlier. Neither do sources alone determine the values in the news, but their values are implicit in the information they provide. Journalists do not, by any means, parrot these values, but being objective and detached, they don't rebut them either.

The one source that best fits the cumulative pattern is the president of the United States. He and, even more so, those who can speak for him or the White House are almost always and easily accessible. In fact, they are available virtually round the clock, except during evening and other hours when "the lid is on," so that no one is available to any reporter. The White House centralizes and releases a great deal of information from other federal agencies; in addition, it regularly creates "photo opportunities" and media events for the electronic and print media. The president's position involves him in a sufficient number of conflicts and world-shaking issues so as to generate a steady supply of suitable and, occasionally, dramatic news. The president is thus also the most productive source of news. At the same time, he is deemed the most authoritative and reliable—if not always trustworthy—source, as well as the best-known and most prestigious.

The president is a particularly suitable source for national news because he is thought to be "speaking for the country," as one editor put it; and according to an executive producer: "For all practical purposes, he is the country." He is also the most economical to cover, for he is almost always to be found in the White House; in addition, he has a large staff of assistants who, paid from federal funds, are responsible for the preparation of suitable news. Besides, White House beat reporters, cameras, and other tools of the trade are already in place and no further funds need be spent to bring source and journalists together. Last but not least, the president is also the source for the biggest story of all. As a Washington bureau chief once told me: "We cover the president expecting he will die."

═ 5 ═

Story Suitability

The New York Times announces every day that it contains "All the News That's Fit to Print." The wording is arrogant, but the phrase makes the point that the news consists of suitable stories. To determine story suitability, journalists employ a large number of suitability considerations, all of which are interrelated. These can be divided into three categories: substantive considerations judge story content and the newsworthiness of what sources supply; product considerations evaluate the "goodness" of stories; and competitive considerations test stories for their ability to serve in the continuing rivalry among news organizations to provide the most suitable news.

I distinguish among the various suitability considerations to emphasize that story selection involves more than story content. This is not accidental, for if story selectors had to rely solely on substantive considerations, they would need many hundreds, and in ranked order, to be able to choose stories from the mass and variety of available ones. Indeed, many suitability considerations are of the exclusionary type; they exist to help story selectors cope with the oversupply of available news. They are also relational: on a "slow news day," story selectors may use stories they would ordinarily dismiss, though never happily so.

Substantive Considerations

Story suggesters and selectors begin with substantive considerations. Stories are bought and sold on the basis of their content summaries; once they enter the story list, the summaries are con-

146

densed further, to four-to-six word labels. In this way, story selectors always remain aware of story content.

Substantively, stories can be either "important" or "interesting," the ideal being an important story that is also interesting. All journalists learn to distinguish these qualities in stories, but in and of themselves, the two terms are meaningless. Since an actor or activity can be important to some sectors of America but not to others, or of interest to some while boring to others, importance and interest are not useful considerations until they acquire subjects and objects which indicate to whom and for whom a particular story is important and/or interesting, and by what criteria. When story selectors apply substantive considerations, they do so in terms of subjects and objects, thereby making the considerations operational.

Story Importance

Importance judgments are applied to both actors and activities; for domestic news, to be discussed here, the judgments are usually determined by four considerations. Stories become important by satisfying one, and increase in importance with every additional one they satisfy.

1. *Rank in governmental and other hierarchies.* The federal government and its activities are always important, but the higher an actor is in the governmental hierarchy, the more his or her activities are of importance. Although this consideration endows the government and its hierarchy with journalistic legitimation and has numerous ideological implications, it exists for very practical reasons. National news media cannot report all stories that affect the nation or the national audience they serve; consequently, they need an exclusionary consideration that automatically limits the number of suitable stories.

Of course, journalists could attribute importance to other national hierarchies: those based on power, wealth, or prestige. These are difficult to identify or to agree upon, however. The governmental hierarchy is visible and nicely rank-ordered, which facilitates journalists in making importance judgments. Equally relevant, it is widely accepted as a symbol of the nation.

It goes without saying that the president is most important. In the past, the newsmagazines ran a special subsection informally titled "The President's Week"; and although it has been eliminated, much of the president's week is still reported. One summer, when the president was on vacation and was clearly not minding the ship of state, a top editor decided to break with tradition and omit the customary weekly picture of the chief executive. Although his assistants supported his decision, he later changed his mind.

Journalists do not slavishly follow the governmental hierarchy below the presidency; for instance, the Speaker of the House is not important solely by virtue of his being fourth in line of succession. He and other federal officials are judged by the extent to which they affect, change, or oppose the president's policies, or affect the nation or the lives of other Americans. On a slow news day, even a minor official can become newsworthy by proposing a new policy or making a dramatic statement; but story selectors may wait until the last moment before reporting it in the hope that a more important story will suddenly break.

Actors outside the governmental hierarchy are harder to evaluate, since journalists have no easy way of determining whether the head of one corporation is more newsworthy than the head of another when both do or say the same thing. This is one reason why nongovernment officials appear in the news less often. Another, perhaps more significant reason is their sheer number: there are so many corporate heads that journalists cannot report on more than a small fraction at best; consequently, they need quickly and easily applied exclusionary judgments.

The most efficient criterion is, once more, the governmental hierarchy. Nongovernmental leaders who come into contact, and particularly into conflict, with that hierarchy become important. Moreover, the higher their governmental contact, the greater their importance. When corporate heads attack a presidential policy, they are more likely to appear in the news than when they challenge an administrative regulation of a lowly government agency. All other things being equal, their general visibility and the size of their organizations are also taken into account; leaders of larger or more prestigious organizations outrank those of smaller or less prestigious ones.

Although this importance consideration overlaps with the source consideration that encourages the use of authoritative officials, it does not simply rationalize the choice of sources but functions as a separate component of news judgment. That the two coincide only facilitates and accelerates story selection.

2. *Impact on the nation and the national interest.* What affects the nation—its interests and its well-being—is a complex question which can be answered in many ways, but journalists resort to answers that enable them to make fast story-selection judgments.

In the case of foreign news, the solution is easy: America is a unit as it deals with other nations, and American citizens or organizations overseas become representatives of that unit when their constitutional rights are threatened. In fact, journalists often follow American foreign policy in selecting foreign news because it supplies a quick and easy importance consideration and because no other equally efficient model is available. This solution also discourages State Department criticism. While journalists do not generally make story choices to minimize government criticism, they gain nothing by unnecessarily provoking official criticism. They know that their audience is not particularly interested in foreign news and would be unlikely to support them if the government chose to attack the news media for harming the national interest.

The criteria that can easily be applied to foreign news, however, do not suit the domestic scene, for the nation cannot often be treated as a unit. Nor is there an efficient way to determine whether and in what ways domestic actors and activities express the national interest. (This is an additional reason why the president is thought to represent the nation.) Story selectors assign importance to activities which are carried out by the entire nation, such as voting; and those which are carried out in behalf of the nation, such as space exploration and national anniversaries.

Because elections and anniversaries occur only periodically, journalists need more frequent domestic news, which they find in actors and activities that express, represent, or affect the nation's values. They do not have a list of national values, however; nor do they have time to decide which of the values constantly pressed on them by sources are truly national. Instead, story selectors fasten on the laws of the land, which are beyond argument most of the time and can be construed as official national values. But in the process, they add the enduring news values (some of which I described in Chapter 2) that they assume to be national values as well: ethnocentrism, altruistic democracy, responsible capitalism, small-town pastoralism, individualism, moderatism, the preservation of social order, and the need for national leadership.

Hundreds of magazine pages and hours of air time would be needed if story selectors were to report every actor or activity expressing these values. Instead, they apply an exclusionary consideration that is virtually part of the definition of news; national values become important only when they are threatened or violated. The role of journalists is to report, in the words of one top producer, "when things go awry, when institutions are not functioning normally." This definition of news awards importance to a wide variety of natural, social, and moral disorder stories.

A finding that institutions are not functioning normally requires standards of institutional normality and abnormality, which can be set either on empirical grounds, value grounds, or both. Political patronage jobs may be awarded frequently enough to be viewed as empirically normal, and they may be evaluated as normal by heads of political organizations but abnormal by political reformers. Story selectors, having neither the time nor inclination to debate standards of normality, rely upon their own expectations about what is, and should be, normal, often mixing the two.[1] These expectations, in turn, involve reality and value judgments that journalists make intuitively (see Chapter 6), but they are particularly guided by the enduring values which suggest what ought to be normal. Accordingly, patronage remains abnormal, and therefore newsworthy.

Many more instances of abnormality occur, however, than can possibly be considered important news. Consequently, story selectors apply a further exclusionary consideration, which regards the rank and power of those acting abnormally. High public officials who engage in abnormal behavior that violates national values are always important news, but lesser Americans who do so must concurrently threaten or engage in conflict or violence. Likewise, high officials make important news when they disagree, but lesser Americans must resort to protest;[2] and the more highly ranked the target of protest or violence, the more important the story becomes. This is why the assassination of a president is the biggest story journalists can conceive, at least in a nation in which revolution is an unlikely prospect.

Protest, especially the violent kind, is an easily applied indicator of abnormality, whether the abnormality resides in the protesters or the target of protest. But since considerations are always relational, indicators change in importance depending on the supply of available news. During the late 1960s, when protest stories were plentiful, story selectors often ignored peaceful protests. During the 1970s, when they became scarcer, protest of any kind once more became a prime indicator of importance; sometimes, new issues did not become important until protest erupted. Medical malpractice developed into important national news only after doctors resorted to demonstrations for the first time. When New York City was threatened with default in 1975, a scheduled mass protest by municipal employees persuaded one top editor to put the default story on the cover; but when the demonstration was called off, the cover story was postponed.

Although the violation of national values is most newsworthy when it involves national institutions, the number of such institutions is limited. Consequently, journalists apply an inclusionary consideration in which they nationalize various institutions and symbolic complexes (see Chapter 2). As a result, even the smallest locality can generate important national news. In 1975, the decision by a tiny California county to drop out of state and national welfare programs appeared in several national news media because it represented an initiative against Big Government. That same year, when five children living in the ghetto of a small southern town died because the city had failed to spray the area against mosquitoes, a top producer told the reporter who suggested it that "you don't even have to sell me."

3. *Impact on large numbers of people.* The most important story of all is one that affects every American. The assassination or attempted assassination of an American president is such a story because it is thought to touch the entire population. But such news is rare; consequently, journalists assign importance to stories that affect large numbers; and the larger the number, the more important is the story. During the stagflation of the early 1970s, for example, story selectors paid more attention to inflation than to unemployment; at the start of the energy crisis, they gave more play to gasoline shortages and price increases than to other ramifications of the crisis.

Lacking data about how many people are affected by an event, journalists make impressionistic judgments. One indicator is their perception of the population, which is derived in part from the people they know best. One newsmagazine often evaluated stories by the extent to which they were thought to affect "our kinds of people," the well-educated upper middle-class to which journalists belong and which is a major constituency in the magazine readership.

A second indicator is the number of people who might eventually be affected. Stories about floods, forest fires, and epidemics become important news, because even if the number of victims is small, the thought that a similar disaster could strike almost anywhere will affect a much larger number of people. A related third indicator assumes a similarity of interests among large sectors of the population. Television producers look for stories relevant to old people, assuming interest on the part of the many older viewers in the audience; thus, a story about a new welfare program for rural old people was deemed important for the urban aged as well.

A final indicator applies journalistic values directly. Perceiving America as a unit, journalists believe that people ought to be interested in important news because they should be informed citizens, even if the news does not directly affect them. The national news media continue to report foreign news for this reason alone, even though journalists know that many viewers and readers do not pay close attention to it.

4. *Significance for the past and future.* News about the American past is usually important, but it can be dealt with easily by keeping track of anniversaries. The future significance of today's news is more important; but because it is more difficult to assess it, journalists may disagree. When, in 1977, James Schlesinger, then a presidential assistant, testified before a Senate committee about the president's proposal to create a Department of Energy, one network's Washington bureau felt that his testimony "didn't amount to anything"; but the other networks decided that his prediction of future energy shortages was important because they could affect the lives of many people.[3]

Prediction is risky, and it is generally eschewed because an incorrect guess impairs the journalists' credibility. Nor do journalists see their role as writers of history; but at the same time, they do not want to be accused later of having ignored events which, in retrospect, ultimately achieved historical significance. This is why they assign importance to record-breaking events and to firsts. Both are easily applied indicators. Firsts are also automatically novel and therefore news almost by definition. The first presidential primary remains important news despite its ambiguous role in, and meaning for, the presidential nomination process.[4]

Variability in Importance Judgments

In the final analysis, importance judgments are made by individuals or small groups; and even if all are journalists, their assessments, particularly in estimating the future significance of a story, will inevitably differ at times. Also, because importance considerations are general but must be applied to specific stories, individual story selectors may arrive at different conclusions as they proceed from the general to the specific.

Moreover, inasmuch as story selectors are competing against their peers at another network or magazine, they may assign news higher importance on the basis of product or competitive considerations, although usually these judgments affect the emphasis given a story rather than its inclusion or exclusion. If a news program or magazine has particularly exciting film or still pictures, or an interview with a high official, the story may be given more importance; and its priority will be further increased if the story is an exclusive. Organizational factors also come into play. If an anchorperson argues strongly for the importance of a story, executive producers may not want to disagree. CBS News has, over the years, given more play to space exploration because Walter Cronkite is an enthusiastic space buff.

At times, story selectors react simply like the people and the members of nation and society that they always are. In the spring of 1975, for example, *Newsweek* decided to run a cover about Ted Kennedy as a possible presidential candidate, partly because the top editors felt the current list of hopefuls was undramatic and they wanted to add some excitement to the race. But the need for excitement was also journalistic, for little important domestic news that could excite the journalists was available at the time, and they were remembering the good old days of Watergate, which had been an unusually exciting period in every newsroom.

Importance in the Back of the Book

Whenever possible, back-of-the-book sections try to use the importance considerations that prevail in the front of the book. At both magazines, two sections can do so easily: the legal section, which emphasizes federal law and the federal government; and the education section, which covers the campuses that train the nation's leaders and the public schools that affect large numbers of people. In addition, both sections can report violations of national values. Other sections adapt these considerations to their own turfs; *Time*'s Press and *Newsweek*'s News Media sections, for example, often deal with the ways in which various news media have reported nationally important stories.

In sections which do not readily lend themselves to front-of-the-book considerations, such as science, medicine, religion, and the "critical sections" on the arts, two conflicting importance considerations are applied. On the one hand, section writers try to go along with what the professional leaders, who constitute their major sources, deem important; on the other hand, editors prefer stories which will have an impact on large numbers of people. Writers also apply a historical consideration, arguing that the magazine cannot afford to ignore currently "far-out" ideas which may one day become as significant as those of Freud or Darwin.

In the critical sections, writers can define importance by the judgments of other critics, so that even unknown artists who have been praised by other critics will be considered important by editors.[5] Still, writers are constantly encouraged to look for news about well-known people in publishing, the arts, and the film industry, since top editors feel that such stories have more popular appeal than reviews. The conflict over whether the professionals or the audience determines importance is endemic to all news organizations. When *Newsweek* decided to run its cover on *Nashville,* a critical success even before its release, some senior editors argued that the cover should wait until there was some evidence of audience enthusiasm. At *Time,* meanwhile, audience enthusiasm for *Jaws* was already virtually assured; however, there the cover choice was questioned because the film had been panned by the critics.

Since fewer agreed-upon importance considerations apply to the back of the book, there is more discussion and negotiation among writers and editors, and more diversity in the stories finally selected by the two magazines. Even so, people working on the back of the book must overcome one additional hurdle: however important they judge their stories, top editors must find them sufficiently interesting or else stories, or entire sections, become prime candidates for prekilling. Since top editors are often chosen from front-of-the-book senior editors, they are usually first given some responsibility in the back of the book so that they can gain experience in handling its more ambiguous importance considerations.

Television Leads and Magazine Cover Stories

Leads for the nightly television news, and the initial stories in the magazines' domestic sections, virtually choose themselves most of the time. When a breaking story is not available, whatever domestic story meets one of the four importance considerations will be selected. Top producers rarely have the luxury or dilemma of having to rank the four considerations; if they must do so, they prefer to choose a story that touches large numbers of people, if only to evoke audience interest. More often, no story meets any of the four, in which case, top producers may choose the latest installment in a major running story. Back-of-the-book subjects are rarely television leads; one day in 1975, a top producer was visibly upset about a rival's news judgment because he had chosen to lead with the death of a prize-winning racehorse.

Most magazine cover stories are national or international breaking or running stories; consequently, the four types of importance considerations can usually be applied. Covers also serve feedback, commercial, and competitive purposes; and more significantly, they are viewed as giving national recognition and assigning national importance to individuals or subjects. As a result, it may be a long time before controversial figures like Ralph Nader appear on magazine covers; others may never appear. One *Newsweek* editor put it diplomatically when he rejected a cover on Paul Goodman, then the elder statesman of youthful protesters, arguing that it "would confer a degree of importance and universality on Paul Goodman which I don't think he has." Another 1968 leader who did not make the cover was Eugene McCarthy. During the spring and summer of that year, he was always on the magazine's long-term list, but the editors could not agree on his importance and kept postponing the decision. McCarthy's last chance came with the issue appearing the week of the Democratic National Convention, but then the editors rejected him because they feared the choice might either influence the outcome of the convention or be taken as the magazine's endorsement of his candidacy.

Back-of-the-book covers must feature individuals or subjects which are easily recognized, as well as important. Few artists or writers meet this criterion, which is why popular entertainers are more readily chosen. Vladimir Nabokov "made the cover" of *Time* only because a top editor overruled senior editors who said they, and the audience, had never heard of him. Unfamiliar and "dry" subjects are also at a disadvantage. One senior editor spent virtually a year persuading his top editor to run a cover on recent advances in the prediction of earthquakes.

Interesting Stories

Important stories are sometimes called necessities, signifying the extent to which their selection is obligatory. Interesting stories are, prototypically, "people stories." A top producer, himself a space buff, bemoaned the end of space stories during the Apollo-Soyuz linkup in 1975 and rejected those on the exploration of Mars then already in the works, because "that's with robots; I want men there."

Interesting stories are used for two reasons. First, important news is often "bad" and must be balanced by interesting stories which either report "good" news or are light. In addition, interesting stories are timeless, so that they can be used when last-minute replacements are needed.

If an interesting story evokes the enthusiasm of story selectors, it is assumed that it will also interest the audience. As a result, journalists do not think about the audience when selecting interesting stories any more than when selecting important ones. The choice of interesting stories is usually a group decision; and if anyone thinks that a story is "boring," it is not likely to remain on the list, unless a top producer or editor announces decisively that he likes it. Because the selection is based on shared personal reactions, it is not governed by considerations; rather, story selectors gravitate toward a handful of story types.

1. *People stories.* These feature ordinary people acting or being acted upon in unusual situations, and public officials acting in unofficial ways or behaving "like people rather than politicians." Thus, the news media always report on the president when he performs in a familial or private capacity, thereby allowing the public a glimpse at his private persona, even if it is created or made visible for public consumption. For much the same reason, the private activities of the president's family are also regularly newsworthy.[6]

2. *Role reversals.* Most people stories are actually what journalists call man-bites-dog stories; they are often humorous features about people who depart from expected roles, such as a college professor who becomes a janitor upon retirement. Role reversals can be serious, too, depicting "hard-core" criminals who go straight or juvenile delinquents who become involved in community development projects. A story about the president's private activities is interesting precisely because politicians are rarely thought to behave "like people."

3. *Human-interest stories.* These are people stories in which ordinary people undergo an unusual experience that evokes audience sympathy, pity, or admiration, such as victims of tragic illnesses or people who act heroically in disasters.[7] Story selectors choose them because they expect the audience to "identify" with a victim or hero; nonetheless, they themselves are often moved.[8]

4. *Exposé anecdotes.* These report, and by implication condemn, actors and activities which story selectors dislike, usually because they violate the enduring values. Lowly public officials who behave like callous bureaucrats or invade people's privacy, members of the business community who desecrate wildernesses, and malfunctioning computers are favorite journalistic villains. *Time*'s Americana section, a page of short items in the Nation section, sometimes uses these anecdotes as miniature editorials.

5. *Hero stories.* Ordinary people who overcome these villains are ready subjects for interesting stories; so are amateur and professional adventurers who climb a previously unclimbed mountain or set an endurance record, thus showing that human beings can overcome nature without hurting it. Charles Kuralt likes to find harmless eccentrics who flaunt social pressure toward conformity and offer testimony to the continued resilience of individualism.

6. *"Gee-whiz" stories.* This is a residual category that includes all

stories which evoke surprise. Although role reversals and hero stories are sometimes labeled gee-whiz stories, these stories are, typically, reports of unusual fads, cults, and distinctive vocations or avocations. One producer defined the genre as "an extraordinary, unusual, but not terribly important item; a story we had one night of a hen laying green eggs."

The selection of interesting stories is free of the tensions and costs that surround important stories. Story selectors cannot be criticized for having missed an interesting one; in fact, because access to them is often a matter of luck, the reporter who is in the right place at the right time can scoop the competition. Reporters who are adept at unearthing interesting stories are therefore held in high regard, especially if they can dig up the humorous ones with which top producers like to end their news programs. These are highly prized, and occasionally executive producers are so excited about them that they will personally edit them, leaving the important news stories to subordinates for more than an hour. The morale in the newsroom always rises when a good, humorous "closer" is available, and even more so when the journalists discover later that the competing network had to end its show with a serious feature.

Product Considerations

Suitable news is, among other things, a product, and journalists want to come up with good stories. "Good" is a simple word, but the "goodness" of a story is judged in several ways. Stories must fit the particular requirements of each news medium, as well as the format within which the news is presented. (*The New York Times* also contains all the news that fits the print medium.) In addition, journalists aim for several kinds of novelty and quality, and they want to provide a balanced product. These product considerations are applied to every story, but the less important a story, the more product considerations enter into news judgment. They also allow story selectors to choose between stories of equal substantive merit; and because these considerations have built-in devices to attract the audience, journalists are thus relieved from having to think about it.

Medium Considerations

Medium considerations connect story selection to technology. More to the point, they enable story selectors to exploit the technological distinctiveness of their news media and to achieve the purposes which news organizations set for themselves to distinguish themselves from and compete with organizations using a different technology.

Television journalists see themselves as providing a headline service, which is meant to supplement the newspapers; but their main purpose and competitive weapon is the offer of "immediacy," bringing the viewer "into" or near important and interesting events through the use of film. Consequently, all suggested stories are automatically judged for whether they lend themselves to filming; and when top producers compile their lists of selected stories, they always begin with, and give most thought to, the films they hope to run that day. At this point, however, quality considerations also come into play, for producers want good film rather than any film, and the prime measure of quality is "action." Action is "something happening," "an incident, not a situation," such as a battle, an interpersonal conflict, or people struggling against nature. Action is also emotion, either a display of anger or other strong feelings, or an activity that evokes an emotional response, such as pity. Conversely, producers eschew undramatic film, and they prefer to avoid "talking heads," that is, interviews or discussions. Even so, for an important story, dull film is better than no film at all.

As a result, television has been accused of emphasizing news that lends itself to filming. The truth, however, is more complicated. When film is not available, the news is presented as a tell story, although then producers worry that the "opposition" has filmed the same story. More important, words are as essential as film. The "text" with which a reporter narrates the film is often the real story, with the film chosen to accompany and illustrate the text, just as still pictures accompany magazine text. Television news, therefore, has rightly been described as visual radio. Also, tell stories are an intrinsic part of the news program. They supply news which producers are unable or unwilling to film, and they complement or update the film story. In fact, a film story is often chosen to fit the tell story, thus becoming its appendage. Since the anchorperson is thought to attract a significant number of viewers, almost a third of the program is given over to independent tell stories, unrelated to available film. At CBS, the practice is institutionalized in "the magic number," which is 6 to 8 minutes of tell stories when Walter Cronkite is the anchorperson, and somewhat less when he is on vacation.[9]

To be sure, television news is dominated by film, but film is chosen after substantive considerations are applied. Exciting film cannot be used if the story for which it provides immediacy is unimportant. Of course, when exciting film is available, producers try to convince themselves of the story's importance, or else they look for an important tell story that justifies the use of the film, even if the connection is tenuous at times. However, using action film that is unimportant is condemned as sensationalism.

The charge against television news is accurate in one respect. Immediacy often requires producers to film dramatic highlights that may be parenthetical to a story's importance, which in turn requires the reporter's narrative "standupper," or the accompanying tell story, to supply the important news. For example, television reported the unrest of the 1960s through films of demonstrations and riots; and important economic news is almost always accompanied by films that feature supermarket cash registers or vignettes of victims of inflation and unemployment.

Television news can be criticized for accompanying important text with unimportant film, but the significant question is whether viewers pay closer attention to the text or the film. Television journalists defend the use of film as the best method of attracting and holding viewer attention, and some studies show that when viewers are asked to state a general preference, they choose film over tell stories. Still, in practice, they may pay as much attention to text as to film, particularly since many are eating dinner or are engaged in other activities while they are watching the news (see Chapter 7).

The newsmagazines lack television's singularity of purpose, but their primary aim is still to summarize the week's news for people unable to obtain high-quality newspapers or unwilling to read them. As a result, their medium considerations are closer to those of television than the differences in technology would suggest. The magazines seek the equivalence of immediacy through "color," an array of important or interesting details about important stories that rival media cannot find or use for lack of time or space. To this they add clever text and a large number of dramatic quotes to create what one writer called "prose pictures."

Equally important, the editors consider still pictures as important as text. In choosing them, they look for precisely the same dramatic action as television producers, the rule being that "you lead with a strong picture to catch the reader; the stronger or more unusual, the better." When stories are of lesser importance, top editors frequently pay more attention to pictures than to text; and periodically such stories are chosen to justify the use of a strong picture. (This practice has become somewhat more frequent with the advent of color pictures.) Once, a story about the best young artists of the year led to a debate between a writer, who wanted to select the best artists, and a top editor, who preferred the artists in the best or strongest photographs. The outcome was a compromise, but the example suggests that the determination of who will receive national publicity does not always hinge solely on a person's merit.

Format Considerations

All communication media—including this book—develop a format, or structure, within which to present their messages. As a result, they also develop format considerations, which both organize and structure the messages and leave out information that does not fit the format. Format considerations are, in theory, tied to medium considerations, but they undergo change from time to time, even though the medium remains the same.

Formats exist for several reasons. They concretize medium considerations and provide the audience with a familiar structure, enabling it in advance to decide whether, when, and how to pay attention to the news. For story selectors, the format is yet another device to facilitate and speed up story choice, and to cope with the oversupply of news, since it dictates certain decisions even before stories are actually selected. Every executive producer knows that he will use between six and eight films, and that most of these should normally deal with domestic news; every senior editor can ignore stories that do not conform to the mandated topics of his or her section. Finally, formats allow journalists to signify levels of story importance, for both television and the magazines arrange their stories roughly in order of decreasing importance. The abandonment of the format signals news of utmost importance; when John Kennedy was assassinated, the television news programs lasted for three days.

The Television Format

Format considerations govern both individual stories and the aggregate of stories that constitutes the program or magazine. Until NBC's 1977 format change, to be described below, television news had traditionally been organized into five segments, with the distribution of stories so "formatted" that, in the words of one top producer, "80 percent of the show determines itself."

Segments are usually organized by story type, with foreign news generally clustered together. Domestic news may be grouped geographically, with all Washington stories in one segment, or topically. For instance, during the 1960s, "trouble" stories were often presented together, reflecting the journalists' assumption, at the time, that all protest, whatever the cause, was inherently similar.

Story format considerations are equally uniform. Tell stories, hard-news film, and features all have prescribed lengths (see Introduction to Part 1), which are violated only by stories of unusual importance. Brevity, however, is not entirely a matter of format, for the deadline limits the amount of information that can be gathered, and the brief-ness of the program limits that which can be presented. Even so, whenever one-hour news programs looked feasible and top producers developed prototypes, they chose to fill the extra time with more brief stories. Brevity is also an audience consideration, for viewers are thought to lose interest in a long story. This is the main product consideration which television journalists regard as a restraint they would like to abolish; nonetheless, they, too, become restive when a story is overly long.

Stories which require lengthy description or explanation are there-fore sometimes dropped from story lists. In the 1960s, economic sto-ries were often omitted for this reason. By the 1970s, they were too important to be killed, even though producers disliked their "talki-ness" and despaired because unexciting films of oil fields or supermar-ket cash registers had to accompany them. They continue to hope that someday an innovative film maker will devise a more dramatic alter-native.

Television's reluctance to use long and therefore complicated stories would appear to be a medium consideration, resulting from the inabil-ity of viewers to go back over them. Nonetheless, newsmagazines also emphasize short articles, because it is feared that the audience will not finish longer ones. Consequently, there is the same reluctance to take on complex issues, although magazines are obviously freer than televi-sion to expand story length and to supply detail should the story be sufficiently important.

The most basic format consideration, which is shared by all news media, is that news becomes suitable only when it is transformed into a story. The networks and the magazines set virtually the same re-quirements for the structure of a story. Every story must always include a lead, a narrative, and a closer. Leads, which are also "hook-ers" designed to attract audience attention, normally state an empiri-cal highlight, raise a moral issue, or question a common expectation (or stereotype). The narrative, whether film or the "body" of the magazine story, documents or illustrates the lead. Often the illustration is a case study, which is or becomes a symbolic signifier. For example, NBC followed the announcement of President Carter's new urban policy in March 1978 with a longer film about how that policy might or might not help Newark, a city regularly chosen as the symbol of urban "decay." Finally, the closer assesses the significance of the original highlight, offers a momentary resolution to the issue, or debunks or reaffirms the expectation.

This story format therefore creates or reinforces symbols, makes it possible for the news to become a morality play, and enables literary content analysts to see the news as today's equivalent of traditional legend or myth (see Chapter 9). Journalists are not aware that they are creating such forms; they often resort to current symbols because these are already well known and therefore likely to interest the audience, even while they save valuable air time or print space. But casting news as a "story" is taken for granted, although it is a major ingredient of news judgment.

In television, news which does not fit the story format, such as stories "which do not make a point" or which lack an ending, can fall by the wayside or be relegated to brief telling unless they rank high on other grounds. During the Vietnam War, news about the possibility of peace negotiations was occasionally dropped from the story list because it was deemed "inconclusive." Battle stories, however, were almost never dropped, even if the reporter's closer indicated the battle itself was inconclusive. An experienced reporter or writer can usually find a point to make in or think up an ending for an inconclusive but dramatic film. The magazines are not fond of inconclusive stories either, but their writers have more time and freedom to find endings because they are not limited by preceding film scenes or, for that matter, by the reporters' files.

The Magazine Format

Newsmagazines, having more space to fill than television, divide the news into many sections; but despite their permanent titles, some are less strictly formatted than television's segments. Front-of-the-book sections are further divided into subsections, which can be created on the spur of the moment to include stories that are not applicable to established ones. The back-of-the-book sections are somewhat less flexible, although some have overlapping topic mandates.

The prime format considerations regulate section dominance and approach. Domestic news is the leading section, not only because it is the first in the magazine, but also because it has the largest readership. Although its approach is political, it is the most general section. If a back-of-the-book story becomes a national issue—such as a Supreme Court decision on an important or controversial case—it moves almost automatically into the domestic section. When *Newsweek* established its new section on the Cities, its editors frequently lost their most important stories to the domestic section; this partially accounts for the section's short lifespan.

Other sections are thought to have narrower constituencies, and therefore more distinctive approaches are used. Stories in the business section normally stress angles relevant to businessmen and women, and top editors must sometimes decide whether an important story about the economy should be approached from these angles or from the more general and political angles of the domestic-news section. Back-of-the-book sections have similarly specialized constituencies; when they lose stories to the front of the book, these are, in consequence, rewritten to appeal to general readers.

Still, story selection is most affected by the format considerations that deal with limited space. The front-of-the-book sections are normally allotted twenty-one to twenty-four columns, and more if they can justify their claim; the back-of-the-book sections are allotted up to six columns but quite often end up with three.[10] As a result, they can usually include only two stories. If the top editor finds only one story of sufficient interest or importance, the section becomes a prime candidate for prekilling; otherwise, the senior editor must find one or two very brief stories (75 to 100 words) with which to round out the section. This creates a perennial cry for "bright shorts"; and in the process, complex stories lacking wide appeal are left out.

The space shortage in the back of the book produces a variety of exclusionary considerations that affect story selection. The book editors, for example, can review only a few of the fifty to one hundred new books that arrive every week. They normally ignore scholarly books, poetry, and first novels; and they do not run negative reviews of the work of little-known authors. As one editor explained: "Why tell anyone about a book he's never heard of if only to say it stinks?"

Format Change

The basic formats are, in most news media, remarkably stable. Of the seventeen sections proposed in the original 1922 prospectus for *Time,* fourteen continue to be published today; likewise, the evening news program has not changed fundamentally since the beginning of the half-hour show in 1964. At the same time, however, all news media make periodic format changes. Most are small, resulting primarily in new ways of packaging the product, which make little difference in story selection. When news media encounter serious economic difficulties, however, more drastic format changes may be instituted. As I pointed out earlier, *Newsweek* underwent extensive renovation in the early 1960s, adding new sections and reorganizing old ones; *Time* followed suit, on a smaller scale, beginning in 1968.[11]

Drastic format change is rare, for news organizations worry that an innovation will interfere with meeting the deadline. Vested interests also develop around formats, as around everything else, one being the audience, which sometimes responds to format change with angry letters. Paul Friedman, an executive producer appointed to alter NBC's *Today* program, was quoted as saying: "It's very scary when you start tampering with an American institution."[12] Although audience anger usually abates once people become used to the new format, there is no guarantee that the change will increase the size of the audience. Other vested interests are less easily placated. For more than ten years television journalists have urged the lengthening of the evening news program to an hour, but their proposal has never been adopted because it would cut into the profits of local stations.

Whether it is minor or major, most format change is instituted in the hope of enlarging the audience. ABC News, which has always been last in the ratings, has over the years made more format (and other) changes than its rivals. NBC, in turn, has made more changes than CBS, which, being the ratings leader since 1967, has made none.

ABC has also made the most dramatic changes. When Barbara Walters was hired in 1976 to co-anchor the evening news program with Harry Reasoner, ABC's evening news program began to use more interviews with public officials, Ms. Walters having earned fame with this story format while she was at NBC. In 1977, the anchorpersons were downgraded in favor of on-air reporters; and in 1978, Harry Reasoner was replaced by three regional reporters. This has encouraged television columnists to predict that the era of the anchorperson is coming to an end.

Eliminating the role of anchorperson would constitute a drastic format change, but ABC's recent moves could reflect its inability to recruit anchorpersons capable of raising its ratings. There is no evidence to suggest that anchorpersons have become less popular with the audience in recent years; consequently, it is entirely possible that when CBS and NBC replace their present anchormen, they will look for people who can attract an even larger audience, particularly among younger viewers. CBS must make a change if Walter Cronkite retires, at age 65, in 1981; but NBC will probably make the first move, since John Chancellor has already indicated his desire to relinquish his anchor post.

Regardless of the final effect of ABC's changes on the ratings, they have, intentionally or otherwise, put an end to the long format uniformity among the three network news programs. NBC's 1977 format change, to a four-segment program with "Segment 3" as its centerpiece, was deliberately made to distinguish the *NBC Nightly News* from its competitors. Indeed, the executives and journalists who created the new format were encouraged, as one top producer explained, "to reinvent the half-hour program all over again." They considered an entirely ad-libbed program, and one with no film whatsoever; but they finally settled on a format that has slightly rearranged the traditional order of film and tell stories, placing them into permanent and titled segments. This in turn has brought the news program closer to the newsmagazine format. The principal innovation, "Segment 3," established a regular daily "slot" for the 3- to 6-minute "in-depth" story, although the in-depth story itself has been around since the 1960s. NBC's new format has raised staff morale—and required enlarging the staff—but like earlier format alterations, it has not increased the ratings.

Occasionally, change comes about as a result of what might be called format rut. Given the pervasive routinization of both story selection and production, journalists become bored with the assembly line and demand changes in the routine. Anchorpersons, who have the most repetitive task but are either unwilling or unable to relinquish their posts, are particularly subject to format rut; in the mid-1960s, for example, NBC News invented "cross-talk," a semi-rehearsed ad-lib interchange between anchorpersons and/or reporters, in large part because the executive producer and his two anchormen found the format tedious. At the newsmagazines, sections sometimes disappear because everyone is bored with them. In addition, newsmagazines revise their graphics and makeup every so often, "for the same reason," according to one top editor, "that women buy new clothes."[13]

Nevertheless, the principal newsmagazine format change is the addition of new sections, the change taking place when news which does not fit easily into the existing array of sections appears regularly on story lists. The establishment of new sections is a momentous decision, for they require new staff, add to the number of sections that must be prekilled, and once started, are not easily eliminated. Newsmagazines do not like to imitate each other, however; and if one starts a new section, the other may abort its plan to do likewise. After the ghetto disorders, both magazines began to plan for a Cities section, but *Newsweek* inaugurated the section first, causing *Time* to cancel its plan. Instead, it started a section on the Environment.

When new top producers or editors take over, they may institute small format changes to place their personal stamp on the product. Staff protest can also produce a change: unhappy writers at *Time* and *Newsweek* pressed for longer, and therefore fewer, stories (see Chapter 3); and *Time*'s section on the Sexes was instituted partly in response to demands from women staff members.

Not all format changes survive, however. In 1967, *Newsweek*'s editor was moved by the ghetto disturbances to publish an "advocacy issue," which analyzed the condition of blacks in America and proposed policies to improve it. Several editors and writers then requested a similar issue on Vietnam; but it took longer to prepare and resulted in a good deal of internal argument between hawks and doves. Thereafter, the idea was abandoned, although both magazines do periodically publish unlabeled advocacy stories and "special sections." *Time* considered running editorials once *Life*, which had an editorial page, ended publication; but it gave up the idea after its initial editorial, which urged Richard Nixon to resign.

Technological improvements come into being from time to time, but they do not seem to alter the format or story selection. The replacement of television film by tape has not visibly changed story content. Conversely, videotape cameras, which allow journalists to put breaking news on the air live and could enable television to compete with radio's speed, have not, thus far, been used extensively. Resorting to unexpected live interruptions would make it virtually impossible to preschedule the rest of the program and would thus essentially destroy the present format. The new camera has been used in local news programs, but because they last an hour or longer, their story lists can be rearranged more readily.

At the newsmagazines, improvements in print technology have led to the replacement of black-and-white photographs by color. The magazines have long used color pages for advertising; but when *Newsweek* published a special color-picture issue for Christmas 1976, *Time* decided to shift to color on its news pages as well, after which *Newsweek* followed suit. (*Time*, which was also replacing its managing editor during this period, departed from its tradition of in-house promotion choosing as its new "M. E." the editor of *Sports Illustrated*, who was a pioneer in the use of color photography there.) Although the change to color was costly, both magazines felt it was necessary (and inevitable), partly to keep up with television, and partly to encourage reader attention to the news. As one news executive put it: "If Walter Cronkite has Zaire in color, the newsmagazines can't have it in black and white."

Initially, some writers felt that color was an "editor's toy," which, like television film, further reduced the primacy of text. While some stories are still chosen because of the availability of strong color pictures, by 1978, the toy had begun to lose its novelty. Like most format changes, the packaging of the news has been affected more than the news itself.

Novelty

Because medium and format considerations are virtually built into story selection and production, journalists do not often have to give them much thought. However, while they are deciding whether a story is sufficiently important and interesting to be chosen, they also ask themselves three other questions: Is the story new? Is it good? Does it contribute to a well-balanced program or magazine?

Novelty is part of the definition of news and is circumscribed by the period between the previous and current deadlines. However, exceptions to this frame are made. For hard news, television producers will use film which has been shot one or two days earlier if it is good and if a more recent tell story can be found to precede it; features can "stay on the shelf" longer because they are timeless. The newsmagazines must often hold stories due to lack of space, but postponed ones are always rewritten before being considered anew, and thrice-postponed ones are usually killed outright. Not all suitable stories can be timed by these measures, however; and journalists must therefore apply other novelty considerations.

1. *"Internal" novelty.* Journalists judge novelty by whether a story is new to them, assuming that it will then also be new to the audience. Many stories, such as scientific discoveries or new fads, may already be old-hat to their sources. More important, journalists create novelty. Unlike sociologists, who divide external reality into social processes, and historians, who look at these processes over long periods, journalists see external reality as a set of disparate and independent events, each of which is new and can therefore be reported as news. They increase the supply of novelty further by being ahistorical; in the 1960s, for example, they "rediscovered" American poverty and hun-

ger—although they did not do so by themselves. More recently, some have begun to rediscover the existence of economic classes, making it news as though classes had not previously existed.

Although it is assumed that what is new to journalists is also new to the audience, television producers realize that some of their viewers have heard the day's major headlines on the radio or from the local news programs that normally precede the network newscasts. Attempts to discourage stations from prior use of national and international news are made from time to time, but these always fail because the networks cannot dictate to their affiliated local stations; neither can the network news division dictate to the five local stations that each network is allowed to own. The network news programs can, however, monopolize the film about national and international stories, forcing local stations that wish to cover this news to limit themselves to tell stories.[14] The need to compete with local news programs is another reason why producers are reluctant to report the big news merely as tell stories, and use film instead.

2. *The peg.* Although story selectors want to maximize the supply of new stories, they must also cope with the resulting oversupply. The primary exclusionary consideration they use in this situation is the peg, a recent event or a public official's statement which is used as a "handle" on which to "hang" their stories, particularly features that can be used at any time. Important news is automatically pegged to the day on which it appears, but all news media keep a supply of features on hand, waiting for a peg to make them topical. When top producers and editors make up their story lists, they prefer to choose pegged features, and pegless ones are almost always the first to be eliminated in order to shorten an overly long story list. This practice raises objections from some journalists because it kills stories they like; however, periodic efforts to de-emphasize the peg have not succeeded, for it is easier to hold the pegless wonder in abeyance, with the hope that a peg can be found for it the next time.

Pegs are useful because they are easily applied. Any actor or activity can be a peg, particularly when journalists are fearful that a competitor is readying the same story. Journalists also have a supply of acceptable pegs on hand: the beginning of the school year is a good peg for educational features; and science stories are often pegged to conferences. Breaking news can serve as pegs for related features, so that a major airplane crash may be used to peg a feature on airplane safety. Most pegs are tied to and, in fact, are often generated by, publicity-seeking sources who know that journalists need pegs; this helps explain why the newsmagazines often notice a new entertainer at the same time. Although some story selectors would prefer to peg stories to audience interests, they cannot easily determine when their audience becomes interested in a new topic. As a result, journalists schedule crime features when the FBI releases its latest statistics rather than when there is rising public concern with crime.

3. *The repetition taboo.* Journalists often see their work as reporting the same story over and over again, perhaps because they obtain most of the news from a small number of sources. The resulting lack of felt novelty is manifested in the journalists' feelings of boredom with a story, and it is assumed that the audience shares these feelings as well.[15] To prevent this situation from arising, a taboo is placed on repetition; stories are thus judged repetitive if similar ones, making the same point or coming to the same conclusion, have been used within the past twelve or even twenty-four months. Story selectors have an excellent memory for past story lists; and while they reject repetitive stories to ward off criticism from peers, they also fear that the audience will switch channels or turn the page—and then question the journalists' competence for tolerating repetition. No one knows how well the audience remembers or whether it objects to repetition; but when any suggested story elicits a "we've-done-it-before" response, it is usually killed on the spot.

Repetition is also discouraged because it wastes scarce air time or print space; but even so, the repetition taboo is applied differentially. Important public figures, as well as dramatic news—such as natural disasters, social disorder, and battles—are exempt from the taboo. Although producers admit that one flood looks much like another, flood stories are almost always newsworthy. During the 1960s, journalists at both media began to feel that they and the audience were becoming bored with protest demonstrations; thereafter, they reported only the largest ones, and those marked by trouble. But stories which do not bore journalists are not defined as repetitious. For example, in the spring of 1975, the news media continued to report regularly, and in some detail, on the final stages of the Vietnam War, arguing that people should be informed about it, despite the fact that story selectors had some indication, from friends and neighbors, that the audience was no longer following it. Likewise, violations of the enduring values are not considered repetitious.

4. *"Freshness" versus "staleness."* Like bakery products, news can be fresh or stale, although staleness is more often a synonym for repetition than for old age. A stale story can become fresh again if novel actors or activities are involved; but usually, freshness has to be supplied by the journalists, as in the form of a new angle. Conse-

quently, both news media continually look for journalists who have a fresh approach: reporters who can think of new sources to contact, film makers who use innovative camera techniques, and writers who can apply new ideas and metaphors to old topics. The newsmagazines, which compete by retelling already known news, are particularly eager for freshness. The portfolios of job applicants are looked over for examples of imaginative writing; and one editor explained that he preferred to hire people who write poetry or parody on the side.

A new story is fresh by definition, but thereafter, it follows a cyclical pattern: the same actor or activity becomes familiar, then boredom sets in. New social movements receive considerable coverage when they first become known to story selectors but are eventually dropped, much to their chagrin, when news about them becomes stale. Moreover, once the movements drop out of the news, they are perceived by others to have become less significant, even though they have only become repetitious to story selectors. Crime news follows a similar cycle. An unusual crime story is particularly fresh, so much so that reporters are encouraged to find further examples, establishing a journalistic crime wave that may bear little relationship to the actual one. In 1964, thirty-eight of Kitty Genovese's neighbors watched her being murdered without calling the police; subsequently, reporters had little difficulty finding similar instances elsewhere, until finally the story became boring and was dropped.[16]

5. *Excessive freshness.* The pursuit of freshness, and of novelty in general, however, is hemmed in by other considerations, which can be illustrated by the handling of trend stories. The magazines actively engage is trend spotting and actively pursue news about the arrival of a promising new entertainer or lifestyle. But trend stories can also be risky, for coverage of a highly touted new personality who does not catch on, or a quickly rising star who declines with equal rapidity, is thought to impair the journalists' credibility. Consequently, the prudent story suggester waits for another news medium to take the lead, then sells the idea partly on the basis that it has been reported elsewhere.

Like fresh news, the trend story is cyclical, and story selectors view both it and its appearance in the media in terms of a bell-shaped curve, which they picture as "ripening, cresting, and declining." The curve does not measure the diffusion of a trend among participants, however, for they are thought to be "trendy" people; instead, the curve measures receptivity to the trend among more conventional people, that is, journalists and their audience. When newsmagazines put a popular entertainer on their cover, they choose one who has already "declined" among adolescents. The journalists' teenage children may scorn the magazine for being behind the times, but top editors are reassured, because they are editing for an adult audience.[17]

The ideal time for selecting a trend story is just before it is thought to crest. If it is selected too early, trend spotters feel they are "too far out." Because editors do not want "to do kooks," suggested fad stories from California are checked out with eastern and midwestern bureaus, and are selected only if "the fad makes sense to them." If a trend is selected after it has peaked, trend spotters expect peer criticism for being imitative. A *Newsweek* editor said it succinctly: "We don't want to be late, but we don't want to be too early either, and mostly we don't want to be scooped by *Time.*"

The risks of trend spotting are increased by the fact that the curve journalists use becomes evident only *ex post facto;* moreover, story selectors are constantly bombarded by press agents and others who are selling a new trend and want the journalist to ignore the curve. Conversely, the risk is reduced by the minimal requirements for legitimating a trend; only a few people need to resort to a new fashion to demonstrate its existence.[18]

Story Quality

Important and interesting stories should be new, but they must also be good. The less important, interesting, or novel the news, the more story selectors worry about story quality, which is judged by five kinds of considerations.

1. *Action.* I have already noted that the best story reports dramatic activities or emotions. Active stories are believed to attract and hold the audience, but they have the same effect on journalists. When journalists are bored by the daily or weekly routine, an exciting story boosts morale; and when there is a long drought of exciting stories, they become restless. In the spring of 1978, some magazine writers, left "crabby" by the drought of dramatic domestic news, joked about their readiness to be more critical of the president and other public officials for their failure to supply news that would "make the adrenalin flow."

News judgment is partly a matter of feel, and excitement is the most easily recognized feeling. As a reporter explained: "Action is a lazy man's way out. Whether in Vietnam or in a ghetto riot, news is happening right in front of you, and you only have to cover it." News judgment also calls for the identification of highlights; and for story selectors, action is the most easily recognized highlight.

2. *Pace.* However, most news lacks action; consequently, journalists try to add what they can during story production. For example, interviewers sometimes ask leading questions in order to obtain dramatic answers from sources. But the main substitute for action is a proper pace that will keep a reader or viewer involved in the story. Television uses a variety of camera angles and cutting techniques to speed up the slow pace of talking-head film; and although the newsmagazines resort to vivid language, they rely heavily on dramatic quotes to interrupt the "tick tock," one editor's label for straight but dull narrative.[19]

3. *Completeness.* Since action is scarce, the most frequent measure of story quality is not very different from that used in all empirical disciplines: the extent to which all possible angles have been considered, all available sources have been consulted, all important issues have been dealt with, and all feasible highlights have been exploited. Television also measures completeness by speed; plane-crash stories are judged by how quickly reporters arrive at the disaster, and how many victims and eyewitnesses they can interview on the scene. Newsmagazines judge completeness by the amount of important or interesting detail journalists can unearth.

4. *Clarity with parsimony.* Whether the medium is film or print, the good story must make its point—what some magazine editors call the billboard—quickly, and set the scene through what television calls establishing shots. The body of the story should strategically locate scarce dramatic components between less dramatic ones; and the ideal ending should make the audience sit up and take notice. It is therefore called the kicker.

Television language must be simple; and writers cannot, unlike their peers at the magazines, play with or on words. Both media also aim for a logical structure that will lead the viewer or reader from beginning to end.

5. *Esthetic and technical standards.*[20] Good film should follow the standards of documentaries but with the pace of the entertainment film; film producers, however, rarely have the time or the cameras to achieve these goals. Also, film and text must be coordinated, the former supplying pictorial evidence for the latter. Underexposed or overexposed film, even with action footage, is never used unless it is an exclusive that cannot be reshot. Films that are out of synch (not completely synchronized lip movements and speech) are also killed if they cannot be corrected. The technical standards for film quality are set by and for peers, and imperfections which cannot possibly be

detected by viewers make television journalists groan with disgust—or with pleasure when it is the competitor's film which is flawed.[21]

Magazine journalists are equally attentive to esthetic and technical standards, but these play a lesser role in story selection, since stories can be endlessly rewritten. On the other hand, although television film can be edited, poorly exposed film cannot be repaired and films cannot normally be reshot. But then, magazine journalists can do nothing if the printers have performed poorly after the last galleys have been set.

When stories do not sufficiently meet one or another quality consideration, they sometimes undergo various forms of restaging, a practice which is considered permissible as long as it does not alter observed events or interviews—or, at least, their meaning. Television interviewers often rehearse their respondents off-camera in order to obtain shorter and more dramatic on-camera answers. Magazine editors follow the same practice *ex post facto* by shortening or editing quotes. In the past, television interviews were often cut so as to begin with the most important or dramatic rather than with the initial question or answer, but the networks halted the practice after it was criticized during a congressional investigation of the CBS documentary "Selling of the Pentagon." Print journalists have not been criticized, however, and thus continue the practice.

Presidential and other ceremonies are sometimes repeated for the cameras, usually if camera crews were in poor position for the actual ceremony. Because some people are self-conscious when they repeat an activity for the camera, producers dislike this type of restaging and are critical of rivals whom they suspect of having done so. Camera crews arriving late for a dramatic incident have been reported asking participants to re-enact it.[22] No one is proud of restaging, but it is treated differently than deliberately creating incidents for the camera (see Chapter 4).

Balance

Top producers and editors select not only individual stories, but also the group of stories that makes up a news program or magazine issue. As a result, they must pay attention to another set of quality considerations, which can be called balance. A balanced news program or magazine issue presents a diverse collection of stories, the assumption being that audience attention is best held by diversity. Balance considerations are therefore a form of audience consideration.

1. *Story mixture.* News programs and magazine issues are governed by pacing requirements similar to those that govern stories. Since most news is serious, bad, and lengthy, it must be balanced and interspersed with light, good, and short stories to avoid depressing or boring the audience and the journalists. Audience feelings remain unknown, of course, but the journalists react to their own, and producers like to end their programs with humorous closers in order to cap off the day's work with a laugh.

2. *Subject balance.* Story selectors also look for diversity of subject matter. Television producers will not, for example, use films on two court trials unless both are "clearly compelling." Although editors will combine similar topics or events in a single story, a book editor will not review two biographies the same week, nor will a science editor include two stories on biology. A writer had to postpone an article on ethnicity in America because his magazine had just run a story on the Holocaust, which the top editors had treated as an ethnic story.

3. *Geographic balance.* Both media ensure that domestic news originates from all parts of the country; in fact, features are occasionally selected because they come from communities or states which rarely get into the news. The two media especially minimize New York stories to compensate for their Manhattan location. "I have to think twice about New York stories, because of my own interest, because it's so close," one top producer (who actually lived in the suburbs and had no particular interest in the city) pointed out. Journalists want to avoid a "New York bias"; as a result, both news media were slow to emphasize New York's fiscal crisis. (The New York bias which upsets critics is not, however, geographical; they are unhappy with stories which reflect excessive liberalism or cultural sophistication.)

The attempt to downplay New York stories is not always successful. Because the journalists live—or at least work and play—in the city, they are more familiar with it and with New York happenings, which subsequently become overrepresented in story suggestions. In addition, breaking stories are always close at hand; consequently, minor floods and disasters in the New York area will appear on television more frequently than similar disasters farther away. The magazines nationalize New York suggestions by ordering a bureau "roundup," and the suggestion becomes a story only if other bureaus find the same phenomenon in their areas.

4. *Demographic balance.* Television producers try to find occasional features about old people. The newsmagazines, on the other hand, look more energetically for news about and for young people. In this

case, they see eye to eye with their business departments (see Chapter 7); they also want to attract young people as a regular and long-term audience. Section writers take constituency balance into account. Religion writers, for example, balance stories on Catholicism with those on Protestantism, and seek out stories on Judaism.

Since the late 1960s, stories which feature or quote several ordinary people as well as public officials have aimed toward racial and sexual balance. In this instance, at least, the balance sought is also political, for journalists are responding to, or anticipating demands and criticism from, sources, the audience, and others. Racial and sexual balance did not become a consideration until blacks and women began to protest their coverage by the news media, although now journalists are seriously trying to become aware of and eliminate their own racial and sexual biases. But religion writers do not have to maintain balance by reporting on minority religions. Generally speaking, then, the search for demographic balance follows outside criticism.

5. *Political balance.* The Federal Communications Commission's "Fairness Doctrine" has made political balance a quasi-legal requirement in television, but it is practiced at the newsmagazines as well. Journalists believe that if they fail to maintain political balance, they will be accused of bias, which undermines their credibility.

Political balance is usually achieved by identifying the dominant, most widespread, or most vocal positions, then presenting "both sides." Producers and editors see to it that both Republican and Democratic politicians are filmed or quoted; that ecology stories quote both environmentalists and businessmen or women; and that an interview with an Israeli leader will soon be followed by an equally lengthy one featuring an Arab leader. *Newsweek*'s columnists are chosen to balance "liberals" and "conservatives"; contributors to the magazine's "My Turn" column are selected in the same way. Sometimes the media strive for balance by counterpointing, or "playing off," stories against each other, juxtaposing a story about black achievements with one about a white anti-bussing demonstration. At times, they will kill a story in order to achieve balance. A Washington reporter explained why his network decided against live coverage of the October 21, 1967, anti-war demonstration at the Pentagon: "We want to do this one because it is news, but next week you may have to do six to eight hours on a pro-war group, and we may not want to do that one. Also, I'm not sure if this demonstration deserves six to eight hours. You have to think who these people represent; they are only a minority."

Reporting both sides of an issue is an easily applied method not only for creating balance, but also for anticipating protest—at least when the chosen sides could be expected to criticize the news media were their positions ignored. In addition, the news is more objective when there are two sides to a story, and it is often more dramatic as well. When the sides involved are not apt to protest, journalists are likely to select two extreme positions in order to achieve highlighting. A television reporter pointed out that "at anti-war demonstrations, we shot the Viet Cong supporters and the Nazis because they were interesting, and also because they are what sells. You always go after the extremes; the same in the South, where we shot the black militants and the Ku Klux Klan." When journalists are unaware that there are at least two sides, letters from the overlooked side are likely to come in; and if they arrive in sufficient numbers, journalists soon become acquainted with at least one other position.[23] Groups on the Far Right and Left, which are normally ignored by the prevailing political-balance considerations, establish their own news media.

Competitive Considerations

The news firms for which journalists work engage in economic competition, but as I will suggest further in Chapter 7, journalists themselves are only tangentially involved in economic competition. Although they do compete with each other, competitive considerations function largely as a form of quality control.

Competition is endemic to the profession. Colleagues compete with each other to make the story lists, and with other news organizations in the same firm. Evening news programs try to prevent morning programs from using a film which they would like to use first. In 1975, the executive producer of the *NBC Nightly News* had to compete with himself in deciding whether to use a feature for the weekday program or hold it over for the weekend shows, which are always in need of features, since the sources for important news rarely work on weekends. *Newsweek* journalists try to beat colleagues at the *Washington Post* to the punch, and *Time*'s journalists occasionally compete with other Time, Inc. publications.

Story selection, however, is more affected by external competition, between news organizations within the same medium. That competition is dyadic, probably because the participants lack the time and energy to worry about more than one competitor. *Time* and *Newsweek* compete with each other but ignore *U. S. News and World Report* as well as other weeklies; NBC and CBS watch each other carefully but pay no attention to ABC—although this might change if ABC catches up in the ratings.

Dyadic competition affects story selection in at least three ways. Rivals still try to scoop each other, but because competing news media have reporters in virtually the same places, the opportunity to be first with a story that, in days past, "stopped the presses" has diminished. Instead, news media compete by getting exclusives, by thinking up original feature-story ideas, and by making small scoops on details.[24] (This undoubtedly hastened the final exposure of the Watergate scandals.)

In addition, competition sets up mutual expectations; as a result, story selectors may choose stories because they expect the rival to do so. From time to time, story selectors use stories they do not consider particularly important or good, for although they can justify their omission to each other, they cannot risk the possibility that an executive will later ask why they left out a story carried by the opposition. They fear that executives give higher priority to competition than to quality; consequently, story selectors are always pleased when executives are recruited from the ranks of journalism, although they are frequently disappointed when it turns out that ex-journalists behave like other executives. The mutual expectations become a common bind: they discourage innovations in story selection that could produce objections from "the brass"; and this in turn contributes to the similarity of the news in competing programs or magazines.

To avoid being viewed as imitating or falling behind the competition, magazine story selectors will also drop or play down a story that has already been used by a rival. The magazines routinely stop work on features the rival publishes first, but they compete most intensely over their covers. Both race to be first to run a back-of-the-book cover on a new trend, and the winner feels superior both in the timeliness of his news judgment and the speed with which that judgment was implemented. The loser, who most likely has been working on the same idea, must now drop the story from the future covers list or at least postpone it for several months.

Front-of-the-book covers are exempt from competition when an important national or international story breaks early in the week; then, top editors expect both magazines to have the same cover subject. If such a story breaks toward the end of the week, however, both top editors must decide whether to "order up" a new cover. If the new story breaks after the cover deadline, each must then determine whether the extra effort and expense involved in making the change is justified. All the while each is wondering if the rival is doing the same thing. In the 1960s, when budgets were looser, last-minute changes were frequently made. After General Charles de Gaulle died, *Time* killed its initial cover even though the presses had already begun to roll, and was pleased to discover that *Newsweek* had not made a change. A week later, the journalists were once more gratified when they noticed that *Newsweek* had buried the story in the next issue, an admission that it had been scooped. On the other hand, in 1975, when Indira Gandhi reorganized India's government, *Newsweek* put the story on the cover at the last minute, while *Time* did not. The following week *Time*'s top editors debated whether the story was sufficiently important to deserve a belated cover, a decision that would put them at risk for being judged imitative; they finally decided that it was not. Once in a while, therefore, a world-shaking event may never appear on the cover of one of the newsmagazines.

Cover competition is spurred by the fact that the two magazines make their decisions independently of each other. Periodically, they learn mid-week that they have both chosen the same cover, usually because a common source will tell one magazine's reporter or photographer that the competitor had been there earlier. By the time editors learn that their covers will be identical, it is usually too late to change; besides, not knowing the rival's plans, they lack the incentive to spend the time or money to come up with a new cover. However, if one magazine learns that both are working on a similar cover for a future issue, it may attempt to come out with the story earlier than planned. Such races are less often run than proposed because a hurriedly commissioned cover may be inferior in quality or because the professional journals make an exposé story out of the race.[25] More often, one magazine will run a shorter, inside story on the same subject the week the competitor's cover appears. In this fashion, the loser admits defeat while at the same time depriving the winner of a complete victory.

When front-of-the-book covers are similar, magazine journalists are not surprised, although they are embarrassed if the titles, or "slashes," are identical. Back-of-the-book covers resulting from similar pegs are taken for granted and are similar for that reason. After the Nixon Administration launched its attack on the news media, however, editors became nervous about having identical covers because they thought, with some justification, that the general public believed them to be in collusion, thus providing evidence of the "media conspiracy" on the part of the "liberal Eastern Establishment," which the Nixon Administration sought to expose.

The anxiety incited by the Nixon Administration remains, inasmuch as the image of a conspiratoral liberal Eastern Establishment is still *au courant*. Even so, journalists, at least in New York, refrain not only from collusion but also from fraternization common among reporters.[26] The offices of *Time* and *Newsweek* are only a few blocks apart, and their staffs see each other at midtown restaurants, at parties, and, during the summer, at the games of a journalists' softball league; but they do not discuss their respective shops.[27]

Despite the lack of collusion, attempts to discover the rival's cover plans are made, either to help in the planning of future covers or, more immediately, to schedule a brief story on the other magazine's cover story. Besides, editors and others like to verify the aptness of their own choice for the week, want advance confirmation that they have planned a more important or attractive cover, and are simply curious. By the end of the week, information or rumors about the rival's cover are always circulating; in fact, sometimes the information comes from high places. Ben Bradlee, writing of the period when he was *Newsweek*'s Washington bureau chief and a close friend of President Kennedy's, reports that "several times, when the editors of *Newsweek* felt they really had to know what *Time* had on its upcoming cover, I was able to get the answer from the President, and he was never wrong."[28]

Television producers do not compete over lead stories because leads are chosen late in the day, and they do not find out about their competitor's leads until air time. For the same reason, there is no concern about imitation, although producers are aware that they can be accused of being in collusion when leads are similar. Besides, television is more ephemeral; and inasmuch as the news programs are scheduled at the same time in most cities, only dial twirlers or viewers with three television sets can spot common leads.

Although dyadic competition involves peers and exists to determine which news organization has better journalists, it is not entirely free of commercial motives. Journalists hope that the winner will, by virtue of its victory, persuade segments of the audience to switch their allegiance, thereby increasing sales or ratings.[29] Their hope may be illusory, for only in some cities can television viewers watch both the *CBS Evening News* and *NBC Nightly News* on the same night. Magazine readers, however, can keep up with both rivals, and fragmentary Simmons data suggest that about a third of each magazine's readers also read the other.[30] But no one knows how many viewers or readers are aware of the competition, or whether those who are aware of it judge it by the journalists' standards, and then switch to the winner for those reasons.[31]

Competition as Quality Control

Journalists use competition to evaluate their own performance, particularly if they are uncertain about their news judgments. They always compare their own work to that of their rivals, and most of the time they believe their stories to have been superior; but they do not deny, among themselves, when they have been beaten in some way. Competition thus creates consensus about the most crucial considerations and supplies the only feedback that journalists take seriously. Audience feedback is sparse and, in any case, not deemed valid or reliable (see Chapter 7); and feedback from superiors is taken into account but fully accepted only when journalists and executives agree.

Dyadic competition has one drawback, however: it is limited to rivals working within the same medium and format considerations. This prevents journalists from judging their work by the more general considerations, notably substantive and quality judgments, which are shared by the profession. Consequently, journalists seem to need a more general standard setter; and that role is played, both in television and at the magazines, by *The New York Times* and, to a lesser extent, by the *Washington Post.*

The *Times* is treated as *the* professional setter of standards, just as Harvard University is perceived as the standard setter of university performance. When editors and producers are uncertain about a selection decision, they will check whether, where, and how the *Times* has covered the story; and story selectors see to it that many of the *Times*'s front-page stories find their way into television programs and magazines.

Book editors will make sure to review a book that has received a big play in the *Times Book Review,* or they will review it because they expect it to be prominently reviewed there. Back-of-the-book writers and editors keep up with *Times* feature stories, especially in the Sunday magazine section. The imitation taboo that operates between the two magazines is ignored as well, so that when *Times* stories wind up on story lists, no one worries about imitation. The role of the *Times* extends beyond story selection, however, for at the magazines, *Times* stories are required reading for writers. Reporters are expected to do as well or better than their peers at the *Times,* and must be able to defend their files if these conflict with what has appeared in the *Times.* [32]

When television and magazine journalists use the *Times* as a standard setter, they make the assumption that the *Times* applies only substantive and quality considerations, and need not concern itself with medium, format, or audience considerations. When pressed, story selectors will admit that the assumption is dubious, but they make it because they need to believe that someone is certain about news judgments—and perhaps more important, that there are professional considerations which transcend those of individual news organizations and firms. If the *Times* did not exist, it would probably have to be invented.

6

Objectivity, Values, and Ideology

Journalism resembles other empirical disciplines and professions in its aim to be objective: to be free from values and ideology; accordingly, journalists practice value exclusion. Of course, objectivity is itself a value, but journalists try to exclude values in the narrower sense of the term: as preference statements about nation and society.

Editorials, commentary, and at the magazines, the endings of some stories are exempted from value exclusion; the primary task in story selection, however, is, as one top editor put it, "to tell the readers this is what we think is important, and we hope they'll feel the same way, but our aim isn't ideological." Yet, because the importance judgments include national values as well as the enduring values, journalists do make preference statements about nation and society. Value exclusion is therefore accompanied by value inclusion, both through story selection and as opinions expressed in specific stories.

The enduring values are built into news judgment; as a result, most values and opinions enter unconsciously (in a non-Freudian sense). "Every reporter operates with certain assumptions about what constitutes normative behavior, if not the good society," Peter Schrag has written, "and the more 'objective' he tries to be, the more likely those assumptions will remain concealed."[1] Since journalists can no more operate without values than anyone else, the ones concealed in their work make it possible for them to leave their conscious personal values "at home."

182

Value Exclusion

Journalists seek to exclude conscious values, and they do so in three ways: through objectivity, the disregard of implications, and the rejection of ideology (as they define it). Value exclusion, however, is not solely a goal but also a practical consideration, for it defends journalists against actual or possible criticism, and protects them against demands by powerful critics for censorship and self-censorship (see Chapter 8).

Objectivity and Detachment

Journalists justify their right to individual autonomy by the pursuit of objectivity and detachment; in a way, they strike an implied bargain, which allows them autonomy in choosing the news in exchange for leaving out their personal values. The outcome restricts the news to facts (or attributed opinions), which, journalists argue, are gathered objectively. This objectivity derives from the use of similar fact-gathering methods; like scientific method, journalistic method is validated by consensus. Equally important, the methods themselves are considered objective because journalists, being detached, do not care how the story comes out.

Most journalists fully realize that objective methods provide no guidelines for the selection either of stories or of which facts go into stories. Nevertheless, in making the selection, journalists strive to be objective, both in intent, by applying personal detachment; and in effect, by disregarding the implications of the news.[2] They do not choose the news on the basis of whom it will help or hurt; and when they cannot ignore implications, they try to be fair.

Objectivity so defined even enables journalists to reach evaluative conclusions and to state opinions. As long as their intent is to exclude conscious personal values, then opinions become "subjective reactions," which follow from objectively gathered facts.[3] Journalistic values are seen as reactions to the news rather than a priori judgments which determine what becomes newsworthy. Investigative reporters, who always end with explicit value judgments, often pick a topic because they smell a good story, not because they have already passed judgment on the target of their investigation. (In addition, the exposé story typically judges the exposed against their own expressed values, and these can be determined empirically by the reporter; as a result, even his or her value judgment is considered objective.⁴) Although journalists may not be aware of it, they are perhaps the strongest remaining bastion of logical positivism in America.

Whether journalists can be truly objective will be discussed in Chapter 10, but they try hard to live up to their definition of objectivity. Most train themselves, or are trained, to practice value exclusion, and many do not vote in order to preserve their political detachment. I found some exceptions: some older journalists described themselves as anti-Communist liberals worried about the dangers of American fascism, and of the Far Right generally; a few were fervent supporters of racial integration, a couple described themselves as moderate segregationists; there were some Zionists and some anti-Zionists; during the Vietnam War, a handful were hawks, and a somewhat larger number were doves; before elections, some became devotees of one or another candidate.

These journalists expressed their values freely in office discussions and, like the "house radicals" and "house conservatives" to be described later, became known for and by them. If they were unwilling or unable to keep their values out of their work, they asked to be taken off a story or were not assigned to it in the first place. Sometimes, however, editors would assign writers with known personal values to work on a story in which their values were relevant, which would ensure their bending over backwards to remain detached. When their values coincided with an organization's conscious stands, they did not need to be excluded; when their values were at odds with a stand but the story had been assigned to them because of seniority or special expertise, discordant values were "edited out" or "toned down." This happened rarely, since experienced writers are also experienced at value exclusion.

However, journalists with conscious values were in the minority, for the news media I studied seem to attract people who keep their values to themselves. Those unable to do so seldom look for work in these media, especially when their values are discordant; and those who come with discordant values do not remain long. But equally important, the national media, and journalism generally, appear to recruit people who do not hold strong personal values in the first place. They have no prior values about the topics which become news, nor do they always develop them about topics on which they are working. Many of the reporters and writers constantly immersed in American politics did not seem particularly interested in it apart from their work. Even women journalists who felt strongly about sexual equality in their firm and profession, and who pressed male colleagues to choose more stories about women, often indicated that they did not share the values of the feminist movement. The abstention from values extended to story preferences, for when I asked people about their favorite story subjects, hoping in this manner to obtain clues to their values, almost all pointed out that they had no favorites. They were only interested in "getting the story."

Although most of the people I studied discovered their future occupation in high school, they did not become journalists to advocate values or to reform society.[5] Some liked to write, and a few magazine journalists are frustrated or "failed" novelists. Others wanted to be storytellers, enjoying the idea of reporting news to an audience; a few saw themselves as teachers, instructing people in current events. But for the majority, journalism offered the opportunity to be in the midst of exciting activities without having to be involved. Daniel Schorr has written: "Participants took positions, got excited, shaped events for woe or weal, but ended up losing perspective on reality. I remained the untouched observer, seeing the whole picture because I was not in the picture. . . . The notion of being the invisible stranger always appealed to me."[6]

A variety of organizational mechanisms exist to reinforce objectivity and detachment. Journalists are rewarded for getting the story, and personal interests or values can interfere. General reporters move so quickly from story to story that they do not have time to develop attachment, while those covering emotionally charged stories like wars and election campaigns are rotated frequently to preserve detachment. Story selectors, on the other hand, rarely are out of their offices long enough to become involved; they are detached by their duties.

The high salaries and perquisites enjoyed by many, if hardly all, national journalists also foster the feeling of objectivity. A *Time* writer, reporting on his own loss of detachment during the 1976 strike at the magazine, noted that even though he himself had covered many strikes as a reporter, he had never felt the need "to choose between capital and labor. In the print and electronic sweatshops of the Manhattan idea business, there are no class divisions."[7] I doubt that many of his colleagues would agree about the absence of class divisions, and he himself describes the news organization, perhaps unwittingly, as a sweatshop. Still, the income and prestige that go with being a national journalist encourage conscious feelings of being "above" many social and political conflicts. Needless to say, being above them is not equivalent to objectivity, but it may feel that way.

Like social scientists and others, journalists can also feel objective when they assume, rightly or wrongly, that their values are universal or dominant. When values arouse no dissent or when dissent can be explained away as moral disorder, those who hold values can easily forget that they are values. Similarly, the journalists' facts remain facts as long as the unconscious value and reality judgments that go into them are not questioned by trusted critics, or when, as Tuchman points out, they are validated by "common sense."[8]

But above all, objectivity is reinforced by necessity: the need to protect journalistic credibility. If journalists were not viewed as being objective, every story could be criticized as resulting from one or another journalistic bias, and the news would be distrusted by even larger numbers of viewers and readers than is now the case. For this reason, objectivity is also a commercial consideration; indeed, the Associated Press is often credited with having invented objectivity in order to sell uniform wire-service news to a politically and otherwise diverse set of local newspapers.[9]

Nevertheless, most journalists see objectivity in positive terms. Proud that it once helped eliminate the partisan news of party newspapers and of journalists bribed by their sources, they also feel a professional obligation to protect audiences, who cannot gather their own news, from being misled by people who, having "axes to grind," would withhold information contrary to their values. Journalists believe, furthermore, that their role is to supply information that will enable the audience to come to its own conclusions.[10] As a result, they were not in favor of either "personal journalism," which includes personal feelings, or "advocacy journalism," which includes personal values.[11] Television journalists were not even fond of commentary, but mostly because it slowed down the pace of the news programs.

Journalists questioned objectivity, however, when it prevented them from reporting what they knew to be lies, although since Watergate, they have been less reluctant either to find sources who will expose liars or to attribute information in such a way that readers and viewers will hopefully realize that the journalists are reporting lies.[12] But much of the time, journalists cannot prove that sources are lying, for they have not been able to do the necessary legwork; this is why investigative reporters, who have done the legwork, are permitted to identify liars more explicitly. Nor do journalists know how to report politicians who are either unaware that they are lying or powerful enough to define honesty to suit their needs.

Compensating for Objectivity

From time to time, journalists have strong opinions about individual issues which they can neither express in their stories nor keep bottled up inside. They voice these opinions in a variety of ways. Magazine editors can reprint cartoons that mirror their feelings, some journalists write on the side for journals of opinion, and most anchorpersons have brief daily radio programs of commentary.[13]

Other journalists express themselves in conversations. In the 1960s, for example, office opinions about the war were more negative in group discussion than in print or on the air. Indeed, one day some CBS journalists were so angry that they rewrote a lead story to read: "The President of the United States today cheapened the nation's highest military decoration for bravery by using a Medal of Honor award ceremony as the occasion for a spite-ridden attack on Americans who dare to disagree with him." They even considered slipping the rewrite into the final script just before air time, but they could not have obtained access to the teleprompter from which the anchorperson actually reads the news. But whatever their feelings about the war, many journalists also objected to the anti-war protesters; at NBC, they were labeled "Vietniks."

In the 1970s, they were mainly upset about the economy; informal discussions usually produced much harsher criticism of inflation, corporate corruption, and greed than could be put in the news. At the same time, the journalists were then, as earlier, privately less comfortable with the racial tolerance of the news and its advocacy of integration, at least judging by the plethora of racial—and ethnic—jokes which were exchanged in informal banter. They also looked askance at the undeserving poor, the very rich, doctors and lawyers who seek an undue amount of profit and publicity, and Pentecostal ministers and faith healers, among others. At all times, however, the main topic of professional discussion was the dishonesty and incompetence of politicians, regardless of party or point of view.

Opinions were also expressed through stories, editorials, and cartoons that appeared on newsroom bulletin boards. At *Newsweek,* many journalists decorated their walls with posters; some were chosen on esthetic grounds and others to shock colleagues. Many, however, were used to take stands, particularly by the researchers, who are less neutral than their superiors—but then again, they are not consulted on the stands their magazine takes. During the Watergate period, some posters were so intensely anti-Nixon that the top editor asked they be taken down, lest nonjournalistic visitors to the magazine get the wrong impression about its objectivity.

Freedom from Implications

Because objectivity is defined as a matter of intent, it includes the freedom to disregard the implications of the news. Indeed, objectivity could not long exist without this freedom, for the moment journalists are required to consider the effects of the news on sources and others, they would have to begin assessing their own intent and to relinquish their detachment, especially if they wanted to prevent injury to someone.

Journalists realize, of course, that news has myriad effects, many of which cannot even be anticipated; consequently, they feel that they are entitled to choose stories, and facts, without first considering the possible consequences.[14] Once more, the crucial ingredient is intent, for objectivity requires only that journalists avoid intended effects. They adopt what Reuven Frank has called an artificial innocence, ". . . the refusal of journalists to alter the story for the purpose of controlling its effects [and] . . . the newsman's necessary deliberate detachment from aiming his work or letting someone else aim it to changing society—even for the noblest motive."[15] But journalists want to be equally free to ignore unintended effects and not to be obligated to consider either the manifest or latent functions (or dysfunctions) of their work.

Freedom from implications exists, like objectivity, to protect journalists from undue criticism, for it makes irrelevant the objections of those who see themselves disadvantaged by the news. As a result, freedom from implications almost becomes an imperative for story selection and production. Story selectors are exempt from the responsibility of worrying whom their choices will help or hurt; and reporters are able to gain access to sources for whom the news might have negative effects, and to ask them any and all questions they regard as newsworthy. Above all, the right to ignore implications eliminates the possibility of paralyzing uncertainty. If journalists had to assess the implications of the stories or facts they choose, and had to determine, much less anticipate, the not immediately obvious implications, they would be incapable of making news judgments—at least, not in time to meet their deadlines.

Objectivity as intent is not difficult to implement at the conscious level, for journalists can know and control their own intentions; however, implications, which are determined by the people affected by the news, are not within their control. Effects cannot be turned on and off by journalists, and they accompany the news regardless of the journalists' intentions or actions. While journalists do not systematically predict story implications, and are therefore less aware of them than nonjournalists think, they also know, from experience, that implications can be expected.

Therefore, in practice, they are not free from implications. The only freedom they have—and it is limited—is the choice of implications (among those expected), which they do take into account. The general consideration has military overtones: to protect the innocent. Accordingly, journalists may sometimes kill or alter stories that can endanger the lives or livelihoods of people who are seen as innocent bystanders at the events that make the news. However, they do not care how the news affects publicity seekers or people whom they consider socially or morally disorderly. Of course, journalists shy away from news that could hurt their own firms, themselves, or their ability to obtain the news; nor do they want, if at all possible, to endanger the national interest or well-being. In wartime, they do not report news that may damage the war effort, and in wartime or peacetime, what may genuinely jeopardize national security (see Chapter 8); and at all times, they seek to prevent panic among the population.

When implications fall outside these areas or are unpredictable, journalists apply a further consideration, which they call fairness. Fairness, like objectivity, is a matter of intent, and journalists who believe they have acted fairly can ignore charges to the contrary. Generally speaking, fairness is determined in accordance with the enduring values, which is why socially and morally disorderly actors need not be treated fairly. Fairness is also regulated by the libel laws, in television, by F. C. C. rules, and more important, by the balance considerations described in Chapter 5.

Producers and editors function as additional enforcers of fairness, for most of their non-stylistic editing is devoted to "softening," the altering of a writer's harsh judgments and/or adjectives thought to be unfair. By softening, reactionary politicians become "conservatives," and lobbyists are sometimes described as "advocates." Conversely, editors rarely "harden" judgments; and if they agree with a writer's critical adjectives, they will not edit them. Unpopular actors and activities may be unfairly described without anyone recognizing, or caring, that the adjectives are pejorative.

The magazines compete against each other and the remaining news media with dramatic writing, and unfair but picturesque adjectives sometimes remain because they liven up a story. Unflattering pictures are chosen for somewhat the same purpose, although *Time* once selected them to put down its political enemies. The safest way to be unfair is to use a cartoon, for it is a reprint; and while cartoons are chosen primarily because they are dramatic, no one can be certain whether or not they represent an editor's opinion.

The Exclusion of "Ideology"

The exclusion of conscious values implies the exclusion of conscious ideology, but the ways in which journalists reject ideology and deal with it when it appears provide further insight into the workings of objectivity—and an understanding of how unconscious values, and thereby unconscious ideology, enter into news judgment.

Unlike European peers working for party or government news media, American journalists do not formulate conscious and consistent political viewpoints; they are not ideologists. This is true even of columnists and commentators. While they tend to develop a set of viewpoints, they do so because they must write or broadcast on a regular basis, and cannot possibly approach every column or program *de novo*. Moreover, they compete with each other by their points of view, particularly now that newspaper "Op Ed" pages, network radio, and local television feature a "spectrum" approach.

In America, conscious ideological thought is mainly left to intellectuals and political activists. Journalists are neither; nor do they have much contact with ideologists and their publications. As a result, most journalists have only a cursory acquaintance with the ideological debates in which activists and intellectuals engage. Although the news constantly touches on ideological issues of moment, journalists are, for the most part, not even aware of this, as I was surprised to discover when I first began my fieldwork. The few American journalists with ideological concerns either work for journals of opinion, the papers and magazines of political parties that stress ideology, or here and there serve as advocacy journalists.

The dearth of ideologically inclined journalists reflects the general dearth of ideologists in America; as many observers have pointed out, America's economic and political structures have thus far not created conditions to encourage the plethora of ideological thought and politics found in Europe. Nor are the news media, including those I studied, likely to attract people with ideological interests. As far as I could tell, few apply for jobs there either because they do not want to work there, their opinions being too far to the right or left of the opinions expressed in the national media, or because they do not expect to be hired. However, even people with conscious centrist ideologies are absent.

More important, ideologists are not wanted by the news media, for most journalists believe ideology to be an obstacle to story selection and production. They see ideologists, rightly or wrongly, as doctrinaire people with axes to grind, and therefore committed to choosing and reporting stories which would advance their ideological interests. While magazine journalists would have liked them around to enliven office discussions, they and their colleagues in television considered them to be inflexible and incapable of applying the source and suitability considerations, especially balance. They would, it is felt, continually pursue the same kinds of stories and sources, which would, among other things, produce boring news. Such news might attract other ideologists, but they constitute only a tiny part of the audience. In addition, ideologists would impair efficiency in story production. "I wouldn't hire a Goldwaterite," a senior editor explained to me in the 1960s. "It would be too much work to argue with him and edit him." But, of course, ultraconservatives (and socialists) would consume precious time and energy only because their political values diverge from the enduring ones.

The view of ideology as rigid doctrine is complemented by the journalists' definition of ideology which, although hardly unique to the profession, identifies ideology with political values at the extreme ends of the political spectrum. In their view, ideology is to be found among the "extremists" of the Far Right and Left rather than among liberals, conservatives, and moderates. However, liberal and conservative groups which support principles rather than explicit economic or political interests, and are therefore viewed as reluctant to compromise in the pursuit of votes or government funds, are also defined as ideological. As I suggested in Chapter 2, the news is suspect about highly principled politicians, and so are journalists.

Nevertheless, ideology is primarily associated with extremism; and while journalists make this association without much deliberation, it also provides a useful defense against outside political pressure, for it automatically excludes political values which, if they entered the news, could generate protest from parts of the audience, management, advertisers, and the government. At the same time, the journalists' definition of ideology is self-serving, if not intentionally so, for it blinds them to the fact that they also have ideologies, even if these are largely unconscious.

Recruitment and the Exclusion of Ideology

Ironically, hiring procedures do not consciously exclude people whom journalists would label "ideologists," for news organizations try to ignore ideology altogether. I studied these procedures more closely at the magazines than at the networks, but both media hire people mainly on the basis of journalistic skill. Other factors are taken into account, notably the amount, type, and quality of college training, and in recent years, race and sex. Editors and personnel officers, as well as recently hired journalists, indicated that values, political or other, were never discussed in job interviews.

Since job applicants must submit samples of previous writing, those who worked solely for ideological publications could have been turned down quietly on other grounds, and perhaps they were. I know of one radical journalist who applied for a network position during the 1960s. He was rejected on the advice of network lawyers because he was facing federal indictment for an illegal trip to a Communist country, but this decision was made over the protest of a news executive—or so he was told—who evidently wanted a radical on the staff. Conversely, at the same time, the presence, at both magazines, of house radicals, as well as other journalists whose portfolios included contributions to radical publications, suggests that ideological screening did not take place regularly.

Although top editors and producers agreed, virtually without exception, that if they had the choice, they would not hire ideologically committed journalists, they were not prepared to delve into the political values of either applicants or colleagues, insisting that such values were irrelevant to the journalistic task. Almost all claimed ignorance of the political values held by colleagues (even those with whom they had worked for years) other than writers whose work required toning down. Nor were they playing dumb; journalists do not ask each other such questions, since values are expected to remain at home. At *Time,* one ultraconservative writer was toned down for years without either him or his editor ever discussing the matter.

Ideological screening is avoided because it implies doubt about the ability of professionals to be objective; it is also unnecessary, for the conformity pressures described in Chapter 3 have the same result. In the end, they drive out ideologists as well as other nonconformists.[16]

The dynamics of these pressures are illustrated by the fate of the house radicals.

House Radicals and House Conservatives

During the late 1960s, both *Time* and *Newsweek* hired a small number of young people of vaguely Marxist bent who were known as house radicals; during my 1975 fieldwork, I found several journalists who were then identified as house conservatives, although most had already been on staff since the 1960s. By nonjournalistic standards, they were not really ideologists, but they were sufficiently interested in political values and sufficiently extreme in their values to be so perceived by their colleagues.

The house radicals worked as reporters or researchers, and had been hired in part to keep the magazines informed about the anti-war movement, much as black reporters had been hired to report on the ghettos when they became newsworthy. The house conservatives were usually writers or editors. Both represented their position in office discussions but also served two important latent functions. By being publicly identified as ideologists, they enabled the other journalists to feel they were free of ideology, and therefore objective. Also, they defined boundaries; in the 1960s, the house radicals stopped their colleagues from going too far to the left in their opinions; in the 1970s, the house conservatives, who had not been so labeled in the sixties, established a point beyond which their colleagues would be too conservative. In fact, one house conservative actually agreed with a number of liberal positions; but because he served as a boundary marker, his colleagues attributed opinions to him which he did not hold.

The house radicals did not remain long at the magazines. Although they had the requisite journalistic skills and were not judged to be prima donnas, they did not fit in. The nonconformity to which their colleagues objected had less to do with politics than lifestyles; they were teased and criticized for their informal dress, sexual attitudes (and alleged practices), and alleged or actual drug (marijuana) use, all of which were, in the late sixties, still disapproved. Even so, the house radicals were more bothered by the political differences; they complained primarily about their inability to participate freely in office discussions or to speak their minds without feeling out of place.[17] In addition, the radicals were uncomfortable about working in the Establishment. They were pleased that they could obtain media visibility for their activist friends, but they felt guilty about their handsome salaries and expense accounts, and about "selling out" instead of being activists themselves.[18]

Had they stayed, conformity pressure might have slackened, because their lifestyle became more acceptable in the years that followed. But political and other differences would have remained, and the inability to conform leads to isolation. Most black journalists who arrived at about the same time but were not deviant in lifestyle left for much the same reason: they could neither persuade editors that news about the black community was newsworthy nor could they find anyone with whom to discuss their interests in the culture and politics of the black community.[19]

The house conservatives have remained, however. Being writers and older, they had more power and status than the radicals, and could better handle disagreements. Moreover, resembling their middle-aged colleagues in lifestyle, they were readily accepted, even if some younger journalists thought them square. They also fit in more easily politically, for the magazines I studied could live with the values of the house conservatives but not with those of the radicals.[20]

Ideological Editing

The lack of attention to ideology and the dearth of ideologically inclined journalists combine to minimize ideological judgments, either in story selection or production. Of course, source and suitability considerations, notably importance judgments and the enduring values within them, have already established ideological boundaries, and the perception of ideology as a form of extremism reinforces these. Consequently, during my fieldwork, I observed the direct entry of ideology into story selection only once: a *Time* story about how the Spanish Communists continued to function during the Franco era was killed because "it made the Communists look too good." Perhaps other stories were left out on ideological grounds in foreign sections, which I did not observe regularly, but none were killed in the domestic sections for this reason. This was also true at the networks.

Ideological editing during story production is also rare. The house radicals did no writing, and thus presented no editing problems. On the other hand, several conservatives prized for their writing skills were often assigned major stories, even though the editors knew them to hold "strong" opinions on some issues. Experience had taught them to keep their personal values out of stories; when they did not, their work was toned down.

The editors, used to the idiosyncrasies of creative people, treat ideological interests as only another, and not very troublesome, idiosyncrasy. As one senior editor explained: "I have one writer who's a bit of a cold warrior, and another who is a conventional Harvard liberal [his term for left-liberal]; but ideological problems rarely come up, and if they do, I just change a sentence or two." However, that same "Harvard liberal" had already, though perhaps not intentionally, reduced the possibility that problems would come up. He told me that he had once criticized South Korea's economy as being based on "the exploitation of cheap labor," but he had actually written that "rapid economic growth had exacted a high social cost. . . . It is based in part on very cheap labor." Later he said that he had never thought of using the phrase he mentioned to me, assuming that "the readers could figure it out for themselves."

Conservative senior editors have more autonomy by virtue of their rank. *Newsweek*'s foreign section was, for a time, edited by a house conservative; the top editor did not interfere because he was more interested in domestic news and because the Cold War was still sufficiently hot to justify the section's fervent anti-communism. However, when the foreign editor wrote an article strongly supporting the Vietnam War in 1968, his opinions were toned down. Another conservative editor, in the back of the book, often fought with his writers; and periodically, the top editors softened the positions he had taken in editing the work of his writers. At *Time,* Henry Luce had appointed a conservative managing editor in the early 1960s; as a result, those senior editors who were less conservative frequently argued with him and sometimes were able to tone him down—although they would not have put it that way.[21]

The unwritten rule is that conclusions or opinions which are deemed to be ideological can survive if they are supported by evidence. During the Vietnam War, television reporters on the scene of a fruitless battle or a search-and-destroy mission resulting in large numbers of civilian casualties could end their stories with critical comments about the war without anyone questioning them. In 1975, a senior NBC reporter sent in a film that favorably reported Castro's domestic economic policies; while one New York producer objected to the reporter's conclusion, the top producer ruled that the reporter had provided sufficient evidence to justify it, and the film was shown without change. The reporter, being a senior journalist who had long covered Central and Latin America, and was trusted for being objective, had a free hand in choosing what to film; but needless to say, favorable stories about a socialist economy are rarely assigned or self-assigned. What is newsworthy about socialist countries is the absence of civil liberties, and the same reporter's first film from Cuba had dealt at length with political repression.

The magazines also house a few invisible ideologists, who are not seen as having ideological interests. Researchers or reporters, they actually are more successful than writers in occasionally getting their point of view into print because they deal in facts rather than in ideas. Moreover, often they alone see the ideological significance of these facts. Once a researcher added an uncomplimentary fact about the CIA to a story about that agency; and although the editor deleted it, the researcher was not sure whether it was the ideological point to which he objected or whether he merely wanted to shorten the story. The researcher considered arguing with the editor, but inasmuch as too much disagreement with superiors types people as "cranks," she decided to save her scarce political capital for an issue about which she felt more strongly.

Value Inclusion

In Chapter 2, I suggested that empirical disciplines must have concepts through which facts can be grasped, and that the concepts themselves incorporate assumptions or judgments about external reality which cannot be tested. Also, no empirical discipline ever has the time or resources to universally apply its methodology, so that many factual statements are actually reality judgments.

In addition, empirical disciplines concerned with their own nation and society contain values, if only in what they choose to study and to ignore. Empiricists can be detached, of course, setting aside conscious personal values; and they can be reflexive, aware of the values they are unable or unwilling to set aside. But journalists cannot write or film some stories without expressing some values; and these take the form of conscious opinions, unconscious opinions, reality judgments (which are sometimes preference statements), and above all, the enduring values.

The Enduring Values

The values that enter the news regularly and most often are the enduring values (see Chapter 2, pp. 42–64). They are included unconsciously, as I argued previously, because they are built into importance judgments; as a result, they do not conflict with objectivity—in fact, they make it possible. Being part of news judgment, the enduring values are those of journalism rather than of journalists; consequently, journalists can feel detached and need not bring in their personal values.

The values are enduring in large part because the basic considerations that underlie news judgment do not change significantly over time—or, at least, have not changed over the last several decades. But not all enduring values are applied at any given moment, for they enter as subjective reactions to available news; and if such news is not available, the values become dormant. When American politics functions according to the dictates of altruistic democracy, this enduring value is not violated, and there is no story to report.

Nor are the enduring values uniformly shared by journalism as a profession. In addition, because they are unconscious values, they are interpreted somewhat differently by every news organization and, insofar as journalists have individual autonomy, by every journalist.

The enduring values are, needless to say, political values, and not all journalists or news media hold the values I found at the networks and magazines I studied. The journals of opinion, for example, earn their living and serve their audience by developing explicit political viewpoints and taking stands on many issues of the day. Consequently, they attract journalists who have developed explicit political values, but even these journalists apply some of the enduring values. They also seek to expose incompetent or dishonest leaders: journals of the Left emphasize moral disorder among business leaders, while those of the Right concentrate on public officials in the liberal wings of the Republican or Democratic party. Even Marxist publications, which argue that moral disorder inheres in the economic and political structures of capitalist society, nevertheless write about moral and other deficiencies of individual economic and political leaders. In that sense, at least, they, too, are under the sway of the enduring values.

Conscious Opinions—Taking Stands

The newsmagazines compete with other news media partly by taking stands. They express opinions, which are topical or story-specific, but these rarely become permanent enough to be called values. True, *Time* still aims to speak with a single voice, but no one examines whether all stands are consistent. Indeed, consistency is sought largely through what both magazines call their "voice" or "attitude." A *Newsweek* senior editor once described his magazine's attitude as that of a "well-educated, decent liberal, in the sense of being an open-minded, fair person, but also one who is bemused and ironic."

Most magazine stands are formulated by individual writers, but they know that they represent the top editor and act accordingly, although sometimes they express their own opinions, expecting the top editor to change them. On major political and economic issues of the day, the top editor determines the stand, sometimes reviewing it with his superiors; occasionally, executives formulate the firm's opinion. As long as Henry Luce was editor-in-chief of Time, Inc., *Time*'s stands favored Republican candidates and causes, even though many *Time* writers were Democrats. Until the early 1960s, *Newsweek*'s opinions resembled *Time*'s; but when Philip and Katharine Graham purchased the magazine, it at once began to take more liberal stands.

Television does not take explicit stands, but it does express opinions. One top producer explained: "I don't want to come out with editorial positions . . . but every night we are saying things. I don't believe in total objectivity." However, evening news programs do not offer a single or consistent voice. Commentators are free to state their own opinions; and anchorpersons can, as autonomous stars, say whatever they want, even when there is protest from local stations affiliated with the network (see Chapter 8). In the 1960s, *NBC News* was anchored by Chet Huntley and David Brinkley. On days when Huntley wrote the major war story, the program was apt to be hawkish, since he wholeheartedly supported the war effort; when the assignment fell to Brinkley, however, the war news often reflected doubt about the war, not because Brinkley was a dove, but because he was (and is) skeptical about all activities undertaken by Big Government.[22]

Even so, commentators, anchorpersons, or top editors and producers do not always take personal stands. They perceive themselves as public figures, and their stands are thus personal interpretations of public stands. An anchorman indicated that while he stated opinions on the air, he limited himself to "only those already held by others"; and Eric Severaid, the recently retired *CBS News* commentator, was often disparaged as "Severalsides" for this reason.

Individual positions are also mediated by audience concerns. A top producer of the 1960s, discussing his program's stand on black power, said: "It's a national audience and it's national subjects we are dealing with, and we can't simply say black power is good. Even if you think it is in Atlanta, you are not sure it is good in Chicago. We've said the opposite quite mildly, that black power is perhaps not quite good." A top editor suggested that his stands were less his own than "a response to the public mood," which he determined from discussions with his senior colleagues and from his reading of other news media. But he also indicated that even his own mood depended "on what I feel as a customer or reader"; he was thus shaping his individual opinions by his role as an audience representative.

Nevertheless, journalists who worked for him often perceived his stands as impositions of his own personal values, and undoubtedly they were correct insofar as, ultimately, *he* determined what he took to be either the public mood or his own feelings as a reader. Likewise, the top producer who took a stand against black power was obviously not concerned that the audience in Atlanta or Chicago might feel differently.

Actually, most of the opinions are derived from the enduring values. Opinions about individual politicians stem from the expectations of political behavior that inhere in the journalistic conception of altruistic democracy. Even if the public mood is favorable to national health insurance, journalistic opinion is not likely to stray too far from the dictates of responsible capitalism. The stand against black power could have been predicted from the journalistic endorsement of racial integration; equally important, the militancy of black power advocates conflicted with the high value placed on the preservation of social order.

Unconscious Opinions

Still, the vast majority of opinions in the news enter unconsciously, largely through the use of connotative, often pejorative words and phrases (see Chapter 2). When journalists describe participants in civil disturbances as "mobs" or "hordes," when they dourly report a rise in the cost of living, or when they describe adolescent behavior in sardonic tones, they are offering opinions, but they are unaware that they are doing so. These opinions are shared by enough journalists so that they are taken for granted; only when they become controversial do journalists realize that they are opinions, after which they may be abandoned, moderated, or transformed into stands.

Opinion Change

Being story-specific, opinions are subject to change. Journalists however, are reluctant to change conscious stands, fearing they will then be charged with inconsistency, which undermines their credibility.

Consequently, conscious opinions generally change only in the wake of highly visible and traumatic events, for positions can then be altered without loss of credibility. Even so, these events are often the culmination of a series of less visible events which had led journalists to doubt their earlier stands. Perhaps the most significant example in recent times is the change of stands toward the Vietnam War, taken by almost all major news media after the Tet offensive of 1968. I noted earlier that many Saigon reporters had long expressed their doubts that the war could be won, and some news organizations were embroiled in internal conflict over whether to listen to them or to their more senior—and more optimistic—reporters in Washington. The Tet offensive was thus the last straw in a lengthy process of increasing uncertainty, not only about the war, but about the government's honesty in informing journalists about it.[23]

A similar process occurs when opinions about presidents and presidential candidates change. Early doubts about President Carter's political abilities were crystallized by the so-called Lance and Marston affairs. After George McGovern forced Thomas Eagleton to withdraw the day after claiming to be 1000 percent behind his running mate, most journalists described McGovern as just another politician; but the strategies of the McGovern staff at the 1972 Democratic convention had already suggested that the candidate was not above using standard campaign tactics.

When journalistic opinions change in response to highly visible events, the events themselves are made visible by the journalists. Furthermore, most of the journalists who alter their positions are not reacting to the events per se but to the news stories they read or see about them.[24] They participate, therefore, in an essentially intraprofessional process, responding to opinion change among large numbers of peers. Dramatic events are necessary to initiate the process but insufficient to complete it. The early exposure of South Vietnamese dictatorship and corruption by Halberstam and his colleagues did not persuade many journalists that the war was a dubious venture, and several years passed before a critical mass of events and the 1968 Tet offensive convinced them otherwise. In this process, journalists are reacting to the same news as their audience while supplying the very information that impels the change in audience opinion.[25]

Unconscious opinions also change with highly visible events, but equally often, they become conscious and may then be altered in response to peer or public criticism. I reported earlier that male magazine journalists consciously reduced their use of sexist terminology after protests from women colleagues, while unconscious racism began to be excised after black criticism of the news media. Some journalists stopped describing the North Vietnamese as the enemy when peers commented on the practice in professional journals, but these commentators were in turn responding to the criticism of the news media by anti-war protesters, and perhaps even more so to the widespread reappraisal of the war reportage after the Tet offensive.

Reality Judgments

Values enter the news most pervasively in the form of reality judgments, the assumptions about external reality associated with the concepts which journalists use to grasp it.[26] These are innumerable; and rather than being preference statements, most are assumptions built into the considerations that journalists apply. When journalists must decide what is new, they must also make assumptions about what is old and therefore no longer newsworthy; when they report what is wrong or abnormal, they must also decide what is normal. If they favor the old or the new, and if they believe that what is normal should be normal, reality judgments then become preference statements.

In any case, journalists cannot exercise news judgment without a composite of nation, society, and national and social institutions in their collective heads, and this picture is an aggregate of reality judgments. When journalists perceive California as the fountainhead of bizarre new fads; look at adolescents as exotic; or, at the magazines, universalize the lifestyles of upper-middle-class Americans and project them onto the entire population, they are making reality judgments. In so doing, they cannot leave room for the reality judgments that, for example, poor people have about America; nor do they ask, or even think of asking, the kinds of questions about the country that radicals, ultraconservatives, the religiously orthodox, or social scientists ask as a result of their reality judgments.

Many reality judgments are stereotypes, accurate or inaccurate, which journalists borrow from elsewhere because of their availability and familiarity both to the journalists and the audience. As Walter Lippmann pointed out many years ago, the news depends on and reinforces stereotypes. At times it also invents them, although more often than not, the stereotypes journalists create coincide with those invented independently by many other people. The stereotype of adolescents as exotic—and highly libidinous—beings is not, after all, limited to journalists.

Strictly speaking, reality judgments develop apart from preference statements, but even so, they are often interconnected. The interdependence of reality judgments and values, and their effect on story selection are perhaps best illustrated by the initial—and continuing—conception of the Vietnam War. From the very beginning, journalists saw the war as a conflict between America and its allies, and a Communist enemy, from which followed the value judgment to support the American side.

It could be argued—and rightly, I think—that the news media should have perceived the American role in the war as a late chapter in a foreign civil war that had been raging for over a generation, but this conceptualization would have required a reality judgment that American journalists—and Americans generally—could not easily make. Civil wars of the kind fought in Vietnam and other developing countries have not been part of the recent American experience from which reality judgments originate. The American Civil War was too distinctive to serve as a model for Vietnam, and the nostalgic image now held of the Revolutionary War ignores the extent to which it was a guerrilla war somewhat similar to that fought in Vietnam.

Prior to American intervention, journalists might have reported Vietnam as a civil war, but even that reality judgment probably would have been accompanied by a value judgment. For at least fifty years now, the first question many Americans have asked about civil wars has been whether Communists were involved in them, and civil wars with Communist participation have rarely been called civil wars either by public officials or journalists. Most often, they have been seen as instances in the Cold War.

The reality judgments about Vietnam and the values associated with them however, were accompanied by a substantive consideration: that domestic news is always more important than foreign news. This consideration preceded the reality judgment, for it discouraged journalists from paying attention to Southeast Asia before the American involvement—and later, to the nonmilitary aspects of South and North Vietnamese life. Once American troops arrived, Vietnam was classified as domestic news, a decision that made the resulting reality and value judgments almost mandatory.

The Journalistic Paraideology

Taken together, the enduring values, conscious and unconscious opinions, and reality judgments constitute what I defined as paraideology—and distinguished from ideology—in Chapter 2. The paraideology that I saw in the news comes, of course, from the journalists, although it expresses the values of the workplace and the profession more than it does the journalists' personal values.

The journalistic paraideology is not inflexible, but then, neither are ideologies, unless they are forcibly imposed party lines. Conformity pressures encourage paraideological homogeneity; but individual autonomy, as well as the organizational divisions of labor and power, makes for diversity. On the whole, top editors and producers adhere to a politically and culturally more conservative conception of the paraideology, just as they take more conservative stands than other journalists, if only because they must keep in mind potential or actual protest from conservative critics and audience members.

When all is said and done, however, the journalistic paraideology is an ideology, an untested and often untestable set of beliefs. That it is an ideology can be illustrated, if not demonstrated, by the fact that those who adhere to it do not conceive of it as ideology. Like other empiricists working within a dominant paradigm, journalists believe themselves to be objective.

The Origins of Journalistic Values

That journalistic news judgment includes values raises the question whether these values are professional correlates of journalistic expertise or lay values that originate from outside the profession. If journalists apply lay values, however, they are selecting stories not only as professionals but also as citizens; in that case, one can ask whether they should do so and whom they are representing when they act as citizens. Furthermore, if professionals are making lay judgments, their claims to autonomy become a matter of debate. These are questions of news policy, to be discussed in Chapter 10, but they presuppose a prior and empirical question: Where do the values that journalists apply originate?

The Enduring Values and the Progressive Movement

The enduring values are part and parcel of news judgment; but even so, they are not, strictly speaking, professional values. They do not reflect technical expertise; rather, they are ingredients in a vision of the good nation and society. As such, they are also lay values, presumably of lay origin.

At the close of Chapter 2, I proposed that these values resembled turn-of-the-century Progressivism. A detailed historical study may show that the resemblance is coincidental, but there is at least one good reason to believe otherwise, for journalists were an intrinsic part of the Progressive movement. Whether they or citizen reformers "invented" the movement's values is another question; but in any case, I suggest that the enduring values originated in the Progressive movement.

This is not the place to consider the origins of Progressivism itself, but its heyday was concurrent with the era of the muckrakers; and the principal muckrakers—among them Ida Tarbell, Lincoln Steffens, and their editor, S. S. McClure—had considerable contact with, and were active supporters of, the national leaders of the Progressive movement.[27] Journalists themselves were part of the national leadership; Chandler's study showed that thirty-six of the 260 Progressive leaders he identified were editors.[28] In addition, many local journalists participated in movement activities in their cities and states.[29] But perhaps the best illustration of the tie between the Progressive movement and the journalism of the period is given by the late Richard Hofstadter:

> The fundamental critical achievement of American Progressivism was the business of exposure, and journalism was the chief occupational source of its creative writers. It is hardly an exaggeration to say that the Progressive mind was characteristically a journalistic mind, and that its characteristic contribution was that of the socially responsible reporter-reformer.[30]

Why Progressives allied themselves with journalists is not hard to guess. Political movements need to communicate with actual and potential supporters; and the Progressive movement came into being at about the time that the mass-circulation newspaper and magazine became the dominant news media. Many of the Progressives were small-town Americans of upper-class or upper-middle-class status who sought to control what they viewed as the corrosive influences of the urban-industrial society into which the economic changes and the immigrations from Southern and Eastern Europe had delivered them.

A detailed historical study would be necessary to ascertain why journalists allied themselves with the Progressives; but those who did, and many other leading journalists of the time, came from backgrounds similar to those of the Progressives; and perhaps they, too, were disturbed by the changes taking place in America. Incidentally, many of today's journalists still come from these backgrounds. The previously cited study of a national sample of journalists by Johnstone and his associates showed that 49 percent were children of professionals and managers (and thus presumably from upper-middle-class homes), and almost three fourths were either "Anglo-Saxon" or descendants of the "old" German, Irish, and Scandinavian immigration.[31] (These data also apply to the news media I studied, except that many top editors and producers, as well as news executives, are Jewish.[32])

That modern journalism should invoke values from the turn of the century does not suggest that the profession is operating with old-fashioned ideas, for Progressivism is hardly dead. Although no longer a movement, its ideas remain central to many political, social, and cultural reform efforts. More to the point, these ideas continue to be salient for journalists today. The values signify and maintain a proud chapter in American journalism, for during the Progressive period, journalists achieved a level of power and influence in American life they have not held since, except during the years of the Watergate scandals.

Today these values also serve journalism as a profession, giving it a respected social role. Insofar as journalists are defenders of a set of values, they are more than technicians who transmit information from sources to audiences. Contemporary journalists do not, for the most part, see themselves as reformers; but the ones I studied were proud whenever a story resulted in official investigations and in legislative or administrative reform. Then, too, Progressivism was, among other things, a professional movement that aimed to bring experts into politics and government; and its values enhance the professionalism of journalism, particularly since journalists are not yet certain whether they deserve to be called professionals. Also, Progressive ideology sidesteps or cuts across the partisanship of the political parties; it was, and continues to be, attractive to people who, like journalists, regard themselves as political independents.

In addition, the enduring values are shared by other segments of society, especially those public officials who are the journalists' major sources. In fact, the enduring values coincide almost completely with the major themes of political rhetoric, which is also centered on the nation as a unit, advocates much the same kind of capitalism and democracy, pays allegiance to small-town pastoralism, supports individualism and moderation, and preaches order. Political rhetoric is not political action, but then news is also a kind of rhetoric; and journalistic assumptions about the need for leadership are often expressed in the speeches politicians make during election campaigns and at ceremonial occasions.

The audience may not agree with all the opinions expressed in the news, but it is not likely to find fault with the enduring values. Middle Americans, for example, also favor social order, honest leadership, pastoralism, moderatism, and individualism. Not all may have faith in responsible capitalism, but neither are they happy with government welfare policies that add to their taxes. It appears as if the original upper-class and upper-middle-class Progressive vision of America has by now diffused to a larger portion of the population.

At the same time, the enduring values also serve the business interests associated with journalism, be they sponsors or news firms. Progressivism was (and is) not antagonistic to private enterprise per se, and the journalistic vision of responsible capitalism does not diverge sharply from the notion of corporate responsibility which, as overt ideology, is supported by the large corporations themselves. Moreover, the concept of individualism in the enduring values not only legitimizes the desirability of entrepreneurship but also views the shortcomings of private enterprise as "bad apples." As a result, the enduring values are blind to possible structural faults within the system, which in turn reduces the likelihood of stories that question the legitimacy of the present economic order.

Values and Working Conditions

The enduring values are values of the journalists' workplace; consequently, their origins must also be sought in the conditions under which journalists work. Journalists themselves argue that values which enter their work are consequences of professional practices and thus value implications rather than values in their own right. Journalists emphasize the president, so the argument goes, because he is a productive and efficient source of news, not because they value leadership; they report social disorder because they are expected to deliver dramatic news, not because they value order; and they stress moderation because, being outsiders who come into contact with diverse sources, they are encouraged to be "open-minded." In a 1970 speech, John Chancellor pointed out:

> Reporters, I think, probably have . . . a bias toward pragmatism and common sense. Reporters are people—and they tend to appreciate . . . competent and honest men; they tend to be hard on scoundrels and buffoons. They learn—firsthand—that things must be done (in effort and money) to solve problems, and that gets them in trouble with the conservatives. They learn—firsthand, in the wars and the riots—that violence and radicalism seldom solve anything, and that gets them in trouble with the new left. Most reporters are members of the extreme center—I am —and it's a difficult place to be these days. . . . If the people in this country could spend their days the way reporters spend theirs, they would turn out the way reporters do: somewhat suspicious of oratory; a bit skeptical of grand plans; committed to rational programs to solve problems; against violence and war; and very worried about the future of the country.[33]

Suspicion of oratory and grand plans, and a commitment to rational programs are not, however, the only possible reactions reporters could have to their work. Journalists might conclude that the slow, incremental change in government is irrational, and they could observe that "violence and radicalism" sometimes force government to act. The appreciation of "competent and honest men," and the hardness toward "scoundrels and buffoons" is Chancellor's personal statement of a major enduring value.

Journalists *do* value the president as a productive and efficient source, and they *do* report social disorder as dramatic news. But that is only part of the answer, for all regular sources become productive and efficient, and journalists could choose other regular sources. If enduring values were not involved, disorder stories could side with the participants in disorder rather than with the restorers of order. While story selection and production cannot be explained by the enduring values alone, neither can these values be left out of the explanation. Work requirements push journalists in certain directions, but their values pull them along as well.

Nevertheless, some values may stem directly from working conditions. For example, the high value placed on civil liberties is almost an instrumental necessity, since journalistic autonomy depends on freedom of the press. Journalistic anti-communism may have a similar basis, at least in part, since Communist journalists lack what American professionals define as autonomy.

Furthermore, it is possible that the journalists' antipathy to bureaucracy does not derive solely from the enduring values but also from the journalists' position as unwilling members of bureaucratic organizations, although they are not alone, either among professionals or Americans generally, in disliking bureaucracy. The journalistic concern with responsible leadership, likewise, may stem from the central role which top editors, producers, and executives play in the working lives and morale of journalists.

Even the journalists' advocacy of individualism and moderatism may relate to working conditions. Group journalism and conformity pressures notwithstanding, news organizations reward the productive individualist; and for many journalists, the self-employed freelance writer—the individual par excellence—continues to be a career ideal, even if it can rarely be achieved. Moderatism is probably a defensive value, inasmuch as journalists subject to criticism are safest near the center. During the 1960s, journalists often said that if they received critical mail both from "Nazis" and "Communists," they saw no need to worry about the stands they were taking. However, moderatism is work-related in yet another way, for journalists who drink heavily or exhaust their energies off the job in other ways cannot maintain the work pace for long.[34] The hard-drinking journalist is a venerable stereotype, but he or she was rarely in evidence at the news media I studied.

The work environment also affects reality judgments, for these judgments derive partly from the small aggregate of sources from whom journalists obtain most of their news. Even when their work places them in an adversary role vis-à-vis public officials, they are still similar in social, economic, cultural, and other background characteristics. They know less about people different from them, and often their information about them comes from secondhand sources. Lacking contact with working-class sources, for example, the journalists' conception of them was influenced by the hard hats who made news during the Vietnam War, and by Archie Bunker, a fictional working-class character developed by upper-middle-class professionals in Hollywood.

Values and Personal Experience

Some reality judgments and values also come from personal experience and background; and from the lifestyles journalists experienced as children, and now as adults, in their own families and communities. The reality judgments they use to determine newsworthy abnormalities generally reflect their own expectations of what constitutes normal parent, neighbor, friend, club member, churchgoer, and other everyday behavior. However, their definition of normality is taken, more often than not, from what they perceive as normal in the upper middle-class. For example, in the last few years, the journalists' perception of the bright side of city life has centered on "urban revitalization," for the journalists are more aware of affluent young professionals (now sometimes called gentrifiers) who restore old inner-city houses than of the remaining 99 percent of urban homeowners. These experiences, frequently translated into story ideas, help explain why the magazines universalize upper-middle-class lifestyles.

But personal experience and background do not explain the enduring values. As I noted before, these values are built into news judgment, and journalists do not have to accept them personally. Perhaps the values they leave at home, which I did not study intensively, differ from the enduring values; but I spent enough time with people in informal conversation to be convinced that this is not the case. In any event, the journalists have no difficulty in going along with the enduring values.[35]

Nor is there any reason why they should disagree with these values, for most journalists are members of the upper-middle-class, middle-aged social order I sketched in Chapter 2. By all the conventional indicators, national journalists are solidly upper-middle-class. All but a small handful of older men and women are college graduates, and many have postgraduate degrees. Newsmagazine journalists still are educated primarily at the Ivy League schools or equivalent private universities in other parts of the country; even most television journalists, some of whom grew up in lower-middle-class homes, have attended "quality" schools.[36]

Journalism was once a poorly paid profession, but now most national journalists are comfortably off. In 1975, reporters and writers, both at the magazines and the networks, were earning between $25,000 and $40,000, depending on seniority, although some network correspondents received considerably more. Senior editors, producers, and bureau chiefs in both media were paid salaries ranging from $30,000 to $50,000 or more; top editors and producers were estimated to earn between $75,000 and $120,000; and anchorpersons, between $300,000 and $400,000. Even magazine researchers, whose starting salaries were then set by the Newspaper Guild at about $12,500, were often earning closer to $20,000 after a few years. These figures do not include either on-air fees paid to television reporters or year-end bonuses and stock options, which benefit mainly the higher-echelon journalists.[37]

Most national journalists, however, are not rich; and in 1975, they were hard-pressed by inflation. Nor do they feel rich, but this stems partly from work-related reasons. As reporters or party guests, many are occasional visitors into the world of the affluent and have seen the public lifestyles of the economically and politically powerful. Equally important, perhaps because their work requires constant attention to novelty, many journalists have an unusually lively interest in the latest fashions, entertainment, and other appurtenances of the "good life." Large numbers live in the fashionable suburbs around, or the more fashionable neighborhoods in, New York City; and by the time they reach their forties, many own weekend or summer homes on Long Island, "the Cape," or elsewhere. Generous expense accounts also expose even people who live modestly to "high living." Perhaps irregular schedules and limited leisure time encourage a compensatory interest in fashionable goods and places; on the other hand, affluent academics and other professionals are also active consumers, although their standards of what is "fashionable" may differ.

National journalists, being at the top of their professional heap, have been upwardly mobile almost by definition. Most grew up in middle-class, or at the magazines, upper-middle-class, homes; and their mobility has often been geographic as well as socioeconomic. Television anchorpersons and reporters aspiring to their jobs in the future come from small towns in the Midwest and the South, whereas most other journalists come from larger cities, and the younger ones, from the surrounding suburbs. Like many professionals now working in New York, they left home to attend a college with a national reputation, and began their careers in smaller cities. Their mobility has left them with considerable empathy for the upwardly mobile, as well as with some nostalgia for their hometowns. Still, even those who grew up in large cities or in New York are not particularly cosmopolitan in their tastes or "urbane" in lifestyle; in any case, whatever their origins, they have no difficulty accepting the small-town pastoralism of the enduring values.

Relatively few journalists came from working-class homes, and those who did lost touch with their origins long ago. However, working-class people are found in the news media, but they work as disseminators. Their values and opinions are often at odds with those of the journalists; and although they express them vocally, they do not participate in editorial decisions.

Journalists from upper-class homes can be found, with a few exceptions, only at the newsmagazines. Some top and senior editors, as well as writers and reporters, are from socially, economically, or politically influential families (including Social Register ones); and daughters from such families sometimes work as researchers after college and before marriage, sprinkling famous names through the magazines' mastheads.

Upper-class status is not an obstacle, especially at the executive level, but the newsmagazines make fun of the very rich as often as do the television news programs. Being in a minority, upper-class colleagues are also laughed at—but behind their backs. They may set a style, after hours, to which others can aspire; but in the office, they are apt to hide their origins. A magazine reporter working on an article about the affluent discovered that colleagues of rich parentage were unwilling to help her with information; similarly, children of the politically or otherwise famous will not use their relatives as sources. At the networks, one seldom finds people from prestigious or famous families; for instance, the production assistants, who are roughly equivalent in rank to magazine researchers, are women who come largely from working-class "ethnic" backgrounds.

Personal Political Values

Being upper-middle-class does not automatically lead to the adoption of upper-middle-class values, but the political values people expressed or implied in informal discussion and in private interviews were consistent with the enduring values. Journalists generally describe themselves as liberals, but liberalism is a synonym for being independent, open-minded, or both. "I am a classic liberal in the ability to see both sides," one anchorman pointed out. "I don't have a party affiliation, but I am not sure if I would even if I were not in the news business."

Johnstone and his associates, reporting on a subsample of journalists in "prominent" publications (which included the networks, newsmagazines, and the more prestigious daily papers), found that 40 percent described themselves as "a little to the left"; 30 percent, "middle of the road"; and 12 percent, "pretty far to the left." Conversely, 17 percent placed themselves "a little" or "pretty far" to the right.[38] The study left it up to the journalists to define the positions on the spectrum; but while one news-media critic has used these data to conclude that the journalists were "leftists," my fieldwork suggests the few who were "pretty far to the left" agreed at most with the left-liberal positions of the Americans for Democratic Action.[39]

My impressionistic data support the findings of the national study.

Some of the people I observed were conservatives, a few were ultraconservatives, and a handful (not counting the house radicals of the 1960s) could be considered democratic socialists; however, the vast majority were independents or liberals. Perhaps the most accurate portrait came from a top producer who, talking about racial integration, said: "We tend to be liberal on civil rights, though not necessarily if a Negro moves next door." But then, journalists are not alone in taking a more liberal position in general than on specific issues. In the end, most of the people I studied could be classified as right-liberals and left-conservatives; they occupy the same positions on the ideological spectrum which I ascribed to the enduring values in Chapter 2. But people in the higher ranks who determine which stands will be taken on major issues are somewhat more conservative.

The conventional ideological spectrum is not always an accurate representation of people's values, however, partly because it does not take into account class position. In America, liberalism is often associated with upper-middle-class values; and positions taken by upper-middle-class people on "ecology," "consumerism," marijuana use, and abortion are defined as liberal. On "social" issues, many of the journalists were clearly liberal, even while they were, at the same time, less interested in, or more conservative on, economic issues or government welfare policies. By the same token, they often favored politicians with upper-middle-class constituencies or backgrounds, some of whom have also been automatically identified as liberal. During the 1950s, I was told, many magazine journalists sided with Adlai Stevenson, and later with John Kennedy, rather than with the populist Estes Kefauver. In 1968, when, for a brief period, liberals had a choice between Eugene McCarthy and Robert Kennedy, most liberal journalists favored the former, but at the time Kennedy was courting blue-collar voters.

If journalists are neither quite as liberal, especially on economic issues, as their critics on the Right believe them to be, or as conservative as critics on the Left think, they are, on the whole, more liberal than their superiors and their colleagues in the business departments, as well as their sponsors and advertisers. Whether they are more liberal than the American people as a whole is doubtful, for while a plurality of people now describe themselves as conservatives when responding to pollsters, they concurrently take quite liberal positions on many economic issues.[40] However, journalists are more liberal than their vocal audience, inasmuch as the people who write letters of criticism are predominantly conservative (see Chapter 7), which helps explain why journalists are frequently under attack.

Lay Values and the News

News judgment, then, is composed to some extent of lay values and lay reality judgments. Like other professionals, journalists practice an expertise that is not and cannot be purely professional. But the lay components of news judgment come from the larger nation and society to which journalists also belong. Even if they conceive of themselves as outsiders, journalists, both as professionals and laypersons, react to the news with the same attitudes and values as some, if not all, members of their audience.

This is not to say, however, that lay values—or the upper-middle-class status—of most journalists can explain the shape of the news, or that the news would be different if other people selected and produced it. True, if journalists were henceforth recruited solely from the working class, they would see America from a different vantage point and would therefore begin with other reality judgments. Bringing with them other lay values, they might also be skeptical of some enduring ones. But they would still have to apply the considerations I described in earlier chapters. In the process, some would have difficulty communicating and establishing rapport with present regular sources, few of whom come from the working class or are sympathetic to its values. They could, I suppose, find more compatible sources; but as I suggest in Chapter 9, present sources might use their power to remain sources. In that case, journalists would have to adapt to these sources. Even if the new journalists were blue-collar conservatives, they would have cultural and other conflicts with their superiors; and while working-class news executives could be imagined, corporate executives are not likely to be recruited from lowly origins.

But barring larger economic and political change in America, journalists could not be recruited from the working class in the first place unless middle-class youngsters decided against entering the profession. Even then, the present educational and credentialist prerequisites for journalistic employment would recruit upwardly mobile, working-class youngsters likely to have shed many of their working-class values and reality judgments. The prerequisites could themselves by altered, however, but not without currently inconceivable occupational and educational transformations. And what applies to hypothetical working-class journalists would apply equally to recruits from other backgrounds or with other political values. In the last analysis, the lay ingredients in news judgment make a difference, but the current ingredients are not there by accident.

═ 7 ═

Profits and Audiences

Since national news is produced commercially, one might imagine that story selectors are under constant pressure to choose news which will attract the most profitable audience. In practice, however, they are not. In the news media I studied, as in most others, editorial and business departments operate independently of each other. Business-department officials would like to influence editorial decisions in order to increase audience size and attract advertisers, but they can only make proposals. Although some feel that journalists do not understand what the audience wants, they also know that they cannot interfere.

Corporate management, which oversees both departments, can of course persuade the journalists to take heed of the economic well-being of the firm, but they have not interfered either. True, the news programs and magazines I studied were in good economic health, but Friedrich's account of the final days of the *Saturday Evening Post* suggests that even when that magazine was going under, the editors remained free from business-department intervention.[1]

Commercial Considerations

Nevertheless, story selectors must attend to some commercial and audience considerations. I distinguish between the two, for commercial considerations are intended to reduce the costs of story selection and production, or to increase revenue from the audience and/or advertisers. Audience considerations, on the other hand, exist to hold the present audience; and while they also have commercial consequences, journalists apply audience considerations for other reasons, as I suggest below. Although journalists pay little direct attention to the audience, they pay even less to costs and profits.

Cost Cutting

Top producers and editors, unlike the rest of their staffs, are expected to consider the cost of producing the news, inasmuch as they must live within budgets not entirely of their own making. During the stagflation of the early 1970s, most news firms tightened their belts, but story selection and production were not visibly affected. Periodic job freezes were instituted; but for the most part, costs were cut by reducing ancillary newsroom services.

The major expenditure items in news budgets are not easily scaled down. Important stories must always be covered, if only because the competition is likely to do so; breaking stories create the greatest havoc on budgets, but again, competitive pressures and organizational pride force the expenditure of additional funds.

The television networks have long been highly profitable ventures, taking advertising, and to a lesser extent, audiences, away from the print media. The evening news programs have also been moneymakers for years; but until recently, the other news programs—and therefore the news divisions themselves—have run in the red. According to *Variety,* however, the three network news divisions showed a 1 percent profit in 1975 and 1976, after having lost 15 percent in 1972.[2] The dramatic change is largely attributed to CBS's *60 Minutes,* the first news program to compete successfully with entertainment programs during prime-time hours.

By 1978, ABC and NBC had also scheduled weekly "newsmagazines" in the hope of imitating the success of *60 Minutes.* Hour-long news documentaries that are costly to produce but attract comparatively small audiences are still being made as well, but the kind that arouse controversy and scare away sponsors have been rarer in the 1970s than in the 1960s, although the current decade has also generated less controversial news. However, the production units that make the longer documentaries have been reduced in size, and recent predictions about the eventual demise of these documentaries may someday turn out to have been correct.

News specials, which are usually half-hour reports on a breaking story, are not likely to disappear, but they are cheaper to produce than documentaries, since the stories are already being covered for the evening news programs. Also, the specials are almost always shown late in the evening, after the end of prime time. Live news-specials have always been rare, and only the president of the United States is able to persuade the networks to preempt profitable daytime or evening programs on a regular basis.[3]

The newsmagazines have also been profitable. In 1975, *Newsweek* had its best year ever, according to Diamond, earning about $12 million on revenues of about $128 million, while *Time* earned "well over 10 million dollars" on revenues of about $157 million.[4] Even so, the magazines appear to have reacted more to the stagflation of the early 1970s than the networks.[5]

Both magazines, however, have sought economy in dissemination rather than in story selection and production—for example, by computerizing printing. Back-of-the-book deadlines have also been advanced so as to prevent the need for overtime payments to disseminators, and *Time* instituted prekilling partly for reasons of cost. Earlier deadlines have some effect on the news, since back-of-the-book stories can no longer be quite as up-to-date as before. The front of the book remains exempt, however. In 1975, when a top editor sent a reporter and photographer on an expensive trip for a minor foreign story, and I asked whether he had to worry about exceeding the budget, he said that "if I had to think about money all the time, I'd be an accountant, not an editor." But post-deadline cover changes are not made quite as often as in the past. *Time* has also cut its editorial staff: in March 1969, its masthead listed 261 editors, writers, researchers, and reporters; by March 1978, it showed 201.[6] During the same period, *Newsweek*'s staff grew slightly, from 221 to 234.

Increasing Income

At the networks, revenue can be increased by enlarging the audience, which in turn raises the price sponsors pay for commercials. The magazines are as much concerned with upgrading the "quality" of the readership—its income and purchasing power—as they are with increasing readership size. Added circulation raises advertising revenue, but it also raises the ever higher costs of mailing issues to subscribers. In fact, many magazines have tried to reduce their total circulation, hoping to discourage less affluent readers whom neither advertisers nor journalists want.

In theory, story selectors could alter story choices in order to enlarge or upgrade the audience; they have not done so, however, out of the belief that they should not choose the news on commercial grounds. Most journalists pay little attention to audience size, although top editors and producers are kept informed of the latest figures, and their staffs know generally whether the numbers are rising or falling. People might begin to worry were sharp declines to take place, but so far, the total audience has continued to rise. Simmons's studies indicate that between 1965 and 1975, the combined audiences of the CBS and NBC evening news programs rose from 14.6 million adults to 26.4 million; those of *Newsweek* and *Time,* from 23.4 million to 38.5 million.[7] The NBC program has, however, lagged behind CBS in the ratings since 1967, and *Newsweek* has never quite caught up with *Time* (see Table 6).

Journalists argue that their job is to inform the audience and to make the news sufficiently attractive so that viewers and readers will become informed. They are opposed to resorting to sensationalism and yellow journalism—stories about crime and sex that might attract a larger audience. Network journalists also object to the various format and other changes that have been instituted by local stations in recent years, such as the informal banter among on-air personnel, called happy news. They lash out frequently and publicly, particularly when they speak at network meetings or during campus lecture tours, against what they consider "show business."

Unless they themselves are under great pressure to increase profits, executives are reluctant to incur the wrath of the journalists, in part because they express it publicly. More important, neither the journalists nor the business departments know how to enlarge the audience (no one can even prove that more sensationalism or show business would be effective); and while there is no dearth of theories about how to accomplish this, existing audience research has not proven them. A proven theory would still have to be accepted by the journalists, however, and for reasons to be discussed below, they are wary of research.

The networks have so far used a trial-and-error approach to audience enlargement, but until now, it has not been successful. Although they have concentrated on format changes, viewers seem to choose one network news program over another largely because of anchorperson or channel preference.[8] Network researchers have conducted studies on the popularity of anchorpersons, but their findings are not often implemented. Anchorpersons are too powerful to be fired easily; their departure could make matters worse; and besides, new faces do not necessarily raise the ratings.[9] After Chet Huntley retired, NBC relied on John Chancellor as sole anchorman; the ratings did not improve. Then NBC brought David Brinkley back as co-anchor, but with similar results. ABC's hiring of Barbara Walters made no noticeable difference either, although it engendered considerable, and somewhat sexist, journalistic protest that it constituted an undesirable resort to show business.

Channel preference is even more difficult to alter, for it is actually a mixture of three viewer decisions: (1) habitual preference for one network; (2) an involuntary choice, based on which channel viewers can receive most clearly on their television screens; and (3) a decision to stay with a channel because of preference for the preceding program, a phenomenon called audience flow.[10] The first two reactions are beyond the control of news executives and journalists, but the networks have sought to influence audience flow by altering the local news programs—at least on the five stations they own—which appear just prior to the network news. NBC, for example, overhauled its local news program in New York by extending it to two hours, altering the format, and hiring new anchorpersons in the hope of raising both local and national ratings (the New York audience constituting 10 percent of the total Nielsen sample), but to no avail. The only sure way of increasing the viewing audience is to persuade additional local stations to show a network's news program, but the NBC and CBS newscasts are already carried by virtually all of their affiliates. However, ABC, which has taken some affiliates away from the other networks as a result of its highly successful entertainment programs, is hoping to attract other affiliates by improving its news programs. Indeed, ABC's recent format changes in the evening news program were made largely for this reason. Journalists can make a program more attractive to affiliates, although they do not try to do so, but they themselves have nothing to do with persuading affiliates to carry it.

Newsmagazine editors are no more knowledgeable than their colleagues in television about how to enlarge the audience. Although they suspect that increases in sensational news and gossip might help, many magazine journalists are displeased with the amount of gossip they already print.

However, magazine editors are able to act in two ways that serve their own purposes, while also pleasing business departments. First, because the magazines are as interested in upgrading as in enlarging their audience, their business departments compete feverishly to prove to advertisers that each attracts a younger, more affluent, and better-educated reader: "more upscale," in business jargon. Story selectors participate in this competition, notably in the back of the book, because they themselves prefer an upscale audience. A better-educated reader is easier to write for and requires fewer space-consuming explanations; more important, journalists are themselves upscale, and can thus write and edit for themselves.

They also try, periodically, to discourage "downscale" readers—for example, by omitting detailed explanations in stories which these readers are thought to need—and they hope that risqué stories and "sex covers," which graphically report on erotica or the liberalization of sexual attitudes and behaviors, will anger them sufficiently to cause them to cancel their subscriptions. Nevertheless, the basic demographic makeup of the readership of both magazines has remained remarkably stable over the last fifteen years, despite changes in format and longer stories, as well as the liberalization of *Newsweek*'s voice in the mid-1960s, and *Time*'s a few years later. For example, in 1975, as in 1965, Simmons reported that about 12 percent of the readership of each magazine consisted of people with less than four years of high school education.

A second, and more frequent, opportunity to satisfy business departments occurs in cover selection, for editors would also like to maximize the number of newsstand sales. Newsstand sales constitute only about 5 percent of total paid circulation (the rest comes from subscriptions), but high sales figures please the business department because newsstand sales are more profitable than subscriptions. Top editors are also pleased because newsstand sales also serve as a feedback mechanism to gauge reader reaction. It is assumed that newsstand buyers make their choice on the basis of the story title and the picture they see on the cover; it is also assumed that their decisions are indicators of how subscribers feel about the covers. Although both assumptions are untested, news editors make them in order to obtain signals about what stories interest the readers on a weekly basis. (This judgment is based on comparative sales figures, since top editors know that some cover subjects always sell poorly.) Moreover, strong cover sales boost morale, suggesting that the magazine is being read. "Newsstand sales are signs of vitality," a top editor pointed out. "If they are up, that also means subscribers are paying attention."

Still, opportunities to be commercial—and to beat the rival—by choosing a better-selling cover are few, for importance considerations take precedence. A breaking foreign-news story will therefore make the cover even though editors know that sales will be poor. Importance judgments being what they are, most covers are about bad domestic news, and these rarely sell well either.

Balance is also a prime consideration. While sex covers are always successful and at both magazines hold the newsstand sales records (together with several Watergate covers), top editors choose them only once every three or four years; they are also unwilling to put "pretty girls" on the cover more than once a year. Nor do they know what will sell (other than sex, health, and religion). They always try to estimate newsstand sales figures for the next cover, but they are as often wrong as they are right.[11]

Then, too, top editors are aware that their colleagues and peers will be critical if too many covers are chosen with commercial motives in mind; in fact, writers at both magazines regularly suspected their superiors of "going commercial" even when they made cover choices for other reasons. As a result, the frequency with which top editors go commercial is difficult to judge, for feeling that it is wrong, they are unlikely to admit to it.[12]

Some back-of-the-book journalists, especially in the critical sections, feel an unspoken pressure "to keep things light in order to build circulation," as one book reviewer put it. "But there's no direct pressure; I just feel it because my senior editor isn't 'serious.' " At the same time, however, other reviewers want to keep things light in order to encourage readers to pay attention to articles about the arts.

Still, most journalists can ignore commercial considerations. Nonetheless, they are communicators who need an audience; and while they are reluctant to treat it as a source of income, they must take the audience into account. Before discussing how they do so, however, I want to describe the actual audience.

The News Audience

Determining the number and characteristics of television viewers and magazine readers is a complicated and very expensive undertaking. As a result, the networks and magazines do little audience research on their own, relying instead on commercial research organizations which provide data for a large number of firms. Most of the data to be reported here comes from W. R. Simmons & Associates Research, whose annual studies both of television viewing and magazine reading make it possible to compare the characteristics of viewers and readers, and with data collected by the same methods.[13] I used the 1974–1975 Simmons report so that I could relate the actual audience figures Simmons collected in 1974 to what I learned about the journalists' images of the audience in 1975. Although some of the percentages have changed by a few points in later reports, the basic patterns have remained constant.[14]

My description will ignore most of the methodological complexities involved in gathering audience data, as well as most shortcomings of the available data. Television sponsors, for example, are not interested in old people, so that the age breakdown for viewers, both in Simmons and in the more widely known A. C. Nielsen reports, ends with people "55 and over."

The actual data come from diaries which people fill out and/or from interviews with them; but whatever the method, researchers are, in reality, studying what the audience reports about its viewing or reading habits. Although researchers can discourage respondents from inflating their reports about how much they read or watch, they cannot determine how completely people attend to the news—whether they watch an entire news program or read an entire issue. Some information on regularity of news consumption and attentiveness is available (see below); but Simmons, like others, asks respondents whether they have "looked at" a program or magazine. Consequently, many of the people who are identified as viewers and readers may be watching only segments of a program and reading only portions of a magazine. In magazine studies, audience researchers identify readers rather than subscribers; in fact, the largest number of readers are "pass-alongs," who get the magazine from the subscriber or purchaser, and may read it at home or elsewhere. In 1977, for example, *Time* had 4.3 million subscribers and newsstand buyers, but according to Simmons, it had 21.2 million readers; *Newsweek* had a circulation of 3.0 million but 17.8 million readers.[15]

Viewer and Reader Characteristics

Table 6 (pp. 222–23) presents Simmons data about the numbers and characteristics of the average adult audiences of *Newsweek* and *Time, CBS Evening News* and *NBC Nightly News.*[16] Although there are slight differences in the audiences of each magazine and program, the greater difference is between the magazines and the programs.[17]

Whereas magazines have a somewhat larger male than female readership, television news programs attract slightly more women than men. More important, the magazine audience is fairly equally divided among all age groups, the median being 36 to 38, with a sharp decline at age 65 (when people may have reading difficulties); television, on the other hand, serves an older audience, for the median is well over 50. Scattered evidence from studies of the aged, as well as inferences which can be made from the levels of education and income of viewers, suggest, in fact, that many of the people whom Simmons and Nielsen

TABLE 6: Selected Characteristics of the Adult Audience for Newsmagazines and News Programs in 1974

| | Newsmagazines | | Evening News Programs | |
	Newsweek	Time	CBS	NBC
Total number (000)	19,013	19,488	16,019	10,395
Sex				
Male	58.2	55.5	47.5	46.8
Female	41.8	44.5	52.5	53.2
Age				
18–24	23.4	20.8	8.4	9.2
25–34	24.5	24.0	12.6	14.7
35–44	16.8	17.2	28.3	28.9
45–54	18.2	19.5		
55–64	10.0	11.4	50.7	47.2
65+	7.1	7.1		
Median (years)	36.3	38.0	55.0	53.0
Education				
College graduate	27.9	31.1	28.1	28.3
1–3 years of college	26.1	26.4		
High school graduate	34.3	31.1	31.2	39.3
1–3 years of high school	7.9	7.7	40.8	32.4
Grade school only	3.8	3.7		
Occupation, Men				
Professional, technical	19.6	20.8	24.2	20.1
Managers, administrators, proprietors	17.7	20.4		
Clerical, sales	14.0	12.9	5.9	6.9
Craftsmen, foremen	14.1	10.7	36.1	39.6
Other (blue-collar)	19.9	19.3		
Not employed	14.8	16.0	33.8	33.3
Household income				
$20,000 and over	34.2	36.8	15.3	16.0
$15,000–$19,999	20.2	19.2	14.6	16.1
$10,000–$14,999	20.8	20.6	17.9	18.5
$8,000–$9,999	7.9	7.7	9.6	13.3
$5,000–$7,999	9.1	8.4	42.6	36.1
Under $5,000	7.8	7.4		
Median (dollars)	$16,091	$16,545	$9876	$10,030
"Index of Social Position"				
I: "Upper class"	8.2	10.2		
II: "Upper middle-class"	21.4	22.6	Not available	
III: "Lower middle-class"	24.9	25.1		
IV–V: "Lower class"	45.5	42.0		

	Newsweek	*Time*	CBS	NBC
Race				
White	90.7	91.1	89.8	93.5
Black	7.9	7.4	9.4	6.0
Other	1.4	1.5	0.8	0.5

SOURCE: Simmons reports. See footnote 16.

describe as over 55 are much older. My 1967 study of New York viewers found that 61 percent of the men and 91 percent of the women over 60 watched a network news program nearly every day.[18]

The second major difference among viewers and readers is along class lines, for magazine readers are better-educated, more likely to be employed in prestigious jobs, and more affluent than television viewers. Even so, readers are not quite as upscale as they appear to be, for over 40 percent have not attended college. To be sure, almost twice as many male readers as male viewers function in professional or managerial capacities (although not all of these are necessarily prestigious); at the same time, however, well over 40 percent of all male readers hold clerical, sales, and blue-collar jobs. The percentage is virtually the same among television viewers, but a greater number of them are blue-collar rather than white-collar workers. (Twice as many male viewers as male readers are not employed, however; and since viewers generally are older than readers, many of them are probably retired.[19]) These occupational and educational characteristics are summarized by Simmons' Index of Social Position, originally developed by August B. Hollingshead, the Yale sociologist. The index is computed only for readers, but the plurality of readers falls into what Simmons calls the lower class, now called the working class by most sociologists.

Class differences among readers and viewers are reflected in income data. In 1974, the national median family income was about $13,000. Although this is not quite the same as Simmons' household income, the magazine audience was about $3,000 above the national median; the television audience, about the same amount below it. A plurality of magazine households had incomes of over $20,000 that year (and 20 percent were earning $25,000 and more), whereas the largest group of television households earned less than $8,000. Still, more than 15 percent of magazine readers were in the same income bracket; and of readers over 55, about a third were living on $8,000 or less.[20] Moreover, the median income from individual jobs was below the median household income: about $11,000 for all adult readers, and $13,000 for all male readers.[21] The two income medians differ partly because of multiple earners and partly because many adult readers have other sources of income: a third derive additional income from stocks and bonds; a fifth, from real estate. But almost a quarter were drawing on social security, unemployment, and welfare payments.[22]

Statistical data do not lend themselves to the development of audience profiles; but as Table 6 and other figures I have cited suggest, readers and viewers can be divided into three categories: 1) affluent, well-educated professionals, technicians, and managers; 2) median and moderate income, high school educated white-collar and blue-collar workers—or Middle Americans; and 3) poorer (but not poverty-stricken), less well educated older people, many of them no longer working. All three types are represented in both media, but the first two types are dominant in the magazine audience. The magazines also attract a numerically small but otherwise significant audience from the national elite: a study of American business, political, media, and other leaders found that *Time* and *Newsweek* were the magazines they read most frequently.[23] Television viewers come more often from the last two categories, however, and especially the last. Of course, some people get the news from several media; and researchers have often found that regular users of one news medium are particularly likely to use others as well. Many television news viewers, however, do not patronize other news media.[24]

Audience Regularity and Attentiveness

The total audience consists of both regular and irregular readers and viewers, with the irregulars in the majority. Simmons collects data on the frequency with which weekly magazine issues are read and daily programs are watched. Table 7 indicates that only about a fifth of all readers look at every issue and a twentieth of all viewers at every program, but over 60 percent see at least half of all issues or programs.[25] Regularity of magazine reading does not vary with age, but it is greatly affected by education: more than a quarter of magazine readers with college degrees, as compared with only 6 percent of those with grade school diplomas, say they read every issue.[26] Conversely, television regularity is higher among women of all ages, older viewers, and the poorly educated.[27]

What portions of a program or magazine people look at is not studied regularly. Some years ago, one magazine asked its subscribers (who are of somewhat higher socioeconomic and educational status than the readership as a whole) what sections they read most often.

TABLE 7: Frequency of Magazine Reading and Program Viewing in 1974

	Percentages	
Magazine issues read (of four):	*Newsweek*	*Time*
1	41.2	37.7
2	24.4	23.3
3	18.4	18.9
All 4	16.0	20.1
Evening news programs seen (of ten):	*CBS*	*NBC*
1	27.6	35.4
2	15.7	15.4
3	10.9	10.6
4	7.7	9.2
5–6	16.3	11.4
7–9	16.5	12.9
All 10	5.3	5.1

SOURCE: Simmons reports. See footnote 25.

I was told that about half responded that they always read the national news; 40 percent, the international news; and nearly 60 percent, the "gossip" section. In the back of the book, regular readership was about 30 percent; higher for the medicine section and lower for the sections on the arts. About 10 percent of the readers reported that they read national news rarely or not at all; but in some of the arts sections, the figure rose to over 50 percent.

Simmons also asks viewers how much attention they pay to the news; three fourths of the men and two thirds of the women claim to give "full" attention.[28] Other studies have shown, however, that only a fourth to a third gave undivided attention to the news, the rest being distracted by concurrent reading, talking, or dining.[29]

A few studies have asked people how dependent they are on the national news media. One third of Albany, New York, viewers studied by Levy reported that they would be bothered a great deal if the news programs were unavailable for a time, and a third each said that they would be bothered somewhat or not at all.[30] A 1969 Harris survey showed, however, that 11 percent of readers would be very upset by the unavailability of their newsmagazine, and 65 percent would not be upset at all.[31] These figures suggest that many people are willing to use other news media instead, but some studies suggest that regular viewers and readers are less willing than others. The Harris survey indicated that 71 percent of the people preferring television news above all others, and 25 percent of those preferring the newsmagazines, would be upset if their favorites were unavailable.[32]

The Uses of National News

That many viewers and readers do not pay regular or undivided attention to the national news should not be surprising, for it may not be very important or relevant to them. Most people do not live in the nation (and society) reported in national news, but in small and localized micro-societies. The actors and activities which matter most to them are to be found among family members, friends, and neighbors; in the places where they work; and in the churches, unions, and clubs to which they belong. News-preference studies generally show the audience to be more interested in local news than in national or international affairs.[33] Even so, the news which most people consider most important and interesting is probably the kind they gather for, and report to, each other about the actors and activities within their micro-societies.

The national and nationwide phenomena reported in national news impinge only periodically, and then indirectly, on the micro-societies in which people live. Admittedly, the federal government and the national corporations, among others, often touch the micro-societies directly; but national news is so general that it cannot be tailored even to the most numerous types of micro-societies. For instance, the news rarely indicates how a new presidential policy will affect different parts of the country, or whether it will have dissimilar effects on high-income and low-income micro-societies. (Even local news must limit itself to general news about the locality; indeed, only the local weather forecast, which helps people decide what clothes to wear, is of direct and immediate relevance to the audience as a whole.) In addition, few people have any control over the actors and agencies which appear in the national news, and are unable to influence national policy merely by becoming regular viewers or readers. Many people could carry on their lives without national news; and in any event, their need for it is not often urgent.

Yet at the same time, people seem to want national news. No one knows to what extent they care to find out about the actors and activities that dominate it, but Levy concluded from his study of television news viewers that "many watched to be reassured that the world both near and far was safe [and] secure, and that . . . it demanded no immediate action on their part."[34] On the other hand, audience studies suggest that people want to be kept informed about news that affects their lives, such as news about the economy and health.[35] In an oligopolistic economy, nationwide increases in the cost of living are apt to be similar for many micro-societies, and all audience members are subject to roughly the same illnesses.

People also use national news to keep up with nation and society. Professionals and managers—and intellectuals—may do so because they participate in, or feel themselves to be a part of, the national agencies which the news monitors; people who participate regularly, however, often subscribe to the specialized newsletters which supply personally or occupationally relevant news to them. For the rest of the population, keeping abreast with the news does not, like a soap opera, require regular attention. Some people also seem to use the news for diversion, not so much as entertainment but as escape from their own problems. They want to learn that their problems are not as severe as the problems of others; but when the news is not reassuring, some people object. A nationwide study made in 1970 found that older, poorly educated, and politically conservative viewers wanted less bad news about social upheavals, sex, and violence.[36] Judging by the letters written to magazines and television networks (see below), this reaction has continued.

Some people appear to be "news buffs"; they become involved in the news as others become involved in hobbies or sports. Such buffs seem to be concentrated among the older population. Perhaps they pay such close attention to the news because they have a good deal of time to fill; or perhaps their involvement is based on more solid existential ground: becoming isolated from, and being made to feel useless by, the micro-society in which they functioned in their younger years, they establish instead a vicarious connection with the larger nation and society. Other television news buffs become fans of the anchorpersons, either developing a one-way "parasocial" relationship with them or perceiving them as public figures who appear to share their own opinions on issues of politics and culture.[37]

Audience Mail

Viewers and readers make their existence known to journalists mainly as statistics in ratings and research reports, but a tiny number also write letters. In 1977 (as in the two preceding years), *Time* received about 60,000 letters, *Newsweek* about 38,000 (up from 32,000 in 1975). Television viewers are less active correspondents; on the basis of a study I made of all letters written during October 1975 about the *NBC Nightly News,* either to the program or to others at NBC, I estimated that the program prompted some 4,600 letters that year.[38] One likely explanation for the larger number of magazine correspondents is that readers are better-educated and thus more likely to write; another is that the magazines publish a weekly letters section, spurring on readers who would like to see their communications in print.

About a fifth of the mail consists of story suggestions and requests for further information, and some letters are written by lonely people calling attention to themselves and their problems. Only a few women write love letters to anchormen, but some write every day. Network news programs, far more than magazines, also receive mail from people who appear to be mentally disturbed. I judged 9 percent of the letters sent to the NBC news program in October 1975 to be partly incomprehensible, and another 9 percent to be totally incomprehensible. These writers were also very active correspondents, six of them accounting for 14 percent of the mail sent to the news program.[39] In addition, television seems to attract what journalists define as crank mail: letters from highly religious people forecasting an apocalypse or the millenium, viewers with paranoid conspiracy theories about government, and those who consider journalists to be Communists.

But most of the mail, to both media, is comprehensible—and critical. In 1974, the chief of *Time*'s letters department wrote: "The single common mood that runs through *Time*'s mail is indignation . . . from mild annoyance to almost incoherent outrage . . . split between those readers disturbed by *Time*'s reporting and those whose indignation stems from events themselves. During 1973, as always, the mad-at-*Time* group was the more vociferous."[40]

The principal targets of indignation are profanity, sacrilege, politics, and above all, sex. At both magazines, sex covers hold the record for cover-story response. *Time*'s 1973 cover on the film *Last Tango in Paris* generated over 12,000 letters, 6,700 of which indicated that the writers had canceled or would not renew their subscriptions. (The previous record response to cover stories [3,500] was held jointly by "Sex in the U. S." and "Is God Dead?"[41]) A 1977 story which featured bare-breasted *Playboy* bunnies drew only a handful of critical letters, however, reflecting either a change in reader attitudes or greater tolerance for stories not featured on the cover.

The domestic news section, which deals mostly with politics, always draws far more letters than all other sections, but the record for political letters is held by Watergate. Of the 80,000 letters (itself an all-time high) sent to *Time* in 1973, 23,000 concerned Watergate stories, with a large number critical of the magazine's reportage or its continued emphasis on the subject.[42] At *Newsweek,* I was told, the mail ran 10 to 1 against the magazine's coverage of Watergate. The networks also received an above-average amount of mail during Watergate; and Daniel Schorr reports that 150,000 people wrote or called the three networks after Vice-president Agnew's 1969 speeches, two thirds supporting his attacks on television news.[43]

Much of the mail comes from people who object to excessive political or cultural liberalism on the part of the magazines and networks, and a member of *Time*'s letters department suggested that this pattern has not changed since the 1950s: "Even when *Time* was conservative, most of the letters came from conservatives, and for them, no one can ever be conservative enough." People who describe themselves as liberals write less often; my analysis of the NBC mail showed, for example, that of the letters which demonstrated an identifiable ideological position, only 7 percent were clearly liberal or populist. The majority of letter writers were explicit conservatives, defenders of Richard Nixon, and above all, critical of government for high taxes, unjustified expenditures, excessive red tape, or interference with personal economic activities.[44]

People who perceive liberal or pro-government biases in the news seem to be more frequent correspondents to the news media than those who see other biases or none at all. People who object, however, are always readier to write than those who praise—and they are writing to news media they consider to be liberal. Sussman has argued that "people write more often when their goals are endangered than when they seem assured"; and the letters to NBC I read were largely from people swimming against one or another tide.[45] Perhaps most important, letter writers are characteristically atypical of the total audience, for a number of studies have shown them to be generally older, better educated, more affluent, politically more conservative, and more involved in community and public affairs than people who do not write.[46] Although most of the studies have dealt with people who write to daily newspapers, the findings probably apply to magazine correspondents as well. But many of the people whose letters to NBC I read appeared to be poorly educated, not affluent, and elderly.

Journalists and Audiences

I began this study with the assumption that journalists, as commercial employees, take the audience directly into account when selecting and producing stories; I therefore paid close attention to how the journalists conceived of and related to their audience.[47] I was surprised to find, however, that they had little knowledge about the actual audience and rejected feedback from it. Although they had a vague image of the audience, they paid little attention to it; instead, they filmed and wrote for their superiors and for themselves, assuming, as I suggested earlier, that what interested them would interest the audience.

That people hired to produce the news for many millions of viewers and readers actually work for themselves may seem incredible, but there are good reasons why they do so. For one thing, journalists cannot keep the audience in mind because of its massive size; for another, they do not believe it to be capable of determining what news it needs; above all, the product considerations, which take the audience into account, exempt journalists from having to do so directly.

The Rejection of Formal Feedback

Journalists have access to formal feedback from the audience, but they use it only rarely. Magazine journalists see the monthly reports analyzing the mail and can request copies of all letters. The networks do not monitor viewer letters as systematically, but television journalists have access to them because newsroom secretaries are responsible for answering them.[48] In addition, journalists can obtain television-rating and magazine-circulation figures, as well as results of audience studies.

Attitudes Toward the Mail

Top producers and editors see all letters written by powerful or well-known correspondents; top editors also keep abreast of the letter reports, and top producers and anchorpersons see a regular but tiny sample of the letters that come to the news programs. Except for one top editor who carefully monitors letters about the magazine (but not those about the state of the world), the journalists ignore or dismiss most of the mail. One executive producer pointed out: "I see the letters about mistakes, and the rest of the mail calls us 'Communist' or asks for a photograph of C. [an attractive woman reporter]."

The lack of interest in the mail stems largely from its predictability. Journalists expect to receive mostly critical letters, particularly from cultural and political conservatives, and their expectations are usually realized. These letters can be disregarded because most journalists believe the writers to be unrepresentative of the total audience and therefore need not be taken seriously. In addition, critical letters are often thought to be unjustified or unfounded, since many accuse the journalists of personal bias or of ignorance about what "really" happened. Television journalists are even more dubious about their correspondents, believing them to be largely "nuts" or "cranks."[49] Their belief is understandable, inasmuch as such people write regularly, and secretaries often tell them about the more bizarre letters.

The cultural conservatives are not ignored entirely because the principal audience consideration, to be discussed shortly, is a set of taste taboos, which inhibit journalists from using words and pictures that offend them. These taboos anticipate audience feedback and undoubtedly reduce the amount of critical mail that would come if the taboos did not exist; the cultural conservatives who are still offended are dismissed as representing an atypical "hinterland." Equivalent taboos to placate the politically conservative correspondents are not necessary because the various forms of value exclusion (see Chapter 6) already inhibit "extreme" ideas, and the political conservatives who nevertheless remain unsatisfied are dismissed as insatiable.

In both media, however, letters which describe factual mistakes are read carefully; as is critical mail when it arrives in unprecedented numbers or when it is unexpected, dealing with topics that do not usually anger letter writers. For example, during Watergate, letters which deplored the use of satirical anti-Nixon cartoons on the cover of *Time* were taken seriously, although the decision to stop using "cartoon covers" was also influenced by staff objections to them.

The Rejection of Audience Research

Top producers and editors keep up with the ratings and circulation reports, but they pay only cursory attention to the audience studies that come across their desks, and the remaining journalists never see them. Many—perhaps most—journalists are suspicious of audience research. First, most of them come from a liberal arts or literature background, and dislike statistics of any kind, even in their own stories. In the 1960s, they refused to accept the possibility that anything useful (or reliable and valid) could be gleaned from studies of small random samples; however, now, as polls are increasingly used for news stories, their disbelief in sampling and probability theory has been somewhat reduced.[50]

Second, journalists have yet to be convinced that audience research is useful, for either it reaffirms the professional "audience lore"—the conventional wisdom about the audience that all journalists come to learn—or it is not relevant to story selection. As one top editor put it: "The studies tell me that the most popular cover is a pretty girl on a red background, but how often can I run such a cover on a news-magazine?" Also, journalists who keep up with existing audience studies know that the demographic makeup of the audience changes very little over time, regardless of format and other changes made in news programs or newsmagazines; consequently, they doubt that audience research can help. Their doubts are not entirely unjustified, for useful research is not easily designed. Researchers can only report on recurring patterns, whereas journalists must make decisions about individual stories.

Even so, the selection considerations are recurring patterns; more significant, they embody assumptions about the audience that have never been tested systematically. Professional audience lore notwithstanding, no one knows whether viewers always prefer film over tell stories, action film over talking heads, and brief magazine stories with pithy quotes; or whether the audience is bored when journalists are. Nor does anyone know the variations in viewing and reading habits between regular and irregular audience members.

But there is a third reason for the journalists' rejection of research: they are reluctant to accept any procedure which casts doubt on their news judgment and their professional autonomy. When a network audience-research unit presented findings on how a sample of viewers evaluated a set of television news films, the journalists were appalled because the sample liked the films which the journalists deemed to be of low quality, and disliked the "good stories." In fact, the viewer sample made its choices on the basis of film topics rather than film quality, preferring films about personally relevant topics to those about important national and international news. The journalists were so involved in judging the films from their own perspective, however, that they did not notice that the viewer sample applied a very different one.

Fourth, journalists are wary of research because it is under the auspices of nonjournalists: of business departments at the magazines; and at the networks, of research departments that report to corporate executives. As a result, journalists are concerned that research findings might be used by nonjournalists to enlarge the audience with people who want more sensationalism or show business. Nor is their concern completely unfounded, for while audience researchers do not view themselves as representing business or management, their own careers depend on impressing them. Their interest is scientific, but the results of their work are evaluated by executives charged with achieving commercial objectives.

Since NBC had established a news audience-research section some years ago, I was able, in 1975, to gather at least some impressions about the relationship between journalists and researchers. The researchers presented their findings with the belief that because everyone wanted higher ratings, the journalists would be interested in their studies; but the journalists were suspicious and, once the researchers left, hostile. The researchers were eager to enlarge the audience by attracting people who disliked the present news programs or did not watch them at all, but the journalists were prepared to add only those viewers who would accept their news judgments.

The conflict between researchers and journalists is over the priority of commercial versus professional considerations in story selection. The news executives are caught in the middle, for while they report to network management, they want to protect their own autonomy and that of the journalists. Besides, they are still journalists and therefore share the journalists' doubts about research.

In 1975, at least, corporate management was also caught in the middle, since it did not want to interfere with the journalists' autonomy. Besides, many executives, like others in the communications and entertainment industries, believe that their trained intuition is superior to research. Perhaps they also fear that the researchers could threaten their autonomy as well. Consequently, the researchers were in a Catch–22. They had findings (about audience news-preferences, as well as criticisms of present formats, stories, and anchorpersons), which they could not prove, having sufficient funds only for small pilot studies. But the widespread skepticism about research prevented them from securing the funds for larger studies that would enable them to come up with firmer findings and stronger recommendations.

Audience research therefore presently plays a marginal role in the news. I reported in Chapter 3 that executives and top producers and editors can be fired or transferred on the basis of declining ratings and circulations. At NBC, anchorpersons have so far not been deposed as a result either of low ratings or audience research attesting to their inability to achieve Walter Cronkite's popularity; but Gates reports that ABC hired Harry Reasoner on the basis of a study demonstrating his audience appeal.[51] Local news formats and anchorpersons have been changed following network studies as well as research carried out by consulting firms.

Moreover, the traditional antagonism to research is beginning to erode; and by 1978, NBC's news-audience researchers appeared to have won the journalists' trust. Partly as a result of earlier conflicts with the journalists, the researchers now restricted themselves to research and did not make recommendations; in addition, they eschewed studies intended to cast doubt on the journalists' news judgments. At the same time, a new generation of top producers and news executives, who have some academic training in communications and who want audience research to test their decisions, are coming to power. Then, too, the competition between the three network news programs has sharpened, and it is always possible that research findings can lead to new ideas and a competitive advantage in the ratings race. Even at the magazines, one or two editors who are ready to use audience research can be found; and if their magazines run into financial difficulties, they might be allowed to go ahead. At present, executive and professional intuition remains dominant; but should commercial considerations become more urgent, the researchers may find themselves with sufficient funds to demonstrate whether they can enhance the corporate balance sheet.

Fear of the Audience

The journalists' reluctance to take formal feedback into account, however, is more than doubt about the representativeness of letter writers or hostility to research. It also reflects fear of the audience and its potential power. One source of that fear is audience size. While critics imagine that national journalists feel great power determining what news millions of people will see or read, story selectors are actually cowed by the magnitude of their audience and by the responsibility of producing news for it. "If we had to think about how our readers feel, all twenty million of them," one top editor said, "we'd freeze." A top producer who made the same point went on to distinguish between what he called the known and unknown audience: "You do the show for a cell of people—the office staff, the wife, and the kids. These are the only known audience. I know we have twenty million viewers, but I don't know who they are. I don't know what the audience wants, and I don't care. I can't know, so I can't care."

Perhaps more important, story selectors feel, as one said, that "you can't edit by readership survey, so we have to take the lead." Journalists see themselves as professionals working for a predominantly lay clientele; and like members of other professions, they believe that they must give the audience what it needs, not what it wants. In addition, they are convinced that the audience cannot know what it wants because it is not at the scene when journalists cover the news. Moreover, viewer or reader reactions to today's news would not be relevant for the future inasmuch as neither the audience nor the journalists can predict tomorrow's news.

Underlying the rejection of audience wants and preferences lurks a further fear, also embodied in journalistic audience lore, that many viewers and readers are not particularly interested in the news they now receive, preferring gossip about celebrities to important activities of important actors. "They only want to know how the astronauts shit while they are in space," a producer working on a space-mission story once pointed out. Television journalists are also fearful that many viewers would prefer attractive or cheerful "news readers" to experienced journalists; and anchorpersons who supply opinion to those who report objective news. In short, they fear that if audience wants were considered, journalistic news judgment would go by the wayside.

These fears are not completely unreasonable either, for while journalists may overestimate the demand for gossip, it is conceivable that were the audience given a choice, a significant proportion would opt for more personally relevant news and less of the current product. Journalists who argue for fewer Washington stories reflect these audience preferences, but even they reserve the right to decide what stories are most important and interesting. Nor do they look for research evidence to support their "news philosophy," for once audience wants become relevant, then journalistic news judgment must be complemented by audience news judgment, and journalists would then have to surrender some of their control over the news.

Informal Feedback

Although journalists reject letters and studies, they make some use of informal, self-generated audience-feedback mechanisms. The primary supplier of journalistic feedback is, of course, the person (or persons) who hold power over the journalists. When I asked journalists for whom they were writing, producing, or editing, they always began with their superiors, and some went no further. Insofar as these superiors are themselves paid in part to be audience-related (see Chapter 3), their feedback has some, albeit indirect, connection with the audience.

A second source of informal feedback comes from what the previously quoted top producer called the known audience. For the most part, these are family members, friends, neighbors, and people journalists meet at parties. "I go after reactions from my neighbors," said one producer, "from my sister in the Midwest, and from my brothers out west." Producers and editors sometimes were concerned about their wives' and children's responses to stories critical of organizations to which they belonged or public figures whom they admired; and a few magazine writers indicated that they occasionally asked their neighbors for their reactions to the magazine. Journalists who seek out or take in feedback from the known audience assume that it is a sufficiently representative segment of the total audience. While this assumption is surely inaccurate, the known audience is recruited from the better-educated people whom the journalists want most to reach.

Feedback is also sought from journalistic and nonjournalistic colleagues who adopt a lay role for the purpose and become what Riesman has aptly called a "near-audience." Secretaries and technicians on staff may be observed by a producer as film is reviewed on newsroom monitors before the show; professionals become a near-audience when they are asked whether they find a story boring or interesting. I reported previously that *Time* top editors sometimes tested sports and entertainment cover stories on colleagues known to be uninterested in these topics.

From time to time, however, informal feedback seems to be insufficient, and the journalists are overcome by what might be called audience hunger. At this point they will generate feedback from the unknown audience. Not trusting "the numbers," and concerned whether anyone "out there" is watching or reading, they select stories guaranteed to produce calls or letters: a risqué magazine story or, on television, a human-interest story certain to elicit letters and donations for a deserving victim.[52]

The Journalist as Audience Representative

Feedback from the known audience is not often used; and the journalists, especially seniors, who rarely get feedback from superiors, indicated that they wrote, filmed, and edited for themselves. In reality, they did so only partially, however, for they always worked within the limits set by the suitability considerations. Nonetheless, they felt as though they were working for themselves. Even when they judged a story by whether it would "grab" or bore the reader or viewer, and I asked them how they made this judgment, they would generally respond: "Well, if it bores me, it will bore them." Although one top producer went so far as to suggest that "the conception of our audience is a reflection of ourselves," most journalists take the congruence of their own and the audience's feelings for granted. In the process, they become representatives of the audience, reacting for it vis-à-vis their sources. "Ego-centered as we are," one reporter commented, "we think we are the delegates of the audience to what is happening. The audience doesn't have independent resources for getting the news; we do it for them."

When journalists decide that what bores them will also bore the audience, they are, in effect, suggesting the equivalence of professional and lay reactions. A. M. Rosenthal has argued to the contrary. Writing about his reaction to a murder story, he pointed out:

> I experienced then that most familiar of newspapermen's reactions, vicarious shock. This is a kind of professional detachment that is the essence of the trade. . . . The reporter or the editor need not [be] and usually is not shocked . . . himself, but he experiences the flashing realization that readers will be.[53]

My impression is different, however, for the journalists I studied were, for the most part, reacting as if they were readers or viewers themselves, rejecting grisly still pictures or overly bloody battle film, for example, because they were personally shocked by them.

But whether or not they project professional or lay feelings, when journalists become audience representatives, they need neither contact with the actual audience nor feedback from it, so long as superiors approve their work and the audience gives no sign of overt or massive displeasure. To be sure, the news media I studied have not experienced significant audience protest or, more to the point, audience shrinkage; and magazine journalists work with the knowledge that subscribers are bound to them for at least a year. Actually, the audience does not have much choice, given the similarity of news programs and magazines; and perhaps it is neither aware of its right to be displeased nor sufficiently involved in the news to care about that right.[54]

Nevertheless, ultimately, journalists can only stand in for the readers and viewers who are most like themselves, sharing their involvement in the news and their political and cultural interests. If and when journalists please this segment of the total audience, it does not need to write critical letters; and insofar as the represented audience, being better-educated, is most likely to resort to letter writing, the journalists thereby help forestall criticism. But the fact remains that the informal feedback mechanisms, and the ways by which journalists act as self-appointed and unaccountable audience representatives, do not represent the entire audience, and probably not even the majority.

The Journalists' Audience-Image

Even if journalists do not have to keep the actual audience in mind, they must be aware of it. Knowing little about it, however, they construct an *image* of the audience, which does not always mesh with the reality. But then it does not really have to do so, for what interests journalists is how the audience (that is, their image of it) reacts to their work.

When I asked the journalists to tell me about the actual audience, they often described their known audience and assumed that it was similar to the unknown one. Others brought up the audience proto- types that exist in some news organizations. Generally, these are professionals outside New York—for example, "a lawyer and his wife, who heads the PTA in a middle-sized town," mentioned by several NBC journalists.[55] A top editor combined his known audience with the magazine's prototype: "I basically edit for my wife. She is *vox populi,* bright and curious but not one of your New York intellectuals; she's not very interested in that, and we're not a cerebral magazine in any case. She's not political, but if a story interests her, it'll interest others—for example, the professional's wife from Winnetka [an afflu- ent Chicago suburb] and the junior-college teacher in the Midwest."[56]

When I pressed the journalists for additional information about the actual audience, they indicated that it spanned all age, income, educa- tional, and other levels; but when I pressed still further, they described what in essence constituted their upscale audience. The magazine journalists saw their readers primarily as affluent and college- educated, with the men holding professional or managerial jobs; at the same time, they were not aware of the white-collar and blue-collar readership shown in Table 6. Some television journalists thought that many of their viewers were older, but others could not understand why so many of the commercials featured denture adhesives and laxatives. Virtually all imagined their viewers to be basically middle- class; the most detailed description was given by a producer: "It's a fairly well-educated group that stays with the show, but there's also a lot without higher education, high school graduates who have the set on and perk up their ears for an occasional piece." But even this dichotomized image overestimated the socioeconomic and educa- tional levels of the actual audience. In fact, I met only one television journalist who correctly saw the audience as consisting of persons mainly of working-class background. Having himself come from a blue-collar home, he argued that television news should be made more attractive to blue-collar viewers; but he also added that he did not know how to do so, having long ago lost track of the people among whom he grew up.

Many other professionals overestimate the status of their clientele, perhaps to raise their own status. Journalists also keep less prestigious viewers and readers out of their audience-image to justify their assumption that they can represent the audience; but in addition, they do so to discourage "writing down," which they assume the audience will recognize and will respond to by rejecting programs or magazines that treat them as inferiors. This is also one reason for the journalists' reluctance to resort to experts who, like academics, are thought to call attention to their informational superiority.

The Effective Audience-Image

The only characteristic of the audience that journalists do keep in mind is its receptivity of the news. This audience-image, which also bears an uncertain relationship to the actual audience, divides viewers and readers into four types, whom I label the interested, uninterested, rejected, and invented audiences.

The interested audience is imagined to care about the news, to keep up with it on a regular basis. The uninterested care less; they are irregular viewers and readers whose attention must be sought and then held, and who are interested mostly in local news.

Journalists, naturally, are most enthusiastic about the interested, for they—or the journalists' image of them—accept journalistic news judgments, thus allowing the journalists maximal autonomy. But when they take the audience into account, they think about the uninterested, who must be pursued continuously. Journalists are often fearful of losing or upsetting them, and many of the product considerations analyzed in Chapter 5 and the audience considerations to be discussed below exist to hold their attention.

The uninterested are treated with a mixture of disdain and resignation: disdain because they care insufficiently about important news, and resignation because they cannot be ignored. Disdain is stronger at the magazines, where the uninterested are thought to be a minority of the readers, than at the networks. They are "not our kinds of people," a senior editor said, "but the others, and you have to throw some crumbs to them."

These images also contain assumptions about audience characteristics. The interested audience is imagined to be well-educated and younger; the uninterested, to be poorly educated, older, and to share the cultural and political conservatism of the hinterland. Whether these images are accurate is uncertain, since audience interest in the news has not been sufficiently studied. If journalists are correct in assuming that the interested audience is equivalent to the regular audience, the magazine journalists are guessing correctly, for the regular readers are better educated. But the television journalists are mistaken, given the previously cited data which suggest that regular viewers are apt to be elderly and poorly educated.

The rejected audience consists of people whom journalists would like to extrude. One group is made up of "would-be intellectuals," who are thought to want more detailed or more analytic—and thus boring—stories than the journalists are willing or able to supply. In addition, they are assumed to be experts who might write letters accusing the journalists of oversimplification. Magazine journalists, however, are ambivalent about would-be intellectuals. On the one hand, they want such readers because they are interested in the news; but on the other hand, they fear they cannot please them without losing the attention of nonintellectual readers.

The second group of rejectees is made up of people thought to be interested solely in sensationalism—viewers who, for example, want only to know about how astronauts defecate in outer space. Television journalists are particularly fearful of this audience, for they worry that because it is numerous, management might therefore want to cater to it in the quest for higher ratings.

The invented audience is one which journalists construct to satisfy themselves that their news judgments guarantee them viewers and readers. In Chapter 5, I showed that all story types are assumed to have built-in constituencies, but perhaps the principal invention is the assumption that the total audience spans all ages and educational levels. On the one hand, this invention enables journalists to ignore the audience altogether; on the other, it allows them to assume that every story is sure to appeal to someone.

In addition, the invented audience can be adjusted to coincide with the journalists' own judgments. When one magazine decided to run a sports cover, the editors decided that at the moment, their readers were utterly bored with politics. They also thought "everyone" was currently following the baseball star who was to be featured on the cover. Every July, magazine story selectors send their readers on vacation, foreign editors seek out news about overseas tourist adventures, book editors review "more light books suitable for hammock reading," and theater critics turn to summer theater "because people are on the road now, going to the festivals." Perhaps they are responding to actual reader interests, but they lack evidence about how many readers are on vacation and whether their reading habits have changed. They do, however, work faster during the summer weeks so that they themselves can get away to the hammocks and festivals of the Hamptons and the Cape.

Audience Considerations

By "audience considerations," I mean those story-selection judgments in which journalists explicitly think about and act on their audience-images. As noted above, most audience considerations are invoked for the uninterested audience, and these fall into two categories: one set exists to attract the audience; the other, to protect it and, in the process, the journalists and the social order.

Most of the time, journalists do not think about the audience while choosing stories but apply audience considerations *ex post facto* when someone suggests that a story could upset, displease, or confuse some viewers or readers. In such cases, the imagined audience becomes a veto group, although most of the time, the story survives and is edited during story production so as to eliminate offending components. At other times, if not very often, stories that do not particularly interest story selectors but are imagined to grab the audience will be chosen solely for that reason.

Attracting the Audience

In one sense, journalists strike a bargain with their audiences, especially the uninterested one. They want viewers and readers to pay attention to important news because "people should know what is going on in the world"; in exchange, they will supply interesting stories to please them. The essential provisions of this contract are already incorporated into the suitability considerations, but journalists also make a special effort to find stories that will attract and then hold audience attention.

1. *"Identifying" stories.* Journalists believe that some stories, notably action stories, are inherently able to engage the audience. Other

stories achieve this aim if people can identify with the news, either because it has personal relevance or because it creates feelings about a hero, villain, or victim. When Reuven Frank developed the initial prototype for NBC's evening news program, he wanted to go further, to "irritate" the viewers, because "irritation means getting the audience involved, not just passive." Years later, he felt that television news had unwisely ignored his objective. If possible, journalists also want "memorable" stories which people will remember and discuss with others. These stories, journalists hope, may generate word-of-mouth advertising, which could enlarge the audience.

2. *Service stories.* The audience can also be attracted by service stories: news of personal relevance, such as health and consumer stories, or periodic reviews of complicated phenomena. In 1975, for example, *Newsweek* ran service stories summarizing the various investigations of the CIA and reviewing funding regulations for presidential campaigns. In both cases, journalists thought the stories dull, or "eyeball-glazing," and chose them reluctantly to "service our confused readers," although they admitted to being confused about the topics themselves.

3. *Non-burdening stories.* Another aspect of the journalists' bargain with the audience is to not burden it excessively with complicated stories, excessive detail, or news in which even interested viewers and readers might lack interest. Journalists' unending effort to achieve clarity exists mainly to minimize the audience's burden; and their belief that the audience must not be burdened reflects their awareness that they are sometimes imposing an unwanted product.

Protective Considerations

A larger set of audience considerations exists to protect the audience from being unduly upset. Some considerations are meant also to protect the social order from the audience, the fear being that news which upsets the audience could lead it to act out its anxieties.

1. *Shock.* Since viewers cannot go back over a story, television journalists are careful to guard them from unnecessary personal upset. News of commercial plane crashes will not be reported until a flight number is available, thereby eliminating potential worry by all viewers whose relatives and friends are currently in the air. News of medical advances must not give false hope to ill viewers. "You have to be very careful with cancer stories," a top producer pointed out, "because people with cancer listen very closely and see a cure where you don't."

2. *Panic.* Television journalists also take pains to discourage panic among viewers as a result of disasters or civil disturbances. In Chapter 2, I suggested that during the hours immediately following the assassination of President Kennedy, television journalists were extremely apprehensive that people might panic in response to the assassination, and repeatedly sought to allay such a response. Local stations are even more concerned about panicking viewers and listeners. Newsmagazines, on the other hand, do not need to worry, since they appear after possible panic-generating news has already been reported. Why journalists fear audience panic despite the absence of actual panic in the past deserves study; however, they are also concerned with discouraging rumors that could cause panic; and there is some evidence that during newspaper strikes, rumor adds to the fear of crime in crime-ridden cities.[57]

3. *Imitative behavior.* Journalists also worry that some audience members might imitate the news, and they take care to reduce this possibility. *Time* and *Newsweek* were criticized for putting Lynette Fromme on their covers after her abortive attempt to assassinate President Gerald Ford, some critics feeling that it prompted Sara Jane Moore to subsequently attempt the same act. As a result of the criticism, neither magazine elected to put her on the cover.

During the 1960s, television and magazine stories on the hippies purposely emphasized the darker side of hippie life to discourage a mass exodus to Haight-Ashbury. Stories speculating on the likelihood of summer ghetto disturbances are also shunned, since journalists do not want to be accused of initiating self-fulfilling prophecies.

Journalists are not alone in fearing imitative behavior; in fact, public officials, religious leaders, and others have voiced such fears since the invention of the first mass media. Accordingly, the journalists' considerations aim less to protect the audience than the larger social order —and, of course, the news media themselves. Local news media have from time immemorial played down local civil disturbances for fear of attracting spectators who might join in them once they arrived on the scene. The national media are concerned with the national diffusion of local disorder; in 1967, television was accused of having encouraged the nationwide spread of ghetto disturbances by its coverage of the Detroit and Newark disorders. The networks worry most about being criticized for publicizing disorder, but the people who attack them do so because they fear the news will incite imitative behavior.

4. *Taste.* The major protecting consideration, and in fact the most important audience consideration, guides the exclusion or editing of stories on the grounds of what journalists call taste. This consideration

is applied by taboos, mainly against nudity, profanity, sacrilege, and the depiction of bloodshed, which exist to protect both the audience from being upset and the news media from massive audience anger.

While journalists feel free to anger the audience with important stories, and are sometimes impelled by audience hunger to violate the taste taboos, they do not wish to unnecessarily encourage a flood of critical mail. They prefer not to risk complaints from executives concerned about the cost of answering the mail, and in television, from owners of local affiliated stations who become aggravated whenever journalists ignore the taste taboos. Consequently, the audience is perhaps most seriously considered on matters of taste.

Television journalists operate with more restrictive taste considerations than do their peers at the magazines, mainly because the evening news is broadcast at the dinner hour, when children are assumed to be watching. As a result, erotic stories are taboo; and although the networks can use stories about nude beaches, nude bathers are filmed only from the neck up and the knees down. However, women's breasts can appear in medical stories and in foreign news. "We can do like the *National Geographic,*" one producer explained. "We can't show American girls topless, but we can show bare-breasted Africans."

Nor can television journalists use profanity. In recent years, interviewees have been allowed to say "hell" and "damn" on the air; but when the CBS evening news program included three "goddamn's" on a single night in January 1970 (all used by interviewees), the network received a "record-breaking" amount of critical mail from affiliated stations.[58]

At the present time, the magazines can occasionally use photographs of totally nude women, but male genitalia continue to appear only in reproductions of sculptures and paintings. Profanity taboos have also been loosened considerably over the last decade; and while writers still cannot use profanity, only a few words are now excised from quotes. "Good taste," however, remains a major consideration for cover art.

People being wounded or killed during disasters or battles are virtually never shown. During the Vietnam War, film editors routinely cut the bloodier scenes from battle and patrol film before top producers reviewed it; and presumably, camera crews did not bother to shoot carnage scenes that they knew to be unusable.[59] Although television has been credited with—and attacked for—showing its viewers the horrors of war, the networks actually reported a highly sanitized version of it.[60] In fact, sometimes the magazines described, with text and pictures, the bloody scenes that were censored by television.

"Taste" is defined broadly enough to also include some political taboos. For one thing, journalists cannot show disrespect to the president or the presidency. Violations almost always elicit audience mail and, of course, White House protest. Journalists can, however, be mildly disrespectful to a president who is losing the respect of the audience, as in the case of Richard Nixon during the latter days of his administration. President Ford's lack of physical coordination was also excluded from the taboo, although magazine editors rejected pictures of the grossest presidential stumbles.

The same taboo extends to other highly placed public officials. Nor do journalists often make disrespectful comments about American wars, patriotism, and democracy. While criticism is permissible and journalists resort to it despite anticipated audience protest, they shy away from satirical comment because it implies disrespect. I reported previously that *Time* ended its use of satirical cartoon covers partly because of sizable audience objection to them.

News about deviant personal behavior of public officials is also off-limits, although many journalists accept this taboo because they deem such news trivial. Off-the-job drinking, premarital and extramarital affairs, homosexuality, and the like are thus kept out of the news, provided journalists do not consider them to interfere with an official's public responsibilities. Until the 1970s, however, even personal behavior that did interfere was usually not reported, except by columnists such as Drew Pearson and Jack Anderson. To this day, journalists are still reluctant to report evidence of alcoholism or senility among members of Congress.

The major national news media finally broke with this long-standing practice to report President Kennedy's alleged involvement with a woman reputedly linked at the same time to two leaders of organized crime; and Congressman Wayne Hays's use of public funds to hire a mistress. Still, both incidents became newsworthy because they involved the men's public roles. But when *Time* and other national media reported President Kennedy's other liaisons which did not impinge upon his public role, some audience members thought they had gone too far. *Time*'s story generated more letters to the magazine in 1976 than any other single story, 750 of the 1,076 letters criticizing *Time*'s decision to report these affairs.[61]

Even so, the taboo was never applied uniformly to all public figures; the private lives of radical activists, for example, were always newsworthy. After Martin Luther King's murder, FBI leaks suggesting that he carried on extramarital affairs were reported; but at that time, no national news medium deemed similar affairs by President Kennedy fit to print.

In recent years, taste considerations have expanded to include taboos on religious, racial, and sexual stereotypes. The news media have long been careful to eschew anti-Semitic stereotypes because Jewish organizations have monitored them closely, but other stereotypes were not excised until the news media were criticized for being racist and sexist. After Vice-president Agnew's 1969 speech attacking the news media, story selectors omitted, for a time, stories that could reinforce ethnic stereotypes—for example, those associating Italo-Americans with the Mafia. (This was probably the major effect of Agnew's attack on the news media.) Yet when an NBC producer argued, in 1975, that a film about old people was unnecessarily patronizing, he was ignored, perhaps because the aged had not yet criticized the news media.

Taste taboos exist almost entirely because of the audience, but some are accepted by the journalists themselves, notably those proscribing stereotypes and grisly or bloody scenes. But journalists would jettison the political taboos if they could, and younger journalists continually argue for relaxing the strictures against nudity and profanity. Indeed, these taboos have been relaxed partly because top editors and producers finally succumbed to their pressure. Picture-picking sessions at the magazines were frequently marked by negotiations over the taboos, and although top editors are paid to be cautious, they may sometimes have given in to "spice up" their pages, hoping that reader reaction would be minimal. And younger top editors and producers adhere to the taboos only because they fear audience protest. In 1975, when an astronaut underlined his eagerness to get out of the space capsule with the word "fuck," and the network journalists feared he could be heard (or seen by lipreaders), one top producer nevertheless wished his expletive had been audible. If a respected public figure used the word, he argued, journalists should, on freedom of press grounds, be able to report it. Magazine journalists have made the same argument, but while sources can now be quoted as saying "bullshit," sexual profanity was still off-limits in 1978.

Audience Enlargement and Cultural Democratization

My observations about the journalists' independence from commercial considerations and their sparse attention to the actual audience hold for the present. But in the last analysis, news organizations are overseen by corporate executives who are paid to show a profit. News judgment is resistant to change, and journalists will fight hard to preserve their autonomy; but if corporate economic well-being is threatened, executives may insist that their news organizations adapt.

For one thing, corporate executives can always demand cost cutting. During the 1975 strikes at NBC and *Time,* they undoubtedly noticed that a small number of producers and editors, supported by nonunion journalists, were able to put on programs and publish magazines without visible effects on quality or ratings and circulation.[62]

In addition, management can call for more profitable news, if only to offset other corporate losses, and thereby require the news programs and magazines to enlarge their audience. Even now, television news appears to be in a period of transition; and if the format and personnel changes being tried at ABC are reflected in an upswing in the ratings, they will most likely be imitated by the other networks.

Nor can anyone predict the future behavior of advertisers and audiences. Present or new advertisers may demand a different or larger audience. Viewers might decide to obtain the national and international news from radio or local television programs; magazine readers might decide to exchange the magazines for the syndicated features that now appear increasingly in daily papers. In that case, enterprising or desperate news firms might shift to include a greater percentage of celebrity biography and gossip, hoping to duplicate the success of *People* magazine.

America itself could change, with consequences for all involved in the news media. Were the country's economic or political problems to worsen, for example, audiences might prefer more entertainment and less news than at present—particularly less bad news about the national and societal phenomena beyond their control. Conversely, they might also decide that they need more analytic news or news which relates national phenomena to their own circumstances and problems. (Political crises may, in fact, attract audiences; Watergate led to a temporary increase of about 10 percent in the number of viewers and readers.) As the population ages, the television news audience will increase, assuming present audience habits persist; as education levels rise, the interested audience may prefer less action and more analysis, driving the news programs and magazines a little closer to the journals of opinion and forcing them to find new ways of holding the rest of their constituency. Audience behavior is only part of the story, however; several magazines died in the 1960s, not because they lost readers but because their advertisers shifted to television.

Journalists fear audience enlargement, for they view it as a threat to their autonomy. Nevertheless, it can also be viewed as cultural democratization, extending to yet larger numbers of people the services of a profession that began centuries ago by supplying news solely to a small elite. Putting it another way, audience enlargement means extending the national news audience much further into the adult and young adult sectors of the lower middle-class, the working class, and the poor than is now the case. However, cultural democratization would concurrently require journalists to pay less attention to upper-class and upper-middle-class sources, and to pay less homage to the social order of these classes.

Elsewhere, I have argued that America is divided into a number of esthetic or taste subcultures and publics, which are differentiated largely by class, principally by education.[63] This observation also applies to the news. Local newspapers and electronic media are already stratified by class, at least in some larger cities. There is no mistaking that the New York *Daily News* is written for a very different set of readers than *The New York Times*. The national news media are less differentiated, if only because they are few in number; more important, in form and substance, national news has so far obeyed the dictates of the subculture of the upper middle-class, even though most viewers and readers are not of that class.

The national journalists have been able to maintain a kind of cultural hegemony because they are a national professional elite. The audience has accepted their hegemony, either because it does not care sufficiently to try to alter its present lack of choice; or because it believes that in order to be informed, it must be supplied with news about and by people of superior status. Perhaps being informed also means that the news must be about high public officials, even when their activities are of little personal relevance.[64] But possibly, viewers and readers would come in larger numbers if the news surrendered some of its upper-middle-class content and tone.

Be that as it may, when journalists worry about increasing sensationalism and show business, they are also reacting to the possibility that the taste subculture of national news will move down a notch— and no one likes downward mobility. Because downward cultural mobility normally goes hand-in-hand with higher corporate profits, it can easily be ascribed to and attacked as an expression of corporate greed. But at the same time, downward mobility is also cultural democratization. I see nothing wrong with either a more attractive anchorperson reading the same news if he or she will attract a larger audience, or more personally relevant news, or more news about Americans who are currently not newsworthy. A greater amount of sensation or gossip would not be desirable, although I am not sure that it would have the deleterious effects journalists predict. But these are issues of news policy, to be addressed in the last chapter.

8

Pressures, Censorship, and Self-censorship

Through the news, journalists give helpful or harmful exposure to the actors whose activities they report. Since many of these actors need publicity to perform their roles, they are, in a sense, dependent on journalists. Thus, journalists' power stems largely from their ability to determine what news enters the symbolic arena, the public stage on which messages about America are presented.

As a result, news organizations are surrounded by individuals and groups wanting to get their messages into the arena with a maximum of helpful and a minimum of harmful publicity. If necessary, they will use their power to pressure journalists for this purpose. By "pressure," I mean criticism, organized or unorganized protest, as well as threats against journalists, their organizations, and their firms. Pressure is applied in order to force journalists to change the news (or to omit a story), which constitutes censorship; or pressure is used to create what journalists call a chilling effect, with the hope of inducing journalists to volunteer the change or omission, which becomes self-censorship. Of course, not all criticism is pressure—for example, when sources request factual corrections. However, when journalists are not convinced that they have been incorrect or when correction is demanded rather than requested, they feel themselves to be under pressure.

Journalists can react to pressure in three ways: they can fight; they can give in, altering the news to placate the exerters of pressure; or they can anticipate their critics, giving in sufficiently and in advance to avoid being pressured.

Story selection and production is, therefore, a power struggle over what messages enter the symbolic arena. Most of the time, the power struggle is covert, for it is built into news judgments; but it becomes overt when unhappy sources, audiences, and others express their displeasure with the outcome of news judgments. This chapter deals mainly with the overt struggles, whereas Chapter 4 can be read as an analysis of the covert ones. Sources try to exert control over the symbolic arena by managing, leaking, and withholding information; journalists try to do so by applying source considerations. Chapter 7 suggests that audiences aim to affect the symbolic arena with critical mail, and by canceling subscriptions or switching stations; journalists fight back by ignoring audience feedback or give in by anticipating, using both audience considerations (mainly those governing taste) and audience-relevant suitability considerations.

The concept of pressure comes from the political arena, where pressure groups try to influence politicians. The term itself implies disapproval of those exerting pressure and sympathy for those having to endure it. Journalists object to pressure, although they rarely use the term. I shall use it, however, without attaching a positive or negative connotation; and in Chapter 10, I will suggest to what extent pressure may be desirable.

In this discussion, I am concerned only with the external kind of pressure, which initially comes from outside the news firm, even though it may be transmitted to journalists by insiders, that is, executives. (Internal pressure, which takes the form of story or editing suggestions from executives, was discussed in Chapters 3 and 6.)

Insofar as the exerters of pressure want to alter what appears in the symbolic arena, their pressures are political; to those concerned with ideology, they are also ideological. For management, the pressures are almost always commercial as well, for whatever the intent behind the exercise of pressure, management must worry about the consequences for the firm. Journalists rarely need to fear these; for them, the primary threat is a reduction of their autonomy, even if, occasionally, individual careers are on the line. But most of the time, they are exposed only to criticism, which they endure no more easily than anyone else, and perhaps less so. Journalists believe their skins to be unusually thin—and they are, but for good reason. Their activities being more visible than those of other professionals, they cannot easily hide from criticism, although it is also true that they often jump too quickly to the conclusion that every criticism is a potential threat.

Problems of Studying External Pressure

Studying external pressure and its outcomes presents both empirical and definitional problems. Surrender to pressure is viewed as an act of cowardice and a sign of powerlessness, and those who must surrender are loath to discuss it. However, journalists are not reluctant to talk about having to accede to a superior's suggestions. Sometimes they suspect that these were prompted by external pressure, but often they do not know for certain, since superiors are not likely to tell them. Daniel Schorr reports that when William Paley urged the *CBS Evening News* to shorten the second installment of an early Watergate story, he did not reveal that he had been under pressure from Charles Colson in the White House. To this day, only Paley knows whether and how much his decision was influenced by White House pressure.[1]

Censorship and self-censorship are difficult both to define and identify. Journalists generally define censorship as killing or altering a story as a result of external pressure, whereas self-censorship is the conscious response to anticipated pressure from nonjournalists. But self-censorship can also be unconscious, in which case journalists may not be aware they are responding to pressure. When journalists announce that chilling effects are in the air, they are pointing out that self-censorship is being demanded of them; however, they are reluctant to admit conscious surrender to these effects, and it is hard to determine when they are responding unconsciously.

Journalists define these terms narrowly, since they are primarily concerned with conscious and perceived censorship and self-censorship. An outside observer can define them more broadly to include the built-in limits to journalistic autonomy. By that definition, value exclusion and other mechanisms that anticipate, and thereby avoid, pressure (to be described below) become institutionalized forms of censorship and self-censorship.[2] I shall move back and forth between the narrow and broad definitions in this chapter; but at its end, I will return to the definitional problem, for it reflects more fundamental issues about the journalistic enterprise.

The Extent of Pressure and Censorship

Journalists believe themselves to be under frequent pressure, with demands for censorship and self-censorship (as they define the terms) always on the horizon. But my fieldwork suggests that successful pressure, leading to censorship or self-censorship, is rare. Beat reporters are, to be sure, often under pressure from sources and must sometimes give in; but other reporters are less easily pressured, since they lack responsibility for what information finally becomes news. The pressures that reach New York are addressed mainly to news and corporate executives, and are usually not passed on to journalists. Specific complaints that question the accuracy of the facts in a story are passed on, however; and journalists are expected to defend themselves, drawing on their files and notes to demonstrate that the story "holds up."

Chilling effects are also few and far between. Moreover, when they appear, they are frequently followed by what I call heating effects, for the journalists, angered by pressure attempts, then seek out news with harmful publicity for the exerters of pressure. They are not always successful, but the Watergate scandals were exposed so quickly in part because investigative reporters increased their efforts after being angered. Probably the most persistent chilling effects come from the audience, whose refusal to view or subscribe is a more direct threat to journalists and their firms than a sponsor's or politician's attack. This is why taste considerations may be the major form of self-censorship. But here I invoke the broader definition, for journalists themselves subscribe to some taste taboos and do not perceive the rest as self-censorship devices.

Successful pressure takes two forms. First, there is occasional censorship and self-censorship of marginal operations, such as television news documentaries. This is not meant to minimize the danger of pressure, however, for attacks on the marginal operations of any institution can weaken the expression of minority viewpoints, which are themselves already on the periphery. But the problems of news documentaries, to be described below, are not transferred to the evening news programs; and there is no equivalent marginal operation at the magazines.

Second, pressure sometimes results in the dismissal or forced resignations of individual journalists. In theory, their departure should produce intense chilling effects, but in practice, this does not appear to be the case, partly because journalists, like other workers, tend to look askance at colleagues who "rock the boat" for the rest. Also, some of the dismissed journalists were previously disliked by colleagues for other reasons. Finally, the role which pressure played in their departure often becomes known only many years later, if at all. Although Edward R. Murrow has long been a hero to journalists for standing up to Senator Joseph McCarthy, it is just now being suggested that his departure from CBS in 1960 was partly a result of corporate surrender to actual or anticipated government pressure.[3]

Business Pressures: Advertisers and Affiliates

Pressure from Advertisers

Advertisers can try to bring pressure to bear on story selectors by demanding that stories which they perceive to hurt them be killed or altered; alternatively, they can withdraw their advertising in the hope that it will have a chilling effect on the journalists. Although local news media and the producers of network news documentaries have been subject to both kinds of pressure for years, the evening news programs and the newsmagazines are virtually free of them.

Perhaps top producers and editors will not admit to having been influenced by advertiser pressure, but other journalists readily talk about this topic. While they occasionally suspect their superiors of using commercial considerations, there is never any suspicion that they had surrendered to advertisers. In our discussions about successful advertiser censorship, the journalists could think of only a few, well-publicized cases, many dating back to the 1950s.[4]

In any case, top producers and editors would not consider killing a story or story suggestion because it might antagonize advertisers; nor do chilling effects lead to unconscious self-censorship. Given their values, journalists do not constantly look for stories that could upset advertisers or the business community, although in light of their feelings about the former (see below), they do not mind upsetting them. However, they are apt to be more cautious in processing news that could antagonize advertisers, making sure that convincing evidence supports their stories. In case of pressure, they must be able to defend what they choose to make news.

Journalists' freedom from advertiser pressure derives from the previously mentioned separation of editorial and business departments. As a result, story selection and the placement of advertising take place independently, so that story selectors do not know until late in the production process what advertisements will run alongside the news.

Top producers and editors are informed in advance of how much advertising they will carry. They know their most regular advertisers but think about them only in cases of possible conflict. If a top producer chooses a story on smoking and lung cancer, he checks whether a cigarette company is listed as one of the day's sponsors; and after first proposing, tongue in cheek, to place the story immediately before or after the cigarette commercial, he informs the business department of the story, which in turn allows the sponsor (or the advertising agency) to postpone the commercial for another day. If the agency decides to run the commercial nevertheless, it will be placed as far away as possible from the cancer story. The procedure is much the same at the newsmagazines, although top editors, having more makeup alternatives than top producers, can always move advertisements elsewhere and do not need to request postponements.

Advertisers cannot, however, put pressure on story selectors to kill or alter stories, since they do not have advance information on what will appear in the news. If they are unhappy, they can complain only *ex post facto,* and if sufficiently upset, they can cancel future advertising. Such cancellations take place from time to time at the magazines, but they are usually temporary, for most advertisers need the newsmagazines as much as the magazines need the advertising. At the networks, I heard of no cancellations due to dissatisfaction with the news; moreover, with multiple sponsors, no single one is that important, provided there is no dearth of interested sponsors. Weekend news programs often have single sponsors, however. An NBC news executive pointed out that Exxon, which sponsors the network's weekend programs, has never complained or interfered; but he also suggested that if a major oil spill occurred on a Sunday, he would have to cancel the day's commercials, "and that might be very difficult."

Interestingly enough, none of the magazine advertisers canceled because of displeasure with news about their own products or firms; rather, they canceled, like subscribers, for reasons of taste or "liberal bias." Some small companies pulled their advertisements because they objected to sex covers; others were unhappy with the magazines' emphasis on Watergate. The only economically motivated cancellation took place in 1974, after *Time* ran a satirical cartoon cover on the economic crisis; in this instance, a major advertiser felt that the cover was an unduly cynical commentary on the crisis. However, even this objection was largely on grounds of political taste.

At that time, many local business people complained about all national media, arguing that news which publicized rising inflation and unemployment could only worsen both; but as far as I could tell, none exerted direct pressure on the news media I studied. In 1975, a southern automobile dealer published newspaper advertisements picturing the three network anchormen and accusing the networks of fostering recession, but these only amused the network journalists.

I could not determine whether the advertiser's discontent with the satirical cover on the economy affected *Time*'s decision to "go slow" on future satirical covers, because both it and earlier cartoon covers (on Watergate) had been criticized by readers and journalists as well. The objections from advertisers to the plethora of Watergate news were not taken seriously, however. Although corporate executives were sometimes nervous about the continuous attention paid to the story, they did not interfere with the journalists; and later, after Richard Nixon's resignation, some advertisers actually apologized for their earlier criticisms.

As might be imagined, journalists resent advertiser interference. Many are also unhappy about advertising *sui generis* because advertisements take up time or space that could otherwise be devoted to news, and because they fear that the lack of credibility of advertising will damage their own credibility. Television journalists will not read or introduce commercials on the air for this reason. Then, too, journalists dislike some advertisements on esthetic grounds: journalists in television often wished they could replace the commercials for laxatives and denture adhesives, which dominate the evening news.

At the magazines, the dislike of advertisers seemed strongest in the business sections, and one writer told me that years ago the business writers informally competed to see how many advertisers they could enrage to the point that they would cancel their advertisements. The story may have been apocryphal, but it symbolizes the attitudes which exist among journalists. Business critics of the news media have pointed to these attitudes as evidence that journalists are anti-business; but the journalists' hostility is limited to advertisers and is not extended to the business community in general.

In fact, there is little reason for advertisers to protest how their firms and products are reported. Television carries little business-related news in any case, while the magazines' business sections are, on the whole, written for business readers. Domestic news sections are less reverent toward business, but neither they nor other sections have much reason to choose anti-business stories. Journalists readily run news about business corruption when it becomes available, much as they do about political corruption, but private firms have been fairly successful in blocking access to investigative reporters out to expose business misdeeds. Still, the journalists' importance considerations and paraideology rarely lead to the general attacks on private enterprise that infuriate advertisers and the business community as a whole.

The freedom from advertiser interference enjoyed by television news and the newsmagazines does not extend, however, to hour-long network news documentaries. For one thing, the high cost of producing documentaries, at least relative to the ratings they earn, sometimes encourages the networks to find sponsors before the final decision to produce a specific documentary has been made, and the sponsors' lack of enthusiasm for news documentaries generally, and those on controversial topics specifically, can discourage their production. Once produced, however, sponsor reluctance does not prevent their being shown; all networks have run their share of virtually unsponsored documentaries, including those in which sponsors backed out a few days before their showing.

Since news documentaries, even when not controversial, are screened in advance so that affiliated stations can decide whether to broadcast them, sponsors as well as sources can view them early enough to protest their content. In 1970, when NBC prescreened "Migrant," its exposé of the treatment of migrant farm workers, the Coca-Cola Company learned that part of the exposé criticized its Florida citrus farms and demanded changes in the program. Perhaps because it is a major television sponsor, some of its demands were met, although its confrontation with NBC executives also became a subsequent news story, resulting in positive publicity for the documentary and negative publicity for the network and the Coca-Cola Company.[5]

Although investigative reporters prefer their exposés to appear on the evening news programs, where they will reach a larger audience, sponsors and sources appear to be more threatened by exposés reported in hour-long documentaries. These are longer and less ephemeral than five-minute segments on the evening news; they are usually reviewed in advance by television critics; and perhaps most important, they are thought to attract an influential audience, including Washington officials. And perhaps they do, for documentaries occasionally inspire speeches on the floor of Congress as well as legislation; and two documentaries, "The Selling of the Pentagon" and "Hunger," became the subjects of congressional investigations.[6]

The journalists' freedom from advertiser pressure actually extends to business in general, since the power that corporations have in America does not seem to permeate the newsroom. To be sure, the corporations have little need to extend it there, but when they do, they seem to be stymied. Instead, business leaders hold conferences on how to influence the news media, appeal to each other to present a more positive image of business, and make speeches on the journalists' lack of enthusiasm about the business point of view. But these are symbolic gestures.

Only one business has the power to censor: the firm to which each news organization belongs. No program or magazine will carry uncomplimentary news about itself or about its firm, except to publicize the firm's defense. Schorr points out, for example, that his story about the study of television violence conducted by President Johnson's National Commission on the Causes and Prevention of Violence was killed by the president of the news division, and that his interview with Sig Mickelson, a former CBS news executive, about CBS cooperation with the CIA was canceled on order of "higher authority."[7] Censorship of uncomplimentary news, however, does not extend to all parts of the firm. During the Vietnam War, for example, NBC News did not omit stories that might have displeased RCA subsidiaries holding war contracts; and CBS News once produced a documentary exposing corruption at CBS Records. (The investigative reporter involved in it wanted it shown on the evening news, however, and lost his job in the resulting argument with a news executive.[8])

Nonetheless, the freedom from successful business pressure enjoyed by the national news media is not shared by local newspapers, radio stations, and television stations. Advertisers and other business people unhappy with the news travel in the same social and political circles as the owners, managers, and news executives of local media, and consequently have easy access to them. More important, they have the economic leverage to demand censorship and to instill a nearly permanent chilling effect on the journalists, who cannot always be protected by the executives.

Although national professional journals constantly publish exposés of local advertiser interference, these do not appear to intimidate local advertisers. During good economic times, when jobs are plentiful, journalistic job seekers can avoid the news media which are under the thumbs of the local business community; but when jobs are scarce, they have little alternative.

National news firms can usually replace advertisers who try to interfere too often; besides, the advertisers are restrained by the glare of national publicity that only national journalists can create. Local journalists are, by contrast, in much the same position as academics in small, "local" colleges, who must also submit when their academic freedom threatens local power holders. The freedoms available to professionals in national news organizations, as in "national" universities, do not always trickle down to the local level.

Pressure from Affiliated Stations

The networks are, however, vulnerable to one kind of local pressure: that from affiliated stations. Since networks can own only five stations, the approximately two hundred stations affiliated with each network not only constitute most of the literal network, but can both refuse to carry network shows and switch their allegiance to other networks. They hold annual meetings with the network, at which time they can make their complaints known; in addition, they are organized into affiliate associations, and their officers, as well as individual station owners, can put pressure on the networks at any time.

Local station owners are local business people, but their pressure on the news has been overwhelmingly political and almost entirely in a conservative direction. During the early 1960s, southern affiliates criticized network coverage of the civil-rights marches; later on, affiliates argued that the evening news paid too much attention to ghetto disturbances and anti-war protestors, and in 1970, about 60 percent of NBC's affiliates voted that the news division was "slanted against the war in Vietnam."[9] Later in the decade, affiliates were upset about the attention paid to the economic crisis and the Watergate scandals.

Network journalists view the affiliate owners as hidebound conservatives who are expressing their personal objections to network news. This view has some justification, for affiliates who were strong supporters of the Nixon Administration also supported Vice-president Agnew's attacks on the networks. Some owners seem to have worked closely with the Nixon White House staff, presenting its opposition to the networks' war coverage as their own.[10] Not coincidentally, ABC, which until its recent ratings successes in entertainment programming had the shakiest hold on its affiliates, almost never offended the Nixon Administration and was consequently not criticized by its affiliates for its news coverage.

Nevertheless, in some cases, local owners are also transmitting the views of local power holders; thus, one owner who attacked NBC's Vietnam War coverage at the 1970 network-affiliate meetings indicated that "there are a lot of important people in my town who are very conservative, and we have to keep that in mind."[11] When affiliates object to the occasional violation of taste taboos, they may be transmitting the objections of those viewers who hold the affiliate station responsible.[12]

Affiliates were never mentioned during the time I conducted fieldwork at the networks, and the executive producers I asked said they had not experienced any pressure. True, at the time the news was not upsetting to affiliates; but even when it is, executives usually handle the complaints, and anchorpersons condemn affiliate criticism at the annual network-affiliate meetings.[13]

While affiliates do not seem to effect censorship or self-censorship, they have been able to bring about, or hasten, the removal of individual on-air reporters. The blacklisting of television entertainers during the McCarthy era, which was itself supported by affiliate pressure, also cost some journalists, then identified as liberals, their jobs, among them Martin Agronsky, Elmer Davis, Don Hollenbeck (who subsequently committed suicide), Chet Huntley, and Raymond Gram Swing.[14] And surely many job applicants with controversial political pasts were not hired during this period. Howard K. Smith was forced out of CBS in the early 1960s because southern stations objected to his support of black civil-rights marchers.[15]

More recently, some affiliates were highly critical of Dan Rather, who was White House correspondent during the Watergate era, although both he and the network have insisted that his transfer to the prestigious but rarely shown *CBS Reports* after Richard Nixon's resignation had nothing to do with affiliate pressure.[16] Conversely, Daniel Schorr, who was asked to resign from CBS in February 1976, felt that some affiliates, concerned about pending congressional legislation on pay TV and cable television, had urged CBS to get rid of him because he had antagonized several high-ranking congressmen by leaking a secret committee report to *The Village Voice.*[17]

Dan Rather's and Daniel Schorr's experiences appear not to have produced a chilling effect on other journalists. The reasons for Rather's departure from the White House post remain uncertain; and Schorr, who had a reputation as an "abrasive" colleague to begin with, antagonized several co-workers by the way in which he leaked the congressional report. Consequently, colleagues and peers could play down possible political threats that might endanger their own careers. They could also note that both Rather and Schorr became national celebrities as a result of their experiences, writing successful books and garnering well-paying lecture invitations. In addition, the total number of journalists who have so far been forced out by affiliate or other pressures over the years has been small. But that is no guarantee for the future, because if news that displeases the affiliates breaks at a time when ratings are low (when networks must find ways of discouraging them from signing with a rival network), the news divisions might be asked to help out by responding to affiliate demands to fire offending journalists.

Political Pressures: Government and Interest Groups

Government Pressures

Journalists are under pressure to censor and self-censor from public officials more often than from business. Private firms can retaliate against harmful news by running self-justifying advertising, but government must defend itself in the same news media that attack it, and defensive statements or denials are never as credible as the initial bad news. Perhaps as a result, public officials are extremely sensitive to news about themselves and are as thin-skinned as journalists when it comes to criticism. The outcome is a predisposition to exert pressure, if only in self- (and agency-) defense.

I shall not detail instances of government pressure, for they have been reported in an ever-growing literature, largely written by worried journalists, covering in particular the McCarthy era, the Vietnam War, and the Johnson and Nixon Administrations.[18] These have been complemented by a handful of defenses of government pressure, mainly by former members of the Nixon Administration.[19] Instead, my analysis will focus on the types of pressure and their effectiveness.

Public officials have five ways of communicating their displeasure. First, and probably most often, government officials complain to a news or corporate executive; but as I have already suggested, executives may not relay the message to the editorial staff. The most widely reported, and partly successful, attempt at political pressure in recent years was the previously noted shortening of the second segment of a two-part October 1972 *CBS Evening News* story on Watergate. In this instance, Charles Colson put pressure on William Paley, charging the CBS journalists with "in effect, working for George McGovern," and threatening revenge against the network.[20] Although Paley did not pass on Colson's criticism and threats, the journalists were finally persuaded, after long and bitter discussion, to reduce the length of the second segment. But in the end, the pressure attempt backfired for all concerned. The White House, which had demanded the killing of the second segment in its entirety, was still angry at CBS. And Paley, according to Schorr, was furious because his network's reputation for "hard-hitting independence" had been damaged when CBS's decision to cut the segment became a news story of its own, even while the White House continued to "[ache] for vengeance."[21]

Watergate may be a poor example for demonstrating the limits of effective government pressure, for the escalation of the scandals, as well as the audience's interest in them, frustrated White House attempts to use pressure to discourage the news media from reporting further scandals.[22] Government pressure can rarely be effective when there is widespread interest in a story.

A second type of pressure threatens to hurt the firm economically if its journalists do not report the news more to the liking of complaining officials. Threats against the firm are, of course, implied in the pressure exerted on executives, although instances of successful threats are few. Still, the Nixon Administration made many threats during its first term and might have implemented them during its second term had it not been for Watergate.

The networks are most vulnerable to economic threats, for their owned stations and affiliates are licensed by the FCC and can be charged with violations of the "Fairness Doctrine." Only one license has ever been withdrawn for violating the doctrine, however, and the networks have considerable power of their own inside the FCC. Perhaps this explains why the Nixon Administration resorted to other threats, such as recruiting wealthy supporters to apply for station licenses held by the Washington Post Company, and proposing to lengthen the license period for local stations from three to five years, allegedly in exchange for more affiliate pressure on network news. The networks are also vulnerable because the government can threaten to revoke government contracts with the corporation to which the networks belong. During the Vietnam War, RCA executives were said to have been concerned that the government might cancel the conglomerate's defense contracts in retaliation for NBC News's reports on the war; but if the government threatened RCA executives directly or indirectly, the executive producers responsible for the NBC news program at the time never knew about it. Powerful politicians can exert pressure through friends owning affiliate stations, as did the Nixon Administration; and they can get in touch with corporate friends who are also major advertisers. "LBJ could tell the Business Council it's un-American to advertise," a top editor pointed out many years ago, "although if it got out, LBJ would be in trouble. But the threat is always there."

Third, government can pressure the news media by launching investigations. Three recent examples are noteworthy: two which followed the CBS documentaries "Hunger" and "The Selling of the Pentagon," and one which resulted from Schorr's leaking of a secret congressional committee report to *The Village Voice*. The investigations of the two documentaries were impelled by the federal agencies whose practices were criticized in the programs (Agriculture and the Pentagon) but were supported by their defenders in Congress.

Neither investigation resulted in legislation or official sanctions, but the networks and the individual producers spent considerable time and money defending themselves.[23] Perhaps the investigations further eroded the enthusiasm of network management for exposé documentaries, and some documentary producers have hinted at being sufficiently chilled to drop story ideas that, they felt, would never be approved by news executives. Even so, *60 Minutes* has not eschewed exposés of government. But Peter Davis, who produced the Pentagon documentary and was associate producer of "Hunger," finally left television altogether; and the congressional investigation of Daniel Schorr supplied the initiative for his departure from CBS. These examples suggest once more that a major effect of pressure is the extrusion of individual journalists.

A fourth kind of pressure, which threatens the journalists themselves more than their firms, is legal. Angry sources and others regularly will bring suit to restrain the journalists from gathering and reporting news that harms their interests. Despite the constitutional guarantees of the Bill of Rights, legal action, if sustained by the courts, can void ancillary rights, thereby restricting and chilling the journalists.[24] In 1970, for example, the Department of Justice attempted to subpoena magazine files and television outtakes about the Black Panthers and other activist groups in order to obtain evidence to be used against them. Had the attempt been upheld by the courts, journalists would have lost access, perhaps permanently, to all activist sources.[25]

From time to time, local journalists have been tried, and in some instances briefly jailed, for refusing to reveal their sources. So far, the pressured journalists have been successful in protecting their sources, but the issue is still before the courts. Were they to rule that journalists do not have a privileged relationship with sources, the effects on the news would be immediate and extensive.

Meanwhile, in June 1978, the Supreme Court ruled that the police have the right to search newsrooms in their hunt for evidence of criminal activities. If the ruling is enforced systematically and energetically, the police can identify sources themselves, even if journalists refuse to reveal them. In any case, sources who wish to withhold information, and their identity, from the police will have good reasons for not talking to reporters.

Two weeks later, the Supreme Court ruled further that journalists could be denied access to a California jail in which, a lower court had decided, living conditions were so debasing that they amounted to cruel and unusual punishment for the inmates. This ruling can set an equally far-reaching precedent, restricting journalistic access to other public agencies which prefer not to be in the news.[26]

Although the eventual consequences of the recent Supreme Court decisions cannot now be estimated, journalists are worried because the Burger Court appears to believe that the Bill of Rights does not require the protection of either journalists or journalist-source relationships. Not only do court decisions stimulate further lawsuits to prevent journalists from carrying out their responsibilities, but these decisions are a form of pressure which journalists cannot fight.

Most lawsuits are brought against local journalists, although adverse court decisions may also chill national journalists. Moreover, whatever their outcome, lawsuits can be used to harass journalists, forcing them to spend time, money, and effort to defend themselves. Riesman, writing in 1942, suggested that libel suits offered a "convenient weapon to punish outsiders coming down to stir up trouble."[27] In the 1960s, lawsuits and investigations sometimes harassed radical publications—which, like other radical groups, lacked the funds to hire lawyers—out of existence. The national news media can afford lawyers, but lawsuits can result in a corporate loss of enthusiasm for future controversial projects. When lawyers make their presence felt in the newsrooms, journalists think twice before making legally risky news judgments.

A fifth type of pressure goes over the heads of the journalists, when critics appeal to the audience in an attempt to impress it with the journalists' failings. Politicians have used this approach through the ages; one of its aims is to generate an outpouring of audience mail that will chill journalists. The prime recent example was Vice-president Agnew's 1969 speeches attacking the networks and other news media, which elicited an immediate response from viewers who had already been upset by bad news about the ghetto disturbances, the Vietnam War, and the anti-war protests; and the number of people (100,000) who contacted the networks to second the vice-president was unprecedented. Their impact was reduced, however, by the fact that the networks had already been receiving audience protest along this line; in addition, Agnew's support was temporary. A poll taken for ABC a month after his first speech indicated that while 52 percent of the respondents agreed with his charges, 60 percent also thought that the news media were fair to the White House.

Meanwhile, the Agnew speeches generated considerable sympathy for the journalists from their peers, from civil libertarians, and above all, from their superiors. When I visited NBC the day after Agnew's first speech, the journalists were cheerful, for the president of the network had, for the first time, spoken out publicly in their behalf.[28]

Whether the Agnew speeches had the chilling effect he intended is doubtful. Stein, making an informal survey of network journalists about a year later, found that they were engaged in more "self-evalua-tion," by which they meant concern with the implications of their written and filmed stories about conservatives and the "silent major-ity."[29] Even though Agnew had attacked television news as being produced by a "tiny and closed fraternity of privileged men," no changes were made in the news organizations; nor did the networks end the "instant analyses" of the president's speeches which Mr. Agnew had criticized.[30]

While journalists feared a chilling effect, it does not appear to have taken place, perhaps because everyone was afraid of it happening. Lowry studied a sample of network news stories before and after the Agnew speeches, and found, among other things, a 9 percent increase in statements attributed to an identified source. Perhaps journalists were more careful, but Lowry's expectation that they would be less likely to draw inferences from the news was not borne out by his data.[31]

My own impression is that Agnew's impressive audience response, and his impact on the news, may have been generated by his populist charge that the journalists, being representatives of an East Coast elite, were ignoring the news preferences of Middle America. His criticism was quickly picked up and developed by other news-media critics of conservative political bent.[32] It was also accepted by the journalists themselves; and Middle America, white ethnics, and Spiro Agnew himself became more newsworthy for a time.

Presumably, the constant availability of a conservative audience which is unhappy both with the state of American society and the journalists, and which is unusually vocal, guarantees that in the fu-ture, other politicians may imitate the Agnew approach or a similar one used by Governor Wallace.[33] I doubt that it can effectively chill the journalists because they already expect and discount that audi-ence.

Should the conservative audience grow measurably larger and an-grier, however, the Agnew approach could be successful, although the news media might respond to the change in the audience even before a politician attacked them. On the evening news programs which reported that California voters had overwhelmingly approved Proposition 13 mandating automatic tax reductions, both David Brinkley and Howard K. Smith endorsed the proposition. Of course, they did not do so to ward off an attack on the networks; they voiced their own feelings. In fact, they had previously expressed their low opinion of high taxes, but this time, they took an explicit stand.

Interest-group Pressures

Journalists are also under surveillance by a variety of organized interest groups, which will protest if they consider the news unfair or inaccurate on issues in which they have taken an interest. They express their objection mainly through letter writing, press conferences, and public meetings. Organized letter-writing campaigns are discounted by the journalists, but letters from officers of major national organizations are taken into account and are apt to be answered by an executive. If sent to a magazine, they may be published in the letters section.

Interest-group pressure appears to be effective when it obtains political support, in Congress or elsewhere; when it threatens advertisers and local television stations; and when it is persuasive to the journalists. However, pressure from powerless groups is ignored.

News documentaries seem to be most vulnerable to interest-group pressure, and for the same reasons that they are vulnerable to other forms of pressure. Robert MacNeil recounts the successful efforts of the National Rifle Association, a powerful national lobby, to strengthen its on-air rebuttal of a 1967 NBC documentary favoring gun control; some years later, similarly effective pressure was exerted on a documentary about hunters;[34] and in 1975, pressure from the American Jewish Committee following a mini-documentary about Syrian Jewry on *60 Minutes* led to an "amplification" in a later program.

Most interest-group pressure has actually been mounted against entertainment television. Child welfare and church organizations, the P. T. A., viewer groups, and most recently the American Medical Association have been successful in reducing the amount of physical violence in prime-time network programming. These groups have not, however, pressured the networks to reduce news violence; they are either sufficiently liberal or unwilling to open themselves to charges of proposing news censorship. Besides, journalists already edit out violent scenes of the kind that appear in entertainment programs.[35]

Pressures from Peers

Like all professionals, journalists are also under some pressure from members of their own profession, especially media reviewers and critics. Although some pressure is aimed against the journalists themselves, much of it is addressed to management.

Most media critics are themselves journalists, but their impact depends on who employs them. At least among the journalists I studied, critics employed by competing media were rarely attended to. Even though they were fellow-professionals, they were almost always thought to express their firm's desire to make the competition look bad. This reaction may be cynical, but it is not inaccurate, for many news-media critics seem to be harshest on other media with which they are in competition.

Magazines and newspapers critically review their major rival, television (and both newsmagazines have television sections); network and public television have, from time to time, carried programs which chastised their primary competitor, the daily press; and other "class" magazines publish critical articles about the newsmagazines. Only the journals of opinion are impartial in choosing their targets; they find flaws in the reportage of all large national news media.

The contents of the newsmagazines and evening news programs are not regularly reviewed anywhere, but news documentaries are almost always reviewed in the daily papers. Some reviews carry weight both with producers and network executives, since the networks schedule documentaries to obtain prestige rather than high ratings. The primary indicator of prestige is a favorable review in *The New York Times.*

During the last few years, the print media have also begun to keep up with personnel changes at the networks, reporting the hiring and firing of anchorpersons and news executives (but not executive producers). These stories are now newsworthy because some journalists have become celebrities. Also, journalists look gleefully at turmoil in the network executive suites, while ignoring similar turmoil in their own.

From time to time, journalists become ad-hoc media critics, taking their peers and even their superiors to task in public—although sometimes they are then punished for attacking their firms.[36] But as I reported previously, network journalists are allowed to criticize local news programs which strike them as muddying journalism with show business.

News that evokes widespread discussion is also likely to generate ad-hoc media criticism from journalists. Editorial writers for conservative newspapers and nationally syndicated conservative columnists have criticized the national news media on the same stories, and along the same lines, as the conservative audience. These criticisms are ignored for the most part, not only because they come from competing news media, but because they are predictable and expected. A dramatic and more effective instance of this took place early in the Vietnam War, when some senior journalists, including Joseph Alsop, Richard Tregaskis, and Margaret Higgins, paid brief visits to Vietnam. Having concluded that America was winning a justified war, they criticized a number of young Saigon reporters for their pessimistic stories. Subsequently, two *Time* reporters resigned from the magazine when its managing editor published a story expressing his agreement with Alsop et al., thereby impugning the credibility of his own men.[37]

A very different and more regular form of news-media criticism is supplied by professional publications, such as the *Columbia Journalism Review, More* (now defunct), and *Nieman Reports.* These journals, local equivalents that have appeared in a number of cities, and unofficial in-house newsletters that occasionally spring up in national news organizations provide supportive criticism, reporting and condemning commercially or politically motivated management interference with journalists. Supportive critics assume that story selection should be based as much as possible on substantive considerations; and while this assumption is in practice unworkable, it establishes a norm that supports the journalists vis-à-vis management and upholds their claim to autonomy.

These journals also award what the editors of the *Columbia Journalism Review* call "darts" and "laurels" to individual media and journalists. They criticize empirical and conceptual sloppiness, such as the use of unreliable sources and stereotypes; laziness in relying on handouts; and corruption, going on "junkets." At the same time, they laud energetic legwork, thoughtful analysis, persistence and extraordinary effort, and the willingness to take risks in reporting on the powerful or in standing up to publishers, advertisers, politicians, and other nonjournalists who pressure them.

In effect, these stories apply the enduring values to journalism itself; they are, in many instances, moral disorder stories which identify villains and celebrate journalists who have clearly behaved heroically in struggling against often overwhelming pressure. Most case studies deal with local villains and heroes, and are thus of little direct relevance to national journalists; but they reinforce journalistic ideals, which journalists can use to inspire themselves to greater effort or to demonstrate to management that journalistic autonomy must be preserved.

Journalistic Reactions to Pressure

As I suggested earlier, journalists have three ways of dealing with pressure: they can fight back, give in, or avoid it by resorting to several kinds of anticipatory mechanisms. Some of their reactions to pressure have already been discussed in this chapter and elsewhere, and require only summary here.

Fighting Back: Defenses Against Pressure

When overt pressure is exerted against journalists, they defend themselves by asserting their moral right to freedom of the press. However, rights do not implement themselves whatever their moral power; but the journalists' claim to autonomy is supported by constitutional guarantees and by a general consensus on the part of the public. These supports in turn restrain exerters of pressure and executives who may, on commercial grounds, prefer to give in to them. As a result, journalists were always surprised when management gave in, while I was surprised by how rarely it did so.

Journalists also use their moral, legal, and consensual power to fight back. They speak out quickly against threats to their autonomy and predict chilling effects so as to discourage anyone from trying to chill them. Despite their reluctance to take stands on current issues, journalists do not hesitate to do so when freedom of the press is at stake. Equally important, journalists have some power to hurt the exerters of pressure; as I pointed out earlier, they can report attempts to pressure them as news.

Journalists can also resist pressure by ignoring it, notably from the audience. Although they give in on matters of taste, they do not respond to the charges of political or other bias that come regularly from the vocal audience. They ignore audience criticism because it is ever-present and unchanging, regardless of what is in the news; and because in the end, letter writers can hurt them only when they complain en masse to advertisers or affiliates.

In theory, freedom of the press, like academic freedom, is total; for that reason, journalists claim the sole right to determine when it should be limited in practice. Press freedom, however, is total only for the journalists themselves; they are less concerned with similar freedoms for sources, audiences, or, for that matter, executives.

Giving In: Forms of Journalistic Surrender

At times, journalists or their organizations give in to pressure. Even so, they often try to camouflage their surrender; for example, when individuals are forced to resign, their departure may be delayed or ascribed to other reasons. In much the same way, journalists respond to criticism, but after the fact and on their own terms. Once the heating effect wears off, they may take criticism to heart, although they are not always aware that they are doing so. After journalists were sometimes criticized for publicizing the ghetto disorders and anti-war demonstrations of the late 1960s, they paid less attention to the smaller disturbances, claiming that they did so because they felt themselves and the audience to be bored with them.

In 1972, Nixon supporters criticized the networks for giving too much time to George McGovern and not enough to the "surrogates" campaigning for Richard Nixon. Although journalists deemed the criticism unjustified, they were careful, in 1976, to give equal time to both candidates. During Watergate, journalists were occasionally charged with reporting unverified charges against members of the Nixon White House staff. As a result, during the exposé of the CIA and FBI scandals in 1975, they were careful not to arouse the same criticism, and held their stories until they had accrued sufficient evidence.

But as already noted, journalists do not pay close attention to criticism from powerless quarters, responding only when the same charges are made by more authoritative, if not necessarily more powerful, people. As long as only anti-war activists charged that the news failed to report the American bombing of North Vietnamese civilians, journalists gave little credence to their complaints; but when *New York Times* editor Harrison Salisbury and others visited Hanoi and supported the charges, the story became newsworthy. Likewise, black and anti-war activist reports of police brutality were discounted until more trustworthy sources also reported it. In this case, as in others, however, the powerless critics may evoke journalistic curiosity, and reporters who sense a fresh story may go out to investigate on their own.

Journalists also ignore criticism to which they cannot respond for various reasons. During the Vietnam War, television was often accused of using too much battle and patrol films; but while some journalists agreed privately, the networks ignored the criticism, partly because they were neither willing nor able to develop a new approach to covering the war.

In Chapter 6, I indicated that although journalists claim the freedom to disregard the implications of the news, they sometimes violate that freedom. Like most other people, they respond more attentively to criticism from those who can hurt them and ignore criticism they cannot deal with. But because they are able to decide what criticism is justified, they can also give in on their own terms. Thus, they do not have to take the power or relevance of their critics into explicit account.

Anticipatory Avoidance of Pressure

Since journalists have neither time nor energy to react to all the possible pressures they might encounter, they anticipate some of them and take steps to avoid them. Some avoidance mechanisms, however, are built into other considerations, resulting in self-censorship (in the broader sense of the term) without the journalists perceiving it as such. Consequently, felt pressure is reduced, as is the likelihood of conscious censorship and self-censorship.

Cooperation with Power Holders

The most effective way to avoid pressure is to cooperate with those who can exert it; and journalists often cooperate with the powerful, even if not solely to ward off pressure. When story selectors postpone or separate advertising that clashes with the news, they are cooperating with their advertisers, both to maintain their good will and to avoid protest and loss of income. At *Time,* stories about the law and medicine are reviewed by a lawyer and doctor before they are sent to the printers. The aim of this practice is to ensure accuracy, although the reviewers are free to question—but not to censor—criticism of their professions.[38]

Since government is the primary source of pressure, however, it is also the recipient of most journalistic cooperation. These days, journalists and government are commonly thought to be in an adversary relationship, although government is not an adversary most of the time. As the major source of news, it is in many ways a member of the journalistic team; and even during the Watergate years, journalists continued to cooperate with many segments of the government, including the White House.

The principal form of cooperation is built into the source considerations, through their skew toward official sources; and into the symbiotic relationship between beat reporters and their sources, which inhibits reporters from displeasing them. In addition, journalists cooperate with government by resorting to self-censorship on matters of national security. In recent years, they have done so in connection with the preparations for the Bay of Pigs invasion, a number of Vietnam War ventures, and many CIA activities. When the CIA tried to raise a Russian submarine from the bottom of the ocean, William Colby, then the director of the CIA, visited the major national news media personally to request their self-censorship; but the story came out because columnist Jack Anderson failed to cooperate, and the other news media then reported it for competitive reasons.

National security self-censorship, even at the expense of scoops, has a long history. Journalists accept it because, as citizens, they are also concerned with national security; and as journalists and citizens, they do not want to contribute to the possible loss of American lives. Even when they are not convinced that the national security is at stake, they may give the government the benefit of the doubt, if only to discourage criticism that they are unpatriotic. Self-censorship is also a self-regulating device that wards off government regulation, that is, official censorship. Journalists justified their cooperation with the military during the Vietnam War by noting that it was the first war not governed by official censorship. Journalists, however, bitterly resent public officials who use national security for political purposes. The Nixon Administration's attempt to stop Watergate leaks on national-security grounds only spurred the journalists on in their pursuit of further scandals.

Many journalists and news organizations cooperated with the government in various ways during the Cold War, evidently without thinking twice about it. Perhaps no one thought twice because the Cold War itself was taken for granted and supported; in addition, cooperation did not interfere with getting the news. The CIA apparently co-opted a number of journalists in ways that are still only beginning to come to light. In some instances, CIA agents used a journalistic role as a cover; in others, journalists worked for the CIA on the side or allowed themselves to be debriefed by the agency. While some foreign correspondents who were suspected of cooperating with the CIA had difficulties obtaining news from sources who considered them spies, many others found CIA ties helpful. Agency officials were well informed and could therefore supply tips, stories, and occasional scoops. During the Vietnam War, I was told, the CIA sometimes provided news about the North Vietnamese, and on an exclusive basis.

Recent congressional investigations, as well as my own fieldwork, also suggest that CIA agents, looking for information in television film outtakes and magazine reporters' files, may have infiltrated some national news organizations without being invited, at least by journalists. Invitations seem to have been extended by some executives, however; Schorr reports, for example, that William Paley allowed the CIA to use both network staff and facilities.[39] During the 1960s, CIA and FBI agents obtained press passes from local news organizations, presumably with executive compliance, to spy on anti-war protesters. At the time, local television stations voluntarily supplied outtakes of films made at anti-war demonstrations to help the CIA, FBI, or local police "red squads" identify individual demonstrators; but I could find no evidence, pro or con, of network cooperation along this line.[40] As long ago as 1967, a documentary producer reported in a public lecture that the CIA had requested that the network allow agents to join camera crews of news documentaries being shot in Eastern Europe. In 1975, a former ABC reporter brought suit against the network, in which he charged, among other things, that it had censored a story about the CIA.

Many of the charges against the CIA have been denied, but then they always are. Conversely, Miles Copeland, a former CIA official, corroborated some of the charges in a letter to *The New York Times,* at least those applying to "every American correspondent serving in the Middle East or Africa from 1947 up to the witchhunts of 1975 and 1976." He pointed out that "foreign correspondents in those good old days were on *our* side, anxious to help their country by passing on such information to its Government as came their way in the normal course of their investigations, and . . . the CIA 'station chief' is normally the safest and most effective conduit."[41]

Journalists often cooperate with the government to gain a competitive advantage in the search for news, but executives do so for other reasons. For one thing, they are the major targets of pressure and may have more difficulty saying no; for another, corporate executives, like their peers in other firms, sometimes play concurrent government roles. They move in the same social circles as highly placed public officials, and they are asked to assist their government or political party in one or another way. Like other corporate officers, they cooperate in order to be responsive to friends and peers, as well as to create good will for their firms, which may occasionally help in dealing with pressure. Some executives have volunteered their services, and for the same reasons. During the mid-1960s, however, one television news executive was described by journalists as a press agent for Lyndon Johnson because he wanted a job in the White House—and eventually he got it.

Founders and owners of news firms have been especially active in cooperating with the government. Halberstam, whose most recent work has chronicled the political activities of founding owners, shows that both Henry Luce and William Paley played a variety of roles in government and Republican party affairs, and that both occasionally used their news organizations to further their political aims. Luce used *Time* to lobby for his China policy, to help elect President Eisenhower, and in his later years, to support the Vietnam War—often over the protest of his staff.[42] Paley encouraged Murrow's departure from CBS, as noted earlier, because of complaints about him from Paley's friends in the Eisenhower Administration and to reduce the threat of government pressure on his network. Later, Schorr reports, Paley helped the CIA in undescribed ways, but as a private individual rather than as the head of CBS.[43]

When appointed executives replace founding owners, cooperation with government slackens, for although they continue to take on periodic government duties, they appear to be less willing or able to use their news organizations for personal political aims.[44] Journalists are aware of their executives' ties to government; and these ties probably chill them more, if still not significantly, than the angry threats of public officials. In the end, executives have greater and more immediate power over the journalists than politicians.

Maintaining Empirical Credibility

Journalists also forestall pressure by preserving their credibility. They work within the limits permitted by libel laws, of course, although these currently favor journalists at the expense of sources, notably public officials. Even so, the news media I studied had lawyers on call to review stories which might initiate lawsuits; and newsmagazine stories reprinted verbatim in their international editions must be written with foreign libel laws in mind.

More important, journalists are aware that their stories have to be based on convincing evidence. They are constantly offered tips which would make dramatic stories, and even scoops, about illegalities and conspiracies but for which convincing and legally defensible evidence is not available. Yet, what makes evidence convincing is not always a purely methodological question. Since journalists usually need only convince themselves and their superiors, the rules of evidence are shaped by their own beliefs and, indirectly, by the power of sources as well. Authoritative sources are believed simply because they are authoritative; those which are not must provide evidence for their claims before reporters and editors will accept them.

Story suggestions and stories that could generate controversy or pressure naturally require more convincing evidence than others, particularly if they must be reviewed by executives. In effect, the standards for what makes evidence convincing become stricter at the higher levels of the organizational hierarchy; top editors and producers, as well as executives, must be more cautious than their underlings.[45]

News that might upset people without power requires less convincing evidence, however. Journalists occasionally report news from distant foreign countries based on slender evidence—for example, most recently, the number of people killed by the postwar Communist government in Cambodia. They also report allegations about criminals, or culturally and politically deviant groups, because they believe these to be true. Stories about the Mafia seem to require less evidence in order to be convincing than other news, although it is also true that convincing evidence in this case is difficult to obtain. During the 1960s, black militants and anti-war radicals were sometimes accused of political and personal activities in which they took no part. Reporters heard rumors from the police or from bystanders and, believing them, failed to collect convincing evidence.

Credibility is further maintained through a taboo on "unbelievable news," so that stories are self-censored when journalists doubt their veracity. The taboo exists because even a normally convincing amount of evidence is not sufficient to persuade journalists that they are true. The phenomenon may be unique, the information may come from untrustworthy sources and could therefore be a hoax, or the story may transcend the journalists' expectations of what people are capable of doing. Every empirical discipline suppresses findings that contradict its common sense, and journalists are trained by experience to develop a cynical attitude toward the incredible.

I have already suggested that although the radical press published exposés of illegal CIA and FBI activities as far back as the 1960s, the national media considered them unbelievable until 1975. For much the same reason, American atrocities in Vietnam, as in other wars, were underreported, for even when reporters had collected evidence that convinced them, New York would have considered the stories sufficiently unbelievable to reject them as "atypical." When CBS finally carried a story about American soldiers collecting the ears of dead North Vietnamese soldiers, the reporter's text was almost entirely devoted to an apologetic statement, explaining the incident was atypical. Many now famous stories, such as Nader's early exposés, the Mylai massacre, and at the very start, the Watergate scandals, were initially slow in becoming national news because they were not considered credible.[46] But even when journalists are persuaded by the evidence, parts of the audience may still consider the stories unbelievable, in which case they write angry letters doubting the journalists' competence and credibility.

Built-in Anticipatory Avoidance

Finally, journalists forestall pressure by a number of devices which, being built into news judgment, serve other purposes as well. Value exclusion is practiced for several reasons, but as I suggested in Chapter 6, objectivity and detachment enable journalists to avoid taking stands that could result in pressure; and the rejection of ideology as "doctrinaire" and "extremist" allows them to claim that they are free of ideology. Ignoring the implications of the news does not avoid pressure and may even encourage it, but journalists need not respond to it. By being fair, they can accommodate the implications that might otherwise anger sources or audience members. And when editors or producers tone down writers, they do so in part to protect their reputation for fairness and their credibility among professional peers.

If value exclusion did not already exist for other reasons, however, it might have to be invented to avoid pressure. As long as journalists are involved in competition and must deal with heterogeneous sources and audiences, the constant expression of conscious values and opinions would surely enrage some sources, viewers, and readers all of the time. Only monopolistic news organizations, in some European countries and some American cities, can disregard value exclusion, for neither sources nor audiences can go elsewhere for the news.

But even some of the enduring values help prevent pressure. I suggested earlier that moderatism is an inherently defensive value; and if journalists stopped favoring ethnocentrism, individualism, and small-town pastoralism, the now vocal audience might be even more vocal. If journalists played down the need for leadership, they might face pressure from their most regular sources, who are, after all, public leaders; if they favored disorder, they would be flooded with protest from these same sources, who are also in charge of maintaining order. The enduring values did not come into being to anticipate pressure, but by their very nature they do.

In addition, criticism is already warded off by source considerations, and in at least two ways. By preferring authoritative sources, journalists pay attention and give publicity to powerful public officials who would be upset were they not deemed newsworthy and who would react accordingly. By avoiding sources which lack authority and those which evoke dissent, journalists also exclude news from, if not about, those individuals and groups whose ideas might result in pressure.

Suitability considerations serve avoidance functions as well. When journalists report controversies from both sides, and elections as contests, they free themselves from having to take sides. Other balance considerations are applied so as not to create unhappy sources and audiences from unreported parts of the nation or the society. And in the final analysis, product considerations, which make the news more attractive to the audience, also reduce pressure, for ultimately, what hurts journalists most is a shrinking audience.

Is There Censorship and Self-censorship?

As the preceding pages have suggested, conscious censorship and self-censorship are rare, as is the unconscious self-censorship that follows a chilling effect. Indeed, successful pressure is surprisingly infrequent; while 100,000 letters to the networks supporting Spiro Agnew's criticism did not materially affect journalistic news judgments, about the same number of letters to the White House forced Richard Nixon to make his tapes public.

By the journalists' definitions, then, there is no serious cause for alarm. But by a broader definition, it appears that through various forms of anticipatory avoidance, journalists are restrained from straying into subjects and ideas that could generate pressure, even if their own inclinations, as professionals or individuals, do not often encourage them to stray in the first place.

The journalistic definition allows journalists to have their cake while eating it. They either do not recognize anticipatory avoidance mechanisms as restraints or, in some cases, they believe them to be desirable. As a result, they do not perceive themselves as forestalling pressure and can therefore feel autonomous.

But are they unrestrained? To be sure, their reliance on unconscious or built-in restrictions puts the lie to simple conspiratorial theories that journalists are "kept," either by monopoly capitalists or by "the liberal Eastern Establishment." Such theories are based on the self-serving assumption that if the journalists' chains were cut, they would line up with the opponents of capitalism or the liberal establishment; that they are, in effect, radicals or ultraconservatives who are forced to suppress their own political values in order to hold their jobs.

But by the broader definition, journalists practice self-censorship; and my observations support the structural analyses of the news media proposed more often by activists or social scientists on the Left than on the Right: that journalists are restrained by systemic mechanisms that keep out some news. These analyses are, typically, combined with a critique of news media, which argues that the systemic restraints prevent journalists from dealing with what radicals—and I use the term loosely—consider to be the fundamental questions about, and the inherent contradictions of, America.

Whether or not journalists accept, endorse, or even recognize the limits under which they work is irrelevant. What matters is that journalists do not ask the questions which are assumed to be important by the framers of this critique: why America fought the Vietnam War; why wealth and power are so unequally distributed in America, and between the developed and developing nations; why corporations have so much power, and citizens so little; why unemployment, inflation, and poverty remain; and why women and racial minorities continue to occupy an inferior position.[47]

At one level, this critique is accurate, for the questions which radicals believe to be vital do not often concern journalists. (The same point can be made about the ultraconservative critique of America, for the news media also ignore its questions.) But the radical critique also has several shortcomings. First, it assumes that news should be based on a conscious and integrated ideology. However, journalists may be correct to argue that such a base would impair their flexibility in covering nation and society. Whether an ideology is of the Right or the Left, it makes some topics more newsworthy than they are at present, but at the expense of those not salient to the ideology. To be sure, the journalists' less integrated paraideology is also an ideology, but in the final analysis it encourages them to be somewhat more open-minded than would an integrated ideology. The journalistic paraideology need not be as conservative as it now is, but ideological news is apt to produce even more propaganda than paraideological news.

More important, news organizations that serve an audience of many millions cannot be expected to operate with an ideology—whatever its location on the ideological spectrum—that is accepted by only a small number in the audience. (Opponents of this argument might reply that the correct ideology should guide the news even if it is not accepted by large numbers, but that raises issues about democracy, to be considered in Chapter 10.) Of course, the news firms serve large audiences to make a profit, but European government-funded news organizations which are unaffected by profit motives do not frame the news in ideologies that are unpopular with large numbers. This is true, at least, in democratic nations.[48]

Third, and even more important, the radical critique is unrealistic, as is the broader definition of censorship and self-censorship. These definitions suggest that journalists can stand outside nation and society, free to report news, raise issues, and present ideas without limit. But no one, including journalists, can stand on the outside.[49] Moreover, while they should be free of restraints, perceived or other, they cannot ignore, any more than anyone else, the existence of pressure and of the power behind it. Were they able to do so, they would be all-powerful themselves and unaccountable to anyone.

As an outside observer, I am not bound by the journalists' definition of censorship and self-censorship; but while the broader definition is empirically more relevant, I cannot fully accept its implications. Whether the anticipatory avoidance mechanisms are called self-censorship or not matters little; however, if pressure and power are inevitable participants in the journalistic enterprise, the more significant issue is whose pressures should be taken into account. This is an issue of news policy and will be pursued further in Chapter 10.

9

Conclusions: The News and the Journalists

This chapter attempts a synthesis of Parts 1 and 2 to suggest which considerations are most significant in news judgment, and therefore in explaining the news. But because an empirical analysis looks at the status quo of the moment and can thus overestimate its permanence, my conclusions are immediately followed by an analysis of how much leeway journalists have to change the news. I ask how much the news could change; and Part 3 then suggests how I think it should change. Because my study has concentrated on journalists, perhaps slighting less visible social processes that may impinge on them and on the news, I append a discussion of some national and societal functions of the news and of the journalists.

The Significant Considerations

My identification of all the considerations that go into news judgment has ignored an important point: not all are relevant to every story. If they were, journalists could not do their work, for they lack the time to take them all into account. The preceding chapters have therefore made story selection and production appear to be more complicated than it actually is. Some considerations are virtually always relevant, but the number and mix that go into specific stories vary.

The most significant considerations show up most clearly in the major running stories. To illustrate with one brief case study: I suggested in Chapter 6 that the overall reportage of the Vietnam War was shaped by an initial importance judgment—that it was a domestic story—and by subsequent reality and value judgments, which framed the story as an American war against a Communist enemy. But the coverage was also affected by source considerations, notably the tendency, until Tet, to favor official sources. A variety of source availability factors came into play as well; these ranged from the news management, and saturation, strategies of the Saigon and Washington Pentagons, as well as the White House, to the inaccessibility of National Liberation Front and North Vietnamese sources, particularly once the news media had described them as the enemy.

The war coverage was further shaped by product considerations, because the search for dramatic action films, pictures, and stories led both television and the magazines to report the war mainly through battles, search-and-destroy missions, and patrols. But once all news media had chosen to emphasize dramatic action, they were locked in by competitive considerations, and no one was prepared to depart from the basic formula. Audience considerations forced television, more so than the magazines, to sanitize battle pictures.

Organizational considerations played a supporting role, for the skew toward official sources was complemented by the practice of top producers and editors placing their faith in the optimistic reports about the war from senior Washington reporters. On the other hand, if the news media had listened more closely to the pessimistic reports from some young Saigon reporters, they would have encountered more pressure than they did from government, as well as from the vocal audience, advertisers, and affiliates, all of whom were predominantly hawkish.

The anti-war protests were, for most of the war, treated as social disorder news. In this instance, journalists applied their own enduring values; they would have been under pressure—from government, sponsors, and the vocal audience—had they done otherwise. As it was, they were often accused of giving the protesters too much publicity and of slanting the war news in their behalf.

Case studies of other running stories would indicate somewhat different mixes, but every story requires a judgment about the availability and suitability of sources, story importance or interest, as well as novelty, quality, and other product criteria. In addition, every story must be judged for its salience to the medium and format of the television program or newsmagazine. These considerations are necessary not only because they prescribe the essential ingredients of any story, but also because they express and represent the interests of the major participants in story selection and production.

All considerations exist, of course, to routinize the journalistic task, thus making it possible for news organizations to function. For example, source considerations represent sources; importance considerations, which are the essence of news judgment, represent journalists. However, the considerations that assume major significance do so because they serve multiple participants simultaneously. Thus, importance judgments also represent the public officials whose activities are usually important. Product considerations, which attract the audience, thereby also benefit the news firm; value exclusion both serves an audience with diverse values and protects journalists from pressure. In fact, considerations that represent only a single constituency are hard to find.

Some considerations turn out, in the end, to be subsidiary. For example, organizational considerations are generally adaptations to the imperatives of story selection and production. More often than not, these imperatives shape the structure and operations of the news organization. The journalists' enduring values are also subsidiary. However essential values may be in putting a story together, and however important the enduring values are to journalism, specific values can be chosen only because they represent other interests. In Chapter 8, for example, I pointed out that many of the values help to anticipate pressure; if journalists did not hold them, these values might have to be invented. The journalistic concern with disorder and order has additional rationales; for instance, disorder news, being dramatic, almost always grabs the audience.

I do not want to explain away the enduring values as mere responses to other interests; like other considerations, they exist because they, too, serve multiple constituencies.[1] Yet, some values do so less than others, notably those which transform journalists into reformers. To be sure, a small constituency for reform is always on hand, for if journalists alone supported these values, they might not get into the news.

Toward a Final Explanation of the News: Power and Efficiency

The length of this book alone should demonstrate that there is no single or simple explanation of the news; but if a handful of explanatory factors had to be singled out, I suggest that of all the considerations, those governing the choice of sources are of prime significance. Most national news, after all, concerns the routine activities (and routine conflicts) of leading public officials.

These sources are chosen because they have power: both to supply the information that makes national news and to exert pressure. Most of the continuing pressures I described in Chapter 8 stemmed from those individuals and agencies which are also the major sources of the news; they do not have unlimited power, however. Journalists choose stories rather than sources, and their stories are hardly limited to handouts from the powerful. While these sources are, therefore, sometimes unhappy with how journalists report them, they would be unhappier still were they not major news sources in the first place. Since the news media constitute their major communication outlet to the citizenry, and are essential to the performance of their duties and the maintenance of their power, they would almost certainly use that power to pressure the journalists were journalists to rely less upon them. Suppose story selectors agreed that the president no longer met their importance judgments. He and his associates might then resort to the arsenal of pressures described in Chapter 8, and beyond them, to more serious threats: mobilizing advertisers and sponsors against the journalists; encouraging new, more compliant news firms that would compete with uncooperative ones; proposing government regulation of the news media; or establishing governmentally run news media that would publicize the president's activities.

Powerful sources usually do not have to resort to such pressures because the news media chose them for another reason: they are, as I suggested in Chapter 4, the most easily and quickly available, as well as most reliable and productive, source of news. The most powerful sources are also the most efficient. This adds further to their power, for efficiency is the other major factor that explains the news.

The need for efficiency and the choice of efficient methods pervade story selection and production. As I noted repeatedly in earlier chapters, many considerations are designed to facilitate quick and easy news judgments, both in choosing stories from the mass of available ones and in gleaning relevant facts from an equally sizable mass. Considerations do not exist solely because they are efficient, but they become significant because they are also efficient.

Journalists do not, it should be emphasized, consciously pursue efficiency—far from it. Journalistic efficiency is not the rationally calculated commercial or industrial kind associated with profit calculations or time-and-motion studies; nor is it merely a means to the highest profit at the lowest cost, if only because news firms are not conventional manufacturers of conventional products. Their profits come from the sale of advertising rather than from the product itself.

Moreover, nonprofit news firms also stress efficiency; the television journalists at Britain's BBC, for example, apply much the same considerations as their American peers, and the news they choose bears a close resemblance to the American product.[2]

Rather, journalistic efficiency exists to allocate three scarce resources: staff, air time or print space, and, above all, production time. News organizations must be efficient because they are expected to deliver the latest news to the audience at a prescheduled time. Efficiency is thus a function of the deadline, for while no one knows whether the audience wants the latest news or whether it would pay more for less efficiently produced news, the news must be on the air or in the readers' mailboxes at a prearranged time.

Of course, profit is sought, and journalistic efficiency has economic causes and consequences. News firms do not hire unnecessary staff if they can help it; and air time and print space are scarce resources because the audience is thought to have a limited appetite for news. Indeed, efficiency is mediated by a second form of power, that of the audience, for in the end, the news must be produced in ways that will create and maintain an audience. Tell stories are more cheaply produced than film, but the assumption is that a program dominated by tell stories would lose viewers. No one knows whether the assumption is accurate, but competing networks do not dare to experiment. And while the audience has power because it is the ultimate fountainhead of profit, nonprofit news firms are also regulated by audience power.

Efficiency and power are intertwined, and it is difficult to say which is more important. Efficiency and source power are parts of the same equation, since it is efficient for journalists to respect the power of sources. If they did not regularly choose influential sources, news firms and journalists would have to spend time and monies to fend off their pressure. Efficiency and audience power are parts of another equation. Without a large audience, the news media could not exist in their present form. A smaller audience would lead to smaller budgets; and if the audience became too small, news organizations would consist of freelance writers, as they do at the journals of opinion.

Source power is greater than audience power, at least presently, for the national news media appear to supply a good deal of news which is not preferred by the audience.[3] But the audience consists of consumers, who rarely have as much power to affect the products they buy as suppliers do. Also, they are spectators, no more able to shape the news than they are able to determine the actions of powerful sources. At best, the audience has an influence on story production. But potentially, the audience has greater power than sources, for if it decided to reject news from or about the present sources, the news firms would have to go along. Even so, the audience could exert such power only by a mass boycott, requiring the nearly impossible task of transforming itself from a heterogeneous aggregate of spectators into an organized and mobilized movement.

Within the twin restraints of efficiency and power, journalists have autonomy, but that autonomy is itself bounded by the two restraints. Journalists are free to apply importance considerations, for example, but these respect the power hierarchy among sources. They can bring in their enduring values, but only when these are supported by other considerations and fall within the limits set by value exclusion, which respects the power of pressure.

Power, as I use it here, is not force, and though unequally distributed, it is not monopolized by a single group. Nor is it predominantly pressure, since most journalists accept the existing distribution of power. As professionals who deem themselves entitled to autonomy, journalists cope with the realities of power by incorporating it into news judgment. They work with apolitical source considerations that are nevertheless sensitive to political power; they apply product considerations that professionalize the commercial imperatives of their firms; they practice value exclusion that similarly professionalizes the avoidance of judgments which could upset the powerful; and in the process, they hide the existence of power even from themselves.

Admittedly, journalists are not alone in this respect, for other professions also use autonomy as a means of coping with the realities of power. Nor is it an irrational strategy, since it enables journalists to feel that they have greater autonomy than they actually have; and when power holders violate enduring values which are widely shared, autonomy to expose the miscreants can make journalists quite powerful themselves for the moment.

A simple summary, then, of the first two parts of this book would suggest that news is about the economic, political, social, and cultural hierarchies we call nation and society. For the most part, the news reports on those at or near the top of the hierarchies and on those, particularly at the bottom, who threaten them, to an audience, most of whom are located in the vast middle range between top and bottom.

Journalists themselves stand just below the top levels of these hierarchies, and their position affords them a better view of the top than of either the bottom or middle. But their best view is of their own position. When journalists have autonomy, they represent the upper-middle-class professional strata in the hierarchies, and defend them, in their own vision of the good nation and society, against the top, bottom, and middle.

Journalistic Leeway

As I indicated before, empirical analyses can reify the status quo. Also, even if the news is shaped by power and efficiency, journalists have autonomy to reinterpret or alter the considerations that now guide them. With autonomy comes leeway for change, and it is therefore worth asking how much the news could change. I can best answer the question by posing some hypothetical changes in the major considerations and by estimating the resulting consequences.

To begin with, journalists could revise their source considerations, paying less attention to public officials and more attention to economic and other nationwide groups that also have power, as well as to ordinary people. Aside from the fact that present sources might object to being deprived of publicity, reporting on groups requires more staff and time than does reporting on individuals. In addition, new beats would have to be established, and some groups can be covered only by specialists. But beat reporters are more costly and less efficient than general reporters. Covering ordinary people all over the country would be more costly than covering Washington officials, and sampling them would require additional time and effort. Furthermore, ordinary people do not hold easily and quickly reported press conferences.

In the same vein, journalists could alter their current definitions of importance, assigning more importance to the political and economic structures—say, of the federal bureaucracy and the corporate economy—and to their often anonymous functionaries and impersonal social processes that so often limit the decision-making autonomy of the president of the United States and his colleagues. But if, as a result, the news also became more impersonal, with fewer people stories and a larger proportion of abstract description and analysis dominating the news, audience members unable or unwilling to accept such news fare might depart.

Current media, format, and product considerations are not immutable either. Television news *sans* film is probably inconceivable, but some dramatic action film could be replaced with important or interesting talking heads. Magazines with fewer but longer sections—or with what the top editor deems to be the best articles produced each week by his journalists—are also possible. These alternatives would even be less costly, for talking heads are more cheaply filmed than action, and magazines with fewer sections require smaller staffs. Whether the present audience would accept these changes is an unanswerable question; but so long as there are only three networks and newsmagazines, it has little choice. Whether the audience cares about novelty, freshness, pace, and balance is also questionable, inasmuch as it now accepts—if not willingly, perhaps—the endless repetition of advertising. Eliminating the product considerations, however, would complicate the journalistic task and slow down the assembly line. Dramatic news is efficient, and so are pegs.

Suppose the news media chose to end the competition, with each network or magazine deciding to go its own way. Network A could, for example, choose important and interesting news for the best-educated third of viewers; Network B, for the next third; and Network C, for the least-educated third. Magazine A could be edited for older readers; B, for the middle-aged; and C, for young adults and adolescents. Each news organization would then have to develop its own brand of news judgment, thereby splintering journalism as a profession. But before then, a drastic reorganization of the news firms, the mass media generally, and Madison Avenue would be necessary.

Value exclusion could be waived; indeed, more personal opinions in the news would probably increase the interest, and perhaps the size, of the audience. Such a change would likely stimulate debate about the news, but it might also intensify protest from people holding other opinions. Eventually, the opinions held by the vocal audience would dominate the news media, and journalists with diverging ones would be dismissed. Journalists could also pay more attention to the implications of the news, but only with difficulty. Were they to do so, they would have to act like politicians, with insufficient time left for reporting the news.

The enduring values "belong" to the profession, but value change by itself might not make much of a difference. As long as disorder news is dramatic and source considerations propel journalists toward leaders, order and leadership values are unnecessary. Changes in other values, however, might upset the now vocal audience—for example, if journalists lost their faith in responsible capitalism and began to supply more critical stories about private enterprise and more information about successful socialist economic policies. Likewise, recruiting journalists from other class backgrounds or with different personal values would not, by itself, bring about change (see Chapter 6).

Commercial considerations are currently not within the power of journalists to change—but suppose they were. News could be supplied without advertising, in which case, the funds would have to come either from government (which would create problems to be discussed in Chapter 10) or from the audience. No one knows whether American viewers would be willing to pay directly for television through license fees as do Europeans; but if the fee system were adopted in America, one could imagine that either politicians or the audience would use power to restrict journalistic autonomy or to require more efficiency in order to keep license fees low. European broadcasting organizations, like their governments, are less responsive to public pressure than American ones. On the other hand, if the federal government had the power to require the networks and local stations to put some of their often extraordinary profits into the news organizations, the television journalists, at least, would obtain higher budgets, which in turn would lessen their need to be governed by efficiency. In that event, they would be free to make dramatic changes in the news. However, if government had power over network profits, it might also have power to restrain the journalists from making any dramatic change that could create adverse publicity about government.

To be more utopian: commercial considerations might disappear entirely if journalists owned their own news organizations and ran them communally or with some form of worker control.[4] Whether national news media, catering to a large audience, could be run in this fashion is an interesting question, especially in light of some successful instances in Europe. A worker-controlled organization could decide to pursue a smaller or more congenial audience of only interested viewers and readers; however, were it to serve today's large audience in the same competitive environment, the workers would probably have to reinvent the news firms that now exist.

If journalists could alter the audience considerations, they could presumably devote most of their attention to the interested audience; yet, this might result in the departure of the rest of the audience to newly minted news firms and entrepreneurs who would invent, and profitably so, a more dramatic and entertaining set of news media with it in mind. The present journalists would have to be satisfied with a smaller audience and a lower news budget. If the interested audience were willing to forego descriptive news, which is expensive, and accept more news analysis, which is cheaper, its news media would remain economically viable, but analytic journalism presupposes prior descriptive news.

A less dramatic step would be the elimination of the present taste taboos, but these could be given up only if the news media could attract a younger audience while extruding the older one. A formula for doing so has not yet been discovered; otherwise, it would have been instituted long ago, given advertiser interest in the young. Television could shed some taboos by moving the news to the end of prime-time programming, when children are asleep; but television journalists lack the power to do so. Besides, the newsmagazines observe many of the same taboos, which suggests that they will not fully disappear without a reduction in the hinterland audience or an end to its willingness or ability to protest.

Finally, journalists could insulate themselves from pressure, but only by ending their own, and their firms', dependence on advertiser and audience income. They would have to be funded by extremely rich and totally independent "angels" who would be willing to grant the journalists total autonomy and who themselves would be concurrently immune from government pressure. In addition, journalists would have to be armed with subpoena power or the threat of force, so that they could obtain information from sources without incurring obligations which could lead to pressure.

Even then, journalists would still be subject to subtler forms of pressure, which come from living in society—unless they chose to insulate themselves from their families, friends, and neighbors as well. At that point, they would be completely unaccountable, but they could also no longer either decide what was newsworthy or communicate with the audience or anyone else. They would be complete outsiders.

Obstacles to Leeway

Journalists have leeway to make changes but, as the preceding observations suggest, with a wide range of consequences. Altogether, five types of consequences seem to act as obstacles to leeway; and while none can with certainty be predicted to occur, no one can be certain that they will not occur either.

1. *Audience reduction.* Given the lack of audience research, it is impossible to predict whether altering the news in ways that "burden" the present audience would result in their departure from the readership or viewership. On the one hand, both television and magazine news have become more complex—however that term is defined— over the past generation; like the entertainment media, the news media have responded to the population's higher educational levels and increased sophistication. On the other hand, journalists and executives

are most likely correct in their belief that many of the present product and audience considerations are necessary to hold the uninterested audience.

2. *Increased pressure.* Some changes in the news are likely to increase pressure from sources, the vocal audience, and others. Although journalists have thus far been able to resist or insulate themselves against a good deal of pressure, neither they nor anyone else can judge their tolerance for increased, more widespread, or more intensive pressure, or to what extent executives will protect them from escalated pressure.

3. *Higher costs.* News innovations that require more staff or a larger proportion of beat reporters would require news firms to increase news organization budgets and audiences to pay more for the news. Journalists do not have sufficient power in the news firms to insist on higher budgets, but the audience seems to be willing to pay more for the news, for both newsmagazines have significantly raised subscription rates and newsstand prices in recent years. Viewers have also paid more for television news, but that cost is hidden in the prices paid for advertised goods.

4. *Organizational obstacles.* News organizations are sufficiently hierarchical to enable executives and journalists at the top to make changes. However, journalists rise to the top by being cautious, and proposals for drastic change must be cleared with management, which is not paid to take unnecessary risks.

5. *The "competitive bind."* News organizations work within a competitive bind that encourages them to offer virtually the same news. Although news organizations occasionally break out of the bind and come up with successful innovations, these are often the result of desperation; firms that are on top rarely try something new but risky. Furthermore, rivals do not want to be too different from each other, for an innovation that is not likely to be successful leaves them defenseless against their competitors.

It goes without saying that journalists always have leeway to enlarge the audience and to take more conservative stands, which will please the vocal audience. In addition, they are relatively free to effect format changes that enhance the packaging of the basic product. But they may have less leeway to implement other changes than is commonly imagined. More correctly, the risks of innovation are sufficiently great to inhibit the incentive to take the first steps. True, journalists, like others, often exhort each other to leadership, but implicit in such appeals is the expectation that leaders will assume risks which no one else is willing or able to take. Although journalism does not lack its share of heroes, news organizations and firms are not often heroic.

As a result, the news will probably change only in response to changing conditions in America which alter audience news preferences or drastically increase the audience's need for national news. Were people required, by necessity or incentive, to participate directly in decisions about the national economy or federal government policies, they would need national news in order to function and would pay attention to the news even if it lacked drama or pace. Indeed, they might resent drama that hindered their obtaining needed information. But participatory democracy would first require a very different America.

More realistically, a drastic economic or political crisis might increase the need for national news, in which case journalists would respond accordingly. And if, in such a crisis, a significant proportion of the audience moved to the left, it is conceivable that journalists would follow, both in their opinions and in the kinds of stories they judged to be important. Still, if a leftward swing damaged their own interests or the economic interests of their firms, it is also conceivable that they would not follow. On the other hand, if a large segment of the audience moved far to the right, and if a crisis spawned a widespread demand for totalitarian leadership in Washington, journalists would be under strong pressure to relinquish their belief in altruistic democracy.

Until there is considerable change in America, however, the journalists' nominal leeway is, in practice, restricted, ultimately for lack of economic incentives. For the moment, journalists are apt to continue to respond to the ever-present incentives for efficiency and to the realities of power.

Some Functions of the Journalists

This study has, thus far, largely ignored the intriguing possibility that journalists and their firms are pawns of larger and more basic social processes to which they unwittingly respond. Perhaps journalists perform unintended or unrecognized (latent) functions for nation and society as a whole, which are necessary enough to force journalists to act as they do.

Despite its many virtues, functional analysis is accompanied by risks, especially when it ignores, as I shall, concurrent dysfunctions (or disadvantages). It can reify nation and society, and thereby the status quo, legitimating as functionally necessary social arrangements which are, from another perspective, outcomes of the current distribution of power. Moreover, functions can be identified only through their consequences, and very little is known about the consequences of the news. Whether journalists perform necessary functions can be studied only if all news media were suddenly to disappear for a time. Consequently, many of the observations to follow are speculative.

Leadership Testers

A functional analysis need not await the disappearance of the news media to suggest that they have become major mechanisms for recruiting and testing the elected national leadership. By emphasizing presidential and other election campaigns, journalists have begun to take over, from the political parties and from primaries, the task of winnowing the rolls of political candidates.[5] The news media do not directly recruit, of course, for it is up to candidates and their agents to decide whether to enter the race. But television, more so than other news media, extrudes candidates who lack the campaign funds to aid their performance before the cameras. In addition, television does not look kindly on candidates who communicate poorly on the small screen, Richard Nixon and Jimmy Carter being exceptions that prove the rule.

Subsequently, journalists test candidates for their competence to answer critical questions and to avoid making mistakes; their ability to conceptualize national issues in a way that will attract an audience; their skill in developing an appealing and consistent public image; and their honesty in dealing with contradictions in their campaigns and their personal lives. Nor do these tests end on Election Day, for successful candidates and the officials they appoint are subject to further scrutiny during their administrations. No one has elected the journalists to participate so intimately in the electoral process; but then, some party conventions and primaries, past and present, have not always been perfectly democratic either.

Suppliers of Political Feedback

The news media's primary purpose is to inform the audience; but elected and appointed officials are, by all odds, the most intensely interested news audience. *The New York Times,* the *Washington Post, The Wall Street Journal,* and a handful of other print media are,

among other things, intragovernmental organs of communication—
professional newsletters for public officials.

Television and the magazines, however, serve public officials mainly
as feedback devices, providing them with early clues to how the general, or the "informed," public feels about their actions and statements. Public officials monitor these media to see how they are received by journalists. Noting how much time or space and how many
leads they obtain enables public officials also to gauge how much
importance journalists attach to them.

In the process, the news media become stand-ins for the national
constituency, at least until public opinion polls or election results are
available. Whether journalists are accurate stand-ins for anyone is an
empirical question, but it is not terribly relevant, since only they can
supply the instantaneous feedback public officials need.

Editorials provide overnight approximations of public opinion; public officials also analyze the news for implicit opinions, believing the
value implications of the news to reflect the journalists' opinions.
When normally objective reporters express an explicit opinion, public
officials become even readier to treat them as agents of the *vox populi.*
That Lyndon Johnson is said to have decided to forego a second term
after hearing Walter Cronkite disavow the Vietnam War is therefore
not surprising.

Power Distributors

But journalists do more than provide feedback; at times they also
distribute power, particularly when they give individuals or groups
helpful publicity, on television and on newsmagazine covers. Of
course, the news media distribute symbolic power, which does not
automatically lead to material power over the allocation of resources.
In addition, the power is ephemeral, for others may receive similar
publicity the following day or week. But when publicity snowballs,
resulting in multiple appearances in the national media and visible
reaction, either by public officials or the general public, symbolic
power lasts long enough to become political capital, which can then
be invested in material power over resources and public decisions.

Moral Guardians

The ability of journalists to distribute power stems in part from
their moral functions. Since they choose moral disorder stories and

frame other news as morality plays, they act as a kind of Greek chorus for nation and society. In fact, this is an intended (manifest) function, for journalists consider themselves "watchdogs." Even when they do not act as such, sources and other people try to be on their best behavior because they are exposed, at least potentially, to public visibility. Consequently, journalists guard not only the moral order embodied in the enduring values but a wide range of ideals, mores, and customs as well. When sources are interviewed by journalists, they demonstrate their adherence to national and societal ideals, and they refrain from picking their noses while on camera.

Moral disorder news therefore reinforces and relegitimates dominant national and societal values by publicizing and helping to punish those who deviate from the values. In doing so, however, the journalists repress other values, and other moralities, which might otherwise come to the fore. If the audience treats journalists as moral guardians and perceives the morally orderly actors in the news as role-models, the audience also enables journalists to protect a particular moral order that it might privately find less worthy of protection.

Prophets and Priests

The moral roles journalists play are sometimes deemed religious. Gerbner has, in fact, argued that television itself is a secular religious institution.[6] Kelly has also resorted to a religious metaphor: watching television news is a ritual, with the anchorperson as shaman.[7] Given the declining power of the churches to influence public morality, whether secular or sacred, journalists are sometimes described as a new set of prophets; but the religious analogy must be taken with a large grain of salt.

Perhaps people do attend to the news media as a daily or weekly ritual, but I think their usage is more habitual than ritual. Moreover, if anchorpersons are shamans, they are less powerful and less eager to use their potential power than the shamans of pre-industrial cultures; nor do they perform the same therapeutic or magical functions. Some investigative reporters have become moral crusaders; but as journalists, they do not develop organized constituencies, and their crusades are usually of short duration. However, commentators, who can hammer away at the same moral disorder over a period of time, can become prophets. Other journalists may perform religious functions occasionally; in 1963, for example, television anchormen may have been secular ministers who led the nation's mourning over John Kennedy.

The religious metaphor overestimates the moral potency of the news; most people attend the news less often than church. Journalists may be moral guardians for the nation, but they are not priests. Although the enduring values coincide at some points with what Bellah has identified as America's civic religion, whether citizens treat these values as religious and whether they do so with the degree of consensus usually assigned to religions remains to be seen.

Storytellers and Myth Makers

Because news is transmitted as stories, journalists are sometimes equated with the storytellers of pre-media times, who passed on the myths and legends which exist in all societies. According to Kelly: "An obvious example of the legend is the story of John Kennedy, the continuous reportage of the young President's quest for the power to do what was morally right. Many of the events of his Presidency, from the Bay of Pigs to the Cuban blockade, were reported as legendary efforts."[8]

Kelly is right to suggest that news stories can be seen as legends or myths, but journalists are more often passive transmitters than active myth makers. The Kennedy family, which appears to have been unusually adept in describing itself in mythic terms, was successful not because of the journalists but in spite of them. Many reporters resented the Kennedys' efforts at persona (and news) management, but story selectors felt that the audience was interested in them, and thus continued to keep them on the story lists.

When journalists are more active, they actually draft myths, only some of which evoke sufficient interest to become memorable and eventually graduate to myth status. Whether John Kennedy will achieve this status will ultimately be determined by the journalists and audiences of the future.

The notion of news as myth reintroduces the religious functions of journalists; and it implies, concurrently, that America is similar to pre-industrial societies wherein, we now believe, myths expressed long-standing and often religious values. In modern societies, however, many myths have a limited lifespan.[9] Also, whether past (or modern) societies actually needed myths is an unresolved question; nor is it certain whether myths expressed societal consensus. Today's news tells stories about the powerful, and the myth makers of old may have done the same; but we do not know if past audiences paid them serious attention. They have left no trace in the historical record, and only the myths remain.

Barometer of Order

Because journalists regularly select stories of natural, technological, and social disorders, the news appears also to function as an order barometer, apprising the audience of the emergence of disorder but at the same time reassuring it through order restoration stories.[10]

Some audience members use disorder news as an early warning system, which alerts them to possible future complications in their own lives.[11] Others use such news to fix blame and identify villains. For example, stories about New York City often provide evidence of its equivalence to Sodom or Gomorrah, even if other cities have higher crime rates or similar porno districts.

Journalists are regularly accused of fomenting disorder by publicizing it; but while there is no evidence that this is the case, it is true that journalists, by highlighting, often exaggerate the extent and intensity of disorder. When they report the most dramatic portions of a disaster or a civil disorder, they may be alarming people more than necessary. On the other hand, journalists often exaggerate the effectiveness of those who restore order.

I previously suggested that journalists try to prevent audience panic and to discourage rumors that could panic it further. When professional news, drawn from official sources, replaces unofficial rumor, journalists assist, and intentionally so, the officials who are charged with maintaining order.

Agents of Social Control

Social control prevents or discourages people from acting and speaking in ways disapproved of by holders of power. To the extent that journalists help maintain order, warn against disorder, and act as moral guardians, they function as agents of social control—although they serve a number of power holders, including segments of the audience. But until sufficient research evidence is available on the extent to which the news—as distinguished from the actors who appear in it—affects people's behavior and attitudes, it is difficult to judge whether journalists are independent agents of social control.

Of course, insofar as the news media carry the messages of official controllers, and insofar as news legitimates their messages, journalists help control the citizenry. However, the distrust of the news media and the lack of audience involvement in the news also suggest that journalists may not be effective controllers. Anchorpersons are more trusted than the news they report, but this trust derives from their detachment and their attempt neither to persuade nor control.

Because the news media supply their audience with common fare, which becomes the raw material for shared experiences, they have also been described as agents of social integration—which can be viewed positively as encouraging social cohesion and negatively as another way of imposing control. Even so, no one knows whether the common fare supplied by the news media is so received or perceived by viewers and readers. During intense national crises in which people have shared interests, such as presidential assassinations or popular wars, the news media undoubtedly contribute to integration, and they do so intentionally. The war in Vietnam polarized the public, however, even though the news media supplied common fare about it.

A different argument maintains that the news media control by depoliticizing their audience. The classic statements of this argument extend to the mass media generally, and they span the ideological spectrum. On the Left, Marcuse has suggested that the mass media lull the audience with modern equivalents of the Roman circus, persuading them to accept the political status quo.[12] On the Right, Ellul has proposed that the mass media supply propaganda rather than information, confusing a poorly educated audience into becoming unwitting victims of the propagandists.[13]

At one level, the charge is accurate, for journalistic objectivity—and in another way, the ironic style of the newsmagazines—do not impel audiences to act on what they see or read. Nor does the reporting of political protest encourage others to join; if anything, order-restoration stories imply the ineffectiveness of protest. Concurrently, journalists celebrate innocuous and nonpolitical citizen participation, such as grassroots activities. Journalists do not often encourage protest, and needless to say, they do not advocate revolution.

On another level, however, the charge attributes too much power to journalists and too little common sense to the audience. If the news media repress protest, purposely or unwittingly, noticeable reductions in protest since the rise of modern journalism should be evident; but as best one can tell, protest has increased in the last generation. Then, too, even if journalists were able or willing to encourage protest, I doubt that the audience would follow, especially into activities that are personally risky. The radical press has not won many adherents to radical protest. If enough people are ready to protest, news that provides them useful information and encouragement would perhaps swell their ranks and reduce the risks of protest, even while legitimizing it. National television appears to have served this function, if unintentionally, for the southern civil-rights movement in the early 1960s.

Likewise, the news media report and publicize the massive power of the federal government and other large organizations, perhaps controlling the audience by informing it of its own minimal power. But people do not need the news media to convince them that they have little power. Even if the news may confuse some people about specific actors and activities, particularly people not interested in nation and society, it cannot often persuade them to alter basic reality judgments about power and other issues, or strongly held values about things that matter to them.[14] It is even possible that the news media boomerang as controllers, for the current public antipathy to government may have been fueled, though not initiated, by the plethora of news about its activities.

The true test of the journalists' political and economic control functions must await a catastrophic economic or political crisis in which large segments of the audience move to the left. I suggested earlier that journalists would either follow the audience or defend their own and their firms' economic interests. European journalists have frequently sided with the Left during major crises, but they are more overtly ideological than their American counterparts; and besides, some were subsequently fired by their governmental "sponsors." In any case, the question here remains moot until the audience swings toward the left and requires that journalists choose sides.

Constructors of Nation and Society

When I first started to think seriously about this study, I began with the question: What does society tell itself about itself? My fieldwork, as well as the changes that have taken place in America and in the social sciences since the 1960s, persuaded me that it was the wrong question for me, because it anthropomorphizes society. However, it has led me to the hypothesis that one journalistic function is to construct nation and society, to put flesh on these otherwise vague concepts, and thus to help make them real.[15]

Strictly speaking, journalists gather information on what individuals and groups do to and for each other in a wide range of institutions, agencies, and communities. But as they translate that information into news, they frame it in a national context, and thereby bring the nation into being. Needless to say, journalists do not do so by themselves, for public officials, among others, also nationalize their actions and statements. But journalists help impose unity on what is otherwise a congeries of individuals and groups acting inside a set of geographic and political boundaries. These boundaries, together with the Declaration of Independence and the Constitution, formally declare America to be a nation, although the federal government, itself an aggregate of agencies, acts and speaks for the nation. (The same boundaries, but no equivalent documents, construct America as a society, with a variety of institutions and agencies proposing to act or speak for it.) But both nation and society are social constructs which, for all practical purposes, do not exist until someone acts or speaks for them.

Journalists report the actions and statements of those claiming to represent nation and, to a lesser extent, society, thus constantly reminding us of the reality and power of these constructs. Journalists do so, moreover, not only to serve interested sources whose legitimacy is enhanced by representing nation and society, but also to inform an audience which lives in micro-societies that are often far removed from nation and society. Whether or not the audience actually needs information about them is a crucial question I cannot answer. Suffice it to say that news supplies that information. But when people say they keep up with the news, they may also be saying that they are maintaining contact with nation and society.

Managers of the Symbolic Arena

Many of the functions I have discussed remain hypotheses until they are empirically tested, and I have tried to suggest that some strike me as unable to survive an empirical test. I feel somewhat more certain, however, about a final one: that one of the journalists' prime functions is to manage, with others, the symbolic arena, the public stage on which national, societal, and other messages are made available to everyone who can become an audience member. Although much of the symbolic arena is given over to entertainment, journalists transmit the only nonfiction that most Americans see, hear, or read.

I argued in Chapter 8 that the symbolic arena is a political battleground, for many people endeavor to get their messages into it and to keep other messages out. Who manages the symbolic arena, therefore, is a major political issue. In many countries, the issue is foreclosed because the government in power is its manager; in other countries, news organizations and journalists manage the arena, with the government retaining veto power. In America, the news firms are the nominal managers, but news organizations and journalists are the actual ones. In the process, they also regulate individuals and groups with messages; and, in so doing, they maintain order in the symbolic arena.

Part 3
News Policy

Introduction

The last chapter is about public (but not necessarily governmental) policy for the news. More correctly, it develops what journalists call a news philosophy, the outline of a national news-media system based on that philosophy, and some specific proposals.

In developing the policy analysis, I have tried to avoid the temptation mentioned in the Preface: that of measuring journalism against and transforming it into sociology. I have also refrained from translating my personal preferences for the news into policy proposals. Like everyone else, I have such preferences. If I could design my own national news media, electronic or print, they would be considerably more liberal versions of newspapers like *The New York Times* or the *Washington Post,* but far stronger on news analysis and explanation —and, to help me do my work as a teacher of sociology, carrying far more news about America as society. In short, I prefer news that fits *my* values and information needs.

Personal preferences, however, cannot be used to justify public policies. These must be based on public values: in this case, the values of all those who participate in and are touched by the news. The public values from which I proceed are, to be sure, those I deem most prevalent and important, but still they diverge from my personal preferences.

The judgments and proposals that follow deal with national news *sui generis* and are not limited to television and magazine news. While my proposals take into account what I have learned about current journalistic practices and are not meant to be utopian, many are presently not feasible. But others could be instituted now.

Multiperspectival News

Discussions of news policy are customarily initiated by evaluating what is good or bad about today's news media and determining how they can be improved. But this approach often ends up with alternative print and electronic news media modeled on either a thicker and more serious *New York Times* or on the journals of opinion—and sometimes even on academic publications. Such improvements, however, are likely to drive away a significant portion of the present audience for national news. They also discourage cultural democratization, that is, making the news relevant for people not now part of the news audience. Consequently, I want to approach policy from another direction, by asking whether the news is distorted.

News Distortion

"Distortion" has become a loosely used equivalent for "bias." In the last ten years, the news has been considered distorted because it favored one or another ideology, or was unfair to one or another set of public officials; because it was overly superficial, too concerned with personalities at the expense of issues, or overly given to dramatic action and exaggeration; because it was too preoccupied with official sources and with media events rather than with "actualities"; or because it reported too much social disorder or other bad news.

Whatever the charges (and some are justified), the assumption is that distorted news can be replaced by undistorted news; but that assumption is untenable. Even if a perfect and complete reproduction (or construction) of external reality were philosophically or logistically feasible, the mere act of reproduction would constitute a distortion of that reality. Thus, objective or absolute nondistortion is impossible.

The concept of distortion is nevertheless valid, but only as a relational one. News can be judged as distorted *in relation* to a specified standard (or ideal) of nondistortion. However, the standards themselves cannot be absolute or objective because they are inevitably based on a number of reality and value judgments: about the nature of external reality, knowledge, and truth; about the proper purposes of the news; and more often than not, about the good nation and society.[1] When the news is accused of favoring one ideology, for example, it is therefore distorted in relation to a standard of ideological balance and the ideal of a pluralist nation of coexisting ideologies. If news is judged to rely too much on official sources, the standard rests on an assumption that government is not to be trusted and, more broadly, on a theory of democracy in which ordinary people are as important as public officials. But when the news lives up to one standard, it may then be distorted in relation to a different one.

Other standards are involved when journalists are charged with gathering distorted facts. Frequently, participants in an event claim that the journalistic account does not agree with their observations; in those instances, the participants are setting the standard. The Langs' classic study of the Chicago parade honoring General Douglas MacArthur demonstrated that television reported a far more enthusiastic and dramatic parade than the one seen by a number of observers watching on the streets. In the Langs' study, the observers set the standard; television, on the other hand, chose to portray the exciting parade intended by its organizers.[2] Social scientists often establish a scientific or empirical standard; the Glasgow University Media Group, for example, evaluated British strike news against an independently gathered survey of all strikes, thus setting an empirical standard.[3] In fact, even the notion that news should report what *is* happening is based on a standard. Radicals who argue that empirical inquiry into the status quo is a conservative posture propose a different standard, by which news is undistorted when it concentrates on the need for radical change, on what *should be* happening.

Relational standards of undistorted news cannot be absolute, but they can be universal. Since they are based on values, however, they can become universal only if there is agreement on these values. Barring such agreement, all anyone can do is choose standards, argue in their behalf, and debate against those that are different. Identifying distorted news and proposing a standard for undistorted news is a political act; and while the act itself is desirable, the actor ultimately must take sides.

Facts and Questions

Basic philosophical concerns about the existence of external reality and about whether it can be grasped by empirical methods are not at issue here, for most critics of the news agree with journalists and most social scientists that empirical inquiry about external reality is possible. Thus, I shall not debate the possibility of determining what journalists call facts. (I will also ignore the problem that many journalistic facts are not amenable to empirical testing but are attributed opinions.)

Rather, the issue is *what* facts should become news. Even empirically determinable facts do not arise out of thin air but are fashioned out of concepts and specific empirical methods. Concepts in turn are based on reality and value judgments, and different judgments produce different concepts. But when concepts—or methods—differ, so do the resulting facts.

To put it another way: facts are, among other things, answers to questions about external reality. The population of New York City does not become a fact until someone asks how many people live in the city. Once that question is asked, in that way, the number of New Yorkers can be empirically determined; in this instance, there need be little debate about the empirical methods. Factual answers to the question of how major party candidates campaign for the presidency can also be determined empirically, although then, problems of selection and summary that always accompany the reporter's tasks begin to appear.

Still, these are not the only questions that can be asked. When journalists emphasize the campaign activities of presidential candidates, they preempt equally significant questions: whether elections materially affect the policies and politics of the federal government; why elections do not seem to make as much of a difference as is commonly assumed, given that a new occupant of the Oval Office frequently retains old policies.

In short, many questions can be asked about the actors and activities which now appear in, or are omitted from, the news. Consequently, news can be considered distorted for asking questions which a standard setter considers to be wrong or for using the wrong concepts to frame correct questions, or for employing the wrong methods. I want to deal with two of these issues: what constitutes the right methods and the right questions.

Methods—and Audiences

The notion that journalists are employing the wrong methods is at the heart of most complaints, by social scientists and others, that the news is too superficial and overly addicted to dramatic action. Ostensibly, the issue is whether journalistic empirical methodology is the best way of approaching external reality; yet it cannot be separated from what questions journalists should ask because superficial facts come from superficial questions, and in order to obtain dramatic news, journalists must ask dramatic questions.

But above all, the issue concerns the audience and how it should be informed. In theory, journalists claim that their responsibility extends only to supplying information, whether or not the audience accepts it; but in practice, the product considerations exist to persuade the audience to accept it. Journalism is an empirical discipline but one which requires that its findings be presented as interestingly and in as few minutes or words as possible.

Many social-science methods are superior to those of journalism; but social scientists are blessed with far more time to do their research, and normally, they delve into narrower topics than journalists. Both disciplines seek to inform; but the social scientists' methods aim for explanation and prediction, whereas journalists' methods are concerned mainly with description. In addition, social scientists spend a larger share of their budget on the empirical phase of their work; journalists, on the production and dissemination of their findings. But perhaps most important, social scientists report to their expert peers, while journalists report to a lay audience.

Charges that the news is superficial or overly dramatic often reflect the implicit standards of experts—and well-educated lay people—who are, in effect, arguing that the news fails to supply the detailed technical description and the explanatory-predictive information to which they are accustomed. In some cases, they may also be criticizing the news for its failure to supply them with the information they want or need as experts. While they have as much right as anyone else to transform their own wants into distortion charges, they are also making three assumptions: (1) that the lay or popular audience is equally entitled to "expert news";

(2) that it will accept such news; and (3) that it should do so.

That the lay audience is entitled to expert news is beyond argument; whether it will accept such news is not. How simple and dramatic the news must be in order to gain a large popular audience remains in question, but explanatory-predictive news seems to be most relevant for people who are, or think they are, involved in shaping nation and society. Lay audiences are not so involved, however, which is perhaps why they seem to prefer dramatic description. In addition, expert concepts and technical vocabularies cannot be understood by people without the requisite education, although today's journalists have become adept at translating expert vocabulary into lay language, which is comprehensible to the better-educated portions of their audience.[4]

Whether the popular audience should nevertheless accept expert news is probably an irrelevant question, since it cannot be forced to do so—except, perhaps, in a dictatorship. Still, the question is often raised. If expert news were essential to bringing about a more democratic society, an argument for the abolition of popular news could be made; however, expert news does not necessarily enhance democracy. News which explains external reality is superior to news which merely describes it, and I personally wish more journalists had the training and time to supply explanation, but understanding the ills of the nation is not sufficient to ameliorate them.

To be sure, if expert news is superior to popular news, then popular news saddles the lay audience with inferior merchandise. Even so, the lay audience cannot and should not, in all fairness, be asked to accept expert news until it can also expect to play expert roles and secure the influence, education, and other perquisites that go along with these roles. Until inequalities between the lay and expert audiences are reduced, condemning the popular audience for not attending to expert news is only another form of what William Ryan has called blaming the victim. Furthermore, the condemnation is reminiscent of the charges laid against popular entertainment and culture by the defenders of high culture, for high culture is, among other things, the culture of scholars and other cultural experts.[5] Equality among lay people and experts is not likely to be achieved soon; in the meantime, the news is likely to continue its emphasis on drama to attract the lay audience, although I suspect that experts, too, sometimes prefer dramatic news.[6]

Is Popular News Harmful?

Whether popular news, like popular culture, is harmful to the audience will remain an open question until research on the effects of the news is available, and until critics and audience members can agree on the definition of harmfulness. My guess would be that popular news is not injurious, even if it fails to discourage some people from behaving in ways that other people consider undesirable.[7]

The news has been criticized for hurting people through exaggeration, and there is little doubt that journalistic highlighting (see Chapter 3), which helps transform news into dramatic stories, can produce an exaggerated construction of external reality (at least as measured by the social scientists' standard), which could, in turn, be injurious to people if and when they act on it. If, for example, viewers saw a highlighted film of a nearby flood, which showed only the worst flooding, and if they unnecessarily fled their homes as a result, the news would clearly hurt them.

The problem is that clear-cut examples of harm are few; and whether exaggerated news is harmful is often a matter of values. The dramatic accounts of police violence against southern civil-rights marchers were considered beneficial by the civil-rights movement because they enlisted public support for federal civil-rights legislation, but they were deemed harmful by southern opponents of that legislation.

In addition, exaggeration may enhance the journalists' ability to inform, such as when it evokes audience interest in topics to which people would otherwise pay no attention.[8] Conversely, highlighting could make external reality appear so intractable that audiences might consider change impossible, in which case exaggeration could reduce audience interest. The trouble is that no one knows. How the news exaggerates and what effects this has on the audience and the issues urgently need to be studied. Afterwards, it may be possible to determine whether and how dramatic exaggeration that is agreed to be deleterious can be reduced. In the meantime, there is some evidence, although not enough, to suggest that at least part of the audience protects itself from exaggeration by "discounting" the news, just as it discounts entertainment.[9]

Television news has been attacked for exaggeration more than the print media, although the magazines' use of dramatic narrative may have the same consequences. Television often *feels* distorted because its media and format considerations diverge from the linearity of what Marshall McLuhan once called the print culture; but no one is certain whether film highlighting is more damaging than that of print. Critics who are certain assume that viewers are more gullible or vulnerable than readers, but that assumption also needs to be researched.

The Right Questions

Whatever the discipline, distortion cannot be judged without reference to the audience. Even so, the major issue concerns what questions are to become facts—and by extension, what sets of facts should be selected, as stories, for the news. In effect, most critiques of the news accuse journalists of asking the wrong questions, and few critics have difficulty in proposing alternatives. For news policy, however, there must be agreement on what constitutes the right questions, which requires prior agreement on the relevant reality and value judgments. However, such agreement is virtually impossible to achieve, since the questions all of us consider correct, or relevant, depend on where we sit or where we stand: on our position in the national and societal hierarchies, and on the value judgments we make, partly as a result of our position in these hierarchies.

In the prototypical homogeneous society, which has never existed, everyone shares the same perspectives; but in a modern society, no one sits or stands in exactly the same place. Consequently, perspectives on reality will vary. Poor people experience America differently than do middle-income people or the rich; as a result, their attitudes toward government will also vary. Different perspectives lead to different questions and different answers, thereby requiring different facts and different news.

Writing in 1922, Walter Lippmann pointed out that "the facts we see depend on where we are placed and the habits of our eyes."[10] A decade later, Karl Mannheim, the European sociologist, put it more systematically, proposing that all knowledge is relational to the knower's perspective.[11] He was primarily concerned with how class position influenced knowledge about society and how it shaped political ideologies, but today it is clear that other factors are also relevant. Organizational studies of the news have shown, for example, that how knowers are organized and for what purposes affect their perspectives, determining what they look for and what they see.[12] In fact, these studies, including my own, suggest that it may be easier for knowers to overcome the perspectives that accompany their class status than

those which are established by the organizations in which they work
and the manner in which their work is organized. Still, organizational
and class perspectives are not mutually exclusive; organizations are
themselves located in the class hierarchy and reflect the class perspectives of the people they represent.

News is a form of knowledge as well, and what journalists (like
sociologists) know is also perspectival. Of course, never totally so, for
journalists and sociologists obtain and pass along information from
sources with a variety of perspectives. Moreover, empirically gathered
information can cut across perspectives, but only when there is agreement on the concepts and methods by which it was obtained and when
the facts answer a relevant question. The population of New York is
the same regardless of where one sits or stands; but for many people,
it is an irrelevant fact because, from their perspective, they have no
reason to ask the question.

Equally important, where one sits or stands can produce knowledge
relevant to others. Poor people, situated at the lowest levels of all
national and societal hierarchies, have a perspective which the affluent, by virtue of being at the top, cannot have—for example, seeing
how government and private enterprise deal with people at the bottom. However, because perspectives are always partially a matter of
values, they also set limits to what knowledge is relevant to others. The
values of the affluent encourage them to remain untouched by what
goes on at America's lowest levels.

Mannheim's perspectival conception shattered the possibility of
complete knowledge or the whole truth about society. He sought to
repair the epistemological damage by a *deus ex machina,* the "free-
floating" intellectual who, being unattached to any class, could therefore transcend and synthesize the class-bound perspectives of others.
Mannheim's intellectual bears some resemblance to the journalist as
objective outsider, but neither exists in the real world.[13] As observers,
journalists and intellectuals can and do take on the perspectives of
others at times, but they cannot totally transcend their own, for they,
too, are attached to organizations, class, and other positions.

Most important, no one can synthesize all perspectives, since some
are in conflict, and in many cases, taking one perspective precludes
taking others. After all, one cannot be a Marxist and a libertarian
concurrently. But if a synthesis is impossible, there can be no one
absolutely right or true perspective, and no single set of right questions. Individuals must choose their perspectives and, in so doing, take
sides. For public agencies like the news media, which serve large
numbers of people, all perspectives are relevant, and all (or virtually

all) questions are right for someone. But if journalists had to consider all perspectives and answer all questions, the news would be nearly infinite in length. News and the news media can exist only if journalists restrict themselves to asking a limited number of questions at any given time.

This book has suggested that journalists limit their questions largely on grounds of efficiency and power. For an inquiry into news policy, however, the issues of what are the right questions and how questions can be limited to make news possible must be reexamined, and their resolution cannot be grounded solely in current practices. The choice of right questions is a political act, requiring, among other things, a decision about the purpose or purposes of the news.

When news has focused purposes, the choice of right questions is relatively easy. If the major purpose of the news is to hasten the revolution or the return to traditional values, to publicize leaders, or to hold nation and society together, some questions are clearly wrong. But these purposes put the news at the service of specific interest groups, whose values are not necessarily public values.

Journalists operate instead with an unfocused and more public purpose: to inform the audience. So stated, however, this purpose is meaningless. Journalists cannot inform the audience about everything; but in deciding what they should include and omit, they skirt the issue of what are the right questions. One can narrow the purpose, as many journalists do, to informing people how to carry out their role as citizens in a democracy, but that formulation is useless without definitions of democracy and citizenship. Anyone who believes in the need for more political equality and economic democracy, and favors more active and adversary citizen participation in government, will supply different news to citizens than do today's journalists.

Instead, I would argue that the primary purpose of the news derives from the journalists' functions as constructors of nation and society, and as managers of the symbolic arena. The most important purpose of the news, therefore, is to provide the symbolic arena, and the citizenry, with comprehensive and representative images (or constructs) of nation and society. In order to be comprehensive, the news must report nation and society in terms of all known perspectives; in order to be representative, it must enable all sectors of nation and society to place their actors and activities—and messages—in the symbolic arena. Or, as the Commission on Freedom of the Press put it in 1947, the news should include "the projection of a representative picture of the constituent groups in society."[14]

Ideally, then, the news should be omniperspectival; it should present and represent all perspectives in and on America. This ideal, however, is unachievable, for it is only another way of saying that all questions are right. It is possible to suggest, however, that the news, and the news media, be multiperspectival, presenting and representing as many perspectives as possible—and at the very least, more than today.

Multiperspectival News

Multiperspectival news is a label, but it also entails a conception of alternative news, which differs from today's news in five ways.

First, multiperspectival news would be *more national.* Moving beyond the current equating of the federal government with the nation, it would seek to report comprehensively about more national and nationwide agencies and institutions, including national corporations, unions, and voluntary associations, as well as organized and unorganized interest groups.

Second, multiperspectival news would add a *bottom-up* view to the current top-down approach. For example, news about federal (and corporate) policies would be accompanied by reactions not just from high officials, but from citizens in various walks of life who would be affected by these policies. If social and moral disorder news remains a news staple, the bottom-up approach would suggest that what ordinary people consider to be disorder also become newsworthy, be it petty delinquency in the suburbs or prosaic labor-management unrest in the nation's factories and offices. At the same time, multiperspectivism would include the disorder that suburban adults create for and among teenagers. Moral disorder news would cover that which a wide variety of people perceive to be amiss in society—from Marxists who see contradictions in capitalism to religious conservatives concerned with the decline in traditional morality. Although the now highly selective list of villains in the news would be enlarged, moral disorder stories would also have to report their perspectives, since these villains, too, are members of society.

Third, multiperspectival news would feature more *output* news, determining how the plans and programs of national and nationwide public and private agencies have worked out in practice for intended and unintended beneficiaries, victims, bystanders, and the general public.

Fourth, multiperspectival news would aim to be more *representative,* reporting on the activities and opinions of ordinary Americans from all population sectors and roles. (By "sectors," I mean groups according to age, income, educational level, ethnicity and religion, etc.; by "roles," I mean what people do as parents and children, employers and workers, buyers and sellers, medical and legal clients, homeowners and tenants, members of organized or unorganized interest groups, etc.) As the term implies, representative news would represent people from all walks of life in the symbolic arena: how they see America and what they deem to be its major problems, as well as what they deem to be theirs—in other words, what they consider to be important national news *about* themselves. Representative news thus means greater coverage of the diversity of opinion, from many positions in different national and societal hierarchies, and from many points on the ideological spectrum.

Fifth, multiperspectival news would place more emphasis on *service* news, providing personally relevant information for specific national sectors and roles: what people consider to be important national news *for* themselves. For example, people of different ages, incomes, and occupations who come into contact with different national agencies and institutions need national news about those agencies and institutions which touch their own lives. Changes in federal tax policy are of little relevance to people too poor to pay taxes; instead, they need news about changes in national welfare and jobs policies. Likewise, homeowners require different news than tenants about federal housing policies and administrative practices.

Multiperspectival Journalism

Most of the ingredients of multiperspectival news are hardly novel, but adding them to the national news, and in larger quantity than they exist at present, would require changes in the journalistic *modus operandi.* For one thing, news would have to be collected from a much larger number of more scattered and less easily accessible sources. Needless to say, the total amount of both available and suitable news would increase, which would demand a larger newshole and, as I suggest in the next section, additional national news media.

The conventional story format would also change. When several perspectives must be taken into account on any given topic, stories will naturally become longer. Moreover, journalists would be required to organize these perspectives and, in some cases, to relate and interpret them; consequently, news analyses would be necessary more often. When the news contains greater diversity of opinion from sources, additional journalistic commentary may also be desirable, thus allowing for personal and advocacy journalists in national news organizations. In the process, the news would become more ideological, with explicit ideological diversity replacing the implicit near-uniformity that now prevails.

Since sources would be recruited from all levels of society, journalists would also have to be recruited and trained to deal with them. This is not to say, for example, that only blacks could report news about and for blacks, or that producers and editors from blue-collar backgrounds would have to choose news about and for blue-collar workers. Although "insiders" might find it easier to obtain access to sources, they would also be limited in communicating to "outsiders."[15] The requisite reportorial quality is sensitivity to many perspectives, empathy with diverse sources, and above all, sufficient contact with them to breed sensitivity and empathy. In effect, beats would have to be established among different sectors of the population; and for this reason alone, multiperspectivism would have little use for today's generalists. Even so, greater heterogeneity in the personal backgrounds of journalists would probably be essential.

As sources multiplied, reporters would almost automatically become more aware of the overt and covert interests that often shape what sources tell and do not tell. Such awareness is essential even now, for as Epstein has argued, the axes that sources grind directly affect what becomes news.[16]

As sources, perspectives, and therefore values multiply and diversify, journalistic objectivity becomes even more necessary than it is today. It may be epistemologically impossible, but it can exist as journalistic intent. Inasmuch as story selectors cannot include every perspective and source, their decisions to include or exclude must be free of political intent. Otherwise, they—and the news—will lose their credibility.[17] Indeed, the differences among objective journalists, news analysts, and commentators would need to be sharpened. But objectivity would also attain a new meaning, for in the final reckoning, story selectors can be objective only by choosing news from several perspectives.

Story selectors would continue to set aside personal values, for their prime value would be perspectival diversity. In the process, the journalists' enduring values would no longer play a major supporting role in story selection, although commentators could continue to apply them. Even so, these values would not disappear; rather, they would be expressed in and by the new diversity of sources. Journalists might be adversaries less often, but they would automatically choose more adversary sources; and in the end, the amount of adversary news would increase.

Basic media and format considerations need not be surrendered. Television could still emphasize film, and the magazines could continue to divide reality into sections. Most of the five ingredients of multiperspectival news could be supplied by current filming and writing techniques. Some, but not all, kinds of representative news could be obtained from public opinion polls, provided these asked people what was on their minds rather than eliciting their approval or disapproval of current policies; and provided, furthermore, that they placed less emphasis on numerical majorities and minorities, and reported instead those opinions held by a variety of population sectors and roles. Kuralt's "On the Road" approach, documentary techniques, and capsule biographies at the print media could be used to alleviate the "dryness" of too many statistics.

With more newsworthy sources and longer stories, some current selection considerations would have to be eliminated, however, and the most feasible candidate would be novelty. Were story selectors to apply multiperspectivism, they could not simultaneously supply all the latest news, even with an enlarged newshole. However, no immutable law requires that a daily television program (or newspaper) or weekly magazine emphasize the events of the day or week. Television news even now could eschew the retelling of the day's headlines, for many viewers know them already. In addition, many stories and sources deserve less topicality and immediacy than they currently receive. There is no intrinsic reason for the president to be in the news nearly every day; since the audience is not immediately affected by his actions or statements until later, these could be dispensed with and replaced by periodic but regular features which would allow for bottom-up reactions, as well as early estimates of how his words and acts might affect beneficiaries, victims, and bystanders.

Giving up novelty and the peg would be difficult for story selectors, for they are easily and quickly applied considerations. Inasmuch as a major purpose of multiperspectival news is audience exposure to many different sources, balance considerations would rise in importance. Story selectors would thus make up their story lists in part by determining which sources had not recently appeared in the news; the kind and degree of balance—which are crucial issues in making multiperspectivism operational—will be discussed in greater detail below.

Multiperspectival News Media

The considerable increase in the sheer amount of news could not be handled by the now existing national news media. The three networks' radio and television news programs (plus documentaries, specials, and magazines), the three newsweeklies, a handful of more or less national newspapers, and a dozen or so weekly or monthly journals of opinion would be inadequate. True, other media also report national news— for example, men's and women's magazines, the racial and ethnic press, and the huge number of magazines that deal with leisure news of interest to hobbyists, sports enthusiasts, celebrity fans, and the like. Professional, trade, and union journals supply national occupational news; and business magazines, as well as industry and Washington newsletters, report news for business and political leaders. But many of these either serve an audience of experts and an educated upper middle-class or do not provide the kind of news I have in mind.

Reaching the millions of people in the lay audience would require an increase in the total newshole for national news, whatever the media, and there are at least two possible models. One model is centralized: it simply expands the present national news media to accommodate multiperspectivism. Each medium would supply its own brand of multiperspectival news to the present large and diverse audience, but one might guess that two-hour evening newscasts, 200-page newsmagazines, and currently non-existent popular national newspapers would be required.

The second model is decentralized: it calls for a much larger number of national news media, each designed to reach different but roughly homogeneous—and therefore smaller—audiences. There might be individual national news programs, magazines, and newspapers for adolescents, adults, and old people; for the rich, the middle class, and the poor; for suburbanites, urbanites, and rural residents; for blue-collar and white-collar workers, and professionals; for ideologically clustered audiences across the spectrum—in theory, at least, for a nearly infinite number of population sectors and roles. Each news medium would supply some uniform news, some stories on the same topics but from different perspectives, and a great deal of distinctive news relevant to each audience.

The centralized model has the benefit of exposing large audiences to a variety of perspectives; moreover, a handful of central media would provide visibility and symbolic power to these perspectives in essentially the present symbolic arena. The decentralized model would supply people with considerably more news in line with their own perspectives, but they would not be exposed to other perspectives; the symbolic arena would thus be decentralized and provincialized as well.

However, both models are probably unworkable. The centralized model requires a multiperspectival news organization, but no top editor or producer could possibly keep all perspectives in mind. The decentralized model fails on economic grounds. Independent news-gathering organizations are very expensive, and those catering to small audiences could not summon up the funds or attract the advertisers to meet these costs. While subsidies could be called for, these would need to be huge, and who would supply them?

A Two-tier Model

A more realistic model, which combines some centralization and decentralization is conceivable, particularly since it is essentially an expansion of the currently existing array of national media. This model assumes the continued existence of the present national news media, with perhaps one or two additional network news organizations (through syndication and public television), newsmagazines, and national newspapers to come in the future, each of which would adopt a modest degree of multiperspectivism.

These central (or first-tier) media would be complemented by a second tier of pre-existing and new national media, each reporting the news to specific, fairly homogeneous audiences. Depending on audience size and interest, these could be daily, weekly, or monthly television and radio programs, as well as newspapers and magazines. Still, many would need to be subsidized (see below); and even then, their news organizations would have to be small.[18] They would devote themselves primarily to reanalyzing and reinterpreting news gathered by the central media—and the wire services—for their audiences, adding their own commentary and backing these up with as much original reporting, particularly to supply bottom-up, representative, and service news, as would be financially feasible. Scattered prototypes of television and radio news programs for specific audiences are already in existence in a few large cities; the newspapers and magazines could be modeled (in makeup and staff size) on the journals of opinion, the publications of the ethnic and racial press, and the newspapers and magazines of small political parties as well as informal political groups.[19]

This model would achieve the prime aim of the news: to present and represent many more perspectives in the symbolic arena. Obviously, the two-tier model would produce somewhat less than equal representation, for the central media would be most prominent in the symbolic arena, which is why they, too, would have to become more multiperspectival.

A Modest Degree of Multiperspectivism

The crucial issue for the central media of my two-tier model, as well as for the national news media as they now exist, is: How multiperspectival should they become? Or, if all questions are right, which right questions should the national news media ask? Other problems aside, the issue is how to allocate a scarce resource—the national newshole—which can never be large enough to accommodate the sources and perspectives that now dominate the news as well as those called for by multiperspectivism.

Philosophers and social scientists have given much thought to how scarce resources are best allocated, but their solutions are difficult to transfer to the news. If news were an economic good, market rules could prevail, although sources and audiences without money would be excluded. If news were a political good, democratic concepts of representation and majority rule could serve as guides, but then numerical minorities would frequently be neglected. When news is centrally planned, it tends to publicize the central planners.

If the symbolic arena must be both comprehensive and representative, however, and if the arena must be so managed that journalists can accomplish their work and attract an audience, then new criteria for allocating the newshole must be developed. I do not know how this is to be done, for there are no simple formulas, and many of the judgments must, in any case, be left to the journalists. I can only make some suggestions that aim toward a modest degree of multiperspectivism.

For one thing, journalists should redefine importance considerations to give greater weight to information that is important to various sectors of the population, and less weight to nation and society as units. By that criterion, public officials—and officials of corporations, national voluntary associations, etc.—become newsworthy when their actions and statements have significant impact on one or more of the major sectors and roles into which America is divided. And stories grow in importance the larger the number of affected sectors and roles, or the more drastic the impact on a few. Impact, however, must be measured by output indicators. Social and moral disorders can be judged similarly, but they become important in two other ways: when they affect public or private policy; and when they are the actions of people who have no other means of appearing in the symbolic arena or of making their demands known to public officials.

But the essence of multiperspectivism is greater balance, which requires a higher priority to balance considerations in news judgment. In effect, journalists have to become knowledgeable about the totality, or "universe," of all possible sources and perspectives, and all sectors and roles, in America in order to represent these in the news in a balanced fashion. Currently, journalists select sources and perspectives from among those they know; instead, they must learn to choose from all those known to exist.

However, this proposal requires a complete "mapping" of all sources and perspectives in American society, by social scientists, statisticians, and journalists, which is not now, and may never be, available. In the meantime, the modest solution is to go beyond current practice by ensuring that more of the now unrepresented sources and perspectives appear in the news.

In some instances, this is relatively simple. For news about government or corporate activities, the prime additional sources, both for bottom-up and output news, are beneficiaries and victims, although identifying them requires a good deal of reporter legwork. Similarly, for the general run of political news, the universe consists of the major political parties, some minor ones, spokespersons for other groups likely to be affected by the story, and representatives of various positions on the ideological spectrum.

When the universe of sources and perspectives is very large, as for representative and service news, feasible balance criteria are harder to suggest, since journalists cannot possibly supply such news for all sectors and roles. Even so, story selectors already apply some demographic balance considerations (see Chapter 5); they would, however, have to add other numerically and politically significant sectors and roles, which they now omit. The modest and not very difficult solution is to report more representative and service news about the now omitted people outside the middle class and professional occupations: notably the poor, blue-collar and lower white-collar Americans, the old, children and especially adolescents, racial minorities, and the people whose economic, political, and cultural opinions are at odds with various "mainstreams." Of course, people from these sectors and roles already appear in the news, but they are either public officials and spokespersons or deviants and oddities. If the symbolic arena is to be comprehensive and representative, however, news about and for such people that treats them, their problems, and their opinions as respectfully as those of high officials must be added for proper balance.

Ideally, multiperspectival balance would be achieved if the news about and for the principal sectors and roles in America were roughly equivalent to their representation in the population. For example, since close to 15 percent of the population is officially designated as poor, and 20 percent earns less than the median income, balance is achieved when roughly 15 to 20 percent of the news for and about income groups deals with the poor.[20] When information about a relevant universe is readily available, journalists should use it, although I do not suggest that story selection be based on census data or that story selectors should start using slide rules. Indeed, they should not be saddled with keeping track of whether they achieve multiperspectival balance; that responsibility properly belongs to media monitors and critics (to be described below).

These balance considerations would, as now, be applied in conjunction with others. There would be times, however, when other considerations might make balance impossible. If the country were involved in a major war or beset by a series of catastrophes, journalists could not supply as much representative or service news. Conversely, if the government were to launch a major anti-poverty effort, story selectors would be justified in paying more attention to the poor than their percentage in the population might otherwise warrant. Then, too, presidents, other major public and corporate officials, and criminals will always be more newsworthy than their number.

Even these proposals overtax the newshole; in addition, journalists will never have sufficient time or staff to apply this kind of balance for a single story. Accordingly, multiperspectival balance can be achieved only over time—for example, over the duration of running stories and, for other news, over a year's time. In that period, journalists should be able to include some stories about all major sectors and roles, both in the news and in commentary.

As a goal, multiperspectivism resembles equality. Both are impossible to achieve completely, but each offers a target toward which to move. Just as changes in income distribution provide a feasible indicator of movement toward economic equality, so increases in the diversity of sources and perspectives in the news provide a feasible indicator of movement toward multiperspectivism.

Nevertheless, the national news media can go only so far. One of the purposes of the second tier is to continue where the central media leave off: to supply further and more detailed news for and about the perspectives of the audiences they serve. In the process, these media would also function as monitors and critics of the central media, indicating where and how, by their standards, the central media have been insufficiently multiperspectival.

Who Should Select the News?

When scarce resources must be allocated, and practical as well as fair formulas are not readily available, who should allocate them becomes a relevant question. Consequently, it is proper to ask who should be responsible for story selection and production. The news may be too important to leave to the journalists alone.

Journalists have always insisted that they should retain sole responsibility over the nation's news. Freedom of the press and the audience's right to know can be preserved, they argue, only if journalists, detached from the political process, are free to decide what is newsworthy. But in reality, journalists are not detached, for their enduring values are political values, which imply the advocacy of one kind of social order. Moreover, because news has political implications, and because journalists choose the news in response to source power, they are unwittingly part of the political process. Whatever their political functions, however, they have not been elected by anyone, nor are they directly accountable to the citizenry.

The issue is not, as Spiro Agnew once put it, whether a small clique of Eastern establishment liberals should select the news but whether that responsibility should be monopolized by a single set of commercially employed professionals. In the last fifteen years, the same issue has been raised repeatedly about many other professionals: about the right of doctors to determine the nature of medical care, of educators to decide what children should learn, of social workers to control the lives of welfare recipients, and of social scientists to decide what topics should be researched.[21] In reality, the question extends beyond the professions, for it concerns the differential rights of all suppliers and users of goods and services. Whether industry can pass the indirect economic and social costs of its operations on to the general public, or whether businesses should sell their goods on a *caveat emptor* basis are only other versions of the same general question.

That question, however, must be answered separately for every set of suppliers and users. Doctors, for instance, have a far greater monopoly over the shape of medical services than journalists have over the symbolic arena: and social workers can exert more control over their clients than journalists can over their audience. Educators deal with a captive audience, whereas journalists must attract and hold a voluntary one; businessmen and women sell their goods and services in ways that journalists do not.

In principle, I would argue that like other professionals, journalists should share their responsibility with others. But principles must acknowledge the real world, wherein the first and most energetic claimants to a share in news selection would be advertisers, powerful sources which prefer to exclude harmful publicity from the news, and the best organized or most vocal audience members. In a world of unequal power, the principle could well enhance the power of those groups which already exert pressure on journalists.

The principle of shared responsibility remains defensible, but only if its implementation results in a widespread and democratic sharing of responsibility by the powerless and the powerful, by those who can express their interests easily and those who cannot. Sharing of responsibility would therefore have to be regulated, but who would regulate? Professional self-regulation has often been proposed, but it tends to regulate the profession first in terms of its own interests. Nor has it been especially effective, for professionals are reluctant to regulate themselves and their peers, except to avoid the possibility of government regulation.

Government regulation has been effective in some professions and commercial enterprises, but government also has a vested interest in the supply of news, being itself a major source and user of news. Sufficient evidence, even from democratic nations, exists to suggest that when government regulates the news media, journalists can be co-opted as spokespersons for the government in power. Those who propose that regulation by elected officials is preferable to regulation by unaccountable corporate executives may have a point, but many elected and appointed officials are themselves insufficiently representative and accountable; moreover, corporate executives have so far maintained a virtually complete hands-off policy toward their news organizations. The journalists' adversary relationship with government, even in its present limited or intermittent form, is too precious to risk, although it should be complemented by a more adversarial relationship with business.

Other alternatives for sharing journalistic responsibility seem to hold little promise. Nonjournalists could be placed on the boards of directors of news firms, just as community control has placed citizens on policy boards to oversee professionals in local communities; but corporate boards do not influence everyday news judgment. Full-time citizen boards designed to oversee top producers and editors are conceivable, but they would probably be co-opted by the exigencies of the assembly line, if by nothing else.

Suppose top editors and producers held elected positions. Requiring them to campaign would open up the political issues in news selection, but the electorate would be difficult to demarcate; and in any case, interest groups with the strongest incentive to influence the news might pack the ballot boxes. The present ways of democratizing organizations are not likely to work in either the existing news media or my proposed central media, but they might be tried in the second tier, for these media would, by definition, be expected to represent their audiences more directly. Indeed, their credibility and their effectiveness in the symbolic arena might be heightened were they democratically organized and were they to use lay people, at least sometimes, to report and comment on the news.

Indirect Sharing of Responsibility

Under present political and economic conditions, I see no ready alternative for continued journalistic responsibility for the news. However, that responsibility can be shared indirectly by giving now unrepresented sources greater access to journalists, strengthening criticism of the news media and the news, democratizing the opportunity to exert pressure, and expanding audience feedback.

If news organizations had extra funds, they could reach out beyond their present array of sources; but sources must also be aided in gaining access to journalists. The difficulties are enormous, for journalists cannot afford to be flooded by sources; and the national media are not easily accessible. In the last analysis, effective access is gained by the provision of suitable news. Now unrepresented sources must therefore avail themselves of the same media specialists that large public and private organizations use to supply anticipated news, create media events, and make newsworthy sources available to journalists. And this requires funds.

News-media criticism is already available but largely within the profession. It could be moved outside, and thus made more visible, were television and radio programs, as well as independent publications, established to review the news. The limitations of intraprofessional criticism could be breached by the use of some lay reviewers.

Media criticism can be encouraged further by establishing commercial, academic, public-interest, and other agencies to monitor the news. Monitors would carry out regular studies of the content of the news in order to evaluate balance, which would help journalists evaluate their success in achieving multiperspectivism. Monitoring studies should be published—and in lay language—so that they are available to the audience and to media critics. Ideally, such studies would be funded and carried out by individuals and organizations disinterested in the results, but I see nothing wrong with ideologically or politically motivated analyses, provided values and value implications are clearly spelled out and the analyses represent all parts of the political and ideological spectrums. Unless monitoring agencies are themselves balanced, however, monitoring may be dominated by more affluent, and therefore more conservative, agencies.

Nonjournalists already have the right to exert pressure on journalists. The problem, as in the case of political pressure, is to expand and equalize the opportunity to be heard and listened to. Until pushbutton devices are invented to permit audiences to talk back instantly to top producers and editors, letter writing will have to suffice; but letter writers will probably always remain a skewed sample of the audience.

However, that skew can be partially corrected by encouraging more letters that offer reasoned criticism and constructive comments on what perspectives have been omitted from the news. After all, journalists pay serious attention only to these kinds of letters. Because writing them requires careful viewer/reader attention to the news, as well as the time and resources to communicate, such letters are probably better written by organizations than by individuals, and by media specialists than by lay people. Those segments of the audience least able to exert pressure by letter writing, however, are also the least organized. If the few organizations that do represent them are to criticize the news, they would need financial help, especially since they have more urgent priorities than monitoring it.[22]

Undoubtedly, journalists will resent additional pressure, even if it comes from now nonvocal segments of the audience. They will also ignore organized letter-writing campaigns, organizational demands for more publicity, and *ad hominem* attacks. But, like everyone else, they must adapt to pressure, even if they deny, like many politicians, that they are doing so.

Probably the best way to democratize pressure is through audience research, for audience researchers reach out to people unwilling or unable to exert pressure. In addition, random sampling is an egalitarian and democratic method that cannot favor the economically or politically powerful. Regular studies among present audiences and nonaudiences to discover how people attend to the news; what they find useful or deficient; and what they want to see, hear, and read are therefore desirable. But in order for the findings to become a form of pressure, these studies must be published. Like monitoring studies, audience research should be carried out by both disinterested and interested agencies (for each will ask different questions), once again provided interested agencies are ideologically and otherwise balanced.

Conversely, one kind of pressure needs to be eliminated: court decisions that threaten to limit the journalists' access to sources (see Chapter 8). Although the courts seem intent, at the moment, on reducing the special privileges of journalists, the court decisions actually restrict the freedom of sources. In particular, they strike at sources that are governmental adversaries, increasing their political and legal vulnerability, and discouraging them from supplying information to journalists. In effect, the courts are, purposely or otherwise, keeping the very sources out of the news whose perspectives are already insufficiently represented.

Multiperspectivism requires the abolition of legal pressure so that the incentives of sources to provide information can be maximized. In turn, journalists may be able to shield sources from harm and maintain their anonymity. Even when a life is at stake and source information has to be revealed, sources themselves must be protected.

Audiences and Funds for Multiperspectival News

I have so far begged two vital, interrelated questions: Where would the audience for multiperspectival news come from? And how would such news be funded? The available data about the actual audience for today's news do not encourage the belief that readers and viewers can easily be found. My proposals for changing the news assume the retention of the product and audience considerations by which today's journalists have attracted and created a large popular audience for national news; but even so, multiperspectivism means more news, and more complex news. As a result, it can be questioned for supplying too much news to an already reluctant audience.

But if I read the existing audience-preference research correctly, there is an interest in personally relevant news and in news that connects the affairs of nation and society to the micro-societies of everyday life. Output, representative, and service news might persuade the existing audience to be more regular and might entice others who find today's news irrelevant. The constantly increasing number of new special-interest magazines suggests that some second-tier media might attract a sufficient audience; on the other hand, most newcomers are leisure magazines, which does not suggest a rising interest in national news designed for specialized audiences. After all, the ability of national news to be personally relevant and to touch on micro-societal lives is inherently limited. In the end, only individually tailored news can achieve a high degree of personal relevance, and only the president of the United States and some corporate officials can afford such news.

In addition, people with little economic or political power and insufficient control over their lives might not want multiperspectival news that would, in effect, demonstrate their inequalities in greater detail. Also, the poor cannot always afford to buy newspapers and magazines. Nevertheless, scattered experiments with news media designed specifically for them have shown that they are as interested as anyone else in relevant news.[23]

News as a Utility

A massive rise in audience numbers and regularity cannot be expected, but I would argue that audience response is not the only significant criterion. In a democratic society, news is not solely a consumer product but also a utility, inherently necessary for the proper functioning of that society. A main purpose of the news is to provide representation in the symbolic arena, and multiperspectivism achieves that purpose even if the audience does not grow larger or become more regular. A major intended audience, in fact, would be public and other officials who need, or should need, to keep their fingers on the pulse of nation and society. Multiperspectival news would supply them with more feedback about the opinions and demands of a variety of constituencies, including some that now rarely provide feedback.

Insofar as the news supplies instantaneous indicators of public opinion to public officials, multiperspectival news would enable journalists to function as more democratic stand-ins for the public than they do now. In addition, multiperspectival news would enrich public opinion polling. Polls do not really measure public opinion; instead, they usually gather reactions to the news; and in some cases, poll respondents merely repeat the ideas and attitudes they have learned from the news.[24] A better-informed news audience would be more competent in responding to pollsters' questions, thereby making the polls themselves more effective providers of citizen feedback.

Funding Multiperspectival News

Virtually all of the proposals I have made in this chapter require additional funds: to expand the news offerings of the present media and to hire the larger staffs necessary to unearth different perspectives from scattered sources; to bring the second-tier media into being; to help now isolated sources gain access to journalists; and to expand news-media criticism, and monitoring and audience research.

Where would the money come from? Some funds might be obtained from national advertisers, since national news is increasingly attractive to them, and they are readier now than in the past to pursue smaller and more homogeneous audiences. Nevertheless, I doubt that they would be enthusiastic until there was some indication of audience enthusiasm; and it is hard to imagine that they would buy advertising time or space in second-tier media for audiences with little buying power, or in any news medium dispensing controversial news or commentary. Foundations have in the past aided media serving small audiences, but their funds and their tolerance for controversy are also finite. I doubt that Americans would accept the European license-fee system for electronic media; and while they seem prepared to pay more for newspapers and magazines, price increases also drive some people out of the audience. Nor does it now seem likely that the government could require the networks to use profits from entertainment programming for the news, and most print media cannot subsidize the news with entertainment profits in the first place.

What About Government?

Since news is not merely a consumer product but a utility as well, I think that the federal government should supply at least some of the funds for multiperspectival news. However, this idea violates the long-standing formal separation of press and state. There are some dangers in ending that separation, which I will come to shortly, but there are also some viable reasons that justify it. First, multiperspectival news will better inform the citizenry; second, it will bring about a more representative symbolic arena; and most important, both will enhance democracy. Whether the government is interested in enhancing democracy may be questioned, but in any event, it should be. In addition, government has long acted as a countervailing force to correct the shortcomings of free enterprise. For example, presidential elections are now subsidized by the government so as to reduce the influence of affluent campaign contributors. By the same token, government support of the news would reduce the inequities resulting from the fact that the news media are commercial enterprises.

I propose, therefore, that the government establish an Endowment for News, modeled in part on the federal agencies that now endow the arts and humanities, which would give grants in the following areas:

1. The Endowment would provide needed funds to entrepreneurs, including journalists, interested in creating new, second-tier national media, who can demonstrate their intent to reach existing audiences (or presently unreached ones) with now unavailable sources and perspectives.

2. The Endowment would provide aid to existing national news media prepared to add new sources and perspectives to the news, and to establish new television or radio programs, or magazine and newspaper sections for this purpose. The Endowment would also aid existing national news firms which wanted to establish new second-tier media.

3. The Endowment would support organized or unorganized sources who can demonstrate their present inability to gain access to national journalists, by supplying them with funds to establish the same facilitating mechanisms by which public agencies and others now obtain access to national journalists.

4. The Endowment would help both new and existing organizations, journalistic and other, engaged in criticism and monitoring of the news; it would also support organizations that seek to exert pressure on the news media.

5. The Endowment would similarly support new and existing organizations, including news organizations, in the creation or improvement of audience feedback mechanisms, as well as news research among present and potential audience members.

6. The Endowment would provide funds directly or indirectly through organizations to people too poor either to obtain national newspapers and magazines or to afford television sets and radios.

The Endowment would not be allowed to participate directly in any way in the selection or production of news. Its sole responsibility would be the provision of funds, and its mandate would limit these funds to applicants who could not find support elsewhere. Applicants would therefore have to demonstrate that alternative funding sources were unavailable; were funds granted, they would still have to find other sources for at least 25 to 33 percent of their budget so as to avoid total dependence on government money. For applicants who need only initial capital, the Endowment would supply or underwrite loans.

The Endowment would be run by an independent board that includes journalists as well as lay people representing audiences and sources. It would give grants on the basis of peer review committee procedures now used in many federal agencies, except that review committees would again include both journalists and nonjournalists.

Administering the six programs I have suggested is not as simple as proposing them; detailed guidelines would have to be developed— for example, requiring applicants to demonstrate that they will add new perspectives to the news and that they cannot obtain funds elsewhere. Moreover, even the wisest guidelines cannot avoid some undesirable consequences. A modicum of legal and illegal corruption is inevitable, as occurs in all private and public granting agencies. Undoubtedly, undeserving and incompetent applicants may sometimes be funded, competent ones will waste money, and many innovations will fail, as they inevitably do.

Even an independent government agency is vulnerable to political pressure, and in turn it will exert some pressure of its own. The Endowment would almost certainly be pressured by other parts of government not to support unpopular ideas and controversial innovations; most likely, it would not be able to fund organizations and individuals associated with "extreme" ideas or causes. At the same time, the Endowment might exert subtle pressures on grant recipients to be kind to the incumbent administration and powerful elected and appointed officials. Conversely, grant seekers might try to please the Endowment, even without being asked to do so; as a result, some may request funds for overt or covert government propaganda.

None of these possible consequences strike me as serious enough to invalidate my proposal, but there are two other possible dangers. One is that when government provides money, it claims the right of review; and once it gains a foothold, it soon begins to regulate. It is undeniable that funding means review, but peer review is not quite the same as government review. That some parts of government might want to regulate the news media is also undeniable; but judging by most existing regulatory agencies, such regulation has often been ineffective, for the regulated have too much power. The present endowment agencies have not regulated the content of the humanities and the arts. Although they have upset "elite" institutions of high culture by funding "populist" ventures, they have not interfered with high culture. Professionals who have secured government funds have not been notably diverted from professional goals as a result, even if they now have to fill out more forms. Just the reverse is true, for the public officials who make funding decisions are frequently fellow-professionals. Were the Endowment to be staffed solely by journalists, it might therefore eschew innovative ideas that run counter to professional goals; this is one reason for including nonjournalists on the board and review committees.

The second danger is that government funding would intimidate journalists, thereby threatening their adversary posture vis-à-vis government. But this fear also strikes me as groundless. If the Endowment for News were run out of the White House, journalists would be justified in worrying about pressure and chilling effects. However, while the White House would appoint the Endowment head, it could not easily dictate agency policy, especially since, with journalists involved, such attempts would surely become news. Perhaps the Endowment would be reluctant to give grants to news organizations which employ journalists or seek out sources that are on a White House or congressional "enemies list"; but this danger, although real, is not serious enough to jeopardize my proposal.

A news medium or organization entirely dependent on endowment funds would have reason to worry or be intimidated; for that reason alone, the requirement for matching funds is desirable. An established commercial news firm which obtains some funds from the Endowment for News would, however, hardly sell its autonomy for a small mess of federal pottage.

The real danger is that government, recognizing that multiperspectival news downgrades public officials as sources, would oppose the establishment of the Endowment in the first place. Alternatively, the government might decide to establish its own news media. The commercial news firms would surely object to another competitor, especially one as well-funded and powerful as the government; but government news media would add to the diversity of national news.[25] In addition, they would relieve the commercial news media of the need and incentive to publicize official sources, thus releasing additional air time or print space for other sources and strengthening the adversarial posture of commercial journalists.

To be sure, ideally, news organizations should be non-commercial and nongovernmental bodies, obtaining funds from various sources without any strings attached. However, the experience of public television suggests that this ideal is illusory.

Multiperspectival News and Democracy

The fundamental justification for multiperspectival news is its potential for furthering democracy. If the honorable cliché that democracy rests on a well-informed citizenry were accurate, no further argument would be necessary. But the cliché is not accurate, for democracies must and do function even when citizens are not well informed. The cliché reflects the Athenian conception of democracy, in which participation in government was limited to the well-informed; but today it also has a hidden agenda: the already well-informed hope that if other citizens are given the same information, they will become political supporters of the causes of the now well-informed.

Multiperspectival news is not designed to gain supporters for any specific political cause. Rather, it will enable people to obtain news relevant to their own perspectives, and therefore to their own interests and political goals, if they have any. In the process, the symbolic arena would become more democratic, for the symbolic power of now dominant sources and perspectives would be reduced.

Obviously, multiperspectivism is not apolitical, since making the symbolic arena more democratic is a political goal. Insofar as such an arena would reduce the symbolic power of now dominant sources and perspectives, it is a goal that includes some redistribution of power. The question is, how much?

A second honorable cliché holds that knowledge is power; but while the news dispenses knowledge, it cannot automatically redistribute power. Already powerful groups can obtain additional power because they have access to politically effective knowledge and because they can withhold such knowledge from others, at least for a time; but powerless people cannot improve their position with further knowledge alone. Most likely, they sense that knowledge without prior power is of limited usefulness.

True, the news media redistribute symbolic power when they act as agenda setters, helping place and publicize issues in the symbolic arena, and thereby increasing the influence of supporters of these issues. Multiperspectival news would set more and different agendas, thus encouraging people to develop opinions and to act if the agenda item were relevant to their interests.[26] In addition, the news disseminates facts, particularly about moral disorder. In the right place and at the right time, moral disorder news can create a wave of sympathy or antipathy, tipping public opinion, and power, on those issues in which public opinion counts. The conditions under which this happens, however, are partly fortuitous; and journalists cannot, by themselves, automatically tip public opinion. Even if news could deliver power, journalists only supply the news; they cannot guarantee that (or how) audiences will use it.[27]

Multiperspectival news will not, therefore, bring about further democratization of America by itself. Democracy is a property of social structure, not symbols, requiring greater equalization of power and of people's ability to exert pressure on their government. But power cannot be equalized without economic change, for unequal economic power breeds unequal political power. Multiperspectival news could supply information about the economic and political inequities that still exist in America; but as radical journalists of every generation have learned, information alone does not alter economic and political hierarchies.

Furthermore, multiperspectival news is likely to encounter opposition, and not only from public officials and others objecting to sharing the news with additional sources. Between 1965 and 1970, Finnish television news implemented a new policy "which stressed the importance of conveying socially relevant information . . . especially from the point of view of those interest groups which were left outside the official channels of information and influence."[28] Although the audience went along with the change, it was opposed by the conservative newspapers and "most of the established institutions in society (church, schools, army, commerce, industry, etc.)."[29] The policy was abolished after the election of a conservative national government.

America is larger and more heterogeneous than Finland; and as of now, it seems unlikely that the equivalent American "established institutions" could coalesce sufficiently amongst themselves or with a conservative federal government. Moreover, Finnish television, being government-run, was vulnerable to begin with; even so, a single American news medium instituting a similar policy might be vulnerable as well, both to commercial and government pressure, and to opposition from other news media.

Yet other forms of opposition to multiperspectival news might develop because the images of nation and society it would construct would also foster the impression that America is not a cohesive unit but an array of diverse, often conflicting groups. While I doubt that today's news media contribute significantly to social or political cohesion, multiperspectival news would, of course, contribute even less.

Whether the news media should aim to depict America as a cohesive unit or as an array of diverse groups depends on one's political values. For those who believe that cohesion and order are prime national and societal goals, multiperspectivism would be objectionable. For those who feel, as I do, that the interests of diverse groups have priority over the needs of nation and society, multiperspectival news and some decentralization of the national media are preferable. Even so, if more people obtain news relevant to their interests, and if that news helps them achieve their own goals, they may feel themselves to be part of a larger whole. In the long run, then, the country would be more cohesive in fact if not in symbol.

Cohesion cannot be achieved without further democratization of the economy and the polity; but if multiperspectival news cannot, by itself, contribute significantly to democratization, why bother with it? In fact, why not put the national news media in the hands of individuals and groups committed and prepared to use them to bring about additional democratization? If anyone knew how to make America more democratic, that possibility would be worth considering, but only if restrictions on freedom of speech and on the constitutional rights of those who oppose further democratization could be avoided.

Nevertheless, bothering with multiperspectival news is justified, for while it is not a sufficient agent of democratization, it does supply some of the necessary information. However, it would be a good deal more effective if it coincided with widespread public demand for greater popular representation in the economy and the polity.

The Feasibility of Multiperspectival News

I am well aware that, at present, many of the proposals in this chapter are not feasible. As I suggested in Chapter 9, journalists have little incentive for significant change. They, or at least their firms, would have even less incentive for multiperspectivism because it undercuts the twin bases of the present journalistic enterprise: efficiency and the power of sources. Journalists might be prepared to reduce the power of present sources, but I doubt that they would accept proposals that created new pressures on them and their work.

Even so, I believe that my basic idea is viable, and it may become more feasible in the future. If the current decline in economic growth becomes permanent, as many economists now predict, the American Dream of continuing improvements in personal and familial standards of living, which economic growth has nurtured, is bound to eventually become an illusion. What Americans will do then remains to be seen. One possibility is that in seeking to maintain their current way of life, they will become more aware than they are at present of their own economic and political interests. But if they also begin to make demands on the government and the economy in line with their interests, they will require a different kind of national news. For one thing, they will need more national news; for another, they will need more news that helps them further their interests. But insofar as these interests will, in a stratified society like America, be diverse, they will need something very much like multiperspectival news.

Of course, people do not always—or even often—get what they need. The news firms, more so than the journalists, are sufficiently beholden to various current holders of economic and political power to be reluctant to respond to popular demands for changes in the government and the economy. Still, the firms also exist to make a profit; and if people require a different kind of news and are willing to pay for it, directly or through advertisers, the firms can be expected to go along.

In other words, multiperspectivism may be relevant to a future America, and one which I believe is likely to come into being. Neither I nor anyone else can now predict its coming, the exact shape it will take, or what news and news media it will need. But who can know what the future will bring?

Notes

Chapter 1—Nation and Society in the News

1. "Topical" content analyses of television news appear regularly in such journals as *Broadcasting, Journal of Communication, Journalism Quarterly,* and the *Public Opinion Quarterly.* Recent book-length studies include Robert Cirino, *Don't Blame the People* (Los Angeles: Diversity Press, 1971); Edith Efron, *The News Twisters* (Los Angeles: Nash, 1971); Robert S. Frank, *Message Dimensions of Television News* (Lexington, Mass.: Lexington Books, 1973); Ernest W. Lefever, *TV and National Defense* (Chicago: Institute for American Strategy, 1974); and C. Richard Hofstetter, *Bias in the News* (Columbus: Ohio State University Press, 1976).

For an excellent qualitative analysis of Vietnam War news, see Michael J. Arlen, *Living-Room War* (New York: Viking Press, 1969). Magazine news is analyzed less often, but see, for example, G. Ray Funkhouser, "The Issues of the Sixties: An Exploratory Study in the Dynamics of Public Opinion," *Public Opinion Quarterly* 37 (Spring 1973): 62–76.

2. A study of all newsmagazines in 1965–1966 found that committee assignments and state size correlated with the appearances of Republican, but not Democratic, senators in the news. David H. Weaver and G. Cleveland Wilhoit, "News Magazine Visibility of Senators," *Journalism Quarterly* 51 (Spring 1974): 67–72.

3. During 1965–1966, Senator Robert Kennedy appeared in the newsmagazines 136 times, more than any other senator and twice as often as the second most frequent subject, Senator Everett Dirksen. Senator Edward Kennedy was fifth on the list, with forty-two appearances, although he was then in his first term of office. Weaver and Wilhoit, "News Magazine Visibility of Senators," Table 1.

4. *NBC News* led with the Rockefeller appointment and, about 19 minutes into the August 20, 1974, program, devoted 20 seconds to the pension story; *Time*'s September 2, 1974, issue carried the Rockefeller appointment as the cover story but did not mention the pension story; *The New York Times* of August 21, 1974, gave Rockefeller a 3-line 5-column head on page 1 and four inside pages, and carried a half-column on the pension story on page 19.

5. Edward Kosner, "Top of the Week," *Newsweek,* 4 July 1976, p. 1.

6. Peter Goldman, "Our America," *Newsweek,* 4 July 1976, p. 13.

7. Ibid.

·8. Henry A. Grunwald, "Loving America," *Time,* 4 July 1976, pp. 35–36, quote at p. 36.

9. William Cohn's study of television historical documentaries concluded similarly that "since most . . . attempt to portray the 'idea' of the American experience rather than the process of historical change over time, images such as American history as a success story tend to dominate the film presentations." William Cohn, "History for the Masses," *Journal of Popular Culture* 10 (Fall 1976): 280–89, quote at p. 281.

10. An additional 5 percent of the columns dealt with black crime and its control, however, whereas 6 percent addressed themselves to white crime against blacks. Of the remaining columns, 9 percent were equally divided between demonstrations and their control; 4 percent reported Adam Clayton Powell's difficulties; and 9 percent were about a wide variety of other topics.

11. Mary Kellogg, "A Farewell to Nirvana," *Newsweek,* 15 March 1976, p. 15.

12. In 1966, Russell Baker satirized the preoccupation with young people in a column which ended by noting that "Like today's teenagers, [grown-ups] are really just like people except for their inability to get themselves probed, prodded and psychoanalyzed by magazine writers and TV crews." Russell Baker, "Observer: Report on America's Grown-Ups," *The New York Times,* 19 March 1966.

13. A breakdown of all television, and domestic and international magazine news in my 1967 sample showed that on television, 48 percent of the news was domestic, 31 percent was about Vietnam, 7 percent was Cold War news (which could be domestic or foreign), and 14 percent was foreign news. For the newsmagazines, the percentages were 39, 18, 15, and 28, respectively.

14. Quoted in John M. Hamilton, "Ho Hum—Latin America," *Columbia Journalism Review* 16 (May/June 1977): 10.

15. In the 1960s, news writers at one network made up what they called a Racial Equivalence Scale, showing the minimum number of people who had to die in airplane crashes in different countries before the crash became newsworthy. As one writer pointed out: "One hundred Czechs were equal to forty-three Frenchmen, and the Paraguayans were at the bottom." The scale was made up to criticize the practice, but it has not changed.

Schlesinger reports that BBC journalists use a similar scale, quoting one in which "one thousand wogs, fifty frogs, and one Briton" are equivalent. Philip Schlesinger, *Putting 'Reality' Together* (London: Constable Press, 1978), p. 117.

Chapter 2—Values in the News

1. How actors and activities are reported and what is emphasized also affect the inference process, however, and result in what Kurt and Gladys E. Lang have called the inferential structure of the news. See their *Politics and Television* (New York: Quadrangle Books, 1968), p. 134.

2. Efron, *The News Twisters.*

3. Foreign news lends itself especially well to this analysis because of a special terminology that is rarely used in domestic news. Some foreign governments are "juntas" or "regimes," but the news does not speak of the "Carter regime." Headlines and their television equivalents are also revealing, for when space is at a minimum, writers must often make value judgments as a kind of forced choice. Even so, the choice is not idiosyncratic. The People's Republic of China was often called Red China because three-letter words are prized by headline writers; however, no color was assigned to the Republic of China on Taiwan.

4. Newfield has made a similar list of values which he calls organic: "belief in welfare capitalism, God, the West, Puritanism, the Law, the family, property, the two-party system, and perhaps most crucially, . . . that violence is only defensible when employed by the State." Jack Newfield, "Journalism: Old, New and Corporate," in Ronald Weber, ed., *The Reporter as Artist: A Look at the New Journalism Controversy* (New York: Hastings House, 1974), pp. 54–65, quote at p. 56.

5. For a more detailed analysis of news-media terminology during the Vietnam War, see Edwin Diamond, *The Tin Kazoo* (Cambridge, Mass.: MIT Press, 1975), chapter 6; and George A. Bailey, "Interpretive Reporting of the Vietnam War by Anchormen," *Journalism Quarterly* 53 (Summer 1976): 319–24.

6. On the underreporting of atrocities, see, e.g., Noam Chomsky, "Reporting Indochina: The News Media and the Legitimation of Lies," *Social Policy* 4 (September/October, 1973): 4–19.

7. In one cover story, *Time* distinguished between "capitalism" and "authoritarian economic systems." "Can Capitalism Survive?" *Time,* 14 July 1975, pp. 52–63, quote at p. 63.

A subsequent cover story distinguished between "Marxism-Leninism," "Social Democracy," and "Third-World Socialism," but then went on to stress similarities among them. "Socialism: Trials and Errors," *Time,* 13 March 1978, pp. 24–36, quote at p. 24.

8. One of the last works of the late Fred Freed, the gifted NBC documentary producer, was a three-hour program on the 1973 energy crisis, which devoted much of its time to wondering whether it would not be better to make drastic reductions in the use of energy, whatever the consequences for the standard of living, in order to preserve the original landscape.

9. Edward J. Epstein, *News from Nowhere* (New York: Random House, 1973), pp. 244–46.

10. Kellogg, *"A Farewell to Nirvana,"* p. 15.

11. Molotch and Lester have developed a somewhat similar typology of the news; they distinguish between routines, accidents, and scandals. Although their typology intersects at various points with mine, it is based on quite a different organizing principle, for they see the news as purposive behavior on the part of "promoters" (whom I call sources), and distinguish types of news by whether it is routinely intended to be issued by sources, whether it appears accidentally despite the best efforts of sources to suppress it, or whether it is leaked by one source to create a scandal for another. My typology, however, is based on values I see implicit in the news, regardless of the intentions of sources. See Harvey L. Molotch and Marilyn J. Lester, "News as Purposive Behavior: On the Strategic Use of Routine Events, Accidents, and Scandals," *American Sociological Review* 39 (February 1974): 101–12.

12. In a study comparing American and Canadian television news for the same time period, Singer found that the former paid far more attention to social disorder news than the latter, carrying twice as many stories about violence, protest, and war. Singer ascribed his results to a greater American interest in violence, although the difference may also be due to the fact that for Canadians, what goes on in America is foreign news, which takes second place to domestic news. Benjamin D. Singer, "Violence, Protest and War in Television News: The U. S. and Canada Compared," *Public Opinion Quarterly* 34 (Winter 1970–1971): 611–16.

13. Twenty-three percent of the sequences depicted "control or containment"; 4 percent, arrests; and 7 percent, "conciliation." Simulmatics Corporation, "News Media Coverage of the 1967 Urban Riots," Final Report, mimeographed (New York: Simulmatics Corp., February 1, 1968), Table IV. The largest proportion of sequences was devoted to "Aftermath," defined as "scenes showing property damage, cleanup and normal activity," and thus a mixture of disorder and order-restoration news. Ibid., p. 18.

14. "The Underclass," *Time,* 29 August 1977, pp. 14–27.

15. I gathered this information from ABC and NBC journalists while serving as an interviewer for a study of television's coverage of the assassination, directed by the late Louis Cowan and Paul Lazarsfeld. The study is partly reported in Ruth L. Love, "Television and the Death of a President: Network Decisions in Covering Collective Events" (Ph. D. dissertation, Columbia University, 1969).

16. A radio story I heard shortly after Gerald Ford's swearing-in noted that Richard Nixon's resignation was handed in at 11:35 A.M.; that Gerald Ford had not taken the oath of office until noon; and that technically speaking, therefore, the country was leaderless for twenty-five minutes. The reporter reassured his listeners, however, that if any foreign power had wanted to take advantage of a leaderless

America to set off an international crisis, Mr. Ford would undoubtedly have taken the reins of office earlier so as to prevent it.

17. Robert Woodward and Carl Bernstein, *The Final Days* (New York: Avon Books, 1976), p. 430.

18. Bernard Berelson, "What 'Missing the Newspaper' Means," in Paul Lazarsfeld and Frank Stanton, eds., *Communications Research 1948–1949* (New York: Harper & Brothers, 1949), pp. 111–29.

19. In recent years, journalists themselves have become aware of what they view as the class bias of the news and of the profession. See, e.g., Michael Novak, "Why the Working Man Hates the Media," *More*, October 1974, pp. 5–7; and Michael J. Arlen, "Report from the Ice Age," *New Yorker*, 11 November 1974, pp. 185–92.

20. Jeanette Hopkins, "Racial Justice and the Press," MARC Paper No. 1 (New York: Metropolitan Applied Research Center, 1968), p. 24.

21. "Leadership in America," *Time*, 15 July 1974, pp. 21–70, quotes at p. 23.

22. In discussing the problem of national leadership, *Time* noted that "the problem is not just a lack of leadership but a lack of followership." "Leadership in America," p. 28.

23. Ibid., p. 22.

24. Ibid., p. 35.

25. Edwin Diamond, "The Chosen People," *More*, November 1974, pp. 14–15.

26. "Leadership in America," p. 35.

27. Diamond's list of eighty-eight individuals who did not appear in the final compilation included one radical leader, Imamu Baraka, and three other men who have sometimes been identified with the Left opposition to the Vietnam War. Diamond, "The Chosen People," p. 15.

28. *Time* apologized for the scarcity of women and blacks, however, by noting that "were a list to be compiled in 1980, say, their number would surely be greater; just now their presence in leadership positions is still limited." "Leadership in America," p. 35. The nominees' ethnic background was almost as homogeneous. Judging by names, not always the most reliable procedure, of the whites, 74 percent were WASPs or bore British surnames; 12 percent reflected other European origins, mainly Irish, German, and Italian; 11 percent were Jews; and 3 percent were of Hispanic or Latin origin.

29. Twelve percent of the leaders went to state universities, and the remaining 25 percent attended lesser-known private colleges, black colleges, or military academies. Since not all biographies included educational data, I analyzed the schools which individuals on the list had attended; this frequently included more than one, and the sum total is all schools mentioned.

30. "Leadership in America," p. 35.

31. Even so, *Time* apologized for their sparsity and explained that at age 45, "most financial and industrial whiz kids are still preoccupied with climbing corporate ladders and their deepest involvement in civic affairs occurs only after they have reached the top." "Leadership in America," p. 35. Diamond also reports that at one point, the editors considered raising the age minimum in order to include more business people on the list. Diamond, "The Chosen People," p. 14.

32. An unkind critic, noting that 10.5 percent of the leaders were from journalism or publishing, might conclude that the list represented the editors' claim to power; but I am sure that this was not one of their values, if only because the individuals were all from competing news media, and journalists normally are not inclined to give publicity to competitors.

Chapter 3—The Organization of Story Selection

1. For an insightful discussion of this point, see Gaye Tuchman, "Making News by Doing Work: Routinizing the Unexpected," *American Journal of Sociology* 79 (July 1974): 110–31.

2. One of the first organizational studies of the news was Warren Breed's now classic "Social Control in the Newsroom," *Social Forces* 33 (May 1955): 326–35. The best recent empirical studies of the news organization are Leon V. Sigal's book on the *Washington Post* and *The New York Times* entitled *Reporters and Officials: The Organization and Politics of Newsmaking* (Lexington, Mass.: D. C. Heath, 1973); and Edward J. Epstein's study of *NBC News* entitled *News from Nowhere*. See also Bernard Roshcoe, *Newsmaking* (Chicago: University of Chicago Press, 1975); and Robert Darnton, "Writing News and Telling Stories," *Daedalus*, Spring 1975, pp. 175–94.

Some studies of local and foreign news organizations are cited in the bibliography. I have also benefitted from Paul Hirsch's sociological analysis of the economics of mass media as oligopolies. See, e.g., Hirsch, "Occupational, Organizational, and Institutional Models in Mass Media Research: Toward an Integrated Framework," in P. Hirsch, P. Miller, and F. Kline, eds., *Strategies for Communication Research*, Sage Annual Reviews of Communication Research 6 (Beverly Hills, Calif.: Sage Publications, 1977), pp. 13–42.

3. An organizational theory that leaves more leeway for individual journalists is David Manning White's gatekeeper theory, which visualizes the editor as opening and closing the newspaper's "gate" to stories he selects. Gatekeeper theory is more easily applied to media which depend largely on wire-service news than to those which also search out their own news. David M. White, "The 'Gatekeeper': A Case Study in the Selection of News," *Journalism Quarterly* 27 (Fall 1950): 383–90.

4. Molotch and Lester, "News as Purposive Behavior."

5. Peter Berger and Thomas Luckmann, *The Social Construction of Reality* (New York: Doubleday & Co., Inc., Anchor Books, 1967). For some applications to the study of news, see Molotch and Lester, "News as Purposive Behavior"; Gaye Tuchman, "Objectivity as Strategic Ritual: An Examination of Newsmen's Notions of Objectivity," *American Journal of Sociology* 77 (January 1972): 660–70; as well as Tuchman, *Making News* (New York: Free Press, 1978).

6. The pioneering work by sociologists is Kurt and Gladys Lang's 1952 study of the reporting of the MacArthur Day parade in Chicago, in their "The Unique Perspective of Television and Its Effect: A Pilot Study," *American Sociological Review* 18 (February 1953): 3–12.

7. The Langs point out, rightly, that "[C]ontrary to the McLuhanites, . . . the way [television] appears depends on the way the men who employ the technology make use of it." *Politics and Television*, pp. 5–6.

8. Philip Schlesinger, "The Sociology of Knowledge" (Paper presented at the 1972 meeting of the British Sociological Association, March 24, 1972), p. 4.

9. The role of power in story selection was already emphasized by Breed, "Social Control in the Newsroom."

10. Personal communication.

11. The journalists' need for certainty has been emphasized by Sigal, *Reporters and Officials*, p. 181.

12 To be correct, the *Nightly News* group is part of a larger news organization, NBC News, which is a division of NBC-TV, which is itself a part of NBC. The last two are news firms, having business departments and aiming to be profitable, even though their major product is entertainment. NBC is, of course, part of RCA, which is now

a corporate conglomerate. The *CBS Evening News* organization is embedded in roughly the same structure. *Time* is one of several news organizations within Time, Inc., a corporation which has now diversified into nonjournalistic ventures; properly speaking, *Time* is itself also a news firm because it has its own business departments. *Newsweek* has the same dual structure and is part of the Washington Post Company, which has diversified itself somewhat less and is considerably smaller than Time, Inc.

13. *Newsweek*'s masthead lists many more senior editors than *Time*'s because it awards senior-editor rank to a number of people, including one writer, who perform other tasks.

14. Most tell stories are translated from wire-story copy into the anchorperson's style and rhythm, a minor art form of its own, which journalists from the print media uncharitably call ripping the wires.

15. The classic critique of newsmagazine checking is Otto Friedrich's "There Are OO Trees in Russia: The Function of Facts in Newsmagazines," *Harper's*, October 1964, pp. 59–65.

16. Computed from Sigal, *Reporters and Officials,* Table 6–1.

17. In Chapter 5, I shall suggest that story selectors work with considerations distinctive to print and electronic media, and others reflecting the formats of their magazines and programs. Scholarly books, like this one, are also governed by medium and format considerations which, among other things, require a linear argument, even though my analysis would sometimes be better served by the intercutting that is possible in films and novels.

18. Daniel Schorr's account of his departure from CBS suggests that although William Paley, the head of the network, wanted him to leave, he may not have requested Schorr's resignation; rather, underlings were projecting their own desires on "the boss." Daniel Schorr, *Clearing the Air* (Boston: Houghton Mifflin Co., 1977), p. 260 and chapter 12 *passim.*

19. Older journalists at *Time* told me that Henry Luce used to flood them with story suggestions, many of which were ignored; but those he deemed most important and urgent were not.

20. David Halberstam, "CBS: The Power and the Profits: Part I, " *Atlantic Monthly,* January 1976, pp. 33–71, quote at p. 34.

21. Anchorpersons can also participate in the selection of news executives. Gates reports that when Fred Friendly resigned the presidency of CBS News, Walter Cronkite and others helped to persuade corporate executives to offer the position to Richard Salant. Gary Paul Gates, *Air Time: The Inside Story of CBS News* (New York: Harper & Row, 1978), p. 128.

In 1978, *Variety* reported that "any succession [to Salant] will have to be approved by Walter Cronkite, second only to Paley in power [at CBS] these days." Larry Michie, "And That's the Way It Is at CBS News," *Variety,* 10 May 1978, pp. 178, 187, quote at p. 187.

22. For some comments by an anchorman who has participated actively in the top producer role, see Philip Nobile, "John Chancellor on the Record," *More,* May 1976, pp. 7–11.

23. *Time*'s managing editor was reluctant to end this practice because he felt that he could select the best sections and stories of the week only by seeing them in finished form. *Newsweek* had instituted prekilling in the 1960s.

24. The protest was also sparked by a Time, Inc. plan to give personality tests to the entire staff, which the journalists viewed as an unconscionable invasion of their privacy and an insult to their professional status.

25. In April 1978, 10 percent of *Time* writers and 37 percent of *Newsweek* writers

were women, as were 21 percent of *Time* reporters and 33 percent of *Newsweek* reporters, in both cases counting only domestic bureaus. At both magazines, the women were mainly in junior ranks. All of the senior writers were men, as were all bureau chiefs, except in *Newsweek*'s one-person Boston bureau.

26. Geoffrey Stokes, "The Time, Inc. Strike: Which Side Are You On?" *Village Voice,* 21 June 1976, pp. 34–39; and Donald M. Morrison, "Bring Back Henry Luce," *Pennsylvania Gazette,* October 1976, pp. 24–28.

27. Morrison's personal account of the strike describes his initial quasi-radicalization and his post-strike feeling that "the company is making an admirable effort . . . to make us feel less like factory hands, more like family members again." Morrison, "Bring Back Henry Luce," p. 28.

28. The problems of women journalists in television are described in Judith S. Gelfman, *Women in Television News* (New York: Columbia University Press, 1976).

29. Gates, *Air Time,* p. 78.

30. Ibid., pp. 219–49.

31. The descriptions to follow are brief summaries of complex processes. They are also generalized summaries, for every news organization handles the process in a slightly different manner. Furthermore, they may be outdated by the time this book is published, as small changes are made all the time. For a more detailed account of the process at the *NBC Nightly News,* see Epstein, *News from Nowhere;* for the process at *CBS Evening News,* with a good account of its origins and changes over the last two decades, see Gates, *Air Time.* The magazine-process description applies mainly to the domestic section; the foreign section operates somewhat differently because its reporters are overseas; and the back-of-the-book sections run on a different schedule and with an earlier deadline.

32. All network news programs are "fed" three times: at 6:30, 7, and 8 P.M. Eastern time. The last two are usually videotapes; but if a late story arrives, part of the second "feed" may be done live. The third feed is intended solely for the West Coast and may be updated by a West Coast correspondent.

Chapter 4—Sources and Journalists

1. Molotch and Lester, "News as Purposive Behavior."

2. The access problems of the powerless are described in detail in Edie N. Goldenberg's study of the Boston newspapers, *Making the Papers* (Lexington, Mass: D. C. Heath, 1975).

3. The Pentagon also discouraged television reporters from showing closeups of wounded or dead American soldiers because it wanted to inform the next-of-kin first; reporters complied willingly because they, too, wanted to spare relatives from the shock of unexpectedly seeing tragic news on television.

4. The same pattern was found in a study of the 155 stories written by the Pentagon press corps between February 15 and March 15, 1973; more than three fourths came from "senior military officials or their spokesmen." Britt Hume and Mark McIntyre, "Polishing Up the Brass," *More,* May 1972, pp. 6–8.

5. Thomas Plate, "The Making of a Godfather," *More,* June 1977, pp. 22–23, quote at p. 22.

6. Daniel J. Boorstin, *The Image: A Guide to Pseudo-Events in America* (New York: Harper & Row, 1964).

7. Sociologists may or may not influence the behavior of the people they study, but since they report to a small audience, their research does not have the same influence as national news.

8. "D. C. Quiz on Staged News Events," *Variety*, 24 May 1972, pp. 31, 42. Conversely, television suffers from chronic staging by sources, for actors behave more dramatically when the camera appears, and film editors must routinely cut from the raw film footage people who wave or make faces at the camera.

9. Epstein, *News from Nowhere*, p. 261.

10. An editor advocating a cover story on E. R. Doctorow when his *Ragtime* was expected to become a bestseller argued that his colleagues had once turned down a cover story on Philip Roth and *Portnoy's Complaint*, only to be sorry later because "everyone" was talking about the novel at dinner parties soon afterwards.

11. Sigal, *Reporters and Officials*, pp. 69–70.

12. A few politicians, such as President Dwight D. Eisenhower and Mayor Richard Daley, whose idiosyncratic use of language has developed into trademarks, are not edited in this fashion. Conversely, an editor going over an interview with Golda Meir explained that he "had to correct her bad syntax and take out her Yiddishisms; otherwise, people will think we are trying to make her look bad." For much the same reason, public officials who use profanity or racial and ethnic slurs are automatically "corrected," except when their resort to such language itself becomes newsworthy. Former Agriculture Secretary Earl Butz's racist remark and Richard Nixon's ethnic slurs that came to light with the publication of the White House tapes became moral disorder stories.

13. During the late 1960s, both *Time* and *Newsweek* hired a handful of young substantive beat reporters for the back of the book; but during the cost cutting that took place in the early 1970s (see Chapter 7), they were either let go or put back on general assignments.

14. Agency beat reporters in Washington have been studied repeatedly; although much of the existing research is about newspaper reporters, the findings are equally relevant for television and the newsmagazines. See, e.g., Leo Rosten, *The Washington Correspondents* (New York: Harcourt, Brace and Co., 1937); Bernard C. Cohen, *The Press and Foreign Policy* (Princeton, N. J.: Princeton University Press, 1953); Dan D. Nimmo, *Newsgathering in Washington* (New York: Atherton, 1962); William O. Chittick, *State Department, Press, and Pressure Groups* (New York: John Wiley & Sons, 1970); and Sigal, *Reporters and Officials*. Two Washington television reporters, Dan Rather and Daniel Schorr, and a Washington bureau chief, William Small, have also written about their work and its problems; their books are cited elsewhere and in the bibliography.

For a study of England's equivalents, see Jeremy Tunstall, *The Westminster Lobby Correspondents* (London: Routledge & Kegan Paul, 1970).

15. Tom Wicker, "The Greening of the Press," *Columbia Journalism Review* 10 (May 1971): 7–14, quote at p. 10.

16. Both newsmagazines issue internal "memos" which are filled with sensational stories that cannot be published because supporting evidence is unavailable. Some reporters suggest that the memos are written to entertain top editors and executives with information that will make them feel like "inside dopesters" (to borrow David Riesman's incisive term), and they disparage the memos, as well as items from them that occasionally appear in *Newsweek*'s Periscope.

17. For an autobiographical account, see Benjamin C. Bradlee, *Conversations with Kennedy* (New York: W. W. Norton, 1975).

18. For similar but more detailed analyses, see Halberstam, "CBS: The Power and the Profits," pp. 52–91; and his "Time, Inc.'s Internal War Over Vietnam," *Esquire*, January 1978, pp. 94–131.

19. On the PBS television program "Behind the Lines," September 15, 1974.

20. Douglass Cater, *The Fourth Branch of Government* (Boston: Houghton Mifflin Co., 1959).

21. For a good analysis of the work of general reporters at *The New York Times,* see Darnton, "Writing News and Telling Stories."

22. Timothy Crouse, *The Boys on the Bus* (New York: Random House, 1973).

23. Dan Rather begins his memoirs as a Washington correspondent with a description of "the time Dan Rather asked the President if he was running for something," and the criticism which followed. Daniel Rather, with Mickey Herskowitz, *The Camera Never Blinks* (New York: William Morrow, 1977), chapter 1, quote at p. 18. White House reporters do not, however, have to maintain decorum or limit themselves to polite questions when they are briefed by the president's press secretaries.

24. Edwin Diamond, "Boston: The Agony of Responsibility," *Columbia Journalism Review* 13 (January/February 1975): 9–15. Diamond is a former *Newsweek* senior editor, but here he writes as a Boston resident and local reporter.

25. John Bird, "The Unyielding Amish: 'We Want to Be Left Alone,' " *Saturday Evening Post,* 17 June 1967, pp. 28–38, quote at p. 38.

26. Harvey Molotch and Marilyn J. Lester, "Accidental News: The Great Oil Spill as Local Occurrence and National Event," *American Journal of Sociology* 81 (September 1975): 235–60.

27. From an unpublished paper by Susan Peterson, written in 1966. Although I have provided quotation marks, the comment is actually Ms. Peterson's paraphrase of the producer's remarks.

28. Sigal, *Reporters and Officials,* Table 6–5. About 17 percent of the stories originated with "nongovernmental foreigners and Americans" and 3 percent with other news organizations.

Chapter 5—Story Suitability

1. The expectations sometimes include a historical component when journalists assume that the present abnormality was preceded by a past normality. In this process, they stipulate an ideal past, if only to make today's abnormality new and thus news.

2. Because television has little room for foreign news, and the magazines must cover the entire globe, both news media use an even more limited exclusionary consideration: in all but the most important allied or Communist countries, governmental change is newsworthy only when it involves violent protest.

3. Eric Levin, "How the Networks Decide What Is News," *TV Guide,* 2 July 1977, pp. 4–10, quote at p. 6.

4. Michael J. Robinson, "The TV Primaries," *Wilson Quarterly* 1 (Spring 1977): 80–83.

5. Writers in these sections have more autonomy than those in other sections. They were the first to receive bylines at *Newsweek* and are still the only ones to be bylined at *Time.*

6. In 1975, the same journalists who were uneasy about President Ford's performance in the White House and embarrassed about his physical clumsiness were also enthusiastic about Susan Ford's work as a photographer.

7. Helen M. Hughes, *News and the Human Interest Story* (Chicago: University of Chicago Press, 1940).

8. Like local journalists, national story selectors choose human-interest stories from time to time in order to invite financial help to the victim from the audience. Although

objectivity and detachment are violated in the process, journalists are always pleased when audience contributions roll in, because they feel they are helping and because the response indicates that the audience is paying attention to the news.

9. At NBC, the balance between film and tell stories is maintained informally, but it is maintained nevertheless; otherwise, as an executive producer pointed out, the anchorperson "would be reduced to the mere role of a master of ceremonies."

10. The letters and gossip sections usually run closer to the maximum because they are popular; the book reviews, because they "close" a week earlier than the rest of the magazine.

11. Richard Pollak, *"Time:* After Luce," *Harper's,* July 1969, pp. 42–52.

12. J. Anthony Lukas, "What Does Tomorrow Hold for 'Today'?" *The New York Times,* 22 August 1976, sec. 2, pp. 1, 20, quote at p. 20.
When Henry Grunwald became managing editor of *Time,* he responded to a writer's request for format change by saying that " . . . the formula must be bent, not broken. . . . *Time* is really part of the American scene, a part of American life, and what you do to it has to be done fairly carefully." Pollak, *"Time:* After Luce," p. 46.

13. In 1977, *Time* received more letters from readers, most of them negative, about its new graphics than about any one of its stories.

14. Film which the network program is unable or unwilling to use is released for syndication and may then be shown by local stations.

15. Because news judgment is partly a matter of "feel," and evaluation of boredom is significant in story selection, journalism may recruit people with short attention spans. Conversely, academia may select researchers who can spend many years on the same study, and teachers who can repeat the same lectures annually. A couple of magazine writers who had previously held university teaching positions indicated that their ennui, the result of having to repeat their lectures every year, was responsible for their switch to journalism.

16. On the dynamic of journalistic crime waves, see, e.g., Daniel Bell, *The End of Ideology* (New York: Free Press, 1960), chapter 8.

17. In commenting on *Newsweek*'s refusal to do the first national story on Tiny Tim, a young ex-researcher wrote that the magazine "was always afraid of venturing into the unknown. They always wanted to catch a story as it crested, but more often they ended up writing about the dwindling foam after the wave went home." Kate Coleman, "Turning on *Newsweek,*" *Scanlan's Monthly,* June 1970, pp. 44–53, quote at p. 51.

18. A *Newsweek* story some years ago about the new bisexuality established the trend on the basis of nine sources. Most were from the East or West Coast, and the majority were professionals. Judging by their quoted statements, all but one appeared to have been bisexual for years, suggesting that bisexuality was an old practice which had become newly visible to the journalists.

19. At the newsmagazines, pace is sometimes described in musical terms. Writers speak of "singing the story," "putting the big gongs [points] at the top," or "starting out with high tones" [a sentimental lead]. *Newsweek* calls its lead article "the violin," in part because it usually has a sentimental tone.

20. For a thoughtful discussion of the esthetics of news film, see Tuchman, *Making News,* chapter 4.

21. The newsroom monitors on which producers review film are of higher quality and larger size than sets at home; but even after several weeks of fieldwork, I could rarely spot the faults which upset the journalists.

22. For the report of one 1957 incident, see Sig Mickelson, *The Electric Mirror* (New York: Dodd, Mead, 1972), p. 41.

23. At the beginning of the 1975 Cyprus crisis, four Greek-Americans called NBC one evening to protest what they perceived as a pro-Turkish slant in a Cyprus story, but the writers who took the calls dismissed the objections as unjustified. As the war progressed, however, and the Greek-American community organized to make its views known, journalists paid closer attention to both sides, particularly the Greek side because it was more vocal.

24. Top producers try to scoop each other by being the first either to film a distant breaking story or, occasionally, to send an anchorperson out to personally report on one. When President Anwar el-Sadat visited Israel in 1977, all three networks competed with each other to be the first to put their anchorperson's interview with Sadat on the air.

25. For a report of one race that resulted in a simultaneous cover about pop singer Bruce Springsteen, see Chris Welles, "Born to Get 'Itchy Excited,' " *More,* January 1976, pp. 10–14.

26. I was told, with some pride, of the only two instances of "collusion" between *Time* and *Newsweek* top editors: one took place when *Newsweek*'s editor called *Time*'s editor to obtain a picture of Henry Luce for a *Newsweek* cover at the time of his death; the other occurred in the spring of 1975, at the end of the Vietnam War, when the two magazines learned that they were planning to feature the same wire-service photo on their covers, and *Time* altered its cover to include two other pictures.

27. One Friday night in 1964, *Newsweek*'s national-affairs writers, having decided to break the taboo against collusion, set off to pay a visit to their equals at *Time,* but at the last minute they turned back. The event was clearly of some moment, for the writer who told me about it in 1968 recounted the story once more in 1975.

28. Bradlee, *Conversations with Kennedy,* p. 50.

29. The magazines and networks also compete with each other in covering party conventions, election campaigns, and breaking events, spending large sums in the hope that the winner will harvest new readers or viewers who will remain loyal afterwards. Journalists participate in the competition and accept the assumptions under which it proceeds, for if nothing else, a victory will add to the budgets and prestige of the winning news organizations.

30. The data is fragmentary because it is based on reader reports for only one week per year.

31. Top editors, however, carefully watch newsstand sale-figures of their own and the rival magazine as a way of monitoring audience reaction to their cover choices (see Chapter 7).

32. In the end, producers and editors go along with their own reporters; but a notable exception took place in 1968 when *Newsweek* editors accepted the *Times*' version of the Columbia University student bust and police action over that of its own writer, even though he had gone to the campus to report it himself. Columbia University is in a unique position, however, several top journalists being alumni; and the editors may have accepted the *Times* story because it sided with the university administration, whereas the writer's report supported the protesting students.

Chapter 6—Objectivity, Values, and Ideology

1. Peter Schrag, "An Earlier Point in Time," *Saturday Review/World,* 23 March 1974, pp. 40–41, quote at p. 41.

2. Here I draw, of course, on Robert K. Merton's distinction between purpose and function. See his *Social Theory and Social Structure* (New York: Free Press of Glencoe, 1949), pp. 25–26.

3. I borrow the phrase, but not his definition, from Peter Braestrup, *Big Story*, 2 vols. (Boulder, Colo.: Westview Press, 1977), 1:708.

4. Michael Schudson, "A Matter of Style," *Working Papers* (Summer 1976): 90–93.

5. Johnstone and his associates found that of a national sample of journalists, over 60 percent had decided to enter their field before the age of 20, the median age being 19. John W. Johnstone, Edward J. Slawski, and William W. Bowman, *The News People* (Urbana: University of Illinois Press, 1976), Table 4–1.

6. Schorr, *Clearing the Air*, p. viii.

7. Morrison, "Bring Back Henry Luce," p. 24.

8. Tuchman, "Objectivity as Strategic Ritual."

9. James Reston, *The Artillery of the Press* (New York: Harper & Row, 1966), pp. 14–15. For a contrary view, see Michael Schudson, *Discovering the News: A Social History of American Newspapers* (New York: Basic Books, 1978), Introduction.

10. Accordingly, Sigelman calls objectivity an "institutional myth," which states and justifies the journalists' "mission in society." Lee Sigelman, "Reporting the News: An Organizational Analysis," *American Journal of Sociology* 79 (July 1973): 132–51, quotes at p. 133.

11. For data on the attitudes of a national sample of journalists about alternative forms of journalism, see Johnstone et al., *The News People*, chapter 7.

12. Edward R. Murrow has become a journalistic hero in part because he was one of the first to call a politician (Senator Joseph McCarthy) a liar. News from Communist sources has, however, always been attributed with the qualification that it could be a lie, or at least "propaganda."

13. Anchorpersons can express opinions on radio that they cannot express on television because radio reaches a smaller audience, is less monitored by other news media, and is therefore even more ephemeral than television.

14. What Louis Wirth once wrote about logical positivism in the social sciences applies equally to journalism: " . . . every assertion, no matter how objective it may be, has ramifications extending beyond the limits of science itself. Since every assertion of a 'fact' about the social world touches the interest of some individual or group, one cannot even call attention to the existence of certain 'facts' without courting the objections of those whose very *raison d'être* in society rests upon a divergent interpretation of the 'factual' situation." Louis Wirth, Preface to *Ideology and Utopia*, by Karl Mannheim, (New York: Harcourt, Brace and Co., 1936), p. xvii.

15. Reuven Frank, "Address Before the 12th Annual Television Award Dinner," NBC xeroxed typescript (January 12, 1970), pp. 16, 20, 33.

16. A similar process is described in studies of local news media: for example, by Breed, "Social Control in the Newsroom"; and Sigelman, "Reporting the News."

17. For a bitter description of the lifestyle differences, see Coleman, "Turning on *Newsweek*"; on ideological differences, see Andrew Kopkind, "Serving Time," *The New York Review of Books*, 12 September 1968, pp. 23–28.

18. Some reporters also worried that their files might be forwarded to the government, making them inadvertent spies on their activist friends; but these worries turned out to be groundless. In fact, just the reverse was true, for the reporters were able to spot CIA and FBI agents masquerading as reporters and to warn activists about them.

19. Blacks from low-income backgrounds left even more quickly because they could not conform to the upper-middle-class ambience at the magazines, and some could not get used to writing in the required ironic style. At the networks, many of the initially hired blacks left when the ghetto was no longer newsworthy, and went to work at local stations in cities with large black populations.

20. Gates reports that CBS News also employed two journalists who may have

fallen into the "house radical" role. One left the network temporarily because he was traumatized by the Vietnam War; the other, who was also the "house hippie" and an investigative reporter, was forced out over a disagreement with a news executive. Gates, *Air Time,* pp. 164, 365–67.

21. These arguments took place before I began my fieldwork at *Time.* Many of the struggles over how to report the Vietnam War are discussed in Halberstam, "Time, Inc.'s Internal War Over Vietnam."

22. George A. Bailey, "The War According to Walter: Network Anchormen and Vietnam" (Milwaukee: University of Wisconsin, 1975), p. 37–70. This is the only study I know of that pays attention to the ideas of individual television journalists. The individuals who write regularly for television and the magazines are thoughtful people; and were they not working for large audiences, their work might by now have been studied as exhaustively as that of essayists working for smaller but more prestigious audiences.

23. Although Braestrup was aware of this process in his detailed study of the opinion change following the Tet offensive, he nevertheless concluded—and I believe wrongly—that it stemmed from "the more volatile journalistic style . . . that has become so popular since the late 1960s. With this style came an often mindless readiness to seek out conflict, to believe the worst of the government or of authority in general, and on that basis to divide up the actors on any issue into the 'good' or the 'bad.' " Braestrup, *Big Story,* 1:726. I am not even sure that journalists had become more volatile; they have always sought out conflict and been skeptical about government. The late 1960s only produced many highly visible events to make this "style" more apparent.

24. Many of the stories are, of course, written or filmed by their own colleagues. Also, opinion change reflects the perception of an event. Thus, journalists perceived the Tet offensive differently from many military experts, who saw it as a North Vietnamese military defeat. They looked only at the military activities, however, and failed to grasp their political implications.

25. Although opinion polls taken before, during, and after the Tet offensive suggest that poll respondents lagged a few weeks behind the journalists in changing their opinion about the war, Roper's analysis of these polls also shows that like journalists, the general public had undergone a slow but evolving disenchantment with the war. The journalists only reacted more dramatically and quickly to Tet than did the public. Burns W. Roper, "What Public Opinion Polls Said," in Braestrup, *Big Story,* chapter 14.

26. Interestingly enough, although journalists develop equivalent terms for many of those used by other empirical disciplines, there is no word for "concepts" in the journalistic lexicon. One writer once described them as "conceits" but only to indicate their lack of relevance.

27. See, e.g., Peter Lyon, *Success Story: The Life and Times of S. S. McClure* (New York: Charles Scribner's Sons, 1963); Harold S. Wilson, *McClure's Magazine and the Muckrakers* (Princeton, N.J.: Princeton University Press, 1970); Justin Kaplan, *Lincoln Steffens: A Biography* (New York: Simon and Schuster, 1974); and the books of the journalists themselves.

28. Reported in Richard Hofstadter, *Age of Reform* (New York: Alfred A. Knopf, 1973), p. 145. Mowry found that of forty-eight leaders of the California Progressive movement on which data were available, fourteen were newspaper owners or journalists. George Mowry, *The California Progressives* (Berkeley: University of California Press, 1951).

29. Among the voluminous literature on state and local Progressives, see, e.g., Fremont Older, *My Story* (San Francisco: Call Publishing, 1919); David D. Ander-

son, *Brand Whitlock* (Boston: Twayne Publishers, 1968); Spencer Olin, Jr., *California's Prodigal Sons* (Berkeley: University of California Press, 1968); Robert M. Crunden, *A Hero in Spite of Himself* (New York: Alfred A. Knopf, 1969); and Charles Larsen, *The Good Fight: The Life and Times of Ben B. Lindsay* (New York: Quadrangle/The New York Times Book Co., 1972).

30. Hofstadter, *Age of Reform,* p. 185. The historical data on the relationship between journalists and Progressives were gathered by James Crispino.

31. Johnstone et al., *The News People,* Tables 2–9, 2–10.

32. In 1975, for example, the executive producers of the three network news programs and the top editors of the two magazines were Jewish. The large number of Jews can be explained in part by the New York location of the news media, and in the case of television, by the traditional Jewish participation in firms providing mass entertainment. For a more general discussion, see Stephen Birmingham, "Do Zionists Control the Media?" *More,* July/August 1976, pp. 12–17.

33. "Chancellor on Reporters," *Variety,* 3 June 1970. I should add that Chancellor, like other anchorpersons, describes himself as a reporter. His statement, which was made at a testimonial dinner honoring Walter Cronkite, not only reflects the professional pride that goes with testimonials but also resonates to the criticism to which journalists were then exposed from both the Left and Right.

34. The "Eastern competition" and "the energy of the East," which *Newsweek* reporter Mary Kellogg ascribes to New York in a previously quoted article, is, in fact, an apt description of the work pace and working conditions inside a news organization. Kellogg, "A Farewell to Nirvana," p. 15.

35. I did not ask the journalists how they personally felt about the enduring values because these emerged from my analysis only after the fieldwork was completed.

36. Of forty-two NBC reporters and correspondents in 1975 for whom I could obtain biographies, 26 percent had taken all or part of their schooling at Ivy League schools; 33 percent at other "quality" private universities; 22 percent at prestigious state universities; and 19 percent at private and public colleges of reputedly lesser quality.

37. National journalists are better paid than most of their local peers; Johnstone and his associates found that the 1970 median income of journalists they studied who worked mostly for local news media was only $11,133. Johnstone et al., *The News People,* Table 8–1. The median salary for male journalists in *The New York Times* Washington bureau, however, was $34,415 in 1977. Philip Nobile, "Mr. Smith Goes to Washington," *More,* June 1977, p. 36.

38. Johnstone et al., *The News People,* Table 5–9. Asked about their party preference, 43 percent of the sample said they were Democrats; 34 percent, Independents; 16 percent, Republicans; 7 percent cited other affiliations. Another subsample included news executives at prominent publications, and curiously enough, 56 percent described themselves as "a little to the left." My own impression was that at least on the job, they were more conservative than the journalists. Barton and his associates, who studied elite opinions on a variety of issues, found that media executives were more liberal than other national leaders, but not so liberal as to support the findings of Johnstone et al. Allen H. Barton, "Consensus and Conflict Among American Leaders," *Public Opinion Quarterly* 38 (Winter 1974–1975): 507–30.

39. Dale Vree, "A Case Study of Distortion," *The New Leader,* 21 November 1977, pp. 18–19.

40. A 1978 *New York Times*-CBS News poll reports, for example, that 42 percent of the national sample classified themselves as conservatives, and 23 percent as liberals; but 80 percent of the conservatives believed that government should help people get low-cost medical care, and 75 percent, that it should guarantee jobs to all

who want them. At the same time, however, only about 20 percent of the conservatives (and 40 percent of the liberals) favored increased government spending on domestic programs. Adam Clymer, "More Conservatives Share 'Liberal' View," *The New York Times,* 12 January 1978, section 1, pp. 1, 30.

Chapter 7—Profits and Audiences

1. Otto Friedrich, *Decline and Fall* (New York: Harper & Row, 1970).

2. Larry Michie, "News Turns Into a Network Money-Maker," *Variety,* 27 April 1977, p. 39.

3. For a more extensive discussion of network profits and cutbacks in the news, see Marvin Barrett, *Rich News, Poor News* (New York: Thomas Y. Crowell, 1978), chapter 1.

4. Edwin Diamond, "The Mid-Life Crisis of the Newsweeklies," *New York,* 7 June 1976, pp. 51–61, quote at p. 56.

5. This was especially true at *Time,* perhaps because *Newsweek* was reducing the gap in advertising income and pages over the last decade. Between 1965 and 1975, *Newsweek*'s advertising revenue grew from 45 to 75 percent of *Time*'s; and its number of advertising pages, from 82 to 118 percent. *Newsweek*'s domestic circulation increased less, from 58 to 66 percent of *Time*'s.

6. The largest reduction was made among researchers, from seventy-four down to forty-six, and the smallest among top editors, from fifteen down to thirteen. Writers and reporters were cut back by 15 to 20 percent. Even so, *Time* still has more domestic and foreign reporters than its rival (fifty-six and thirty-three, as compared to fifty-one and twenty-two at *Newsweek*), but some of *Newsweek*'s eighty-six researchers also report.

7. Computed from W. R. Simmons & Associates Research, *Selective Markets and the Media Reaching Them* (New York: W. R. Simmons & Associates Research, 1965 and 1975). I am indebted to Edward Barz of the Simmons organization for making these and other Simmons data available to me.

8. In a 1967 study of a New York City sample of viewers, I found that about 40 percent chose the network news program on the basis of the anchorperson, and about 20 percent each on the basis of channel preference and broadcast time. (That year, *ABC News* was shown an hour earlier than the others.) About 10 percent cited the quality of the news; the rest gave other reasons. Herbert J. Gans, "The Uses of Television and Their Educational Implications," mimeographed (New York: Center for Urban Education, 1968), p. 90.

In a more recent study of viewers in Albany, New York, Levy found that 41 percent chose the network news program on the basis of anchorperson, 28 percent on the basis of channel, 9 percent on the basis of news quality or program format, and 22 percent gave other or no reasons. Mark R. Levy, "The Audience Experience with Television News," *Journalism Monographs,* no. 55 (April 1978): 7.

9. ABC is an exception, having frequently changed its anchorpersons over the last ten years in the hope of catching up with its two competitors.

10. For a detailed discussion of audience flow, see Epstein, *News from Nowhere,* pp. 91–97.

11. Andrew Walfish, "Sex Is In, Politics Is Out," *More,* September 1977, pp. 25–31.

12. One top editor went commercial insofar as he accepted business-department research and recommendations for redesigning the cover; but this was a packaging change, and the editor continued to decide what stories would appear on the cover.

13. The A. C. Nielsen Company, which supplies the most frequently used television

ratings, also collects data on viewer characteristics but not on magazine readers. Also, Simmons interviews a larger sample of viewers and can therefore supply greater detail about viewer differences. The total audience-size figures reported by Simmons are lower than Nielsen's, but there is little variation in the data on viewer characteristics between the two research organizations.

14. Simmons, *Selective Markets* (1975). The small changes mean a great deal to the news firms because they compete with their rivals by emphasizing differences in the number and "quality" of the audience, but they are not significant for my purposes.

15. In 1974, Simmons found that *Newsweek* had just about as many readers as *Time,* despite the fact that its circulation was about two thirds of *Time*'s. As a result, *Newsweek* began to call attention to the large number of pass-alongs, while *Time* sued Simmons for supplying inaccurate data, although it later withdrew its suit. Chris Welles, "The Numbers Magazines Live By," *Columbia Journalism Review* 4 (September/October 1975): 22–27.

16. Most of the data in this section, and in Table 6, are taken or computed from Simmons, *Selective Markets* (1975), vol. 1, Tables A01 to A10; and vol. 5, Tables C1 to C6.

17. *Time* has a slightly larger, older, and somewhat more upscale readership than *Newsweek.* CBS has a considerably larger number of viewers (who are also somewhat older) than NBC, but they are also slightly more downscale. The demographic differences are not distinctive to the news programs, however, for other NBC audiences have long been somewhat more upscale than those of CBS.

18. Gans, "The Uses of Television," p. 81.

Additional evidence can be gathered from the fact that about 20 percent of the viewers (and 31 percent of the women viewers of *CBS News*) are divorced, separated, or widowed. Data for widows and widowers are available only for the magazines; they made up 3.6 of *Newsweek*'s and 3.8 percent of *Time*'s readership. Simmons, *Selective Markets* (1975), vol. 5, Table C2; and vol. 1, Table A05.

19. The magazine studies supply employment data for both men and women. About a fifth of the women readers hold professional or managerial jobs, about a quarter are in clerical and sales positions, and only 10 percent are blue-collar workers. The remainder are not employed. Simmons, *Selective Markets* (1975), vol. 1, Table E03. Among women readers over 55, more than two thirds are not employed. Ibid., vol. 2, Table I09.

20. Simmons, *Selective Markets* (1975), vol. 2, Table G03.

21. Ibid., vol. 1, Tables A04, C04.

22. Ibid., Table A10.

23. *Time* is read by 70 percent of all industrial executives; 57 percent of "owners of great wealth"; 66 percent of congressmen and women, and senators; 76 percent of mass-media executives; 31 percent of labor-union presidents; and 48 percent of voluntary association heads. (For *Newsweek,* the equivalent percentages are 59, 42, 68, 81, 40, and 48, respectively.) Carol H. Weiss, "What American Leaders Read," *Public Opinion Quarterly* 38 (Spring 1974): 1–22, Table 3.

24. A study showing that college-educated men and women of all educational levels use both electronic and print media is reported by Harold Israel and John P. Robinson, "Demographic Characteristics of Viewers of Television Violence and News Programs," in Eli A. Rubinstein, George A. Comstock, and John P. Murray, eds., *Television and Social Behavior* (Washington, D.C.: U. S. Government Printing Office, n. d.), vol. 4, pp. 87–128.

25. The frequency data reported here and in Table 7 are taken or computed from Simmons, *Selective Markets* (1975), vol. 3, Table A000, for the magazines; and vol. 6, Tables A49 and B49, for the networks. I should note that these figures are mathe-

matical projections from raw frequency data about two magazine issues and ten network programs. For methodological details, see appendices to volumes 3 and 6.

26. Simmons, *Selective Markets* (1975), vol. 3, Tables A001 to A012.

27. Ibid., vol. 6, Tables A50 to A62, B50 to B62.

28. Ibid., vol. 5, Tables G1 to G5. Seventy-eight percent of the men and 72 percent of the women report giving full attention to prime-time entertainment programs. Ibid., Tables B3, B8.

29. Levy reported that three fourths of his sample was involved in other activities while watching the news: 25 percent said that they were reading, 23 percent talking, and 41 percent eating dinner. Levy, "The Audience Experience with Television News," p. 11.

Stern, who studied a Bay Area sample, found that one third watched the whole program, another third did so but with distractions, and a third were distracted enough to have watched only part of the program. Andrew A. Stern, "Presentation to the Radio-Television News Directors' Association, Boston, Massachusetts, September 29, 1971," mimeographed (Berkeley: University of California, Graduate School of Journalism, 1971), p. 2.

A 1972 study of Swedish viewers found that half had watched the entire program, 15 percent complaining that distractions prevented them from paying closer attention. Sveriges Radio, "Audience and Programme Research," no. 3 (July 1973): 3.

30. Levy, "The Audience Experience with Television News," p. 10. My 1967 New York study found, however, that 19 percent of the viewers would be bothered a great deal, 25 percent somewhat, and 56 percent hardly at all. Even 40 percent of all regular viewers felt that they would not be bothered at all. Gans, "The Uses of Television," pp. 83–84.

Levy's data and my data both suggest that older viewers would be bothered to a greater extent. Levy also found that about 25 percent of those who missed their favorite anchorman when he was on vacation reported being "upset." Levy, "The Audience Experience with Television News," p. 19.

31. Louis Harris and Associates, *Time-Harris Poll on the Press,* mimeographed (New York: Louis Harris and Associates, 1969), Table 14. *Unavailability* was defined as "for the next month."

32. Ibid., Table 3c.

33. A recent major study by the Newspaper Advertising Bureau has found, however, that its respondents considered national news more important and interesting than local news. Newspaper Advertising Bureau, "How the Public Gets Its News: An Address by Leo Bogart Before the Associated Press Managing Editors, October 27, 1977" (New York: Newspaper Advertising Bureau, 1977), p. 14. Conversely, a 1977 Harris poll reported 60 percent of respondents expressing strong interest in national news, but 74 percent in local news. *The Harris Survey,* 9 January 1978, p. 2.

34. Levy, "The Audience Experience with Television News," p. 13.

35. Ibid.; and Newspaper Advertising Bureau, "How the Public Gets Its News," pp. 13–14. For a detailed analysis, see "Two Dimensions of News: Interest and Importance Ratings of the Editorial Content of the American Press," mimeographed (New York: Newspaper Advertising Bureau, January 1978).

36. Levy reported that 60 percent of his respondents agreed with a statement that news helped them forget their own problems. Levy, "The Audience Experience with Television News," p. 13. The nationwide study is reported in Robert T. Bower, *Television and the Public* (New York: Holt, Rinehart & Winston, 1973), p. 113.

37. Donald Horton and Richard Wohl, "Mass Communication and Parasocial Interaction," *Psychiatry* 19 (August 1956): 215–29. In a study of the mail received by *NBC News* in October 1975, almost all of which was addressed to John Chancellor,

who was sole anchorman at the time, I found that of the correspondents writing directly to him, 15 percent addressed him "Dear John." Herbert J. Gans, "Letters to an Anchorman," *Journal of Communication* 27 (Summer 1977): 86–91.

38. Ibid. In 1972, Leo Bogart reported that "only 27 people of every 10,000 in the audience of a popular television program write a letter after a typical broadcast." *Silent Politics: Polls and the Awareness of Public Opinion* (New York: Wiley-Interscience, 1972), p. 53.

39. Gans, "Letters to an Anchorman." I should note that my judgments about comprehensibility were based purely on content, and I did not include letters which were difficult to understand because of poor grammar.

40. Maria L. Cisneros, "*Time* Letters Report," mimeographed (New York: Time, Inc., February 7, 1974), p. 7.

41. Ibid.

42. In 1972, the domestic news section averaged 219 letters a week; in 1973, during Watergate, the number rose to 561. Between April 1973 and the end of June 1974, *Time* received altogether 34,832 letters about the subject, of which 15,723 attacked the magazine; and 7,974 letter writers canceled subscriptions or threatened not to renew them. *Time*'s November 1973 editorial calling for Richard Nixon's resignation attracted 17,800 letters: 9,400 supported the president; 8,400 supported *Time*'s stand.

43. Schorr, *Clearing the Air,* p. 40.

44. Gans, "Letters to an Anchorman."

45. Her conclusion was based on letters written to President Franklin Delano Roosevelt; she also found conservatives to dominate the mail. Leila Sussman, *Dear FDR: A Study of Political Letter-Writing* (Totowa, N.J.: Bedminster Press, 1963), p. 166.

46. For a review of the literature, see Lawrence W. Lichty and George A. Bailey, "Violence in Television News: A Case Study of Audience Response," *Central States Speech Journal* 23 (Winter 1972): 225–29.

47. For pioneering studies of journalists' conceptions of the audience, see Raymond A. Bauer, "The Communicator and the Audience," and Ithiel de Sola Pool and Irwin Shulman, "Newsmen's Fantasies, Audiences and Newswriting," in Lewis A. Dexter and David M. White, eds., *People, Society and Mass Communications* (New York: Free Press, 1964), pp. 125–40, 141–59. My own early study of audience conceptions dealt with Hollywood; see Herbert J. Gans, "The Creator-Audience Relationship in the Mass Media: An Analysis of Movie-Making," in Bernard Rosenberg and David M. White, eds., *Mass Culture* (New York: Free Press, 1957), pp. 315–24.

48. The magazine letter departments hire correspondents who answer the mail, although normally with various form letters. Copies of incoming letters also go to the editor of the letters section, who chooses the most interesting and articulate for publication. When a story attracts an unusually large number of letters, the editor leads off with one or two particularly emphatic or indignant ones as a way of reflecting both the tone and the amount of mail.

49. English television journalists also see their viewers as "usually cranky." Schlesinger, *Putting 'Reality' Together,* p. 115. A London producer claimed that "most viewers who write letters are psychopaths." Philip Elliott, *The Making of a Television Series* (London: Constable Press, 1972), p. 142n.

50. For an interesting attempt to persuade journalists of the relevance of statistics and sampling theory, see Philip Meyer, *Precision Journalism* (Bloomington: Indiana University Press, 1973).

51. Gates, *Air Time,* p. 237.

52. The most remarkable instance of audience hunger took place at NBC. During

every NASA space mission, an anonymous viewer, whom the journalists named the "mystery lady," sent an expensive bouquet of roses, and after the final story on the mission, she called to congratulate the journalists. Once, however, she called in the middle of a space mission and got into an argument with the producer who answered the phone. The next day, everyone was disappointed when she failed to make her regular congratulatory call. The mystery lady had indicated that she suffered from emotional problems, and was thus classified as a "crazy" viewer; but at times, journalists feel so isolated from the audience that they will welcome reactions even from a crazy viewer. Presumably their sense of isolation is increased by knowing that only a crazy viewer will pay them such regular attention.

53. A. M. Rosenthal, *Thirty-Eight Witnesses* (New York: McGraw-Hill, 1964), p. 24.

54. In entertainment television, where audiences must be won anew for every series, television producers do not see themselves as audience representatives but as having "higher" taste than the viewers. Muriel G. Cantor, *The Hollywood TV Producer* (New York: Basic Books, 1972), p. 183.

55. In the 1930s, Ed Murrow had proposed that CBS radio journalists "talk to be understood by the truck driver while not insulting the professor's intelligence." Alexander Kendrick, *Prime Time: The Life of Edward R. Murrow* (Boston: Little, Brown & Co., 1969), p. 278.

56. In the early 1960s, *Newsweek*'s prototype had been a "tool and die executive from Cincinnati."

Back-of-the-book writers and editors develop dichotomous images, composed of professional and lay readers; thus, a religion writer mentioned "the laity plus a Diocese chancellor," and a law writer cited "the general audience, but I also want to be respected by lawyers." Sigal found that *Washington Post* journalists, who pay more attention to public officials in the audience than the journalists I studied, distinguished between "policy players" and "policy makers." Sigal, *Reporters and Officials,* pp. 60–61.

57. Jerome Aumente, "City of Rumors: Detroit's Year Without News," *The Nation,* 14 October 1968, pp. 363–66. Crime rates themselves do not seem to rise during newspaper strikes, but no one has yet studied these rates during a total news blackout. David E. Payne, "Newspapers and Crime: What Happens During Strike Periods," *Journalism Quarterly* 51 (Winter 1974): 607–12.

58. "News 'Goddams' Ire Affils," *Variety,* 14 January 1970, pp. 47, 66. Seventy-nine percent of the sample of New York City viewers I studied in 1967 indicated that they thought it improper for someone being interviewed on television to use "goddamn." Gans, "The Uses of Television," p. 13.

59. Gates pointed out that when Morley Safer made the now classic film of Marines using Zippo lighters to burn down peasant huts during a search-and-destroy mission, he did not film the troops who were killing peasants with grenades and flame-throwers. Gates, *Air Time,* p. 160.

60. After American troops began to leave Vietnam, however, the taboo was relaxed —once more, for foreigners only—and some films of South or North Vietnamese soldiers committing atrocities were shown.

61. Mary L. Cisneros, "*Time* Letters Report," mimeographed (New York: Time, Inc., January 20, 1977), p. 9.

62. Executives must also respond to stockholders. Some years ago, a group of Texas investors bought a significant amount of stock in Time, Inc., which led to rumors that *Time* would be moved out of New York City, partly for ideological reasons, partly to reduce costs.

63. Herbert J. Gans, *Popular Culture and High Culture* (New York: Basic Books, 1974).

64. By the same token, the critical sections of the newsmagazines supply news about a high culture in which most readers do not participate, but no one knows whether they accept such news willingly, although *Time* advertisements periodically suggest that cultural news can be used to impress one's friends and neighbors.

Chapter 8—Pressures, Censorship, and Self-censorship

1. Schorr, *Clearing the Air,* pp. 53–56, 266–71. Halberstam concludes that Paley surrendered to White House pressure: "CBS: The Power and the Profits: Part II," pp. 83–90. Gates adds that Colson was actually trying to reach Frank Stanton, who Gates thinks could have fielded the pressure better than William Paley. Gates, *Air Time,* p. 306. I should note that many of the examples of pressure on journalists cited in this chapter involve CBS. This is because CBS News has been written about more extensively than other news media and because its journalists seem to have taken greater risks and provided more harmful publicity about the powerful than did other news organizations.

2. This definition is from the perspective of the news organization. An editor's changes in a writer's story could, from a writer's perspective, also be defined as censorship; but writers do not consider it censorship (unless the change has been demanded externally), and I shall not do so either.

3. Halberstam suggests that William Paley wanted Murrow to leave because the Eisenhower Administration, to which he was close, was displeased with him and with CBS News generally. "CBS: The Power and the Profits: Part I," pp. 67–71.

Alexander Kendrick, writing in 1969, ascribed Murrow's departure to both a long-festering dispute with Frank Stanton and the latter's displeasure over a Murrow speech attacking Stanton for his public criticism of a Murrow program. Kendrick, *Prime Time,* pp. 482–526.

4. During my fieldwork, the most frequently mentioned instance was *Life*'s 1968 killing of Chris Welles's exposé article on the oil industry's exploitation of publicly owned oil shale, the killing allegedly resulting from a Shell Oil Company threat to withdraw its advertising at a time when *Life* was already suffering from heavy losses in advertising revenues. J. R. Freeman, "An Interested Observer Views an Oil Shale Incident," *Columbia Journalism Review* 8 (Summer 1969): 45–48. For Welles's own account, see his *Elusive Bonanza* (New York: E. P. Dutton, 1970).

5. Fred Ferretti, "Coca-Cola Denies Link to Farm Ills; NBC Alters Documentary on Migrant Farm Workers," *The New York Times,* 17 July 1970, p. 51.

6. Talk and interview programs which also have a Washington audience are sometimes vulnerable to sponsor pressure. Fred Powledge, *The Engineering of Restraint* (Washington, D.C.: Public Affairs Press, 1971), p. 30n.

7. Schorr, *Clearing the Air,* pp. 119, 202–03.

8. Gates, *Air Time,* pp. 365–67. The reporter in question was also the house hippie mentioned in Chapter 6, footnote 20.

9. Bill Greeley, "60 Percent Say TV Web Slanted Vs. War," *Variety,* 27 May 1970. As far as I know, only one local station owner, Stimson Bullitt of Seattle's King Broadcasting Company, ever came out against the Vietnam War, and he did so in 1966.

10. Powledge, *The Engineering of Restraint,* p. 35.

11. Greeley, "60 Percent Say TV Web Slanted Vs. War."

12. "News 'Goddams' Ire Affils," p. 47.

13. Steven Knoll, "CBS TV Affils Meet in a Two-in-One Affair, Costarring Wood and Cronkite," *Variety,* 13 May 1970.

14. Winston Burdett, who had been a Communist before going to work for CBS, chose to cooperate with congressional investigators, after which, according to Gates, CBS sent him to Rome. Gates, *Air Time,* p. 157.

15. Ibid., pp. 37–39. The decentralization of public television brought about the removal of another liberal reporter, Sander Vanocur, although in this instance, affiliate displeasure seems to have originated in the Nixon White House.

16. Rather, *The Camera Never Blinks,* chapter 15. Gates comes to the same conclusion, suggesting that William Paley was pleased that Richard Nixon was giving a CBS staffer a hard time. Gates, *Air Time,* pp. 372–76. Gates indicates that affiliate pressure was strong, however; and Schorr concludes that it was a major factor in Rather's transfer. Schorr, *Clearing the Air,* pp. 128–29.

17. Schorr, *Clearing the Air,* pp. 212–14. Both Schorr and Gates report that some news executives wanted Schorr to return after the congressional investigation but that several Washington colleagues objected, since Schorr implicated one of them in the leak of the Pike Committee report to *The Village Voice.* Gates, *Air Time,* pp. 390–96. See also Schorr, *Clearing the Air,* pp. 252–57.

18. To name just a few, in alphabetical order: James Aronson, *The Press and the Cold War* (Indianapolis: Bobbs-Merrill, 1970); Ben H. Bagdikian, *The Effete Conspiracy* (New York: Harper & Row, 1972); Eric Barnouw, *Tube of Plenty* (New York: Oxford University Press, 1975); Edward J. Epstein, *Agency of Fear* (New York: G. P. Putnam's Sons, 1977); Hillier Krieghbaum, *Pressures on the Press* (New York: T. Y. Crowell, 1972); Dale Minor, *The Information War* (New York: Hawthorn Books, 1970); Powledge, *The Engineering of Restraint;* Schorr, *Clearing the Air;* Harry Skornia, *Television and the News* (Palo Alto, Calif.: Pacific Books, 1968); William Small, *To Kill a Messenger* (New York: Hastings House, 1970), and *Political Power and the Press* (New York: W. W. Norton, 1972); and David Wise, *The Politics of Lying* (New York: Random House, 1973). Most of the books about the Watergate scandals also include instances of governmental pressure. Annual reports about governmental pressure on television can be found in the Alfred I. du Pont–Columbia University Surveys of Broadcast Journalism, written by Marvin Barrett and published under various titles, first by Grosset & Dunlap and, more recently, by T. Y. Crowell. For the earlier history of White House pressure, see James E. Pollard, *The Presidents and the Press* (New York: Macmillan, 1947).

19. These can be found in their books about Watergate. For a pre-Watergate defense, see James Keogh, *President Nixon and the Press* (New York: Funk & Wagnalls, 1972). Other defenders of the Nixon Administration or its policies have used content and analyses, for example, Efron, *The News Twisters;* and Lefever, *TV and National Defense.*

20. Halberstam, "CBS: The Power and the Profits: Part II," p. 88.

21. Schorr, *Clearing the Air,* p. 56.

22. If the Watergate scandals had not been uncovered, and if Edward J. Epstein's analysis of a White House scheme to establish an intelligence agency that would have subverted both the federal bureaucracy and the press is correct, the Nixon Administration's attempt to censor and chill the journalists might have been successful. Epstein, *Agency of Fear.*

23. See, e.g., Robert Sherrill, "The Happy Ending (Maybe) of 'The Selling of the Pentagon,' " *The New York Times Magazine,* 16 May 1971, pp. 25–27, 78–80, 87, 90–94.

24. For discussions of recent court actions, see, e.g., Benno Schmidt, Jr., *Freedom*

of the Press Versus Public Access (New York: Praeger Publishers, 1976); and Fred W. Friendly, *The Good Guys, The Bad Guys, and the First Amendment* (New York: Random House, 1976).

25. In the spring of 1978, the Supreme Court also agreed to hear a case in which Colonel Anthony Herbert, a former army officer, charged a producer of the CBS *60 Minutes* program with libel. The Court agreed to rule whether the producer is required to disclose the thoughts and opinions he held in preparing the program segment about Colonel Herbert. The case is, in that sense, similar to cases about the relevancy of notes and outtakes.

26. In 1972, a temporary injunction against *The New York Times* to cease publication of the Pentagon Papers appears to have discouraged the networks from reporting on them, although after the injunction was lifted, the networks—as well as the print media—paid more attention to the dramatic story of how Daniel Ellsberg copied and leaked the papers than to their content. Steven Knoll, "When TV Was Offered the Pentagon Papers," *Columbia Journalism Review* 10 (March/April 1972): 46–48.

27. Quoted in Isidore Silver, "Libel, A Weapon for the Right," *The Nation,* 20 May 1978, pp. 594–97, quote at p. 597.

28. The journalists were confused by the vice-president's assertion that they had immense power, and they were also angry about being attacked. As it turned out, they found an immediate chance to retaliate, for a space-mission film that day included a conversation in which one astronaut called the other Tricky Dicky.

29. M. L. Stein, "The Networks: First Round to Agnew," *The Nation,* 7 September 1970, pp. 178–81.

30. Four years later, William Paley ordered a temporary cessation of instant analyses by CBS News, but paired it with a decision to allow the opposition party time and opportunity to react to presidential speeches. The journalists objected to his order, and it was later rescinded.

31. Dennis Lowry, "Agnew and the Network TV News: A Before/After Content Analysis," *Journalism Quarterly* 48 (Summer 1971): 205–10. Lowry did not attempt to explain his findings, and he did not study whether journalists paid less attention to stories of the kind that aroused the vice-president's ire; but such a study would require a comparison of matched before/after samples of news about similar actors and activities.

32. See, e.g., Novak, "Why the Working Man Hates the Media."

33. Conversely, liberal politicians who want to attack the news media for being too conservative probably cannot resort to this type of pressure because the audience which considers the news too conservative is either too small or too silent to make its views known. More important, the Agnew supporters were actually protesting the emphasis on bad news. A corresponding liberal attack on good news would not be credible. Radical attacks on the news are equally inconceivable because the radical consituency is too small and because radical spokespersons are unlikely to be sufficiently authoritative to become newsworthy. Thus, they can neither obtain publicity for their views nor mobilize audience support.

34. Robert MacNeil, *The People Machine* (New York: Harper and Row, 1968), pp. 268–72.

35. In recent years, a broader media-reform movement has developed, largely resulting from long-standing efforts, particularly by the United Church of Christ, to enable members of the television and radio audiences to participate in FCC proceedings. The movement, also spurred by former FCC Commissioner Nicholas Johnson, the Nader organization, public-interest law firms, and others, is also attempting to bring about more public-service programming, increase citizen access to local media, and reduce local cross-ownership monopolies in local print and electronic media. The

---

movement is not, at the moment, concerned with the national news media, however. The Network Project, a radical organization, sought to document and organize against monopolistic and other practices by the networks, including network news; but it had minimal resources and folded after about five years of existence.

36. According to Gates, Roger Mudd was accused of "biting the hand that feeds you" for publicly criticizing television news practices soon after Spiro Agnew's speeches. Gates, *Air Time*, pp. 266–68. Schorr's popularity at CBS declined similarly after he made a speech in which he attacked management; he was later accused of attacking some of his colleagues for "softening" their analyses of Richard Nixon's speeches. Schorr, *Clearing the Air*, pp. 116–19.

37. For a detailed account of the incident, by a colleague of the two men, see David Halberstam, *The Making of a Quagmire* (New York: Random House, 1965), chapter 16.

38. This is a far cry, however, from the practice of entertainment television producers, who work directly with the American Medical Association in the preparation of shows about doctors, as well as with local police departments and the FBI. See, e.g., John E. Cooney, "If a TV Script Needs a Medical Checkup, A Doctor Is on Call," *The Wall Street Journal*, 8 November 1977, pp. 1, 17.

39. Schorr, *Clearing the Air*, pp. 274–80.

40. Cowan and Newfield have suggested that in 1970, the Department of Justice had to resort to subpoenas to obtain outtakes and files about the Panthers and other radical groups because the "collusion" that existed during the Democratic era had ended. Paul Cowan and Jack Newfield, "Media Response: Medium Fool," *The Village Voice*, 12 February 1970, pp. 1, 66–68.

41. Miles Copeland, "The News Media's 'CIA Agents,'" *The New York Times*, 30 September 1977, pp. A26. [Emphasis in original.]

42. Halberstam, "Time, Inc.'s Internal War Over Vietnam."

43. Schorr, *Clearing the Air*, p. 276.

44. Halberstam, "Time, Inc's. Internal War Over Vietnam," pp. 127–31.

45. When Seymour Hersh, the investigative reporter, was convinced by his evidence but felt that editors might not be, he would turn his stories in late in the evening, after the editors had gone home, and his work could not be changed or killed. Leonard Downie, Jr., *The New Muckrakers* (New York: New Republic Book Co., 1976), p. 84. According to Downie, Hersh used this technique both at the Associated Press and *The New York Times*, but it cannot be used in the news media I studied, since a top editor or producer is always on hand until the news program or magazine goes to press.

46. On Mylai, see Seymour M. Hersh, *My Lai Four: A Report on the Massacre and Its Aftermath* (New York: Random House, 1970), chapter 10.

47. For thoughtful recent statements which coincide generally, if not always specifically, with this position, see Todd Gitlin, "Fourteen Notes on Television and the Movement," *Leviathan*, July/August 1969, pp. 3–9; Molotch and Lester, "News as Purposive Behavior"; Herbert I. Schiller, *Mass Communications and Empire* (New York: Augustus M. Kelley, 1969); and Gaye Tuchman, "Professionalism as an Agent of Legitimization," *Journal of Communication* 28 (Spring 1978): 106–13.

48. Journalists in Communist and fascist countries have a monopoly and can therefore promulgate unpopular ideologies. But as far as one can tell, journalists in Eastern Europe must abide by the party line, and they are censored or forced to censor themselves when the party line and the national ideology diverge. They, too, must respond to pressure.

49. To be sure, journalists consider themselves outsiders; but insofar as they func-

tion under restraints, they are not. However, they are able to have the best of both possible worlds, since they can perceive themselves outside society by virtue of being detached, and do not perceive the avoidance mechanisms as restraints.

Chapter 9—Conclusions: The News and the Journalists

1. In addition, I suggested in Chapter 6 that some of the values may also be responses to the conditions under which journalists work, even if, for example, journalists do not apply anti-bureaucratic values solely because they dislike news organization bureaucracy.

2. See, e.g., James D. Halloran, Philip Elliott, and Graham Murdock, *Demonstrations and Communication: A Case Study* (London: Penguin Books, 1970); Jeremy Tunstall, *Journalists at Work* (London: Constable Press, 1971); and particularly, Schlesinger, *Putting "Reality" Together.* Schlesinger's study of the BBC news organization repeatedly suggests the essential similarity of television news organizations in Britain and America.

3. My observations on source power suggest that the study of sources deserves far more attention from news researchers than it has so far obtained. To understand the news fully, researchers must study sources as roles and as representatives of the organized or unorganized groups for whom they act and speak, and thus also as holders of power. Above all, researchers should determine what groups create or become sources, and with what agendas; what interests they pursue in seeking access to the news and in refusing it. Parallel studies should be made of groups that cannot get into the news, and why this is so. And researchers must ask what effect obtaining or failing to obtain access to the news has on the power, the interests, and the subsequent activities of groups who become or are represented by sources.

4. Incidentally, a worker-controlled news organization could, presumably, choose to be more democratic and less hierarchical, electing top editors and producers, provided they had sufficient power to get the work done on time. This would do wonders for staff morale, even if it might increase internal conflict. A democratically run news organization would probably take more liberal stands, reflecting the dominance of young people in the organization.

5. David S. Broder, "Political Reporters in Presidential Politics," *Washington Monthly,* February 1969, pp. 20–33.

6. George Gerbner, "Television: The New State Religion?" *Et cetera,* June 1977, pp. 145–50.

7. John E. Kelly, "Information Theory and the Ethnography of Television News" (Ph.D. dissertation, Brown University, June 1976), p. 29.

8. Ibid., pp. 175–76.

9. Some myths—for example, those about the Founding Fathers and Abraham Lincoln—survive for a much longer time; but while journalists also repeat them, the major perpetuating agencies are the schools, and the public officials who justify their decisions by the Founding Fathers and other now mythic politicians of the past.

10. Robert Park, "News as a Form of Knowledge," *American Journal of Sociology* 45 (March 1944): 669–86, especially at pp. 682–83.

11. In the uses and gratifications paradigm, this is part of the surveillance function of the news media. See, e.g., Levy, "The Audience Experience with Television News," pp. 12–19.

In this connection, Arlen has described the journalists as outriders. Writing about audience lack of interest in the news, he notes that "the mass public, while appearing not to care, cares enough to dispatch its own outriders into the future. . . . In the end, and sometimes in the nick of time, the new messages are accepted." Michael J. Arlen, "The News," *New Yorker,* 31 October 1977, pp. 119–27, quote at p. 122.

12. Herbert Marcuse, *One-Dimensional Man* (Boston: Beacon Press, 1964).

13. Jacques Ellul, *Propaganda* (New York: Vintage Books, 1973), particularly chapter 3. For a more detailed discussion of Marcuse and Ellul, see Gans, *Popular Culture and High Culture,* pp. 43–51.

14. For an argument and some empirical data to the contrary, see Michael J. Robinson, "American Political Legitimacy in an Era of Electronic Journalism: Reflections on the Evening News," in Douglass Cater and Richard Adler, eds., *Television As a Social Force: New Approaches to TV Criticism* (New York: Praeger Publishers, 1975), pp. 97–139, especially pp. 118–20.

15. This hypothesis resembles, in some way, Durkheim's argument that preliterate tribes, and by implication modern populations, construct their societies with and through their religions. Emile Durkheim, *The Elementary Forms of the Religious Life* (Glencoe, Ill.: Free Press of Glencoe, 1947). I have never been entirely convinced by Durkheim's imaginative argument, however; nor do I mean to suggest that journalists serve religious functions. Durkheim, moreover, did not believe that society is a construct.

Chapter 10—Multiperspectival News

1. For an excellent analysis that makes this point in reviewing a number of recent bias and distortion studies, see Alden Williams, "Unbiased Study of Television News Bias," *Journal of Communication* 25 (Autumn 1975): 190–99.

2. Lang and Lang, "The Unique Perspective of Television."

3. Glasgow University Media Group, *Bad News* (London: Routledge & Kegan Paul, 1976).

4. There is some evidence, particularly from England, that many viewers do not comprehend all of the news they see on television. Elihu Katz, *Social Research on Broadcasting: Proposals for Further Development* (London: British Broadcasting Corporation, 1977), pp. 61–63.

5. Consequently, the experts, who believe that popular culture, like lay news, is superficial and excessively dramatic, want it replaced by high culture. For my argument against this position, see Gans, *Popular Culture and High Culture,* chapter 1.

6. The social sciences hold theorists who develop dramatic concepts and theories in high regard; evidently, highlighting for dramatic effect is marketable in expert as well as lay endeavors.

7. For my argument against the harmfulness of popular culture, which I think is applicable to popular news as well, see Gans, *Popular Culture and High Culture,* pp. 30–36.

8. Gitlin has argued that television's endless repetition of patrol films during the Vietnam War, which showed the war to be senseless, also induced war weariness among the viewers. Todd Gitlin, "Spotlight and Shadows: Television and the Culture of Politics," *College English* 38 (Spring 1977): 789–801. Unfortunately, pollsters at the time were so interested in counting hawks and doves that no one, to my knowledge, asked viewers how they reacted to the war news. For some evidence that the battle footage made some people hawkish and some dovish, see Gans, "The Uses of Television," p. 14.

9. Levy, for example, found that 70 percent of his respondents agreed with a statement that "the TV news programs try to make things seem more dramatic than they really are." Levy, "The Audience Experience with Television News," p. 16.

Their response, however, does not prove that they were therefore discounting television news. On discounting, see Eliot Freidson, "Adult Discount: An Aspect of Children's Changing Taste," *Child Development* 24 (March 1953): 39–49.

10. Walter Lippmann, *Public Opinion* (New York: Free Press, 1965), p. 54.

11. Mannheim, *Ideology and Utopia*. His central thesis, that all knowledge is relational to the knower's perspective, can, I realize, be logically questioned for being stated in absolute form. Mannheim's thesis is itself relational, however; it stems from the perspective of an intellectual embedded in a heterogeneous society marked by political and other conflicts. Knowers in homogeneous societies, and those who accept the infallibility of gods, popes, or public officials, will therefore come to different conclusions. Still, knowledge cannot exist without a knower, any more than news can exist without a journalist. Even the person who assumes, as do journalists, that external reality exists in the absence of a knower is a knower. And a knower's choice of perspective, when he or she is free to choose, is a matter of values.

12. Hofstetter, among others, has applied organizational research to the issue of distortion in his analysis of "structural bias." Hofstetter, *Bias in the News*, chapter 1.

13. For a similar observation but a different assessment of Mannheim's ideas, see Schlesinger, *Putting 'Reality' Together*, pp. 169–70.

14. Commission on Freedom of the Press, *A Free and Responsible Press* (Chicago: University of Chicago Press, 1947), p. 26.

15. Robert K. Merton, "Insiders and Outsiders," *American Journal of Sociology* 78 (July 1972): 9–47.

16. Epstein, *Agency of Fear*, pp. 265–66.

17. When too many conflicting perspectives appear in the news, objectivity can, in fact, become what Smith calls a "yardstick of reality," a perspective that is credible simply because it is detached. Anthony Smith, *The Shadow in the Cave* (Urbana: University of Illinois Press, 1974), p. 109.

18. The size and profitability of the present daytime and weekend television audience suggest that news programs for women and children could be established without subsidy. News programs for children and adolescents have, in fact, appeared from time to time, but so far none have lasted.

19. Good recent examples of publications on the Left are the weekly newspaper *In These Times* and the biweekly newsmagazine *Seven Days*.

20. Jones has suggested that the amount of crime news should bear some relation to the crime rate (assuming that an accurate rate can be developed). E. Terence Jones, "The Press as Monitor," *Public Opinion Quarterly* 40 (Summer 1976): 239–43. Even if journalists continue to emphasize dramatic crimes, they can "tag" stories by reporting the rates for such crimes, thus providing some balance to the exaggerations that accompany highlighting.

21. For many of my general observations about professionals, here and elsewhere, I am indebted to the work of my teacher Everett Hughes and a fellow-student, Eliot Freidson, at the University of Chicago. See, e.g., Everett C. Hughes, *Men and Their Work* (Glencoe, Ill: The Free Press of Glencoe, 1958); and Eliot Freidson, *The Profession of Medicine* (New York: Dodd, Mead, 1970).

22. People who lack organizations, however, can demonstrate. Demonstrations against the news media, although rarely tried, might be effective if only because they would be newsworthy.

23. See, e.g., Cecilie Gaziano, "Readership Study of Paper Subsidized by Government," *Journalism Quarterly* 51 (Summer 1974): 323–26, reporting on a newspaper published for residents of a model-city area in Minneapolis.

24. For some empirical evidence, see Funkhouser, "The Issues of the Sixties."

25. Lee M. Mitchell, "Government as Broadcaster—Solution or Threat?" *Journal of Communication* 28 (Spring 1978): 69–72.

26. Maxwell E. McCombs and Donald L. Shaw, "The Agenda-Setting Function of Mass Media," *Public Opinion Quarterly* 36 (Summer 1972): 176–87. On the role of the media in opinion formation, see Elisabeth Noelle-Neumann, "The Spiral of Silence: A Theory of Public Opinion," *Journal of Communication* 24 (Spring 1974): 43–51.

27. For a comprehensive and systematic analysis of the relationship between knowledge and power, see Amitai Etzioni, *The Active Society* (New York: Free Press, 1968), chapter 8.

28. Yrjö Littunen and Kaarle Nordenstreng, "Informational Broadcasting Policy: The Finnish Experiment," in Kaarle Nordenstreng, ed., *Informational Mass Communication* (Helsinki: Tammi Publishers, 1973), chapter 1, quote at p. 23.

29. Ibid., p. 41. Audience studies showed that the viewers deemed the news to be somewhat more credible and reliable, although informationally and economically privileged groups saw the news as conflicting with their interests. Ibid., pp. 37–39. Whether audience size or regularity increased was impossible to determine, however, because television ownership grew from 75 to 92 percent of the population during that decade and because changes in news content were, by one researcher's opinion, gradual and not dramatic. Juha Kytömäki, Finnish Broadcasting Company, personal communication, 1978.

Bibliography

This bibliography contains most of the items about the news media cited in the chapter notes (other than newspaper and other brief articles), and some of the many uncited books and articles on the news media which I have read and found useful while working on this study. For reasons of space, I have not included standard textbooks or brief articles about the news media (even if useful) which appear regularly in *Newsweek, Time,* and other magazines and journals. I have also excluded general items about television and other mass media (as well as other items cited in chapter notes) that either did not pertain directly and explicitly to the news media or did so only in passing.

Altheide, David L. *Creating Reality: How TV News Distorts Events.* Beverly Hills: Sage Publications, 1976.

Arlen, Michael J. *Living-Room War.* New York: Viking Press, 1969.

———. "The News." *New Yorker,* 31 October 1977, pp. 119–27.

Aronson, James. *The Press and the Cold War.* Indianapolis: Bobbs-Merrill, 1970.

Bagdikian, Ben H. *The Effete Conspiracy.* New York: Harper & Row, 1972.

———. *The Information Machines: Their Impact on Men and the Media.* New York: Harper & Row, 1971.

Bailey, George A. "Interpretive Reporting of the Vietnam War by Anchormen." *Journalism Quarterly* 53 (Summer 1976): 319–24.

———. "The War According to Walter: Network Anchormen and Vietnam." Milwaukee: Department of Mass Communications, University of Wisconsin, 1975.

Balk, Alfred, and Boylan, James, eds. *Our Troubled Press: Ten Years of the Columbia Journalism Review.* Boston: Little, Brown, 1971.

Barnouw, Eric. *Tube of Plenty.* New York: Oxford University Press, 1975.

Barrett, Marvin, ed. *The Politics of Broadcasting: Alfred I. du Pont–Columbia University Survey of Broadcast Journalism, 1971–1972.* New York: Thomas Y. Crowell, 1973.

———. *Rich News, Poor News: The Sixth Alfred I. du Pont–Columbia University Survey of Broadcast Journalism.* New York: Thomas Y. Crowell, 1978.

Bauer, Raymond. "The Communicator and the Audience." In *People, Society and Mass Communications,* edited by Lewis A. Dexter and David M. White, pp. 125–40. New York: Free Press, 1964.

Berelson, Bernard. 'What 'Missing the Newspaper' Means." In *Communications Research 1948–1949,* edited by Paul Lazarsfeld and Frank Stanton, pp. 111–29. New York: Harper & Brothers, 1949.

Bernstein, Victor, and Gordon, Jesse. "The Press and the Bay of Pigs." *Columbia University Forum,* Fall 1967, pp. 4–15.

Bethell, Tom. "The Myth of an Adversary Press." *Harper's,* January 1977, pp. 33–40.

Blumler, Jay G., and McQuail, Denis. *Television in Politics.* Chicago: University of Chicago Press, 1969.

Bogart, Leo. *Silent Politics: Polls and the Awareness of Public Opinion.* New York: Wiley-Interscience, 1972.

Boorstin, Daniel J. *The Image: A Guide to Pseudo-Events in America.* New York: Harper & Row, 1964.

Bower, Robert T. *Television and the Public.* New York: Holt, Rinehart & Winston, 1973.

Bradlee, Benjamin C. *Conversations with Kennedy.* New York: W. W. Norton, 1975.

Braestrup, Peter. *Big Story.* 2 vols. Boulder, Colo.: Westview Press, 1977.

Breed, Warren. "Social Control in the Newsroom." *Social Forces* 33 (May 1955): 326–35.

Broder, David S. "Political Reporters in Presidential Politics." *Washington Monthly,* February 1969, pp. 20–33.

Busch, Noel. *Briton Hadden: A Biography of the Co-Founder of* Time. New York: Farrar, Straus and Co., 1949.

Calmer, Ned. *The Anchorman.* New York: Doubleday & Co., 1970.

Cater, Douglass. *The Fourth Branch of Government.* Boston: Houghton Mifflin Co., 1959.

Chittick, William O. *State Department, Press, and Pressure Groups.* New York: John Wiley & Sons, 1970.

Chomsky, Noam. "Reporting Indochina: The News Media and the Legitimation of Lies." *Social Policy* 4 (September/October, 1973): 4–19.

Cirino, Robert. *Don't Blame the People.* Los Angeles: Diversity Press, 1971.

———. *Power to Persuade: Mass Media and the News.* New York: Bantam Books, 1974.

Coase, R. H. "The Market for Goods and the Market for Ideas." *American Economic Review* 64 (May 1974): 384–91.

Cohen, Bernard C. *The Press and Foreign Policy.* Princeton, N. J.: Princeton University Press, 1953.

Coleman, Kate. "Turning on *Newsweek. " Scanlan's Monthly,* June 1970, pp. 44–53.

Commission on Freedom of the Press. *A Free and Responsible Press.* Chicago: University of Chicago Press, 1947.

Crouse, Timothy. *The Boys on the Bus.* New York: Random House, 1973.

Darnton, Robert. "Writing News and Telling Stories." *Daedalus,* Spring 1975, pp. 175–94.

Davison, Phillips W.; Boylan, James; and Yu, Frederick T. *Mass Media Systems and Effects.* New York: Praeger Publishers, 1976.

Diamond, Edwin. "Boston: The Agony of Responsibility." *Columbia Journalism Review* 13 (January/February 1975): 9–15.

———. "The Mid-Life Crisis of the Newsweeklies." *New York,* 7 June 1976, pp. 51–61.

———. *The Tin Kazoo: Television, Politics, and News.* Cambridge, Mass.: MIT Press, 1975.

Dominick, Joseph R. "Geographical Bias in Television News." *Journal of Communication* 27 (Autumn 1977): 94–99.

Downie, Leonard, Jr. *The New Muckrakers.* Washington, D.C.: New Republic Book Co., 1976.

Edelman, Murray. *The Symbolic Uses of Politics.* Urbana: University of Illinois Press, 1964.

Efron, Edith. *The News Twisters.* Los Angeles: Nash, 1971.

Elliott, Philip. *The Making of a Television Series.* London: Constable Press, 1972.

Ellul, Jacques. *Propaganda: The Formation of Men's Attitudes.* New York: Vintage Books, 1973.

Elson, Robert T. *Time, Inc.: The Intimate History of a Publishing Enterprise, 1923–1941.* New York: Atheneum, 1968.

———. *The World of Time, Inc.: The Intimate History of a Publishing Enterprise, 1941–1960.* New York: Atheneum, 1973.

Epstein, Edward J. *Agency of Fear.* New York: G. P. Putnam's Sons, 1977.

———. *News from Nowhere: Television and the News.* New York: Random House, 1973.

Fisher, Paul L., and Lowenstein, Ralph L., eds. *Race and the News Media.* New York: Frederick A. Praeger, 1967.

Fowler, Joseph S., and Showalter, Stuart W. "Evening Network News Selection: A Confirmation of News Judgment." *Journalism Quarterly* 51 (Winter 1974): 712–15.

Frank, Robert S. *Message Dimensions of Television News.* Lexington, Mass.: Lexington Books, 1973.

Freeman, J. R. "An Interested Observer Views an Oil Shale Incident." *Columbia Journalism Review* 8 (Summer 1969): 45–48.

Friedrich, Otto. *Decline and Fall.* New York: Harper & Row, 1970.

———. "There Are 00 Trees in Russia: The Function of Facts in Newsmagazines." *Harper's Magazine,* October 1964, pp. 59–65.

Friendly, Fred W. *Due to Circumstances Beyond Our Control.* New York: Random House, 1967.

———. *The Good Guys, The Bad Guys, and the First Amendment.* New York: Random House, 1976.

Funkhouser, G. Ray. "The Issues of the Sixties: An Exploratory Study in the Dynamics of Public Opinion." *Public Opinion Quarterly* 10 (Spring 1973): 62–76.

Galtung, Johan, and Ruge, Mari H. "The Structure of Foreign News." In *Media Sociology,* edited by Jeremy Tunstall, pp. 259–98. London: Constable Press, 1970.

Gans, Herbert J. "Letters to an Anchorman." *Journal of Communication* 27 (Summer 1977): 86–91.

———. *Popular Culture and High Culture: An Analysis and Evaluation of Taste.* New York: Basic Books, 1974.

———. "The Uses of Television and Their Educational Implications." Mimeographed. New York: Center for Urban Education, 1968.

Gates, Gary Paul. *Air Time: The Inside Story of CBS News.* New York: Harper & Row, 1978.

Gaziano, Cecilie. "Readership Study of Paper Subsidized by Government." *Journalism Quarterly* 51 (Summer 1974): 323–26

Gelfman, Judith S. *Women in Television News.* New York: Columbia University Press, 1976.

Gerbner, George. "Television: The New State Religion?" *Et cetera,* June 1977, pp. 145–50.

Gieber, Walter, and Johnson, Walter. "The City Hall 'Beat': A Study of Reporter and Source Roles." *Journalism Quarterly* 38 (Summer 1961): 289–97.

Gitlin, Todd. "Fourteen Notes on Television and the Movement." *Leviathan,* July/August 1969, pp. 3–9.

———. "Spotlight and Shadows: Television and the Culture of Politics." *College English* 38 (Spring 1977): 789–801.

Glasgow University Media Group. *Bad News.* London: Routledge & Kegan Paul, 1976.

Goldenberg, Edie N. *Making the Papers.* Lexington, Mass: D. C. Heath, 1975.

Habermas, Juergen. *Strukturwandel der Öffentlichkeit.* Neuwied: Luchterhand, 1962.

Halberstam, David. "CBS: The Power and the Profits: Part I." *Atlantic Monthly,* January 1976, pp. 33–71; Part II: February 1976, pp. 52–91.

———. *The Making of a Quagmire.* New York: Random House, 1965.

———. "Time, Inc.'s Internal War Over Vietnam." *Esquire,* January 1978, pp. 94–131.

Halloran, James D; Elliott, Philip; and Murdock, Graham. *Demonstrations and Communication: A Case Study.* London: Penguin Books, 1970.

Halperin, Morton, and Hoffman, Daniel B. *Top Secret: National Security and the Right to Know.* Washington, D.C.: New Republic Book Co., 1977.

Herschensohn, Bruce. *The Gods of Antenna.* New Rochelle, N. Y.: Arlington House, 1976.

Hirsch, Paul. "Occupational, Organizational, and Institutional Models in Mass Media Research: Toward an Integrated Framework." In *Strategies for Communication Research,* edited by Paul M. Hirsch, Peter V. Miller, and F. Gerald Cline. Sage Annual Reviews of Communications Research. Vol. 6, pp. 13–42. Beverly Hills: Sage Publications, 1977.

Hofstetter, C. Richard. *Bias in the News.* Columbus, Ohio: Ohio State University Press, 1976.

Hohenberg, John. *The News Media: A Journalist Looks at His Profession.* New York: Holt, Rinehart & Winston, 1968.

Hopkins, Jeanette. "Racial Justice and the Press." MARC Paper No. 1. New York: Metropolitan Applied Research Center, 1968.

Hughes, Helen M. *News and the Human Interest Story.* Chicago: University of Chicago Press, 1940.

Huntley, Chet. *The Generous Years: Remembrances of a Frontier Boyhood.* New York: Random House, 1968.

Israel, Harold, and Robinson, John P. "Demographic Characteristics of Viewers of Television Violence and News Programs." In *Television and Social Behavior,* Vol. IV: *Television in Day-to-Day Life: Patterns of Use,* edited by Eli A. Rubenstein, George A. Comstock, and John P. Murray, pp. 87–128. Washington, D. C.: U. S. Government Printing Office, 1971.

The "I. F. Stone's Weekly" Reader, edited by Neil Middleton. New York: Random House, 1973.

Johnstone, John W.; Slawski, Edward J.; and Bowman, William W. *The News People: A Sociological Portrait of American Journalists and Their Work.* Urbana: University of Illinois Press, 1976.

Jones, E. Terence. "The Press as Monitor." *Public Opinion Quarterly* 40 (Summer 1976): 239–43.

Kaplan, Justin. *Lincoln Steffens: A Biography.* New York: Simon and Schuster, 1974.

Keeley, Joseph. *The Left-Leaning Antenna: Political Bias in Television.* New Rochelle, N. Y.: Arlington House, 1971.

Kelly, John E. "Information Theory and the Ethnography of Television News." Ph.D. dissertation, Brown University, June 1976.

Kendrick, Alexander. *Prime Time: The Life of Edward R. Murrow.* Boston: Little, Brown, 1969.

Keogh, James. *President Nixon and the Press.* New York: Funk & Wagnalls, 1972.

Kimball, Penn. "Journalism: Art, Craft or Profession?" In *The Professions in America,* edited by Kenneth S. Lynn and the Editors of *Daedalus,* pp. 242–60. Boston: Houghton Mifflin Co., 1967.

Knopf, Terry A. "Media Myths on Violence." *Columbia Journalism Review* 9 (Spring 1970): 17–23.

Kopkind, Andrew. "Serving Time." *The New York Review of Books,* 12 September 1968, pp. 23–28.

Kraslow, David, and Loory, Stuart H. *The Secret Search for Peace in Vietnam.* New York: Vintage, 1968.

Kraus, Sidney, and Davis, Dennis. *The Effects of Mass Communication on Political Behavior.* University Park, Pa.: Pennsylvania State University Press, 1976.

Krieghbaum, Hillier. *Pressures on the Press.* New York: Thomas Y. Crowell, 1972.

Kueneman, Rodney M., and Wright, Joseph E. "News Policies of Broadcast Stations for Civil Disturbances and Disasters." *Journalism Quarterly* 52 (Winter 1975): 670–77.

Lang, Kurt, and Lang, Gladys E. *Politics and Television.* New York: Quadrangel Books, 1968.

———. "The Unique Perspective of Television and Its Effect." *American Sociological Review* 18 (February 1953): 3–12.

Lefever, Ernest W. *TV and National Defense.* Chicago: Institute for American Strategy, 1974.

Lemert, James B. "Content Duplication by the Networks in Competing Evening Newscasts." *Journalism Quarterly* 41 (Summer 1974): 238–44.

Levin, Eric. "How the Networks Decide What Is News." *TV Guide,* 2 July 1977, pp. 4–10.

Levy, Mark R. "The Audience Experience with Television News." *Journalism Monographs,* no. 55 (April 1978).

Lichty, Lawrence W. "The War We Watched on Television." *American Film Institute Quarterly* 4 (Winter 1973): 29–37.

Lichty, Lawrence W., and Bailey, George A. "Violence in Television News: A Case Study of Audience Response." *Central States Speech Journal* 23 (Winter 1972): 225–29.

Liebling, A. J. *The Press.* New York: Ballantine Books, 1961.

Lippmann, Walter. *Public Opinion.* New York: Free Press, 1965.

Littunen, Yrjö, and Nordenstreng, Kaarle. "Informational Broadcasting Policy: The Finnish Experiment." In *Informational Mass Communication,* edited by Kaarle Nordenstreng, chapter 1. Helsinki: Tammi Publishers, 1973.

Love, Ruth L. "Television and the Death of a President: Network Decisions in Covering Collective Events." Ph.D. dissertation, Columbia University, 1969.

Lowry, Dennis. "Agnew and the Network TV News: A Before/After Content Analysis." *Journalism Quarterly* 48 (Summer 1971): 205–10.

Lyon, Peter. *Success Story: The Life and Times of S. S. McClure.* New York: Charles Scribner's Sons, 1963.

MacNeil, Robert. *The People Machine: The Influence of Television on American Politics.* New York: Harper & Row, 1968.

Marcuse, Herbert. *One-Dimensional Man.* Boston: Beacon Press, 1964.

McClellan, Grant S., ed. *Censorship in the United States.* New York: H. W. Wilson Co., 1967.

McCombs, Maxwell E., and Shaw, Donald L. "The Agenda-Setting Function of Mass Media." *Public Opinion Quarterly* 36 (Summer 1972): 176–87.

Merril, John C., and Barney, Ralph D., eds. *Ethics and the Press: Readings in Mass Media Morality.* New York: Hastings House, 1975.

Meyer, Philip. *Precision Journalism.* Bloomington: Indiana University Press, 1973.

Mickelson, Sig. *The Electric Mirror.* New York: Dodd, Mead, 1972.

Minor, Dale. *The Information War.* New York: Hawthorn Books, 1970.

Minow, Newton N.; Martin, John B.; and Mitchell, Lee M. *Presidential Television.* New York: Basic Books, 1973.

Mitchell, Lee M. "Government as Broadcaster—Solution or Threat?" *Journal of Communication* 28 (Spring 1978): 69–72.

Molotch, Harvey L., and Lester, Marilyn J. "Accidental News: The Great Oil Spill as Local Occurrence and National Event." *American Journal of Sociology* 81 (September 1975): 235–60.

———. "News as Purposive Behavior: On the Strategic Use of Routine Events, Accidents, and Scandals." *American Sociological Review* 39 (February 1974): 101–12.

Mott, Frank L. *American Journalism: 1690–1900.* 3d rev. ed. New York: Macmillan, 1962.

Newfield, Jack. "Journalism: Old, New and Corporate." In *The Reporter as Artist: A Look at the New Journalism Controversy,* edited by Ronald Weber, pp. 54–56. New York: Hastings House, 1974.

Newspaper Advertising Bureau. "How the Public Gets Its News: An Address by Leo Bogart Before the Associated Press Managing Editors, October 27, 1977." New York: Newspaper Advertising Bureau, 1977.

———. "Two Dimensions of News: Interest and Importance Ratings of the Editorial Content of the American Press." Mimeographed. New York: Newspaper Advertising Bureau, January 1978.

Nimmo, Dan. D. *Newsgathering in Washington.* New York: Atherton, 1962.

Noelle-Neumann, Elisabeth. "The Spiral of Silence: A Theory of Public Opinion." *Journal of Communication* 24 (Spring 1974): 43–51.

Novak, Michael. "Why the Working Man Hates the Media." *More,* October 1974, pp. 5–7.

Park, Robert. "News as a Form of Knowledge." *American Journal of Sociology* 45 (March 1944): 669–86.

Patterson, Thomas E., and McClure, Robert D. *The Unseeing Eye: The Myth of Television Power in National Politics.* New York: G. P. Putnam's Sons, 1976.

Payne, David E. "Newspapers and Crime: What Happens During Strike Periods." *Journalism Quarterly* 51 (Winter 1974): 607–12.

Pilat, Oliver. *Drew Pearson: An Unauthorized Biography.* New York: Harper's Magazine Press, 1973.

Pollak, Richard. *"Time:* After Luce." *Harper's,* July 1969, pp. 42–52.

Pollard, James E. *The Presidents and the Press.* New York: Macmillan, 1947.

Pool, Ithiel de Sola, and Shulman, Irwin. "Newsmen's Fantasies, Audiences and Newswriting." In *People, Society and Mass Communications,* edited by Lewis A. Dexter and David M. White, pp. 141–59. New York: Free Press, 1964.

Powers, Ron. *The Newscasters: The News Business as Show Business.* New York: St. Martin's Press, 1977.

Powledge, Fred. *The Engineering of Restraint.* Washington, D. C.: Public Affairs Press, 1971.

Pride, Richard A., and Clarke, Daniel H. "Race Relations in Television News: A Content Analysis of the Networks." *Journalism Quarterly* 50 (Summer 1973): 318–28.

Quinn, Sally. *We're Going to Make You a Star.* New York: Simon and Schuster, 1975.

Rather, Dan., with Mickey Herskowitz. *The Camera Never Blinks.* New York: William Morrow, 1977.

Reston, James. *The Artillery of the Press.* New York: Harper & Row, 1966.

Rivers, William L. *The Opinionmakers.* Boston: Beacon Press, 1965.

Roberts, Churchill. "The Presentation of Blacks in Television Network Newscasts." *Journalism Quarterly* 52 (Spring 1975): 50–55.

Robinson, Michael J. "American Political Legitimacy in an Era of Electronic Journalism: Reflections on the Evening News." In *Television as a Social Force: New Approaches to TV Criticism,* edited by Douglass Cater and Richard Adler, pp. 97–139. New York: Praeger Publishers, 1975.

―――. "Television and American Politics, 1956–1976." *Public Interest,* no. 48 (Summer 1977): 3–39.

Rosenthal, A. M. *Thirty-Eight Witnesses.* New York: McGraw-Hill, 1964.

Roshcoe, Bernard. *Newsmaking.* Chicago: University of Chicago Press, 1975.

Rosten, Leo. *The Washington Correspondents.* New York: Harcourt, Brace, 1937.

Schlesinger, Philip. *Putting 'Reality' Together.* London: Constable Press, 1978.

Schmidt, Benno, Jr. *Freedom of the Press Versus Public Access.* New York: Praeger Publishers, 1975.

Schneider, Lawrence. "White Newsmen and Black Critics." *Nieman Reports* 25 (September 1971): 3–7.

Schorr, Daniel. *Clearing the Air.* Boston: Houghton Mifflin Co., 1977.

Schudson, Michael. *Discovering the News: A Social History of American Newspapers.* New York: Basic Books, 1978.

Sherrill, Robert. "The Happy Ending (Maybe) of 'The Selling of the Pentagon.' " *The New York Times Magazine,* 16 May 1971, pp. 25–27, 78–80, 87, 90–94.

Shibutani, Tamotsu. *Improvised News: A Sociological Study of Rumor.* Indianapolis: Bobbs-Merrill, 1966.

Sieber, Fred; Peterson, Theodore; and Schramm, Wilbur. *Four Theories of the Press.* Urbana: University of Illinois Press, 1956.

Sigal, Leon V. *Reporters and Officials: The Organization and Politics of Newsmaking.* Lexington, Mass.: D. C. Heath, 1973.

Sigelman, Lee. "Reporting the News: An Organizational Analysis." *American Journal of Sociology* 79 (July 1973): 132–51.

W. R. Simmons & Associates Research. *Selective Markets and the Media Reaching Them.* New York: W. R. Simmons & Associates Research, annual reports in several volumes.

Simulmatics Corporation. "News Media Coverage of the 1967 Urban Riots." Mimeographed. New York: Simulmatics Corporation, February 1, 1968.

Singer, Benjamin D. "Violence, Protest and War in Television News: The U. S. and Canada Compared." *Public Opinion Quarterly* 34 (Winter 1970–1971): 611–16.

Skornia, Harry. *Television and the News.* Palo Alto, Calif: Pacific Books, 1968.

Small, William. *To Kill a Messenger.* New York: Hastings House, 1970.

———. *Political Power and the Press.* New York: W. W. Norton, 1972.

Smith, Anthony. *The Shadow in the Cave: The Broadcaster, His Audience, and the State.* Urbana: University of Illinois Press, 1974.

Stevenson, R. L.; Eisinger, R. A.; Feinberg, B. M.; and Kotok, A. B. "Untwisting 'The News Twisters': A Replication of Efron's Study." *Journalism Quarterly* 50 (Summer 1973): 211–19.

Talese, Gay. *The Kingdom and the Power.* New York: NAL World Publishing Co. 1969.

Tuchman, Gaye. *Making News: A Study in the Construction of Reality.* New York: Free Press, 1978.

———. "Making News by Doing Work: Routinizing the Unexpected." *American Journal of Sociology* 79 (July 1974): 110–31.

———. "Objectivity as Strategic Ritual: An Examination of Newsmen's Notions of Objectivity." *American Journal of Sociology* 77 (January 1972): 660–70.

———. "Professionalism as an Agent of Legitimation." *Journal of Communication* 28 (Spring 1978): 106–13.

———. "The Technology of Objectivity: Doing 'Objective' TV News Film." *Urban Life and Culture* 2 (April 1973): 3–26.

Tuchman, Gaye, Daniels, Arlene K., and Benét, James, eds. *Hearth and Home: Images of Women in the Mass Media.* New York: Oxford University Press, 1978.

Tunstall, Jeremy. *The Westminster Lobby Correspondents.* London: Routledge & Kegan Paul, 1970.

———. *Journalists at Work.* London: Constable Press, 1971.

Walfish, Andrew. "Sex Is In, Politics Is Out." *More,* September 1977, pp. 25–31.

Weaver, David H., and Wilhoit, G. Cleveland. "News Magazine Visibility of Senators." *Journalism Quarterly* 51 (Spring 1974): 67–72.

Weaver, Paul H. "Captives of Melodrama." *The New York Times Magazine,* 29 August 1976, pp. 6, 7, 48.

———. "Is Television News Biased?" *Public Interest,* no. 26 (Winter 1972): 57–74.

———. "The Metropolitan Newspaper as a Political Institution." Ph.D. dissertation, Harvard University, 1967.

Weiss, Carol H. "What American Leaders Read." *Public Opinion Quarterly* 38 (Spring 1974): 1–22.

Welles, Chris. "The Numbers Magazines Live By." *Columbia Journalism Review* 14 (September/October 1975): 22–27.

Wenglinsky, Martin. "Television News: A New Slant." *Columbia Forum,* Fall 1974, pp. 2–9.

Whale, John. *The Half-Shut Eye: Television and Politics in Britain and America.* New York: St. Martin's Press, 1969.

White, David M. "The 'Gatekeeper': A Case Study in the Selection of News." *Journalism Quarterly* 27 (Fall 1950): 383–90.

Wicker, Tom. "The Greening of the Press." *Columbia Journalism Review* 10 (May 1971): 7–14.

———. *On Press.* New York: Viking Press, 1978.

Williams, Alden. "Unbiased Study of Television News Bias." *Journal of Communication* 25 (Autumn 1975): 190–99.

Wilson, Harold S. *McClure's Magazine and the Muckrakers.* Princeton, N.J.: Princeton University Press, 1970.

Wise, David. *The Politics of Lying.* New York: Random House, 1973.

Wolf, Frank. *Television Programming for News and Public Affairs: A Quantitative Analysis of Networks and Stations.* New York: Praeger Publishers, 1972.

Yellin, David. *Special: Fred Freed and the Television Documentary.* New York: Macmillan, 1973.

Index*

ABC and ABC News, 4, 164, 165, 177, 218, 233, 247, 263, 272; affiliates, 258. *See also* television news
ACLU, 65
action, 158, 171; defined, 158; in news-magazine pictures, 159–60; in television film, 158–9
advertisers and advertiser pressure, 166, 221, 247, 253–8, 268, 282, 288; and documentaries, 256; journalists' attitudes toward, 255; news role of, 73, 254–7
advocacy journalism, 166, 186, 315
affiliate stations, 218, 256, 268; pressure from, 258–60; and Vietnam War news, 258
Africa, 35, 36, 37
agenda-setting, 332
Agnew, Spiro, 26, 78, 229, 246, 258, 263–5, 276, 322
Agronsky, Martin, 259
Alsop, Joseph, 267
altruistic democracy, 43–45, 55, 68, 69, 149. *See also* democracy
American Jewish Committee, 265
American Medical Association, 265
anchorpersons, 3, 4, 75, 86, 99, 106, 259, 266, 293, 348; audience relationships, 217–18, 227; commentary, 187; eliminating role of, 164–5; format rut, 165; income, 209; morale role, 104; and news executives, 342; power of, 85, 99, 152–3; and ratings, 108, 217–18, 233; source access of, 119, 125; story opinions, 198
Anderson, Jack, 134, 245, 271
anti-communism, 195, 207
anti-war movement, 27, 40, 53, 54, 58, 127, 139, 175, 176, 187, 258, 263, 269,

272, 274, 280. *See also* protests and protest news; Vietnam and Vietnam War news
anticipated stories, 87–88, 109, 122
anticipatory avoidance, 270–6
assassinations, 18, 151; Kennedy, 11, 20, 55, 76, 160, 243
Associated Press, 86, 186
audience, 73, 220–40, 295; changing the news and, 290; channel preference, 218; demographic characteristics, 220–5, 248, 352; and enduring values, 206; and format change, 164; and generalists, 143–4; and ideology, 278; interested and uninterested, 239–40; invented, 240–1; journalist fear of, 234–5; journalist as representative of, 236–8; known, 235, 236; lay vs. expert, 307–8; media images and prototypes, 93, 238–41, 355; news needs and uses of, 226–7; and objectivity, 186; possibility of change in, 286, 288–9; and political pressure, 263–5; power of, 283–4; regularity and attentiveness of, 224–6, 353; rejected, 240; size of, 216, 217–19, 220–6, 246–8, 288–9
audience considerations, 159, 214–48, 280, 288–9, 351; balance, 173–4, 175; boredom, 236–7; defined, 241; and expert news, 308; financial, 214–20; and multiperspectival news, 326–7, 334–5, 363; and panic, 55, 243; possibility of changes in, 247, 287–8; protective, 243–6; vs. source considerations, 89–90; story importance, 154; story interest, 155–6; story length, 161; and story opinions, 198–9; and story repetition, 169

tim, 84; and sociology, compared, xiv, 24, 39, 63, 82, 92, 126, 140, 167–8, 307; Supreme Court decisions on, 262–3; value exclusion, 183–96; value inclusion, 196–203; yellow, 84. *See also* journalists; news; professional autonomy

journalist-audience relationships, 89–90, 143, 168, 169, 229–41, 244, 354–5; informal feedback, 235–6. *See also* audience feedback

journalistic autonomy, *see* professional autonomy

journalistic credibility, *see* credibility

journalistic efficiency, 282–4

journalistic evidence, 195, 273–4, 359. *See also* facts

journalistic leeway, 285–90

journalistic methodology, 307–8

journalistic values, 183–213; and bureaucracy, 207; and class, 208–11, 213; enduring values as, 204–6; and individualism, 208; lay values and, 203–4, 213, 237; and multiperspectival news, 315–16; origins of, 203–13; and personal experience, 208–11; personal political, 211–12; and professional practice, 206–8; and Progressive movement, 68–83, 204–6; role in story selection, 207, 281; and working conditions, 206–8. *See also* news values; values

journalists, xii, xiii–xiv; as agents of social control, 295–7; attitudes toward audience, 229–35, 236, 354–5; audience hunger of, 236, 244, 354–5; as audience representatives, 168, 169, 236–7; audience- vs. source-related, 89–90, 143; black, 121, 194, 348; bureau chiefs, 91, 209; celebrities, 266; class and cultural background of, 107, 205, 209–11, 213, 248, 315; commentators, 198, 293; co-opted by CIA, 134–5, 136, 137, 271–2; cynicism of, 130; dismissal or forced resignations, 252, 259, 262; fraternization between, 139, 178–9, 347; ideology and values of, 190–6, 211–12, 277; importance judgments, 151–3; income of, 209–10; media critics, 266–8; muckrakers, 204; opinions and stands, 183, 197–201, 268; organized protest, 105–6; prima donnas, 98, 99; as profession-

als, 248, 322–4; reactions to pressure, 268–76; reality judgments, 39, 150, 196, 201–2, 208, 305, 310–12; recruitment of, 184, 190–1, 192–3, 213; social roles and functions, 57, 69, 205, 206–7, 281, 290–9; as sources, 127–8, 138–9; sources and, 81, 89; story design function, 88; as storytellers and myth makers, 294; task of, 5; term, xiii; TV and magazine, compared, 133–4; view of America, 143; women, 184–5, 201; working class, 210, 213; working conditions, 105–6, 206–8. *See also* journalism; reporters; story selection; writers

journals: of opinion, 187, 190, 197, 317, 318–19

Kefauver, Estes, 212
Kellogg, Mary, 27, 51
Kelly, John E., 293, 294
Kennedy, Edward, 11, 153
Kennedy, John F., 11, 29, 56, 179, 212, 294; alleged sexual involvements, 245; assassination of, 20, 55, 76, 160, 243; rapport with journalists, 134
Kennedy, Robert F., 11, 92, 212; assassination of, 18
Kerner Commission, 22, 54
King, Martin Luther, 18, 245
Kissinger, Henry, 10, 55
Kraft, Joseph, 24
Ku Klux Klan, 13, 30, 176
Kuhn, Thomas, 68
Kuralt, Charles, 3, 15, 48, 50, 156, 316

labor and labor news, 8, 12, 14, 15, 18, 24–25, 46, 65, 67. *See also* business and business news; economy and economic news
Lang, Gladys E. and Kurt, 305
Latin America, 24, 32, 36, 37, 195. *See also* foreign news
law, 19, 132, 270
lawsuits, 263
leaders and leadership value, 12–13, 62–68, 149, 206, 276, 286, 340; journalists as testers of, 291; *Time* story on, 63, 64–65. *See also* government; president and the presidency; public officials
leads, 111, 154, 161; and competition, 179

class, 151; commercial and financial considerations, 84, 214–20, 286–7; competitive considerations, 176–81; contexts, 74; cover stories, 154–5; efficiency and, 282–4; executives' role, 95–96; final, 109–10; format considerations, 160–7; freedom from implications, 188; "freshness" versus "staleness," 169–71; and ideology, 194; inclusionary and exclusionary considerations, 83, 183–203; interest criteria, 155–7; medium considerations, 157–60, 316; mirror theory, 79; in multiperspectival news, 315–16; national values and, 149–51; novelty considerations, 167–71; organizational considerations, 78, 93–109; peer pressures on, 266–8; peg, 168–9; political pressures on, 260–5; primary task in, 182; process of, 109–15, 343; product considerations, 157–76; quality considerations, 171–3; repetition taboo, 169; responsibility for, 322–6; role of power in, 81, 83, 249–50; seasonal variations in, 240–1; sellers and buyers, 90–91; significant considerations, 279–81; source considerations, 128–31, 280, 281–2; source- vs. audience-related, 89–90; substantive considerations, 146–57; taste considerations, 243–6; and technology, 79, 80; theories of, 78–80; TV news leads, 154. *See also* news; suitability and suitability considerations

story selling, 90–1

story suggesters, 87–88, 90

story suitability, *see* suitability and suitability considerations

substantive considerations, 146–57; back-of-the-book, 153–4; importance judgments, 147–54; interest, 155–7; leads and cover stories, 154–5; and multiperspectival news, 319–20; possibility of changes in, 285. *See also* importance considerations; news; story selection

suburbs, 48, 49, 51

suitability and suitability considerations, 146–81, 250, 276; action, 158–60, 171; clarity, 172; competitive, 176–81; completeness, 172; freshness, 169–70; defined, 81–82; pace, 172,

174; product, 157–76; sources, 128–31; substantive, 146–57. *See also* story selection

Supreme Court decisions, 11, 17, 163; as legal pressure, 262–3

Sussman, Leila, 229

Swing, Raymond Gram, 259

symbolic arena, 249, 250, 298–9

taking stands, *see* story opinions

talking heads, 158

Tarbell, Ida, 204

taste considerations, 231, 243–6, 355; and news executives, 95; political, 245–6; possibility of changes in, 287–8; as self-censorship, 252; and subcultures in the news, 248; and Vietnam War news, 244

technical standards, 172–3

technological disorder, 53, 58

technology, 49–51, 69, 166; fear of, 50–51; format change and, 166–7; and news values, 49–50; print, 166; and story selection, 79, 80, 128, 157–8

television news, 22, 37, 54, 91; advertisers, 221, 254, 255; affiliated stations, 218, 256, 258–60, 268; age-related stories, 29; anchorpersons, 3, 4, 75, 85, 86, 99, 104, 106, 108, 109, 125, 152–3, 198, 209, 217–18, 233, 259, 266, 293, 342, 348; audience image of, 238–9; audience mail, 227–8; audience size, xi, 217; autonomy and, 103; camera crews, 86, 87–8, 128; channel preference, 218; commentary, 198–9; commercials, 255; costs and income, 215–18; criticism of, 159; daily production of, 85–86, 93–94, 109–10, 111–13; disaster stories, 17; and distortion, 309–10; division of power and labor, 99; documentaries, 19, 57, 173, 215, 252, 253, 256, 261–2, 265, 266, 272, 337; economic threats to, 261; on education, 27–28; exaggeration, 309–10; features, 3; filmed stories, 84, 87, 112, 158–9, 172–3; foreign coverage, 31, 160; format, 3–4, 160–2, 164–5, 166, 218; highlighting, 91–92; interviews, 131, 173; language, 42, 172; lead stories, 111, 154, 179; media events in, 123; medium considerations, 157–9; middle class in, 26–28; network competition, 176–9; network variations,

About the Author

Herbert J. Gans was born in Cologne, Germany, in 1927, and came to this country at the age of thirteen. He holds an M.A. in Social Sciences from the University of Chicago and a Ph.D. in City Planning from the University of Pennsylvania. By profession both a sociologist and a planner, he is widely known for his writings on many aspects of the current American scene, including urban and suburban life, poverty, equality, ethnicity, and popular culture. His articles have appeared in numerous magazines and professional journals. In addition, he is the author of five earlier books, including *The Urban Villagers, More Equality, Popular Culture and High Culture,* and *The Levittowners,* the well-known study of suburban life. Since 1971 he has been Professor of Sociology at Columbia University and Senior Research Associate at the Center for Policy Research.